BLACK CORONA

E D I T O R S

Sherry B. Ortner, Nicholas B. Dirks, Geoff Eley

A LIST OF TITLES

IN THIS SERIES APPEARS

AT THE BACK OF

THE BOOK

PRINCETON STUDIES IN
CULTURE / POWER / HISTORY

BLACK CORONA

RACE AND THE POLITICS OF PLACE

IN AN URBAN COMMUNITY

Steven Gregory

PRINCETON UNIVERSITY PRESS

PRINCETON, NEW JERSEY

Copyright © 1998 by Princeton University Press
Published by Princeton University Press, 41 William Street,
Princeton, New Jersey 08540
In the United Kingdom: Princeton University Press,
Chichester, West Sussex
All Rights Reserved

Second printing, and first paperback printing, 1999

Paperback ISBN 0-691-02936-9

*The Library of Congress has cataloged the cloth edition
of this book as follows*
Gregory, Steven
Black Corona: race and the politics of place in an
urban community / Steven Gregory.
p.   cm. — (Princeton studies in culture/power/history)
Includes bibliographical references (p.   ) and index.

ISBN 0-691-01739-5 (cloth : alk. paper)
1. Corona (New York, N.Y.)—Race relations.   2. New York (N.Y.)—
Race relations.   3. Afro-Americans—New York (State)—
New York—Politics and government.   4. Urban ecology—
New York (State)—New York—History—20th century.   5. Political
culture—New York (State)—New York—History—20th century.
I. Title.   II. Series.
F128.68.C65G74   1998
306.2′089′9607307471—dc21   97-39537

This book has been composed in Times Roman

The paper used in this publication meets the minimum
requirements of ANSI/NISO Z39.48-1992
(R1997) (*Permanence of Paper*)

http://pup.princeton.edu

Printed in the United States of America

3   5   7   9   10   8   6   4

TO THE MEMORY OF MY FATHER

Raymond Edward Gregory

Contents

List of Illustrations   ix

Acknowledgments   xi

PART ONE   1

Chapter One
Introduction   3

Chapter Two
Making Community   20

Chapter Three
The Movement   55

Chapter Four
The State and the War on Politics   85

PART TWO   107

Chapter Five
Race and the Politics of Place   109

Chapter Six
A Piece of the Rock   139

PART THREE   179

Chapter Seven
Up Against the Authority   181

Chapter Eight
The Politics of Hearing and Telling   218

Chapter Nine
Conclusion   248

Notes   253

References Cited   267

Index   279

List of Illustrations

MAP

Research area, North Corona and East Elmhurst, in relation to nearby Queens neighborhoods.   2

FIGURES

5.1. Schoolchildren crossing the Long Island Expressway on their return home to Lefrak City. (Photo by the author)   112

5.2. Lefrak City teenagers speak out at the Concerned Community Adults Youth Forum. (Photo by the author)   122

5.3. Jonathan Bates, chair of the Youth Forum, and Edna Baskin listen to complaints about police harassment. (Photo by the author)   124

5.4. Edna Baskin poses with members of the cleanup team and "Leo the Greek," a local merchant. (Photo by the author)   127

6.1. Arthur Hayes, president of the East Elmhurst–Corona Civic Association, during neighborhood inspection. (Photo by the author)   142

6.2. Fashion show held during the Ericsson Street Block Association's annual block party in East Elmhurst. (Photo by the author)   171

6.3. Calvin Wynter and John Bell of SAVE oversee final preparations for the reception of Queens College dean Hayward Burns at the Corona Congregational Church. (Photo by the author)   178

7.1. Edward J. O'Sullivan, director of the Port Authority's airport access program, poses with a model of the AGT light rail train. (*Daily News* LP Photo)   197

8.1. Congresswoman Carolyn Maloney responds to audience questions about immigration reform at the United Community Civic Association's town hall meeting. (Photo by the author)   237

9.1. City Councilwoman Helen Marshall discusses election returns with campaign workers at the Frederick Douglass Democratic Association on election night, 1994. (Photo by the author)   250

9.2. Arthur Hayes presents John Bell with the East Elmhurst–
Corona Civic Association's Pioneer Award for lifelong
community service at the association's 1995 Scholarship
Dinner Dance. (Photo by the author)   251

_____ *Acknowledgments* _____

ONE SUMMER in the early 1970s, when I was seventeen, my father and I drove down to Richmond, Virginia, from our home in Brooklyn. I had never been further south than Washington, D.C., and I was both intrigued and apprehensive about visiting the place where he had been raised. My father hated the South. He never spoke to me about it—about living under Jim Crow, about the Depression, or about leaving for Harlem in the 1930s with his ten brothers and sisters. Had it not been for the fact that my grandfather and a few relatives still lived there, he probably never would have returned.

Every now and then something would slip out. Once he told me how, during the Depression, he and his brothers would hop freight trains passing through Richmond's black belt and throw coal down to people waiting along the tracks. More often, I would overhear these things at family gatherings or hear them secondhand from my mother. Once she explained to me that my father hated avocados because their texture reminded him of the lard that his family used to make sandwiches during the Depression. But never, ever did he speak to me about segregation or about his experiences with racism in the South.

To be sure, he was not a very talkative man when it came to his own life. Nor was he very political, at least in the ways in which I then thought about politics. (I was a high school militant at the time and dismissed anything short of armed insurrection as "reactionary.") My father practiced his beliefs with a quiet and unembellished determination, not uncommon for his generation: one that had lived the mundane details of life as potentially deadly encounters with American racism. In fact, I only recently remembered the morning in 1963 when my father left for the March on Washington, a suitcase in one hand and a Stetson hat in the other; he had left quietly and without a fuss.

When we got to Richmond, my father took me on a tour of the city, which seemed a bit curious given his usual lack of interest in sightseeing anywhere. He took me first to the area of the city where he had lived and that had since become Interstate 95. For thirty minutes we stood by the highway, cars barreling by, as he perused the few surviving landmarks. "We used to live over there somewhere," he said, frowning and pointing to a spot in the northbound, center lane. "Must've been somewhere over there, near that overpass."

Next, we took a bus downtown. I used to like sitting in the back of the bus—in the last row next to the window, where you could see everything happening up front. I had just started down the aisle when my father bellowed after me in a tone that was at once angry, impatient, and perplexed. "Why you goin' all the way back there? Come sit up here." Frowning, he pointed to a row of seats directly behind the driver and then dropped some change in the fare box. Feeling humiliated and put upon, I sat next to him, avoiding eye contact with the gawking passengers. When the bus pulled off, he turned to me. "Took us a hundred years to get here, and you wanna sit all the way in the back." An elderly woman sitting across from us smiled and, looking at me, raised her eyebrows as if to say, "You listen to what he's telling you, hear?" My father nodded to her as they do in the South and then peered out the window to get his bearings.

Despite my youthful conceits, my trip to Richmond with my father made a lasting impression on me. It was as though he wanted me to see the places where he had endured and overcome the day-to-day brutalities of racism in America. It was not enough to talk about them—to give words to experiences that were far too life-shaping to convey through language. Rather, he wanted me to relive them with him—to rehearse the constraints and struggles of the past against the noisy promises of the future. And in the process he taught me a great deal about human dignity, courage, and resolve.

If my father provided the inspiration for this book, there are many, many others who made it possible. Above all, I would like to thank the people of Corona and East Elmhurst, Queens, who, during the course of my fieldwork, gave generously of their time, hospitality, and knowledge. I am deeply indebted to Edna Baskin, John Bell, John Booker, the Reverend Irvine Bryer, Barbara Coleman, Joyce Cumberbatch, Jacob Govan, Selma Heraldo, Blanche Hubbert, City Councilwoman Helen Marshall, Calvin Wynter, and Elwanda Young. These persons supported my research in ways too numerous and indispensable to convey adequately here. I hope that this book does justice to their generosity and good faith.

Within the academic world, many people contributed to the development of this book. I would especially like to thank Susan Hirsch, my friend and former colleague at Wesleyan University, for the intellectual stimulation, encouragement, and sound advice that she has given me over the years. Many friends, colleagues, and students read and provided comments on this manuscript at various stages in its preparation. Particularly helpful were George Bond, Brett Williams, Dorinne Kondo, T. O. Beidelman, Manthia Diawara, and Roger Sanjek. I would also like to thank Sherry Ortner and George Lipsitz who reviewed the manuscript for Princeton University Press. The detailed comments and thoughtful suggestions of them all improved the book considerably. During the final stages of preparation, Yemi Benedict and Rene Simpson, my undergraduate assistants at NYU, provided me with invaluable research and office help. Finally, I would like to thank Mary Murrell at Princeton University Press for her expert advice, encouragement, and support of this book.

This project was generously supported by the National Science Foundation and by the National Research Council. A Rockefeller Postdoctoral Fellowship at Princeton University's Afro-American Studies Program provided me with time, space, and collegiality to pursue my writing in 1992–93, as did a one-semester residency at Wesleyan University's Center for the Humanities in 1994.

PART ONE

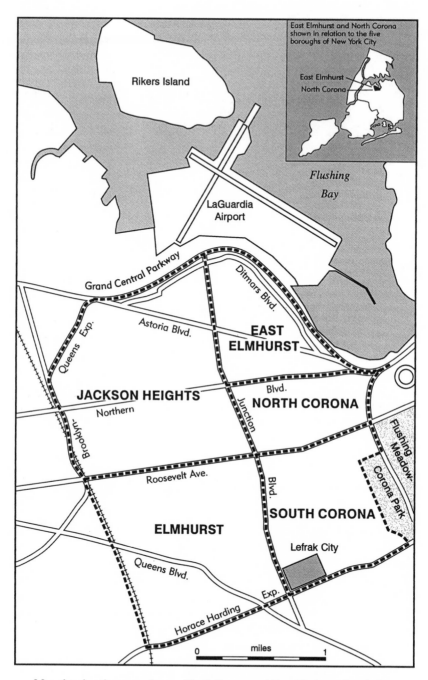

Map showing the research area, North Corona and East Elmhurst, in relation
to nearby Queens neighborhoods.

CHAPTER ONE

Introduction

JACOB GOVAN pushed aside the venetian blinds covering the windows of his enclosed porch and pointed to the Antioch Baptist Church, a small white brick building across the street. "Used to be the El Dorado Moving Picture Theater," he remarked, matter-of-factly. John Booker, who had arranged my interview with Govan, listened attentively, punctuating each statement with an enthusiastic nod of his head. At ninety-two Jake was still active in community affairs despite the trouble he had getting around when his arthritis "kicked up."

"And that's the building the Corona Congregational Church bought back then," Govan continued, sifting through a huge pile of papers and photographs on his lap. He found the photograph he had been looking for and showed it to us. It was a large, sepia-toned print of the Corona Congregational Church taken in 1922, not long after the congregation had moved to the building across the street. About sixty church members posed before the two wide arches that once framed the building's entrance, women in large floppy hats and fur stoles, men in stiff white collars and oversized topcoats.

"Are you in the picture?" I asked.

"Yeah, I'm down there in the corner somewhere," he replied, motioning to a group of hatless young men squatting in the front row. He chuckled and drew his lean hand across his head.

Born in 1897, Jake still lived in the house his father had built nearly a century ago on a lot purchased on the northern fringe of Corona, then a farming and light manufacturing village on the north shore of Queens, Long Island. During his lifetime, Corona had undergone an evolution repeated in various forms in many northern cities. Early in the century, the once rural village on the outskirts of Manhattan was incorporated into the city's expanding industrial economy absorbing in the process waves of European immigrants and, soon after, African-Americans from the southern United States and Caribbean.

When Govan graduated from Newtown High School on the eve of World War I, his parents' home on 102nd Street in Corona was in the heart of a small but prosperous black community. Between the world wars, Corona's African-American population continued to grow as the children and grandchildren of its European immigrants fanned out into surrounding areas and into neighborhoods farther out on Long Island. By the late 1950s large sections of North Corona were predominantly black and, like many urban black communities at the outbreak of the civil rights movement, confronted with escalating problems of neighborhood deterioration, poor public services, and political powerlessness.

Although the Great Society did little to change the face of Corona, the post–civil rights era witnessed the arrival of new immigrants from South America, the Dominican Republic, Mexico, and the West Indies. The El Dorado Moving Picture Theater, once a hub of black middle-class life in Corona, would, not long after my interview with Govan, become home to the Iglesia de Dios and to new generations of desires, convictions, and struggles.

Govan was both amused and annoyed by this history. As our interview progressed, he would dismiss decades of people and events with an impatient wave of his hand. "That bunch didn't do nothin' for the colored folks out here," he remarked, frowning with irritation at the memory of a group of 1940s race leaders. His lack of reverence for the past complemented his enthusiasm for the present. Often, in the midst of recounting events that had taken place a generation earlier, he would pause to draw a biting parallel with current affairs, chuckling and shaking his head from side to side as he explained why a local development project was failing; why, as he would often put it, rubbing his legs to ease his arthritis, "you can't get nothin' done around here, can't get nothin' followed up."

John Booker, retired from the real estate business and approaching a youthful eighty, listened intently, now and then posing a sharp question to clarify some fragment of Corona's past that had preceded his own arrival in 1953. A long-time community activist, Booker beamed in anticipation when one of Govan's stories promised to add a new gloss to personalities still shaping community events or make sense of some hitherto puzzling political act or affiliation. When I asked Govan about the Great Depression, Booker nodded in approval and then tightened his eyebrows to attention.

"Well, you see," Govan began, "the depression didn't affect people too much 'cause they had the WPA. You worked three days. And you did something. Construction. That's how they built LaGuardia Airport. That's how you got over the depression. They should have that Conservation Corps now. You see this welfare thing, I think this is some kind of thing put together to try to demean our people."

"That's right!" Booker exclaimed, cutting his eyes to me to make sure that I was listening. "To demean the black race," he added, striking his knees in a gesture of conviction.

For Govan, there was little mystery to the problem of the Negro, a term he continued to use interchangeably with "colored," "black," and "African-American," depending on the context. Nor was there anything particularly baffling about the young crack addicts who hung out at night in front of his house, believing or disbelieving the sign, BEWARE OF DOG, posted on his front door. The twentieth century held few moral lessons for Govan, little cause to reflect on the values, attitudes, and self-esteem of the race. History had to do with *how* things got done and why too often they did not; it had to do with the everyday play of power and powerlessness, action and inaction, commitment and indifference. For Govan the social and economic problems facing African-Americans on the eve of the millennium were as they had always been: political problems requiring political solutions.

Govan's political and deeply historical perspective on African-American experience contrasts sharply with the ways in which the problems and issues facing contemporary urban black communities have been framed in public policy debates, the mass media, and academic research. In many such forums the concept of an "inner city" isolated from the American "mainstream" and plagued with escalating rates of welfare dependency, crime, and teen pregnancy has served as a dominant trope for representing urban black experience in the post–civil rights era, conflating, in the minds of many, black identity, urbanism, and the "tangle of pathology" of the poor (Wilson 1987:21).

What is perhaps most alarming about the trope of the black inner city and its equivalent, the "black ghetto," is the degree to which both have served to block or screen alternative and, for want of a better word, *ordinary* ways of understanding the lives of African-Americans. Narratives of black urban life in the mass media and scholarly research have tended to focus on poverty and its impact on the culture and social organization of the black poor. In pursuing this line of inquiry, investigators have addressed an extremely narrow range of social behaviors and relations: crime, teenage sexuality, family disorganization, and "ghetto street life" have dominated both the research agendas of academics and the imagery of the mass media. History, political organization, work and leisure, and other everyday dimensions of urban life that de rigueur have guided and informed the research of social scientists working elsewhere fade from view within the epistemological frontiers of the black inner city.

This book sets out to challenge and put to rest the trope of the black ghetto that has shaped what we know and do not know about black urban life and that has strongly influenced, if not defined, the terms of political debates in the United States concerning race, social inequality, and the changing political economy of American cities. My general aim is to restore both history and politics to discussions of contemporary black urban life through an analysis of community activism in Black Corona. By shedding light on the political lives and struggles of people such as Jake Govan and John Booker, I hope to contribute to our understanding of the complex and shifting interrelation of race, class, and power in American society.

THE CRISIS IN INNER-CITY THEORY AND ETHNOGRAPHY

During the 1980s the nation's attention became riveted once again on urban poverty and other serious problems in U.S. cities. In the conceptual arsenal of Reagan and Bush-era conservatives, this "crisis" in the inner city was held to be proof positive that the welfare state had failed and that the origins of black poverty rested not in racialized forms of inequality but in a breakdown of family values and structure. The rhetorical figure of the "welfare-dependent mother" raising generation after generation of criminals and unwed mothers in fatherless families provided ideological support for budget-cutting attacks on the social welfare system and massive increases in public expenditures for law enforcement and prison construction.[1]

This discourse of inner-city pathology, popularized in the mass media, depoliticized the problem of black poverty and related social inequalities by locating their origins in the moral economy of the isolated "ghetto" household, rather than in the political economy of the greater society. In this view, the problems facing African-American and other poor populations would best be solved not through political struggles for social and economic justice but rather through the punitive rehabilitation of the family and its weakened moral values. When President George Bush assured the American public on nationwide television that the May 1992 outbreak of widespread social unrest and violence in Los Angeles was "not a message of protest" and "not about the great cause of equality," he gave voice to this depoliticized vision of black identity and community life: a race- and power-evasive view that rendered the political struggles of African-Americans either invisible or as senseless expressions of "black rage" and criminality.[2]

Among scholars, the intensification of poverty in black urban communities during the 1970s and 1980s led to a renewed interest in explaining the origins and persistence of ghetto poverty and the social problems with which it was said to be associated. While some researchers supported the arguments of conservative policy makers and linked continued black poverty to the putative welfare dependency of female-headed families,[3] others challenged this "blame the victim" approach and focused attention on joblessness in inner-city areas brought about in part by the postwar deindustrialization of the U.S. economy. This latter perspective, most notably developed in the research of William Julius Wilson, grounded the problem of black poverty in the changing structure of the U.S. economy. Though the link between unemployment and black poverty had been long recognized (see DuBois 1996 [1899]), Wilson's widely disseminated writings became a lightning rod in debates about the origins of inner-city poverty and its impact on the lives of the minority poor.

Wilson's thesis, developed in his influential book, *The Truly Disadvantaged* (1987), was that the minority poor in certain cities had become concentrated in ghetto neighborhoods and isolated from the socioeconomic resources of the wider society. Wilson argued that this concentration and isolation of the poor resulted from the interaction of two social forces: a restructuring of the U.S. economy since 1970, which accelerated increases in the jobless rate among blacks, and a "social-structural dislocation" in inner-city areas that Wilson associated with an out-migration of nonpoor blacks from ghetto communities.[4]

For Wilson, economic restructuring exacerbated the labor market exclusion of blacks and other urban minorities but did not suffice to trigger the concentration of urban poverty that he associated with the inner-city poor or "ghetto underclass." Increased rates of joblessness, Wilson argued, interacted with an out-migration of the black nonpoor from inner-city areas, concentrating the poor in "extreme ghetto neighborhoods" and producing a qualitatively new form of urban poverty, characterized by "acute social and economic marginalization" (Wacquant and Wilson 1989:9).

Building on arguments developed in his 1978 book, *The Declining Significance of Race*, Wilson argued that middle-class African-Americans or, more generally, the black nonpoor were better positioned than the poor to benefit from civil rights era reforms, such as antidiscrimination legislation and affirmative action programs. More educated and skilled than the poor, the black nonpoor were able to exploit newly opened white-collar and professional job opportunities at the very time that changes in the economy were eliminating entry-level job opportunities for the unskilled and minimally educated. As higher-income blacks consolidated income gains, Wilson reasoned, they moved away from ghetto neighborhoods. This "exodus" of the nonpoor incited a social transformation of inner-city areas, not only increasing the concentration of the poor within them but also contributing to an increase in "social dislocations," such as crime, welfare dependency, and out-of-wedlock births (1987:46–62).

Wilson's account of the transformation of inner-city communities in the wake of the deindustrialization of the U.S. economy challenged the views of conservative poverty policy analysts who attributed the persistence and intensification of inner-city poverty to a culturally reproduced "cycle of welfare dependency" rather than to the complex socioeconomic effects of prolonged joblessness. Equally important, Wilson raised key questions about changes in black class structure and in the social organization of black communities in the wake of civil rights era reforms.

The view of black urban life that emerged from Wilson's writings was one of ghetto communities, socially isolated from the values and resources of not only "mainstream society" but of the black working and middle classes as well. From this perspective the black nonpoor, armed with civil rights era gains in income and citizenship rights, had abandoned segregated black areas, leaving behind neighborhoods that were as a result less equipped culturally and institutionally to withstand the socioeconomic strains of prolonged joblessness.

In *The Truly Disadvantaged*, Wilson explained the impact of the removal of this working- and middle-class "social buffer" on the communities that the nonpoor left behind:

> This argument is based on the assumption that even if the truly disadvantaged segments of an inner-city area experience a significant increase in long-term spells of joblessness, the basic institutions in that area (churches, schools, stores, recreational facilities, etc.) would remain viable if much of their base of support

comes from the more economically stable and secure families. Moreover, the very presence of these families during such periods provides mainstream role models that help keep alive the perception that education is meaningful, that steady employment is a viable alternative to welfare, and that family stability is the norm, not the exception. (1987:56)

It was Wilson's account of the exodus of the nonpoor from ghetto areas, more than his analysis of economic restructuring, that aroused the attention of critics. Some argued that Wilson had overestimated the economic and social mobility of the black working and middle classes and thereby minimized the effects of contemporary racism on their ability to accumulate wealth and overcome deeply entrenched practices of job discrimination and residential segregation.[5] Others took issue with the normative role that Wilson attributed to the black middle classes as cultural "role models" and as a social buffer against joblessness and economic hardships.[6] On this score, some argued that Wilson had not only discounted the resiliency and sociocultural resources of the black poor but had also elevated an idealized and deeply patriarchal model of the middle-class family to a universal norm against which the "pathology" of the poor was defined and statistically measured.[7] Equally important, Wilson's analysis of the effects of the loss of the middle-class "social buffer" on inner-city areas seemed to imply that class had been relatively unimportant in structuring social relations in black communities during earlier periods.[8]

These concerns highlighted critical weaknesses in Wilson's analysis of the transformation of black communities in the post–civil rights era and focused attention on important research issues that had been relatively unexplored in studies of black urban life. High on the list among these was the process of black class formation and, more generally, the social complexity of black urban life and identities.

With rare yet important exceptions social science research on black urban populations has tended to focus on the black poor or, more accurately, on aspects of "ghetto life" that were viewed as differing from an often evoked but seldom defined "mainstream culture." Pursued in the name of understanding the uniqueness of "ghetto subculture" and the deft survival techniques of the poor, this ghetto research agenda emphasized, and at times celebrated, what Lee Rainwater opined to be the "limited functional autonomy" of black ghetto culture (1970:6).[9]

This notion of the relative autonomy of black ghetto culture served as a leitmotiv for the surge of ethnographic research on black urban communities during the 1960s. By emphasizing the relative autonomy of ghetto culture, anthropologists and, to a lesser extent, sociologists hoped to demonstrate that the behavior of the poor was a creative and adaptive response to an oppressive society and not merely a pathological deviation from its norms. Moreover, in contrast to the view, associated with the culture of poverty thesis, that the behavior of the black poor demonstrated the "tragic sameness" of life in poverty, anthropologists and other social scientists stressed the distinctiveness of black ghetto culture.[10]

In the introduction to his 1969 ethnography, *Soulside*, Ulf Hannerz explained:

> [T]he general question here is, "What is different about ghetto living?" This also means that all ghetto dwellers will not get equal time here. There are many who are in the ghetto but not of the ghetto in the sense of exhibiting much of a life style peculiar to the community. (In some ways, of course, everybody in the ghetto has special problems to cope with by virtue of his residence there.) There are people in the ghetto who have good, stable jobs, help their children with their home work, eat dinner together at a fixed hour, make payments on the car, and spend their Saturday night watching Lawrence Welk on TV—to their largely mainstream way of life we will devote rather little attention. This neglect may distress those who profess their friendship for the people of the ghetto, yet feel that conformity to mainstream standards is a prerequisite for full citizenship. (1969:15–16)

Although researchers during the period assigned different weight to the notions of ghetto cultural distinctiveness and autonomy, those who were "in the ghetto but not of the ghetto" received scant attention. For not only did ghetto research focus narrowly on the impact of poverty on the lives of the ghetto poor, but it also riveted its gaze on areas of black urban life that were taken to differ most markedly from an underconceptualized and monolithic conception of an "American mainstream." In fact the distinctiveness of ghetto culture was often, if not typically, defined in precisely the same terms as the racial stereotypes held by backers of the culture of poverty thesis. As a result, researchers tended to discount, implicitly or explicitly, the significance of social practices which, like eating dinner at a fixed hour, were taken to be "mainstream."

Although this notion of ghetto distinctiveness acquired very different political and moral connotations during the post-liberal 1980s and 1990s, the sharp distinction it drew between ghetto subculture and what Rainwater coined "the rest of society" continues to frame both the questions asked and the answers given about the lives of African-Americans (1970:6). For despite the perfunctory gestures that many have made to the diversity of black urban life, this socioeconomic, political, and cultural complexity has remained largely invisible. In the binary "ghetto" versus "mainstream" conceptual economy, which continues to drive much of the research on black urban life, working- and middle-class people are either absent or taken to be unproblematically integrated into the vague topography of "mainstream society."[11]

If researchers have focused on the poor at the cost of obscuring the diversity of black urban life, they have presented a surprisingly thin account of their lives *in* poverty and of the communities in which they live. In contrast to both an earlier tradition of "race relations" research in sociology and more recent scholarship on black urban history, postwar ethnographic accounts of black urban life have focused on an extraordinarily narrow set of social relations and settings (Valentine 1971).[12] Whereas the desire to demonstrate the creative and distinct cultural adaptations of the ghetto poor to poverty led ethnographers during the 1960s to the kitchens, street corners, and nightclubs of the black ghetto (rather than to its political groups, public offices, voluntary associations, and churches), more recent accounts of inner-city black neighborhoods have stressed their socioeconomic isolation from "mainstream" society and a related breakdown of social and institutional organization.[13] As a result, little attention has been devoted to the social and institutional structure of urban black communities and, most notably, to relations of power.[14]

Rarely substantiated in the literature on the inner-city or ghetto underclass, this notion of the social disorganization of the urban poor has roots reaching far back into the history of discourses about poverty.[15] Anthropologist Charles Valentine, writing in the wake of the Black Power movement and ghetto rebellions of the 1960s, criticized this notion of the disorganized poor as it was expressed in the culture of poverty doctrine of the period: "A major element in the stereotypes associated with this dogma pictures the poor as collectively weak and ineffective, incapable of organization, planning or sustained purposeful action, irresolute and lacking in will, dependent, helpless, and resigned. It is no doubt because Americans have been bemused by these myths that they have been so shocked by recent rebellions" (1971:222–223).

The tendency to view the black poor as collectively weak and ineffective or, in its updated version, as socially isolated and institutionally disabled by joblessness and by the exodus of the middle classes, has not only obscured the struggles that black urbanites have continued to wage against racial injustices; more broadly, it has also elided the role that relations of power and political processes play in determining the significance of race, class, and place in contemporary American society.

This is not a book about a "black ghetto" or an "inner-city" community. Whatever service these categories might have once rendered toward heightening recognition of the ferocity of racial segregation and urban poverty, they today obscure far more than they reveal. These concepts have become (and perhaps always were) powerful tropes conflating race, class, and place in a society that remains organized around inequalities in economic resources and political power that stretch beyond the imagined frontiers of the inner city. And it is precisely these relations of power and privilege that the trope of the black ghetto has served so well to conceal.

Black Corona is about political activism as it has been exercised by black Americans in a community in Queens County, New York City.[16] Corona is a "black community," not because its residents share a common culture or class position. Rather, it is a black community because, through much of its history, its residents have been subjected to practices of racial discrimination and subordination that inextricably tied their socioeconomic well-being and mobility to their racial identity *and* to the places where they lived and raised their children. And equally important, Corona is a black community because its residents fought back as a black community.

My use of "community" here requires some comment. Though social scientists have been much more critical and reflexive in their use of the concept of community than in their appeal to the notions of "ghetto" and "inner city," it remains a fuzzy and contested category. Often the idea of community has been used in ways that exaggerate the commonalities of the people it names and understate the heterogeneity of the institutional and social relations that they sustain through time and space (Suttles 1972).[17] The notion of a community "bounded" by a common history, social identity, or sense of attachment to place not only elides this heterogeneity but also obscures the central role that efforts to define the meaning and limits of community play in the political lives of urban residents and in the construction of their collective identities and commitments.

For communities *do* exist. People move into them and are excluded from them. Public authorities chart their borders and "develop" them. Financial institutions invest and disinvest in them. Politicians represent and appeal to them. And those who inhabit these bewilderingly complex fields of political and socioeconomic relations struggle to define their needs, interests, and identities by constructing and mobilizing their own often oppositional versions of "community." From my perspective, community describes not a static, place-based social collective but a power-laden field of social relations whose meanings, structures, and frontiers are continually produced, contested, and reworked in relation to a complex range of sociopolitical attachments and antagonisms.[18]

It is this enduring struggle over the social construction and political exercise of community by black residents of Corona that is the subject of this book. By framing my focus in this way, I highlight the interrelation of two social processes that have been neglected in the anthropological and, more generally, empirical studies of contemporary black urban life: the social construction of identity and political activism.

Social theorists have stressed the heterogeneity of social identities and their contingent relations to social practices and matrices of power. Against "essentialist" views of race, gender, and sex identities, for example, which fix social differences in biology or metaphysics, scholars working from a variety of disciplines and political commitments have argued that identities are constructed through social practices that "position" people as subjects within complex hierarchies of power and meaning.[19] These identities, or "subject positions," are neither static nor uniform since their constituent meanings and relationships are practiced and rearticulated across a variegated political and socioeconomic field shot through with social antagonisms.

This critique of essentialism has led scholars and activists to emphasize the diversity of racial identities and to investigate the ways in which racial hierarchies of social power and meaning operate in concert with those tied to class, gender, sex, ethnicity, and other constructions of difference. Thus researchers have underscored the heterogeneity of black identities and pointed to how the latter are differentiated along the axes of class, ethnicity, and gender while demonstrating how essentialist views of black identity have served to mask complex forms of oppression and disable strategies for resistance.[20]

Despite this emphasis on the diversity and plasticity of racial identity in contemporary theory and criticism, scholarly and mass-mediated narratives of black urban life have rarely attended to this complexity. Accounts of black urban identity in the mass media have stressed a radical socioeconomic and moral rupture between an inner-city underclass, typically defined in relation to deviant values and behaviors, and the "black middle class," treated as unproblematically integrated into a shapeless American mainstream. Although ethnographic studies have sketched a more variegated portrait of contemporary black urban life, much of this research has remained firmly tied to the problem of explaining or interpreting the deviant-coded behaviors of the inner-city poor. As a result, not only have the lives of the black nonpoor remained largely obscure, but we also know little about the social processes and power arrangements through which black identities are socially constructed and exercised.

This book argues the diversity of black urban experience by directing attention to the political struggles through which Corona's black residents have contested the practice of racial exclusion and, in the process, negotiated multiple and shifting meanings of race, class, and community. By attending to the political construction of black identities, I want not only to dismantle the trope of the black ghetto but also to show that the exercise of political power and resistance consists precisely of those social practices that enable or disable people from acting collectively as political subjects.[21] Simply stated, this book is about the everyday *politics* of black identity.

As Nicholas Dirks, Geoff Eley, and Sherry Ortner have pointed out:

> At one level, the observation that identity or subject positions are complex and nonfixed is banal. But the important thing is that politics is usually conducted as *if* identity were fixed. The question then becomes, On what basis, at different times and in different places, does the nonfixity become temporarily fixed in such a way that individuals and groups can behave as a particular kind of agency, political or otherwise? (1994:32)

This line of inquiry, pivotal to conceptualizing and practicing emancipatory forms of political activism, requires a broader view of politics and a deeper conception of identity than are usually applied to studies of black urban life. Politics, if addressed at all, is often treated as a distinct, relatively autonomous arena of urban life which more often than not falls beyond the purview of the researcher. By the same token, politics is rarely considered as a social process implicated in the formation and reformation of urban black identities.[22]

For my purposes, politics refers to a diverse range of social practices through which people negotiate power relations. The practice of politics involves both the production and exercise of social relationships and the cultural construction of social meanings that support or undermine those relationships. Politics does not delimit a pre-given set of institutions, relations, or actions, as much as describe a variable field of social practices that, imbued with power, "act upon the possibilities of action" of people (Foucault 1983:221). Thus the social construction of identity or the "fixing" of racialized, gendered, and other subject positions within a given social order is not only political, it is also the precondition of politics. From this perspective, the identity of black people in the United States has everything to do with politics.

If the construction of identity is a political process, implicating a range of social, economic, and cultural practices and locations, it is a deeply historical one as well. For not only are social identities transformed over time, but they are also grounded in social relations, experiences, and commitments that endure through time. People recollect and rework the past through social practices of memory that bring the meanings of the past to bear on conditions in the present. These practices of memory shape the formation of collective identities.[23]

As David Thelen has noted, "People depend on others to help them decide which experiences to forget and which to remember and what interpretation to place on an experience. People develop a shared identity by identifying, exploring, and agreeing on memories" (1990:xii). The construction of identity thus involves social relations and practices that articulate subject positions simultaneously in space *and* time.

I opened this introductory chapter with an ethnographic vignette meant both to unsettle conventional knowledge claims about the "black ghetto" and to underscore the eminently political and historical dimensions of black identity. For Jake Govan would not fit comfortably in the discourses and categories that have been enlivened through decades of research on ghetto culture and the pathology of inner-city poverty: he was too concerned with politics, and he remembered much too much.

But equally important, this ethnographic experience and many others that would follow impressed upon me the degree to which black people in Corona have remained not only committed to the goals of social justice and equality but also willing to devote substantial portions of their lives pursuing them. During the course of my fieldwork, I was inspired and at times puzzled by the enthusiasm, resolve, and endurance with which activists conducted their politics, struggling interminably with armies of public officials, attending countless meetings, and organizing and re-organizing around a dauntingly complex array of social needs and issues. And, more often than not, the rewards of their efforts seemed few and far between. For me, the writing of this book has been in part a process of coming to terms with this question of political commitment: an attempt to understand how the commitments held by Jake Govan and other residents of Black Corona had been historically formed, politically exercised, and oftentimes disabled on the power-laden terrain of community.

Understanding how and why people act collectively has political and theoretical significance that stretches beyond the study of black urban life. In recent decades students of social movements have focused attention on the processes through which people constitute group identities in order to enable collective action (Escobar and Alvarez 1992). This emphasis on the formation of collective identities, often associated with New Social Movements (NSM) approaches, directs attention to the role that cultural practices play in constructing or "framing" the meaning of political antagonisms, goals, and activity (McAdam 1994). In underscoring the political significance of culture, NSM theorists have argued against approaches that stress the determining effects of "structural" social contradictions or, alternately, that treat collective mobilization largely as a function of the political resources and opportunities available to people in a given social formation.[24]

This book sets out to contribute to our understanding of the relationship between the formation of collective identities *and* structural arrangements of power. For though NSM theorists have directed needed attention to the role culture plays in the fashioning of collective identities, they have often done so at the risk of obscuring their "concrete practices, constraints, and possibilities," thereby removing the problem of identity from a wider or structural analysis of power relations in general and class hierarchies in particular (Escobar and Alvarez 1992:5).[25] Through an ethnographic study of neighborhood activism in Corona, I argue that the process of forming collective identities is not only key to our understanding of how and why people collectively act; it is also a critical axis of conflict in struggles between the people, the state, and capital.

Part 1 of this book traces the history of Black Corona from roughly the turn of the century to the present. My concern in these three chapters is less with presenting a seamless, let alone comprehensive account of Black Corona's past than one of emphasizing the important role the past plays in the lives of contemporary residents and activists. While doing my fieldwork it quickly became apparent that activists continually recollected and reworked Corona's history to provide meaning and context, as well as narrative authority, to interpretations of contemporary social conditions. In public ceremonies, political gatherings, and everyday conversations, activists drew on and communicated a rich knowledge of social networks, institutions, and political struggles reaching far back into Corona's past and that of the greater society. To have shunned that history or treated it as a mere backdrop for an otherwise atemporal "ethnographic present" would have rendered the political culture, antagonisms, and struggles of the present unintelligible, if not banal.[26] For what would have been lost, as Marshall Sahlins has pointed out in a related context, "is not merely history and change, but practice—human action in the world" (1981:6).

For this reason I am less concerned with presenting an exhaustive chronology of political activism in Black Corona than with illuminating the meanings that the practice of politics has held for activists as they worked toward the future. "Too often," historian Robin Kelley has pointed out, "politics is defined by *how* people participate rather than *why*" (1994:9). Indeed, when Corona activists recalled the past, it was more often than not to interpret and communicate why they acted in the past, and why they should continue to act in the future.

Not surprisingly, my account of Corona's history has been shaped by the purposeful acts of memory of the people with whom I worked. Much of my historical material was collected in the form of oral narratives in open-ended interviews and through my participation in a variety of conversational settings. Most of the people with whom I worked, like Jake Govan and John Booker, were still involved in neighborhood affairs and had continuing stakes in the lessons of the past. Their present-oriented accounts of Corona's history served as signposts, directing me toward many of the topics that I would pursue in greater detail.

If my writing of this history has been skewed by the ways in which activists selectively reuse the past, it has also been shaped by my own, equally particular, theoretical and political commitments. Like the people with whom I worked, I have pursued the past to illuminate social processes in the present and raise theoretical problems and issues that are central to my political commitments as a scholar. Paramount among these is my desire to argue the heterogeneity of black identity through an analysis of community activism. As a result, important historical questions have been necessarily neglected or summarily addressed.

Chapter 2 explores the social construction of Black Corona from roughly the turn of the century to the civil rights period.[27] I focus on the processes through which black residents of Corona organized a collective social life and endeavored to construct a shared yet by no means static or undisputed sense of community and racial identity. By highlighting these contested processes of community building, I stress the diversity of black identity and direct attention to the social practices and sites through which that diversity has been politically and culturally negotiated in the face of racial exclusion.

In chapter 3 I turn to the political mobilization of Black Corona during the civil rights era. I show how postwar changes in the organization of the economy and racist government policies fueled poverty and neighborhood deterioration in Corona, galvanizing black resistance around a wide spectrum of political issues. Driven by state policies promoting racial segregation and cen-

tral-city disinvestment, urban deterioration exposed the vulnerability of Corona's black residents across class lines to far-reaching relations and processes
of economic and political subordination, spurring the formation of interclass
alliances that linked the national civil rights agenda to a neighborhood-based
"politics of place."

This concern with stressing and unpacking the relationship between the
economy, state activism, and the political formation of black identities is taken
up in chapter 4 where I consider the impact of the War on Poverty on neighborhood-based activism. Here I argue along with other scholars who have highlighted the role that War on Poverty programs (and, in New York City, elite-
generated initiatives for "decentralized" governance) played in "regulating"
black political protest.[28] Locating this issue in a historical context, I tease out
the practices and shifting arrangements of power through which various state
agencies not only funneled activists into "a segregated 'arena' of poverty politics" (Jackson 1993:41) but also propagated and lent authority to race- and
power-evasive discourses and strategies for addressing "neighborhood blight."
Furthermore, by restructuring the public sphere of black community activism,
state practices also incited a rearticulation of the social and political significance of racial identities and class divisions in Corona. More than regulating or co-opting black protest, the state's "differential absorption" of the political networks and demands of black activists in Corona cultivated new ways of
both conceptualizing and acting on black poverty, community, and identity
(Laclau and Mouffe 1991:65; cf. Foucault 1991).

Part 1's analysis of the political construction of Black Corona and of the
formation and rearticulation of racial and class identities provides a crucial
historical and conceptual framework for the ethnographic sections to follow.
In parts 2 and 3, I explore the complex and far from transparent legacy of civil
rights era activism and reform by directing attention to the ways in which
neighborhood activists construct, negotiate, and exercise diverse and oftentimes antagonistic conceptions of race, class, and community identity in a
range of political struggles over the built environment and black "quality of
life."

In chapter 5, I focus on grass-roots activism in a black housing complex in
Corona where tenants mobilized to get better services and resources for black
youth. Here I direct attention to how black women in Lefrak City contested
discourses of "black family pathology" and local power arrangements that
imposed significant limits on their participation in neighborhood politics. By
disclosing the links between discourses about black identity and the exercise
of power over black people, I stress the concrete political and material stakes
that are at issue in struggles over "representation" and, more widely, identity
politics. For it is precisely in struggles over the social meanings of places like
Lefrak City that we see most clearly the constitutive relation between the symbolic economy of representations and the political economy of urban spaces.[29]

As David Harvey has pointed out, "The fierce contest over images and counter-images of places is an arena in which the cultural politics of places, the political economy of their development, and the accumulation of a sense of power in place frequently fuse in indistinguishable ways" (1993:23).

This struggle over the cultural meaning and political economy of space provides the analytic framework for chapter 6, where I turn to black homeowner activism in East Elmhurst, a largely middle-income area adjoining Corona. My focus here is on the problem of black class formation, and I attempt to show how the identities, interests, and political commitments of black homeowners are formed and negotiated through struggles over the built environment that pit residents against a medley of public authorities and private sector interests.

In contrast to discussions of black class stratification that treat class identities, such as "middle class" and "underclass," as either transparent categories, needing little or no conceptualization, or as unmediated reflections of the economic rewards received—or not received—from occupational status, I direct attention to the social processes through which black class identities and interests are elaborated and contested in everyday life and in relation to a plurality of cultural, political, and economic determinations.[30]

This practice-oriented approach to black class formation stresses the ways in which power relations shape and reshape how people experience, interpret, and act from their positions within the social relations of production. The economic benefits and forms of consciousness that accrue or do not accrue from where people are positioned in the economy are mediated by relations of power and social hierarchies that articulate in complex and, typically, disparate ways to those of the labor market. For not only are relations of race, sex, and gender subjugation (to name a few) irreducible to those of production—in the restricted, if not orthodox sense—but the apparatus of the state also plays a critical role in governing the social benefits (housing, credit, public services, etc.) that derive from occupational status and income.[31]

Sociologists Melvin Oliver and Thomas Shapiro have recently shown how racialized state policies "impaired the ability of many African-Americans to accumulate wealth" despite gains in income and occupational status associated with civil rights era reforms (1995:4; cf. Massey and Denton 1993). Practices of bank "redlining" in black communities, race-based disparities in the provision of public services, and equally racialized practices of environmental "dumping" continue not only to impede the ability of African-Americans to achieve economic and social security but also to inflect the specific ways in which they experience and interpret their class positions as well as define and act on their class interests.[32]

By examining the cultural politics of place through which residents of Corona-East Elmhurst constituted and exercised their identities, I not only illuminate how racial and class differences are negotiated and culturally elaborated in their everyday lives and politics but also stress the state's role in governing the meanings and political consequences of these distinctions. For as I argue more directly in part 3, struggles over the social meaning and political economy of space turn precisely on the ability of various sectors of the state, capital, and urban populations to disclose or obscure economic interests and the social identities they implicate; that is, both to make and unmake classes in time and space.

Part 3 presents a case study of Corona-East Elmhurst's struggle with the Port Authority of New York and New Jersey over the latter's plan to build a "people mover" to provide transportation between midtown Manhattan and the Queens airports, LaGuardia and JFK International. In these chapters I demonstrate how Port Authority officials and neighborhood activists produced and exercised disparate accounts of the identities and interests of residents and of the social meaning and limits of "community" in order to mobilize support for their respective positions.

On the one hand, Port Authority officials maintained that improved airport access was key to strengthening New York City's economic competitiveness in increasingly global markets of labor and capital. In their view the people mover would contribute to retaining jobs and businesses in the region. On the other hand, neighborhood activists, concerned about the environmental impact of an elevated rail system, disputed the Port Authority's claims about the region's global development needs and reframed the issue of the people mover as one of "environmental justice."

During the course of this conflict, which pit the global interests of capital against the environmental needs of "local" neighborhoods, I show how activists worked to build interracial coalitions with surrounding communities by emphasizing regional environmental concerns about the people mover and by recasting their identities and interests in transneighborhood terms. By contrast, Port Authority officials and their public and private sector boosters acted to fragment and disable resistance to their proposals by not only funneling neighborhood opposition through local or "place-bound" political venues but also by inciting activists to formulate and pursue their broader and potentially generalizable interests within the bureaucratically defined frontiers of the local community. This enclaving of political resistance not only undermined coalition building around wider social justice issues but also encouraged activists to fall back on parochial identities and construct their resistance to the people mover as a defense of the rights and privileges of black property owners.

As in earlier chapters my concern in part 3 is one of illuminating the relationship between the construction of social identities in time and space and the exercise of power relations. Social identities and community-based solidarities are not given "ready made" to politics; rather, they are formed and reformed through struggles in which the "winning of identification," the articulation of collective needs, interests, and commitments is itself a key stake in the exercise of domination and resistance (Hall 1992). This theoretical position has important political implications that have both inspired and driven the writing of *Black Corona*.

In the wake of our critique of essentialism and the philosophies of history that it has served, the political problem of social emancipation looms as a daunting and, in some circles, unfashionable line of inquiry. Many, myself included, have bid farewell to the working class as a universal subject of history in favor of a still fuzzy vision of an emancipatory politics that will attend to multiple forms of subordination and to a plurality of social needs, interests, and desires; in short, a politics of *difference* rather than one of identity. Though we have become adept at reading and writing differences, at disclosing the conceits of "tradition," "the nation-state," and other totalizing narratives about who people are, we have been less able or willing to imagine or plot the formation of a political bloc that would be capable of effecting fundamental political and economic changes. We need to learn a great deal more about how and why people develop and act on collective political commitments. Evading this problem, whether through an appeal to a peculiarly postmodern or "postindustrial" political horizon or through a celebration of the ironic, runs the risk of deferring an "essentialism of the totality" for an equally disempowering "essentialism of the elements" (Laclau and Mouffe 1985:116).

The complexities and dilemmas facing those of us who are trying to think about social transformation after Nietzsche are by no means new; even less are they privileged afflictions of intellectuals. Social activists and those whom they organize against grapple with the problem of constructing "unity in difference," as Stuart Hall put it (1985), of shaping political constituencies and building alliances. They invent places and traditions, they fabricate narratives about the past and future, and they construct and deconstruct social identities and differences. In short, they know a great deal about politics.

This book attempts to break through the power-evasive shell of "black ghetto" research so that we might learn something about social change and the politics of difference from the people of Black Corona, people who have lived and struggled at perhaps the most brutal juncture of race, class, and power in U.S. society.

CHAPTER TWO

Making Community

And God stepped out on space,
And He looked around and said,
"I'm lonely
I'll make me a world."
    (James Weldon Johnson, "The Creation")

AT THE TURN of the twentieth century, Corona was growing in leaps and bounds as real estate developers purchased and subdivided the farms and private estates that surrounded the old village center for development as working-and middle-class housing. Italian, German Irish, and other first- and second-generation immigrants, many abandoning the crowded tenements of Manhattan's lower east side, found work in construction, transportation, and other industries supporting this development, as well as in local ceramic, garment, and other light manufacturing firms. By the time of its incorporation as a town in 1897, the Long Island Railroad and electric trolleys companies linked Corona's growing population to Brooklyn and to Manhattan-bound ferries based in Long Island City (Chamber of Commerce of the Borough of Queens 1922; Seyfried 1986).

Interspersed with this influx of immigrant and native-born whites to Corona was a trickle of African-Americans also drawn by employment opportunities and by the prospect of homeownership and suburban living. Jake Govan's parents moved from East Harlem to Corona in 1892. Born in Virginia in 1861, Jacob Govan, Sr., had arrived in New York in the mid-1880s, working as a custodian at a YWCA in lower Manhattan, and later as a mechanical engineer for the Consolidated Laundry Company of Manhattan. Emma Govan, also from Virginia, worked as a live-in domestic worker for a wealthy family in Lakeforest, New Jersey. In 1900 the Govan household appears on the Twelfth United States Census, owning clear title to their Corona home and employing an eighteen-year-old black "servant," Margaret.[1]

In that same year Martha Butler, a fifty-six-year-old African-American widow from South Carolina, rented a house not far from the Govan family, along with her five unmarried adult children and a granddaughter. "These young immigrants to New York," W.E.B. DuBois wrote in *The Black North in 1902*, "cannot afford to marry early. Two-thirds of the young men twenty to twenty-four years of age are unmarried, and five-eighths of the young women" (1969). Like their counterparts elsewhere in the North, black residents of Corona were concentrated in low-paying, labor intensive jobs in domestic and personal service, unskilled and low-skilled trades, and in nonfactory-based, "piece work" manufacturing.[2] Three of Martha Butler's four daughters were employed: Marie and Julia as dressmakers, and Jean as a stenographer. Thadeus, her twenty-three-year-old son, worked as a fireman.

The 1890s and 1900s saw an increase in demand for black female domestic and personal service workers throughout the North (Trotter 1985). By 1905, 90 percent of black working women in New York City were employed as domestic servants (Jones 1985). African-American women, often recruited in the South by labor agents on "justice tickets," were employed as domestic workers in private households and in local Corona businesses, as were Irish, German, and other immigrant women (Osofsky 1971).[3] Near the town center, Virginia Yeats and Clara Marna, both eighteen years old and Virginia-born, were employed in 1900 as a live-in maid and cook, respectively, at the Scott boarding house, which catered to Corona's growing white professional class.[4] Next door, twenty-year-old Corry Davis, also from Virginia, worked as a servant to a county judge.

Not all Corona's black residents were born in the United States. Rudolf Beaslie, a forty-nine-year-old-white insurance agent from Germany was enumerated as owning a home with his wife Eleanor, a "colored" woman whose birthplace was reported as England. Though a sizable black population had existed in Britain since the eighteenth century, Eleanor Beaslie was more than likely part of a growing population of immigrants from the British West Indies who, by 1900, formed a sizable portion of the city's black population (Haynes 1968). Interestingly, the census enumerator declined to indicate the "color or race" of the Beaslies' four children.[5]

A few doors from the Scott boarding house lived sixty-five-year-old black "oysterman" and native New Yorker, Edward Hicks, along with Lottie Davis, his seventy-four-year-old white "housekeeper." Jacob Berry, who also made a living harvesting oysters in nearby Flushing Bay, owned the house next door with his wife Mary.

Edward Hicks and the Berrys were among a small population of Long Island-born African-Americans living in Corona and the wider township of Newtown at the turn of the century. This locally born population, which included descendants of enslaved and free-born African-Americans, had been declining since the abolition of slavery, which occurred gradually in New York State between the passage of the Manumission Act in 1799 and the year 1827 (Sanjek 1993).

By 1830 the black population of Newtown, which included a number of villages, farms, and estates in West Flushing (renamed "Corona" in 1872), had decreased to 206 from 585 in 1790. Many newly emancipated African-Americans resettled in Manhattan, which offered relatively more employment opportunities than did rural Queens, as well as a growing African-American community, which supported churches, schools, and beneficial societies (DuBois 1903; Curry 1981; Sanjek 1993).[6] Other African-Americans fanned out into nearby towns, such as Jamaica and Flushing, which were home to sizable black populations (Rose n.d.). Still others settled on the outskirts of Newtown in areas such as Winfield, which had not yet become desirable for white property owners, demonstrating a widespread antebellum pattern in which free blacks were segregated and "pushed toward the periphery of the city" (Curry 1981:79; see also Sanjek 1993).

The dispersed African-American population that remained in Newtown established a colored Presbyterian church and parsonage in 1828 on land deeded to the United African Society by a white farming couple. In later decades African Methodist Episcopal (AME) and AME Zion congregations met in the colored Presbyterian church and at other locations in the Newtown area. African-American children attended Newtown's colored school, authorized by Newtown Village in 1868 but abolished in 1884, possibly because of low enrollments (Sanjek 1993).

Although Newtown's black population remained small, numbering 376 in 1845, ties to neighboring communities, sustained through religious and other associational networks, ensured their political visibility. On August 20, 1862, black Queens residents gathered in Newtown for a mass meeting to present their rebuttal to President Abraham Lincoln's speech "on the subject of being colonized in Central America or some other foreign country" (*Long Island Daily Press*, 4 August 1935).

"We the colored citizens of Queens County, N.Y.," the assembly declared, "rejoice that we are colored Americans, but deny that we are a 'different' race of people, as God has made of one blood all nations that dwell on the face of the earth." Emphasizing their attachment to the nation as "loyal Union colored Americans and Christians," the assembly buttressed their citizenship claims with a catalog of contributions that had been made by African-Americans to the nation's prosperity: reminders directed as much to their neighbors in Queens, no doubt, as to the president in Washington.[7]

We are interested in [the nation's] welfare above every other country; we love this land, and have contributed our share to its prosperity and wealth. This we have done by cutting down forests, subduing the soil, cultivating fields, constructing roads, digging canals. We have, too, given our aid in building cities and villages, in building and supporting our churches and schools. We have aided in procuring its mineral resources such as coal, iron and the precious metals; helped in construction of railroads, bridges, telegraph lines, steamboats and ships; assisted in cattle breeding, raising various kinds of produce such as corn, wheat, oats, potatoes, cotton, rice, tobacco, the leading staples of the country. In these ways and many others too numerous to be named here, we have aided the nation in the growth and progress and contributed to the general prosperity. (*Long Island Daily Press*, 4 August 1935)

At the turn of the twentieth century Newtown's African-American population remained small. The small number of black residents in the Corona

area enumerated in the 1900 census included the relatively prosperous oys-
termen, farm laborers, dressmakers, and service workers, employed in such
occupations as "railroad porter," "servant," "laundress," and "brass pol-
isher."[8] Like African-Americans throughout the North, blacks in Corona
and the wider township of Newtown were being displaced from some unskilled and semiskilled occupations by European immigrants arriving in the
latter decades of the nineteenth century (Spear 1967; Kusmer 1976; Trotter
1985).[9]

In 1911 the congregation of St. Mark AME Church, where construction had
begun three years earlier at the site of the former colored Presbyterian church
of Newtown, had still not raised enough money to install windows and was
threatened with condemnation by the Queens Buildings Department (*Newtown
Register*, 13 April 1911). When dedicated in November of that same year, the
pulpit, chairs, and three of the memorial windows were provided by white
patrons "in memory of family members and old family employees" (*Newtown
Register*, 9 November 1911).

In 1914, still struggling to pay its debts, St. Mark AME sponsored a fund-
raising event at the white Elmhurst Presbyterian Church of Newtown, featur-
ing Booker T. Washington as its keynote speaker. "It is not common," the
Newtown Register reported, "for smaller suburban centers to have the privilege
of hearing locally prominent men. This famous Negro educator is known
throughout the world for his grand leadership among his own people," the
writer added (30 April 1914).

In the opening decades of the twentieth century the center of gravity of
Newtown's black community shifted from the village of Newtown proper (renamed "Elmhurst" by real estate developer Cord Meyer) to the northern outskirts of Corona Village, incorporated as a town in its own right in 1897.
Continuing a trend that had begun with emancipation, black Newtown residents were pushed out of areas of prime commercial development and excluded by racial covenants from new residential developments.

In 1922 a dispute erupted between the trustees of the St. Mark AME Church
of Elmhurst and the Long Island AME leadership over control of the church
which, the *New York Times* reported, occupied frontage "very valuable for
business and industry": "The business men of the district want the controversy
settled so that some one with authority who will be recognized by the courts
will be able to consider the offer made for the property. These business men
would like to see the plot taken over and improved as a business or industrial
property for the *general benefit of the community*" (*New York Times*, 4 June
1922; emphasis added). By the end of the decade, St. Mark had sold off its
property in Elmhurst and relocated to North Corona.

The opening decades of the twentieth century saw a gradual but steady increase in Corona's African-American population, fed in part by the pre–World
War I migration of African-Americans from the South. Gilbert Osofsky estimated that between 1890 and 1910 the black population of New York City

increased from 36,183 to 91,709, the majority of which was southern born in 1910 (1971:17).[10]

Like the parents of Jake Govan, many of these new arrivals were unskilled and semiskilled laborers, domestic and personal service workers, and, in smaller numbers, professionals leaving congested and increasingly segregated areas of black settlement in Manhattan in search of better living conditions in rapidly developing Queens. As a second settlement area for upwardly mobile African-Americans, Corona, like Bedford-Stuyvesant in Brooklyn, offered an alternative to congested and increasingly segregated Manhattan (see Connolly 1977).

African-Americans from the South were also recruited as unskilled laborers on local public works projects, typically filling the least desirable jobs. Black southern workers were hired by private contractors as "sand hogs" in the building of Corona's sewer system, which began in 1913 (Seyfried 1986). Poorly paid ($2–$3 per day) and involving dangerous underground tunneling, sand hog work was shunned by native-born whites. Vincent Seyfried reported that Corona's largely foreign-born sewer workers agitated for higher wages, prompting contractors to purge their workforce of noncitizens in March 1915 (1986:78). The subsequent hiring of African-Americans for work not desired by native-born whites suggests that black workers were being used as strikebreakers, a common practice in the North during this period (cf. Bodnar, Simon, and Weber 1983; Spear 1967; Trotter 1985). Black laborers were also employed in housing construction, which skyrocketed during the 1910s and 1920s in Corona, and in the building of the elevated IRT subway that reached Corona in 1917 (Seyfried 1986).

The pre–World War I northern migration, more than doubling the black population of Manhattan between 1890 and 1910, fueled racial hostility and violence against black New Yorkers, provoking an intensification of de facto, and to some degree de jure, forms of social, occupational, and residential segregation (DuBois 1903; Meir and Rudwick 1976; Osofsky 1971). As black enclaves in New York City grew in size and population, African-Americans were increasingly excluded from white churches, public facilities, occupational areas, and trade unions, reflecting a general trend toward a hardening of the "color line" in northern cities receiving the first waves of the Great Migration (Osofsky 1971; Trotter 1985; Ward 1989; Kusmer 1991).

In August 1900 a race riot broke out in "the Tenderloin" section of Manhattan, following a violent confrontation between a recent southern migrant and a white, plainclothes police officer. Extending roughly from Twenty-third Street to about Fifty-third Street in present-day midtown Manhattan, the Tenderloin embraced scattered enclaves of African-American settlement, many only one or two blocks in size, surrounded by largely white immigrants. White mobs, aided and abetted by the police, went on a rampage through this center of black life, attacking and beating African-Americans at random (Osofsky 1971).[11]

Like the infamous New York "draft riots" of 1863 and the Chicago riots of 1919 that would soon follow, the riot of 1900 prompted many African-Americans with the means to do so to leave the Tenderloin, "San Juan Hill," and other expanding enclaves of black settlement, where experience had shown that vulnerability, as much as safety, rested in numbers. Throughout the century, white vigilante violence would remain a critical factor in the enforcement of residential segregation in the urban North (see Drake and Cayton 1945; Hirsch 1985; Sugrue 1995).[12]

As the northern Migration picked up steam in the years leading up to World War I, black settlement in New York was shifting "uptown" to Harlem and, increasingly, across the East River to Brooklyn, Queens, and other areas of Long Island where African-Americans moved when, as a New York Times article put it, "they amass a comfortable fortune" (quoted in Connolly 1977:22).

Following a real estate depression in the early years of the century, Harlem property owners began renting apartments to African-Americans. Subject to a discriminatory housing market, black residents of Harlem and elsewhere typically occupied the worst housing and paid the highest rents (DuBois 1903; Osofsky 1971). For example, between 1880 and 1910, Seth Scheiner noted, blacks paid from 10 to 30 percent more in rents than whites did (1991:310–311). Later, during the 1920s, a government report revealed that blacks in Harlem paid, on average, $9.50 per room, per month, whereas the typical white working-class family in New York paid $6.67 (Osofsky 1971). Exorbitant rents in relation to household incomes (African-Americans often paid as much as 45 percent of their income in rent) aggravated housing overcrowding as black tenants and homeowners took in boarders to help make payments (Osofsky 1971; Haynes 1968; cf. Hirsch 1985; Trotter 1985).

The New York Age, the city's leading Negro weekly, alarmed by the growing in-migration of African-Americans from the South and by their concentration in rapidly deteriorating sections of Harlem and Brooklyn's Bedford-Stuyvesant, appealed in a 1924 editorial to the New York Urban League, churches, and other organizations to manage better the distribution and assimilation of the new migrants:

> There is a steady and continual growth of population, and it should not be centered in already congested localities. Harlem, the Bronx and Brooklyn have already an excess population. But there are other communities in the immediate neighborhood that have not become so thickly populated. Out on Staten Island, some sections of Long Island, and upstate at Geneva, Albany, Schenectady, and a number of other places, there is only a small percentage of the addition to the Negro

population, and these communities could easily assimilate many others, both industrially and economically. But—this will mean the sorting out and sending to these communities trained help, both domestic and industrial. There is no room for the untrained migrant in these small communities. (*New York Age*, 19 January 1924; see also 16 February 1924)[13]

As a rapidly developing town, linked to Manhattan by the Long Island Railroad and, after 1917, by the New York City Rapid Transit System, Corona provided a suburban alternative to Harlem and Brooklyn where housing prices were skyrocketing and living conditions rapidly deteriorating. And in contrast to the "exclusive" housing being developed in Elmhurst to the south and Jackson Heights to the west, sections of Corona's working-class housing were not restricted by racial covenants and were within the means of many of its relatively prosperous African-American arrivals.[14]

For example, the family of Harriet Easton (née Hill) moved to Corona in 1905 from Forty-first Street in Manhattan where the 1900 riot had begun and rented the second-floor apartment in a house owned and occupied by first-generation Italian immigrants. Easton's father, Daniel Hill, worked as a clerk for an interior decorating firm in Manhattan and later assumed Arthur Schomberg's position as head of the mail department at the Bankers Trust Company. After renting for a few years from the Scelepis, the Hill family purchased their own home not far away.

Corona's African-American households were dispersed through northern areas of Corona and lived on racially mixed blocks along with first- and second-generation Italian, Irish, German, and, to a lesser extent, Eastern European immigrants. "We didn't have no problems with this prejudice business," Jake Govan remembered, referring to his Italian and Irish neighbors. "They used to come sleep in my house, and I used to go sleep in theirs."[15]

Like the Govans, the Hill family exchanged food, child care help, and other forms of assistance with their Italian-speaking neighbors. "You see," Harriet Easton recalled of her landlord's family, "they couldn't speak too much English. So my father, just to show you how things happen in life—well, they asked him, 'Mr. Hill, would you like to go in business with us?' They were builders, and, whenever they had letters to write, they would come upstairs and ask him. But my father didn't like Corona. He told them no, because he didn't think we were going to stay. It was too *country!*"

Barbara Coleman's family moved to 104th Street in Corona in 1913 and lived on a block that was predominantly Italian but included a handful of West Indian families. "We grew up with Italians. We ate Italian. And we went to Italian homes." The Coleman family's West Indian neighbors included a carpenter, a self-employed taxi driver, and a New York City policeman, one of Harlem's four "black horsemen."

Coleman lived with her mother, a clerical worker for the New York Urban League, and members of her mother's family: two grandparents, two uncles, and two aunts.

> My uncle worked in a factory that made buttons. And we had the best damn button collection you ever saw. Pearl buttons, and pearl buckles and stuff like that. Because my aunt was a dressmaker, so she made all my clothes and she made all my mother's clothes. We all were poor, but poor—we were not at the poverty level. We were all poor because no one really had the kind of money that you have today. So we were all poor, but we all ate well and we all dressed well. And my mother dressed better than anyone 'cause my aunt made all her clothes. She worked in a factory that made clothes for the rich, in Manhattan. And at the end of the season, the leftover material would be sold to the employees, so she would always bring home material and make suits for my mother. My mother always looked *good*, always looked great in suits and stuff like that. And I had homemade clothes. In those days you cried 'cause you didn't have anything that was store-bought. Everything was homemade in those days.

For many of Corona's new arrivals, before the depression, Corona was a second settlement area. Many southern-born and West Indian residents had lived in Harlem and Brooklyn before moving to Corona. For many, residence in Corona offered the opportunity for homeownership, suburban living, and social mobility.

"My mother's family," Coleman explained, "is from Barbados and they lived in Harlem for a short while, and then they moved out here like all good West Indians. You buy a home and then you get a job working for the government, because you can't get fired, except for malfeasance. And all West Indians did that. We all owned homes, you know."

African-Americans attended predominantly white schools in Corona and nearby Flushing but preserved social, religious, and political ties to black communities in Manhattan as well as in Brooklyn, where many worked and continued to attend church. The Hill family, for example, attended the Leverich Memorial Church, a white Presbyterian church in North Corona, but they continued to send their two daughters to Sunday school at St. Philip's Protestant Episcopal Church in Harlem. Founded in 1818, St. Philip's was reported to be the richest black church in the world in 1919 (Scheiner 1965). Black Corona residents also attended Abyssinian Baptist Church, St. Mark's AME (Harlem), Harlem Congregational, and other black churches in Manhattan, many of which were relocating to Harlem from the Tenderloin district (Osofsky 1971; Scheiner 1965).

Although personal ties with white Corona residents rarely, if ever, extended to institutional settings, such relationships did sometimes provide access to jobs and, on rare occasions, to skilled industrial work from which African-

Americans in New York, as elsewhere, were generally excluded (cf. Trotter 1985). During World War I, Jake Govan and two of his friends found jobs in the booming war industry in Queens through their acquaintance with a Corona white. Govan remembered:

> John W. Rapp had a place in College Point, where he used to make hand grenades.[16] They used to do the welding. And there was an Italian fellow we knew over here [in Corona] who became the foreman. So he got us all jobs over there. And he learned us, we used to sit twelve hours up on a bench, how to weld. That's how I learned how to weld, burning stuff over there. And we stayed there until after the war was over. And that's how I got into the building construction line, making steel doors, barn doors and things—fireproof doors.

Similarly, Harriet Easton's father was able to intervene with an Irish ward boss shortly after the World War I when her membership in the Republican Party barred her from getting a job through the Democratic Party patronage machine:

> They were offering jobs in the city to young people. And you didn't have to take any tests or anything, just be a Democrat. Most of my friends got jobs. My sister and I were the only two who didn't get the job. So I said to my father, "This is funny. All my friends have been called and we haven't." There was this Irishman who lived on Thirty-fourth Avenue—he was a big man in politics. My father said, "I'll go around and talk to him." And the Irishman said to him, "Find out how your daughters are registered." We were, of course, registered Republican. And he said to my father, "Sorry, they have to be Democrats." So, from then on, I've been a Democrat.

Black settlement in Corona was boosted when the Pennsylvania Railroad completed construction of the Sunnyside Yards in Long Island City, just west of Corona, in 1910. The opening of this enormous railroad marshaling and service yard, linked to recently completed Penn Station in Manhattan, led to the relocation of Pennsylvania Railroad crews, service personnel, and other employees from Jersey City, New Jersey, to Queens (Seyfried 1961–66). African Americans, employed as Pullman porters, maids, cooks, and in other railroad-related jobs, moved to Corona to be closer to the Sunnyside Yards, often relying on friendship and kin ties to established residents to find housing. As Shirley Ann Moore noted, black Pullman porters often served as "scouts" disseminating information about neighborhoods to prospective settlers (1991).

An employment advertisement, appearing in the *New York Age* in 1917, suggests the importance of the railroad as a source of black employment.[17]

> HELP WANTED. 100 Cooks, 100 Waiters (colored). Young men 17 to 25 years as 3rd and 4th Cooks, no experience needed. Experienced 2nd Cooks and Waiters.

Penn. R.R. Commissary, Sunnyside Yards, L.I. (*New York Age*, 11 January 1917)

As Corona's black population grew, creating a sizable but still scattered enclave in North Corona by the end of the World War I, white resistance increased. Although there is scant documentation of organized opposition to black settlement in Corona during this period, a 1915 article in a local newspaper records the play of a familiar pattern of white homeowner anxiety, resistance, and flight:

> The invasion of Negro families in the section of pretty homes on 42nd Street between Polk Ave. and Siboutsen St. has the neighborhood greatly stirred up. Recently, August Dietrich of 20 42nd Street sold his home to Negroes and moved to Elmhurst. This made the second colored family in the block and other property owners have become so aroused that they say they will sell to Negroes also in order to get away from the neighborhood. Property values always take a sudden drop when an invasion of this sort occurs. While the Negro families mentioned are apparently very respectable and quiet in every way, the residents do not feel that their rights have been respected by those who sold their homes to Negroes. (*Newtown Register*, 7 October 1915)

In 1922 the *New York Times* reported that residents of neighboring Jackson Heights and Elmhurst were expressing "much interest" as the black Knights of Pythias prepared to hold their national conclave on farm land in the area. Local property owners, the *New York Times* reported, had discovered that the week-long conclave would be attended by two thousand African-Americans who were to be housed in tents "in the heart of the *restricted sections* of Elmhurst" (*New York Times* 15 August 1922; emphasis added). Similar alarm was voiced by white property owners in Corona when an African-American congregation made overtures to buy a building occupied by a declining white Evangelical Lutheran congregation (*Newtown Register*, 10 July 1913). And in May 1913 the *Newtown Register* reported that a storefront Zion AME church pastored by a Brooklyn minister was vandalized by "bad boys" in Corona although their racial identity was not noted (quoted in Seyfried 1986:99).

Racial hostility toward Corona's African-American community was perhaps mitigated by its slow growth and dispersed pattern of settlement, the relative prosperity of its black citizens, and by the diversity of the white population.[18] In Corona, as elsewhere, tensions and conflicts among whites along class and ethnic lines, and between immigrants and the native born, persisted well through the peak of nativism in the 1920s, confounding if not muting the significance of the color line in some social arenas.

In 1924 a beauty contest in nearby Flushing was canceled when officers of the elite Green Twig Society, the contest's sponsor, discovered that the candidates receiving the highest number of votes were not "society girls." Among the leading contestants for the Queen of Flushing's "Spanish Fiesta" were Dorothy Derrick, an African-American college student and the granddaughter of a bishop of the AME church, Violet Meyer, "whose Hebrew father" owned a newsstand in Flushing, and Mary Hussey, a white garment worker who, the *New York Age* reported, was "equally distasteful to the society leaders" (12 April 1924).

The *New York Age*, ever vigilant to issues of racial discrimination during the period, stressed distinctions based on social class in its reporting of the incident: "All sorts of reports and speculations were rife as to the reason for stopping the contest, and it was pretty well understood that the basis of that action lay in the fact that the only girl who might be described as a 'society' girl stood something like No. 11 in the voting" (12 April 1924).

Subsequently, Flushing residents and merchants called on the *Flushing Evening Journal* to organize an alternative "Miss Flushing" contest in which, the *New York Age* expressed confidence, "all contestants, without regard to social or racial affiliations, will be given an equal chance" (12 April 1924).

Whereas Dorothy Derrick's participation and standing in the Green Twig contest suggests the limited permeability of the color line for some African-Americans, the contest's cancellation and reorganization highlights the complex interplay of social class, religion, ethnicity, and race in the reckoning and negotiating of social relations, hierarchies, and identities during this period.

In the decades leading up to and immediately following World War I, much resentment among native-born whites in Corona and elsewhere in Queens focused on foreign-born whites and, in particular, Catholic and Jewish immigrants. During the 1890s Corona's Protestant clergymen organized campaigns against the sale of liquor on Sunday that were directed largely against Irish, Italian, and German immigrants (Seyfried 1986). Corona and other Queens towns formed "law and order" societies that railed against the working-class "ruffians" from Manhattan and Brooklyn who visited the parks and saloons on the north shore of Queens on their days off (Kroessler 1993).

In the 1890s the *Long Island City Star*, protesting the "disorderly elements of New York City" who spent Sundays at the People's Recreation Ground in Long Island City, described a baseball game "between nine colored gentlemen, the Gorhams, and a team of white trash called the Senators. The blacks were from Sullivan and Thompson Streets [in lower Manhattan]. The entire place was filled by a noisy yelling mob whose shouts and curses were heard a mile away but no effort was made by either the 'mounted calvary' or the footmen of the police to put a stop to the disgraceful proceedings" (quoted in Kroessler 1993:174–175).

The Ku Klux Klan, which reached its heyday in Queens and Long Island in the 1920s, directed its propaganda and activities primarily against immigrants, Catholics, Jews, and alcohol, with some chapters maintaining close ties to local Protestant churches (Betten and Mohl 1970; Connolly 1977; cf. Blee 1991). The Klan was strongest in south Queens and Suffolk County, where three successive chairmen of the Republican Party had been Klan members (Caro 1975).

A KKK palm card, distributed by the Jamaica, Long Island, "Klavern" in the 1920s, provides an eclectic tour of the nativist worldview and suggests the relative lack of focus on the "Negro problem" among even the most xenophobic elements in Queens:

THE JEWS own this country, the IRISH run it, the BRITISH envy it, the GERMANS cuss it, the NEGROES enjoy it, the FRENCH style and perfume it, the CHINESE wash it, BOOTLEGGERS irrigate it, the GREEKS feed and shine it, the JAPS fear it, MEXICANS hate it, RUSSIANS pity it, the ITALIANS fruit it, ALL NATIONS cigarette it, EVERYBODY likes it, and the AMERICANS—well, those poor simps just pay the bills and can keep out of jail if they behave themselves and are very careful about their driving and parking. (*New York Newsday*, 18 February 1987)

Southern Italian immigrants, who occupied the lowest strata of white Corona society, were frequently the target of civic ire. Italian residents kept goats and other farm animals that wandered about, often becoming the subjects of police action.

In 1915 the *Newtown Register* reported and warned:

Officials of the Board of Health are making a canvas of Corona Heights rounding up the owners of goats, pigeons, chickens, etc., that are kept in violation of the law. Goats must not be allowed to roam about at will. If put out to pasture, they must be tied with a rope to a stake. Pigeons are not allowed to fly about and cannot be kept without permits, the same rule applying to chickens. The new law relative to roosters is also being enforced. Many residents were summoned to court during the past week and fined $1 for the above violations. (Quoted in Seyfried 1986:53)

As a result of such actions, Queens had the highest number of licensed chickens in the five boroughs by 1914 (Seyfried 1986).

Although the heterogeneity of Corona's white population may not have lessened racial hostility and resentment toward African-Americans, it did shape the way in which black residents both conceptualized white identity and constructed and presented the public identity of the black community. In interviews, longtime black residents carefully marked distinctions among white ethnic groups when discussing relations across the color line, particularly before World War II. Jake Govan recalled that after his father had been promoted to fireman by a "German" supervisor at a Negro YMCA in Manhattan, he was denied by a later one: "It seems that my father was supposed to be the superintendent, but they got some Englishman. And the Englishman brought some English friend of his that was an engineer and put my father down to a lower level. So he didn't like it, and quit there and went to work for some big laundry company."

White identity lacked the uniformity it would later achieve, and class and ethnic differences were important factors in shaping the quality of race relations and the meanings of racial categories (Sacks 1994). Moreover, African-Americans were attuned to these intraracial distinctions and antagonisms among whites, and to their socioeconomic and political implications in everyday negotiations of the color line. The emphasis placed on Christian "respectability," temperance, and patriotism in sermons delivered in Corona churches during the period was as much a claim to "American" identity vis-à-vis European immigrants as an assertion of middle-class values against, what one *Age* commentator called, the "shiftless class" of black migrants (12 April 1921; cf. Higginbotham 1993).

THE POLITICAL CULTURE OF THE "NEW MIDDLE CLASS"

Negro genius to-day relies upon the race-gift as a
vast spiritual endowment from which our best
developments have and must come.
(Alain Locke, "Negro Youth Speaks")

By the outbreak of World War I, Corona's black population had grown large enough to support its own local institutions. Writing in 1967 for the Corona Congregational Church's fiftieth anniversary book, Harriet Easton (née Hill) recalled: "In the early part of the year 1916, a group of men felt the need for a religious institution wherein they could worship with freedom and give their families the necessary religious and educational training" (Easton 1967). Though some residents report that hostility and exclusion from local white congregations provoked the church's founding (suggested by the phrase "worship in freedom"), it registered a wider and deeper process of institution building, tied to the formation of a new black elite and articulated in the philosophy of "race pride" and racial unity.

Historian Joe Trotter observed:

In Milwaukee, as in other cities, Afro-Americans responded to the socioeconomic, political, and racial restrictions by intensifying their efforts to build a separate black institutional life. An emerging new elite looked toward the Booker T. Washington-inspired ideology of self-help, race pride, and solidarity as a model for such an undertaking. Even the old elite modified its stand in the face of the increasingly hostile racial climate. As early as the 1890s, the Milwaukee Afro-American League explicitly enunciated the philosophy of self-help and racial unity. The idea, however, gained its fullest expression in the black press and the proliferation of black clubs, fraternal organizations, mutual benefit societies, social welfare organizations, and churches. (1985:29)

Like Harriet Easton's father, a white-collar worker, the Congregational Church's other founders were members of Corona's growing elite and included a physician, a school administrator, skilled craftsmen, and a Pullman porter. Meeting at first in private homes, and later in a rented storefront, the congregation quickly established a missionary society, a literary society, a "Girls Friendly Society," and a youth fellowship called the Young People's Christian Endeavor (YPCE), which would remain an important focal point of cultural life for decades to come (Easton 1967).

By 1918 seventy children were attending the church's Sunday school, and the congregation had embarked on a fund-raising campaign to buy property (*New York Age*, 7 September 1918). The *Age*, reporting the congregation's purchase of three building lots in the same year, noted that the church's "ten divisions" had already reached their hundred-dollar fund-raising goals and that "the white people of Corona are also giving great help in raising funds" (12 October 1918). "Division No. 8," the *Age* informed its readers, would be holding a benefit concert later in the month.

Through the 1920s the *New York Age*, the city's premier Negro weekly, reported news from Corona in its regular feature, "Out of Town Correspondences." While the *Age*'s metropolitan area reporting focused almost exclusively on Harlem, "Correspondences" published bylines that had been written in "out-of-town" areas, such as Corona, Flushing, Yonkers, and Plainfield, New Jersey.

"Correspondences" provides an important record of unreported aspects of community life, revealing how black Corona residents chose to represent themselves before a black reading public. Though the authors of the columns were never identified, Corona's bylines were probably written by someone affiliated with the Congregational Church since they tended to focus on this church and its elite social networks and cultural activities.

During the 1910s and 1920s the *Age*'s Corona column methodically documented the growth of the Congregational Church, stressing its educational activities and cultural resources and performing the black press's "dual function of reporting news and stimulating racial solidarity" (Drake and Cayton 1945:411). Corona's columns played as critical a role in the building of community through the "accumulating memory of print" as in the recording of important local events (Anderson 1983:80).[19]

For example, an October 1918 byline provides a concise map of the measures of "progress" central to the self-representation of Corona's emerging new black elite.

CORONA, N.Y.—Missionary Day was observed Sunday at the Corona Congregational Church. A missionary sermon was preached by the Rev. Hinton in the morning service. The Sunday School had a review of the lessons of the quarter by the teachers, after which the Rev. Hogans spoke to the school. At the Christian Endeavor Society, Mr. Wilson presiding, there was a discussion [of] the topic, "Favorite Hymns." Dr. Percy Green addressed the society on the Church and the

Theater. Mrs. Angrum, who has spent two years in Africa, told of some of her experiences. The paper on the Negro and the War by a representative from Nutley, N.J. was greatly enjoyed as was the patriotic solo. Delegations from the Nazarene Church of Brooklyn, and from the Baptist Church of Nutley were present. (5 October 1918).

The Reverend George W. Hinton, who became the church's full-time pastor in 1918, delivered sermons on such subjects as "Labor and Its Various Aspects for the Future" and "Saloon Power and How to Overthrow It," and, in 1919, purchased a "stereopticon machine" with which he gave weekly, stereopticon lectures on Africa and other subjects (*New York Age*, 13 September 1919; 27 September 1919). In that same year Reverend Hinton asked the men of Corona to "begin to think about forming a Civic League" and cooperative grocery store, and announced his plan to "survey Corona and find out how many colored people are living here" (20 September 1919; 13 September 1919).

Guest speakers from churches throughout the region, as well as prominent figures in black intellectual and cultural life, were regularly invited to speak to the Missionary Society, youth-oriented YPCE, and other church-affiliated groups, underscoring the complex institutional and social networks that linked black communities through space, as well as the importance that Black "Coronaites" placed on cultivating a cosmopolitan worldview.

For example, in 1920 a Professor Maxwell Hayson was invited to deliver a lecture entitled, "Princes Shall Come Out of Egypt; Ethiopia Shall Stretch Forth Her Hand unto God," and, in 1921, "[t]he [church] was filled in the evening to listen to the able sermon delivered by Prince Madarikin Deniyi of Lagos Nigeria, West Africa" (14 September 1920; 15 January 1921). Like communities elsewhere, black Coronaites represented themselves as deeply interested in and attuned to the cultural, political, and intellectual life of the nation and African diaspora.

Correspondences also provided an important forum through which the comings and goings, accomplishments, social life, and health of residents were publicized. Social gatherings and events were reported in meticulous detail, often accompanied by complete guest lists, not only indicating the latter's social and professional affiliations but also describing how the former were received by residents.

A 1918 column reported on Corona society, before ending abruptly with a somber reference to the devastating influenza pandemic of the same year:

The usual interest was shown at the Y.P.C.E. Society. There was an interesting discussion by Thomas Moore on temperance. In the evening the pastor preached from the topic, "The Great Invitation." On Tuesday night there will be a parlor social at the residence of Mrs. Samuel Page. Thursday night there will be a masked Halloween party at the residence of Mrs. Randolph, 18 East Hayes avenue. Mrs. Baker, grandmother of Thos. A. Baker, was in Corona Sunday. Many of our people are ill. (2 November 1918)[20]

Such commentaries did not merely record what was enjoyed and of interest, but, more important, they indicated what *should* be enjoyed and what *should* be found interesting, and therefore, like the metropolitan press in general, they played a critical role in constructing and legitimating both class- and gender-inflected norms and models for urban living (cf. Barth 1980). Moreover, "Correspondences," and the black press in general, chronicled the visiting patterns of black Coronaites and their relations, publicizing the strategies being used "to mend taxed family relations, rekindle old friendships and maintain primary social relationships" during times of great social mobility and dislocation (Trotter 1991:31; see also Lewis 1991c). For example, a 1918 column included the report that "Mrs. Lula Howard of Alexandria, Va., is visiting her sister, Mrs. J. A. Darnell of 47th Street. Mrs. Sutton and daughter are visiting friends in Amityville. Mrs. Samuel Page and son of 44th Street are visiting relatives in Stonington, Conn." (*New York Age*, 7 September 1918).

In 1920 the Corona Congregational Church purchased the site of the former El Dorado Moving Picture Theater, which earlier had housed a Jewish temple. Skilled craftspersons in the congregation donated carpentry, plumbing, and electrical and other services toward renovating the building. The Reverend Hinton acquired an organ from a white congregation that was about to leave the neighborhood (Easton 1967).

Not long after the move, Corona's "Correspondents" provided an enthusiastic progress report that highlights the black church's role as a "nation within a nation" (Frazier 1964).

CORONA, N.Y.—Services at the Corona Congregational Church are reaching a level of interest such as has not here before been displayed. The whole community has been aroused in behalf of the institutional features which are being considered for the immediate future. The building committee reports that plans shall be completed by July 6, at which time the second quarterly meeting will be held. Rev. Hinton preached an interesting sermon Sunday morning for Education Day. The Young People's Christian Endeavor is continuing with much interest. The choir is improving under the able directorship of Mr. Guerrant. The mother's club will be started soon. Special medical advice will be given by Dr. Albert S. Reed. A day nursery will be started in the fall for the benefit of mothers who are forced to go out by day. (*New York Age*, 19 June 1920)

Between the world wars, black Coronaites organized an infrastructure of churches, clubs, fraternal organizations, and mutual benefit societies, such as the Elks, Prince Hall Masons, Odd Fellows, and Knights of Pythias, while maintaining a variety of social and cultural ties to Harlem and other black communities. Like the Congregational Church, rapidly growing congregations at the First Baptist Church, The Church of the Resurrection (Episcopalian), and St. Mark's AME (formerly of Elmhurst) formed networks of auxiliary units that organized social welfare and educational and recreational activities.

Corona women, although excluded from high church office, played leading roles in these and other activities. The Phyllis Wheatley Sewing Circle, for example, held "parlor socials" to raise money for the Congregational Church's Missionary Society, which provided relief to poor black and white Corona families during the Great Depression. Corona women established local chapters of the Urban Big Sisters and Helping Hand Settlement Workers Society, which monitored the proceedings of Children's Court in Jamaica, Queens, and assisted in the care and placement of black orphans (*New York Age*, 21 February 1920). Far from being mere auxiliaries in a male project of community building and racial uplift, Evelyn Brooks Higginbotham pointed out, black women played "a crucial role in the formation of public sentiment and in the expression of a black collective will" (1993:7). Just as black women's labor was critical to the socioeconomic viability of black households, their organizational and fund-raising labor was pivotal to the construction of black collective life.

Corona residents often speak of the period between the world wars as a "Golden Age" when there was "a good class of people" and a "better society." Kenneth Ancrum, who arrived in Corona in 1926, described the neighborhood as "hoity-toity," noting that his parents were first refused an apartment by its black owners because they had a large family and, although Baptists, did not attend Harlem's Abyssinian Baptist Church, a center of black middle-class society during the era. Before the Great Depression, Black Corona could be viewed as a middle-class suburb of Harlem—a tie that was strengthened when the building of the Triboro Bridge and the Grand Central Parkway during the 1930s provided a direct road link to Harlem from northern Queens.

Although few if any black Coronaites would have viewed themselves as part of the "upper tens," the black aristocracy that Willard Gatewood has brought to light, many of them were solidly middle-class and cultivated a lifestyle and "society" not unlike that of black elites elsewhere (1993). And, like black elites elsewhere, "the better class of Negroes" in Corona embraced an occupationally diverse grouping of people that included civil servants, physicians and lawyers, and skilled and semiskilled workers, as well as the upper echelon of domestic and personal service workers (see Higginbotham 1993). Although income and occupation were far from unimportant, black elite status in Corona rested on an elaborate and seemingly opposed set of characteristics that blended race-conscious social activism with the cultivation of "respectability."

Willard Gatewood highlighted this tension:

What is especially noteworthy about this "aristocracy" was its cross-cutting definition of itself in regard to the black and white worlds, and the tenuous place that it occupied between them. These aristocrats laid claim to elite status within a subgroup, the black Americans, by defining themselves in terms of prestige, tradition, culture, and other considerations reflective of values drawn from the white majority of American society. The aristocrats of color also dramatized the fact that there have been numerous variations of *the* black experience. Because they were upper-class *black* Americans, not simply upper-class Americans, their "we" feeling was defined by both class and race. Their behavior mingled these variables in ways that often perplexed whites and sometimes enraged other blacks. (1993:x)

Between the world wars, residents of Black Corona worked to produce this "we feeling," which melded race consciousness with an elite politics of respectability. Black Coronaites organized the Corona Playcenter Tennis Club on land owned by the Congregational Church, which competed with Harlem's Cosmopolitan Tennis Club and offered free instruction to local "juniors who have rackets" (*New York Age*, 15 July 1939). Daisy Reed founded a black women's athletic club, whose basketball team, "the Coronettes," hosted cocktail parties and competed with "their lighter opponents" in affluent and white East Elmhurst to the north (*New York Age*, 6 June 1938).

Black social clubs sponsored picnics, bridge parties, and annual "jumps" at the Savoy and Alhambra ballrooms, which were billed as "Corona Night in Harlem" and seldom failed to arouse the society columnists at the *Age*. Corona-based entertainers, such as "Uncle" Frankie Allen, Sidney Easton, and Joe Culberson's Jazz Stompers performed at community events and brought popular entertainers out to Corona's after-hours clubs following their performances in Harlem. "Big George," a former bouncer at the Savoy and the owner of a popular Corona nightclub, organized a riding club whose members arrived at its inaugural jump "on their prancing mares and stallions" (*New York Age*, 27 May 1939).

And when Daniel Hill, deacon and founding member of the Corona Congregational Church, refused to turn over financial control of the Young Peoples Christian Endeavor Club to its young constituency, Jake Govan and other club members founded the Clubmen of Corona, which quickly became one of the city's premier black social clubs.[21]

Through the 1930s and 1940s social clubs, such as the "Musketeers," "Top Hatters," "Hopperets," "Zeniths," and "Les Copains," proliferated, carving up Black Corona society into cross-cutting and often competing "social sets" along age, gender, class, and political lines (cf. Drake and Cayton 1945; Frazier 1962). George Lopez, whose Jamaican-born father opened a popular nightclub in Corona after the repeal of prohibition, underscored the ranked, status-conscious social life of Corona's elite families, as well as the important role the church played in shaping elite identities (Drake and Cayton 1945):[22]

Social life? I thought my social life was fantastic. It was really separated in terms of the "socials" and the "nonsocials" like any community, you understand. And having strict parents, they would try to guide me as to who to hang out with.

Social life was built around the Congregational Church. 'Cause in the evenings
they would have what they called Christian Endeavor. On Sunday evening we
would meet there. And from there you'd take your gal to get some ice cream, or
go by somebody's house and have a party. Everybody had playrooms. It was a
good environment. We'd go to the Savoy Ballroom, which would make my parents very unhappy. We'd get there at 3:00 P.M. and stay until 3:00 in the morning.
My mother would pitch one! But you know, you would have Chick Webb battling
Benny Goodman—now how you gonna leave that?[23]

By the early 1930s "Corona Chatter," a weekly *New York Age* feature written by seven anonymous Coronaites, had replaced the staid correspondences of
the previous decades. The "We Seven" systematically reported on club activities and other community events during the 1930s and early 1940s, providing
a glimpse of the complex contours of Corona associational life where political
activism fused with entertainment:

> A grand time was had by all at the installation of officers of the Les Copain Social
> Club last Saturday evening at the Recreation Hall, 104–16 32nd avenue. The clubs
> represented were: the Royal Gents, the Hi Crest, the Trotters, the Progressive
> Democrats, the Cotterie of Players, the Progressives, the Odd Girls, the Veterans
> of Foreign Wars, and the Regal Social Club. The guest of honor was Eddie Blunt,
> heavyweight. There were [*sic*] a large group of guests from all parts of the Metro-
> politan District and they enjoyed swing music and a delightful collation. (12 June
> 1938)

Boasting a *New York Age* mail drop at Dorothy's Dress Shop on Northern
Boulevard, "Corona Chatter" provided black Coronaites with visibility that
was lacking in the white as well as black press. A gossip column in format,
"Corona Chatter" offered its readership detailed and usually deeply coded information about the social activities, affiliations, and schisms in Corona society. For example, a 1938 column announced: "George Lopez, secretary of the
Musketeers, wishes to express his feelings to the so-called "four hundred" of
Corona.[24] He wants us to remind them of the good time that they had at the
Musketeers' Christmas party and the way that the Musketeers cooperated with
them in the surprise party for Olive and Ruth Bishop. We agree with George
in his sentiments" (12 June 1938).

More than publicizing social debts and cultural capital, "Corona Chatter"
provided an important public forum where claims to status and class identity
were aired and contested, often in the idiom of gender. Black women, who
bore a disproportionate share of the burden of creating elite respectability,
were frequently the targets of anti-elitist sentiments. For example, in a caustic
response to the announcement of a cocktail party hosted by "sub-debutantes"
of the Glamour Girl Social Club, editors of the "Junior Chatter" column wrote,
"There are several chippies in Corona who claim to be sub-debs. Where did

they get this? A point in reality, they are just a bunch of plain Corona chicks. The meaning of sub-debs is to be found in the dictionary and you will find that they are far from that so-called society class. Is the name to hide the dirt, or is it on the up and up?" (*Age*, 11 March 1939).

Socially and politically sensitive issues concerning class divisions, gender relations, and racial inequalities found their way into the "Chatter" column, often shrouded in innuendo, sarcasm, and irony and typically embedded in "chatty," seemingly trivial narrative contexts. "We have little or no legislative power," the "We Seven" complained, "but we do believe that something should be done about the sharp edges of exposed automobile license plates" (25 February 1939). Reporting on an interracial dance competition held after a Coronettes basketball game, the "We Seven" noted, "[T]he jitterbug contest prize money was practically a gift to our white friends of East Elmhurst" (22 April 1939).

When reporting proudly that a Corona soldier in Harlem's celebrated 369th Infantry Division had organized a "militaristic picket" in front of the segregated Palace Theater, the "We Seven" used the soldier's club name, Private "Rough Rider," to mask his identity (25 March 1939). In another column the Musketeers social club voiced an appeal to the people of Corona to cooperate in the boycott of the Palace Theater, whose owner had been quoted as telling club members, "It would be an insult to my white patrons to hire a colored usher."

Far from merely providing "status without substance," as E. Franklin Frazier wrote of black bourgeois society, social clubs in Corona formed a flexible, heterogeneous, and, from the vantage point of white society, largely invisible network of constituencies which could be mobilized for political activities that would have compromised the tenuous, patronage-producing ties of "recognized" leaders to the white political establishment (1962:162). Although black society, with its social clubs, voluntary associations, and frenetic social calendar, was an important arena where black Coronaites constructed and negotiated status claims in the face of racial exclusion, the social calculus of status in black communities was more complicated and, indeed, contested than Frazier admitted.[25] Not merely an "imitation" of white society, black club life was a pivotal and dynamic social field where the symbolic and political terms of engagement with white society were articulated and publicly performed through cultural practices that blurred, rather than sublimated, the boundary between entertainment and politics.[26]

Robin Kelley has underscored the analytic importance of this variegated arena of African-American political culture: "Knowing what happens in these spaces of pleasure can help us understand the solidarity black people have shown at political mass meetings, illuminate the bonds of fellowship one finds in churches and voluntary associations, and unveil the *conflicts* across class and gender lines that shape and constrain these collective struggles" (1994:47).

Indeed, during the 1930s "Corona Chatter" both documented and in part enabled the formation of a new, African-American counterpublic in Corona that fused the politics of race with the politics of pleasure. In contrast to the older, largely church-based "settler" elites, who had found voice in the "Out of Town Correspondences," Corona's growing new middle class was younger, Corona-raised, and less committed to both white sources of patronage and elite definitions of black respectability.

The Musketeers Social Club, for example, whose secretary would go on to study dentistry at Howard University, was referred to as the "mighty club of potential businessmen," registering the younger generation's shift to occupations serving largely black clienteles (25 February 1939). And in that same column, the new editors of "Junior Chatter" flaunted elite conventions of respectability, boldly announcing: "Under new management. Look out, pops! My boy and I are taking this column over. We're going to do our best to keep this jive jumpin' steady. So keep on sending in your drags!"

This debut of hep-cat jive and the broader celebration of hipster culture in "Junior Chatter" by "the Zippers" registered one face of an emergent youth-oriented political culture that would constitute an important social base of activism during World War II, fusing alternative constructions of black identity, style, and modernity with an increasingly confrontational race politics.

As St. Claire Drake and Horace Cayton noted, the depression years not only weakened the established, black professional class, it also

> laid the basis for association between a heterogeneous group of young college trained men and women who had not yet been able to establish themselves economically and a group of people who had stable incomes but were short on education. Most important, however, it brought to the upper class the almost traumatic experience of facing the implications of life in a Black Ghetto. As a result, there was a sharp increase in civic activity, a general restlessness which found expression in the support of radical and labor groups by professional and business people, and a tendency on the part of many to seek prestige through race leadership rather than through conspicuous consumption. (1945:546)

African-Americans in Corona and in other urban areas were severely affected by the Great Depression, which witnessed a more than 50 percent drop in manufacturing production between 1929 and 1933. By October 1933, 17.8 percent of the black population of the United States was on relief, compared to 9.5 percent of nonblacks. In urban areas the Federal Employment Relief Administration reported that three times as many blacks were on relief as whites (Wolters 1974). And in New York City, four out of every ten black families were living on welfare in 1935–36, almost double the ratio among whites (Blumberg 1979).

As Raymond Wolters pointed out, black urban workers were particularly vulnerable to depression-era job losses. The largest concentrations of black industrial workers were in building construction and coal mining, both of which were stagnant during the depression. In addition, the vast majority of African-Americans were employed in marginal, unskilled, and semiskilled jobs which, like domestic service, were "dispensed with most easily when the first distress of the depression was felt" (Wolters 1974:92).

Black working women, heavily concentrated in domestic service jobs, were especially hard hit by unemployment. A 1935 *Crisis* article, "The Bronx Slave Market," described a daily "shape-up" in which black women waited for work:

> As early as eight A.M. they come; as late as one P.M. they remain. Rain or shine, cold or hot, you will find them there—Negro women, old and young—sometimes bedraggled, sometimes neatly dressed—but with the invariable paper bundle, waiting expectantly for Bronx housewives to buy their strength and energy for an hour, two hours, or even a day at the munificent rate of fifteen, twenty, twenty-five, or if luck be with them, thirty cents an hour. (Quoted in Blumberg 1979:153)

Moreover, as the "last hired and the first fired," black workers found it not only difficult to compete for scarce jobs, but they were often purged from jobs to make room for whites who, as T. Arnold Hill of the Urban League put it, were "content to accept occupations which were once thought too menial for white hands" (quoted in Wolters 1974:92). In some areas of the United States black workers were subjected to intimidation and violence to force them to leave their jobs. Walter White of the National Association for the Advancement of Colored People (NAACP) charged that lynch mobs were being used to terrorize black workers and their employers, noting that lynchings had increased from eight in 1932 to twenty-eight in 1933 (Wolters 1974).

Black workers in Queens suffered severe job losses across occupational categories but particularly in service occupations. Black working women in Queens were concentrated in domestic and personal service. As late as 1940, 77 percent of black working women in Queens were employed in domestic service work compared to 7 percent of white women (Frost 1947). "Many women," a black Corona woman remembered, "just had to stop working. Those kinds of jobs, you know in service, just dried up during the depression. And when you could find work, it was by the hour."

Thirty-five percent of black male workers in Queens had service jobs in 1940, though largely in nondomestic areas (e.g., janitors, porters, waiters, and cooks), compared to 11 percent of white males. Black male workers were also concentrated in unskilled occupations, 16.9 percent working as laborers in 1940, compared to 4.9 percent of white males (Frost 1947). And although black male workers compared favorably with whites in semiskilled occupations (18.4 and 18.0 percent, respectively), only 10 percent held skilled jobs in manufacturing, compared to 25 percent of white male workers (Frost 1946).[27]

"See," Jake Govan recalled, "the depression didn't hurt you too much if you had a trade, just like it is today. 'Cause if you didn't have a job, the WPA [Works Progress Administration] picked you up. But out here in Corona, the people who had the most trouble during the depression were the day laborers, 'cause they didn't have no skills."

In New York City the most effective of the Roosevelt-era New Deal experiments in stimulating the economy and relieving the unemployed was the Works Progress Administration, which in 1935 assumed many of the functions of the Federal Emergency Relief Administration and Public Works Administration. The WPA provided work and aid to jobless persons drawn largely from the home relief roles and, between 1935 and 1943, employed 700,000 New Yorkers in construction-related jobs and, in lesser numbers, white-collar professions, "housekeeping," and the arts.

Federal WPA funds were used to hire workers for a variety of public works projects in New York City, ranging from the construction of LaGuardia Airport, just north of Corona, to the building and renovation of libraries, public parks, roadways, and sewers throughout the city.[28] Although black workers received a significant share of WPA jobs, they were assigned to the least skilled work. In 1937, for example, three-quarters of black WPA workers in New York City worked as unskilled laborers, whereas only 5 percent held professional and technical jobs (Blumberg 1979). Similarly, black women were largely relegated to domestic service work through the WPA's predominantly black Housekeeping Project (Blumberg 1979). Racial discrimination in WPA hiring and job assignments, particularly during the early years of its administration, provoked persistent protests from the National Urban League, the NAACP, black clergy, and other leaders (Wolters 1974; Blumberg 1979).

Many black male workers in Corona found work through WPA public works projects, a considerable number of which, like the building of LaGuardia Field, road repaving, and the clearing of the 1939 World's Fair site in Flushing Meadows–Corona Park, were sited in Queens.[29] Jake Govan, laid off from a welding job with a private company, was employed by the WPA's City-Wide Department in the modernization of the docks along the North River waterfront.[30] However, Govan's experience as a skilled worker was no doubt exceptional. The vast majority of black workers, when assigned to the WPA, worked in the lowest-paying jobs as laborers; given rules limiting WPA assignments to one member of a family, black households that relied on multiple wage earners suffered as a result.

People who lived through the depression in Corona reported that many households survived by "doubling up" in apartments and private homes and pooling resources, and by taking in boarders. Black Corona churches and voluntary associations provided relief in the form of food, clothing, and, in some cases, emergency loans to their members and to others who were experiencing severe hardships. The Corona Congregational Church under the Reverend George Hinton also provided relief services to impoverished black and white families in Corona. In fact, a smaller proportion of black Queens homeowners lost their homes during the depression than did whites. Between 1930 and 1940 black homeownership in Queens fell from 36.6 to 30 percent, a decline of 7 points. In contrast, white homeownership dropped from 45 to 37 percent, a loss of 8 points (Frost 1947).

The outbreak of World War II and rearmament did little to alter the pattern of job discrimination for black New Yorkers. As private industries converted to wartime production, unemployment declined. Between July 1, 1940, and June 30, 1941, the number of unemployed in the nation dropped by nearly four million. By the end of 1940, WPA workers in New York City were resigning at the rate of two thousand per week to take jobs in war production (Blumberg 1979). Black workers, however, found themselves largely excluded from this wartime boon.

As Barbara Blumberg pointed out:

Blacks found all too true the old saying that they were the first fired in hard times and the last rehired when prosperity returned. Civil rights groups, Governor Lehman, and Mayor La Guardia all charged that management and unions were excluding blacks from defense jobs and industrial training programs. Because of this discrimination, blacks tended to remain on the WPA long after their more fortunate white colleagues left. In November 1937 a little over 13 percent of the WPA personnel in the metropolis was black; by April 1941 the figure had climbed to 22 percent; and as of 30 of October 1942 nearly one-third of all those still on the WPA were black. (1979:268)

Although at the outbreak of the war Queens was already a major industrial center (fifteenth among U.S. cities in the value of manufactured products), many corporations practiced outright discrimination against black workers (Frost 1947). For example, the Ledkote Products Company of Long Island City (Queens) barred black and women workers from its factory and refused at first to hire both groups of WPA-trained workers as permanent wartime employees (Blumberg 1979).

Nor did the limited gains of the wartime economy prove long lasting. Writing in 1947, after massive numbers of black workers had been laid off from their defense industry jobs in Queens, Olivia Frost concluded:

In general . . . union officials admitted that especially in difficult times, such as the present, because of the Negroes' more disadvantageous position with respect to seniority, the bulk of Negro workers previously induced into the war plants were not being rehired to any appreciable extent. In the metal trades industry, particularly, because of the tight employment situation, hardly any of the large numbers of Negroes laid off after the war had been rehired. Seniority provisions had resulted in the few job openings being filled by white workers with longer seniority. (1947:20)

"DON'T BUY WHERE YOU CAN'T WORK"

> It is the race-conscious black man cooperating
> together in his own institutions and movements who
> will eventually emancipate the colored race, and the
> great step ahead today is for the American Negro to
> accomplish his economic emancipation through
> voluntary, determined cooperative effort.
> *(W.E.B. DuBois, 1934)*

If the depression underscored the vulnerability of African-Americans across class lines to the vagaries of the economy, the New Deal's failure to address the needs of black workers exposed the inability of black organizations to shape, let alone improve, the economic conditions of black people (Wolters 1974). During the 1930s civil rights groups such as the National Urban League and the NAACP came under increasing attack for their focus on civil liberties at the expense of what many argued to be more fundamental economic issues facing the masses of black people. Signaled in part by the NAACP's 1933 Amenia Conference, black activists such as W.E.B. DuBois increasingly stressed the need to develop independent bases of power within black communities that could be brought to bear on the government and private sector to win economic objectives.

In Corona this far-ranging, albeit hotly contested, shift in strategy and consciousness gave rise to new leadership cadres and forms of political activism that stressed direct political action toward eliminating racial discrimination in employment.

An important focus of this emergent oppositional politics in Corona was the 1939 New York World's Fair, held in nearby Flushing Meadows–Corona Park. Despite assurances given by fair organizers that African-Americans would not be discriminated against, New York NAACP and black church leaders charged that African-Americans were being systematically excluded from all occupations "except in the capacities of maids and porters" (*Crisis*, April 1935:116). In response to these charges of discrimination in employment, wage levels, and access to public facilities, the fair's managers stonewalled, contending that there was "absolutely no discrimination as to race, color or creed" (quoted in Rydell 1993:183).

Underscoring the hypocrisy of the fair's organizers, led by World's Fair's president and former police commissioner, Grover A. Whalen, the New York

NAACP declared in a March 1939 resolution: "In an exposition which purports to indicate the trend toward the world of tomorrow, this association believes that among the first considerations should have been a recognition of the unfairness of discrimination between peoples, and the justice of opportunity for all on the basis of merit" (*Crisis*, April 1939:116).

As Robert Rydell pointed out, African-Americans recognized that the nation's world's fairs "had always been battlefields for control of the future," providing a monumental stage on which to display a "corporate-run, white supremacists' world of tomorrow" (1993:157). For black Coronaites engaged in building community and "uplifting the race" within walking distance of the world of tomorrow, the fair became a cause célèbre, galvanizing political activism and inciting new and renegotiated constructions of racial, class, and political identity.

In April the Greater New York Coordinating Committee for Employment, based at Harlem's Abyssinian Baptist Church, picketed fair offices at the Empire State Building, following through on a threat that had been made by A. Philip Randolph in 1937. On the opening day of the fair, the Committee, led by the Reverend Adam Clayton Powell, amassed five hundred demonstrators outside the fairgrounds while President Franklin Roosevelt delivered his opening address (Rydell 1993).

"Corona Chatter," reminding its readers of the fair's May 1 opening, alluded to a protest planned by the Musketeers social club, masking its details with ellipses. "We all hope to see you on the [fair] grounds for this gala occasion. That is, if we are fortunate enough to come across tickets of admission. Watch for the connection between Mr. Grover Whalen's enterprise and the Mighty Musketeers" (11 March 1939). Days after the fair's opening, Corona Chatter announced that the protests had produced results: "Three of our friends have received jobs at the [World's Fair]. Dot Daniel, who now works for 'Pop' Knickerbocker, is a she-male peace officer [policewoman?], Ham Hamilton and William Reese of Corona at Bell Telephone Co." (6 May 1939).

A leading organization in the fair campaign and in other collective protests in Corona during the period was the Negro Youth Association (NYA), founded in 1938 by West Indies–born realtor, Walter Reifer. As Corona's most prominent black real estate agent, Walter Reifer had gained notoriety as a "block buster" who enabled African-Americans to move into previously white sections of Corona and later East Elmhurst.

Black youth associations like the NYA of Corona were active throughout the country during the 1930s and were often organized under the auspices of the NAACP as parallel "junior branches." In Corona, as elsewhere, these youth associations often pursued social action programs that were more controversial, if not militant, than those of the senior leadership. For example, in an article on youth councils in Detroit, the *Crisis* reported, "Ofttimes the attitude of the seniors was 'quell and control the youth councils lest they wreck the association.' That attitude is no longer prevalent" (May 1939:155). The youth division of the Jamaica, Queens, branch of the NAACP played a leading role in demonstrations and marches in support of the antilynching bill in 1938 (as did NAACP youth councils in Brooklyn), low-income housing construction, and other social action work during the 1930s (*Crisis*, March 1938:88). Although Corona's NAACP chapter was not formed until 1940, the NYA and its young activists cooperated with NAACP branches throughout the city.

George Lopez, who had served on the NYA's Youth Council, highlighted Reifer's twin qualities of business acumen and race pride which, in the minds of many residents, epitomized the post–depression era generation of "race leaders."

> Slick as goose grease. He was slick, boy. What I admired about him was that he didn't take no crap off the white folks. But people didn't like him 'cause he would bring a tenant to you and get the commission and then take the tenant over to someone else. That's why he and my old man didn't get along, see. But he did good on the other hand. He wouldn't take no crap from the folks. He'd go down to city hall and raise hell. He didn't care who it was. And that's the kind of fire we need that we don't have now among black people. Walter didn't give a damn— he'd tell the president of the United States off.

The NYA pickets at the 1939 World's Fair produced jobs for youth in Black Corona and incited a broader campaign to force white-owned businesses in Corona to hire black workers. The "We Seven" documented the progress of the picketing, publicizing the names of businesses that had complied and not complied, as well as the names of Corona youth who had been hired.

> Who's who and who did it—The NYA Negro Youth Association is at it again. After a mass meeting at the [St. Mark] A.M.E. Church Monday night, the group got underway to some fine picketing. This time it's anti–Prosperity Cleaners and Dyers who refused to hire colored help . . . Owen Birkett now holds down the job in Corona's Wine and Liquor Store . . . Owen, who is a freshman at good ole N.Y.U., intends to bring home the letters. (*New York Age*, 21 October 1939)

The NYA's practices of direct action protests did not go uncontested. The "We Seven," in their typically cagey narrative style, provided an account of a struggle over the leadership of the NYA, which suggests a deepening conflict between the youth-oriented, race politics of the NYA and sectors of Corona's established black political leadership.

> Getting back to the affairs of the N.Y.A. we find that the head executive, W. Reifer, is peeved over the action taken by many of Corona's leading "professional" men and women. It seems that a certain political group had it arranged for their choice to take the office of chairman but were defeated by the popularity of his opponent, W. Reifer, who believes that the complete absence of politics is

essential for the proper functioning of this worthy movement. (*New York Age*, 1 April 1939)

The dispute over the control of the Negro Youth Association registered a division, which developed in other black communities during the period and was tied to a rearticulation of black class identities and their social and political meanings.[31] For many residents of Black Corona, Walter Reifer and other race leaders symbolized an emerging cadre of the black middle class that derived its livelihood from within the black community and was relatively free of the political obligations that tied Corona's largely church-based, old settler elites to white political institutions. "The thing that was different about Walter Reifer and that young crowd," one woman recalled, "was that he didn't owe anything to white people. He had his own business. And as far as he was concerned, they could take it or leave it."

This intraclass division between old elites and emerging sectors of the new black middle class, although emphasized by contemporary residents, did not align neatly along generational, institutional, or economic lines. The Corona Congregational Church, a longtime focal point of old settler activism and influence, played an important role in the citywide struggle against job discrimination at the 1939 World's Fair and, later, at LaGuardia Airport. The Reverend Hinton, pastor at the Congregational Church, also organized a campaign to house black visitors to the fair who were excluded from the area's hotels. As Higginbotham pointed out, "Arguments over the accommodationist versus liberating thrust to the black church miss the range as well as the fluid interaction of political and ideological meanings represented within the church's domain" (1993:18).

Social and political divisions did not neatly follow class lines but were shot through with distinctions based on length of residence, place of birth, and ethnicity. The complex and often contradictory manner in which these distinctions intersected is illustrated by a resident's remarks about Black Corona's class structure during the Great Depression:

> Yes, there was a class distinction in terms of "Were you working or not working?" It didn't matter *what* you were doing: "Are you working, or are you not working?" Then there were people who came up from the South, and let's face it, West Indians and Southerners don't get along very well, you know. But it wasn't an overt prejudice, it was sort of a snobbish prejudice. You might nod to them because you were raised to be gracious.

The formation of Corona's "new middle class" should be viewed less as an abrupt changing of the economic and political guard than as a gradual, uneven, and contested rearticulation of black class, political, and cultural identities: a process which, although shaped by the changing economic orientation of the new middle classes, was collectively realized in modes of political activism and cultural expression that publicly challenged white racial domination. It was this shift in political strategies, tactics, and identities that marked the "newness" of Corona's political culture during the 1930s and 1940s.

George Lopez described an NYA action during World War II whose confrontational tactics no doubt alarmed Corona's black and white political establishment:

> There was an Italian bakery on Northern Boulevard. That's the one we wrecked 'cause they wouldn't hire nobody. What happened was, Reifer went to speak to those people [at the bakery] and they said, "Hell no, we ain't gonna hire no blacks." So he got us together. For example, we'd go into the bakery and take something, and say, "We ain't gonna pay for it unless you hire somebody." And there'd be a whole lot of things—we'd turn over the cakes, and then they'd call the cops, and that kind of stuff. And we did the same thing all along Northern Boulevard. Finally, they broke down.

This growing political and cultural militancy of African-Americans in Corona sometimes alarmed the "We Seven." Reviewing a play produced by the Corona-based, Long Island Dramatic Group in support of the antilynching bill, the "We Seven" criticized its "heavy-handed" treatment of the topic, charging that the play was carried to a "state of vulgarity and antisocialism":

> We appreciate the theme, "Pass the anti-lynching bill," but not the lengths used to put that idea over. We all realize the importance of the passage of that vital bill, but we were so impressed that it [seemed to be] enough for us sepias to go out and cuff the first white person we met. [But] I believe the author didn't realize the emphasis he placed on that point. As for the posterity of that group, the public will be a little skeptical about your future efforts. In dealing with the working class (as we all are, at the end of the day, [looking] for relaxing entertainment), lighter themes instead of such heavy dramatics. (5 May 1940)

Between 1930 and 1940 Corona's black population grew by nearly 50 percent, from 2,963 to 4,381, or 6.6 percent of Corona's population (Frost 1946). Some of this growth was associated with the employment of black workers in the WPA-financed construction and operation of LaGuardia Airport on the north shore of Queens and in the expanding war industries. Corona also continued to be an important second-settlement area for upwardly mobile working-and middle-class people from Manhattan and the other boroughs, and for southern migrants, during and after the war.

Some residents associated the construction and operation of LaGuardia Airport with the arrival of "lower-class" migrants from the South. One old settler recalled:

> The transition of Corona was devastating to watch. When they opened [La Guardia Airport], they brought a lot of blacks from Newark, New Jersey, over here to

work at the airport. That's when this town started going downhill. That influx of blacks. Nothing to say about Southerners, but most of them were Southerners from Newark who came up here to take the jobs. And the complexion, the whole atmosphere of the community, started to change, and it went downhill.

Completed in October 1939, the LaGuardia Airport project employed twenty-three thousand WPA workers in three eight-hour shifts during peak construction periods (Blumberg 1979). Given that black workers, heavily concentrated in unskilled occupations, formed 13 percent of the city's WPA labor force in 1937, they no doubt constituted a significant part of the project's labor force during the more than two years taken to complete the airport. When LaGuardia Field opened, black workers were employed as "sky caps" and in other service occupations on the airport's labor force.

Other migrants from the south moved to Corona to work in service industries which, even during the depression, offered better wages than in the South (Jones 1985). For example, the mother of Eunice Waynes left North Carolina in 1937 at the age of eighteen to live with an aunt who was the founder and pastor of Corona's Mount Horizon Holiness Pentecostal Church. The first of ten children to migrate north, Waynes's mother did domestic work in Corona, Flushing, and Jackson Heights. When Waynes's mother married a West Virginia–born Corona man in the 1940s, her aunt provided the down payment for their house in Corona. After the children were born, Waynes's father worked nights as a custodian and took care of the children by day.

Although by 1940 Corona's black population had grown and become more diverse, it remained an economically stable, working- and middle-class community. An indication of the prosperity of Black Corona relative to other areas of black settlement in New York City can be gleaned from homeownership figures. In 1940 Queens as a whole showed a higher rate of black homeownership than did the other four boroughs. In 1940, 31 percent of black Queens residents owned their own homes, compared to only 0.4 percent in Manhattan, 8 percent in Brooklyn, 2 percent in the Bronx, and 21 percent in Staten Island. Black homeownership in Queens had actually fallen from 37 percent in 1930, because of the depression, but white losses during the same period in Queens were higher. Olivia Frost estimated that at least one in five black families in Corona in 1940 owned the homes in which they lived. When Langdon Post, the city's tenement house commissioner, toured Long Island City, South Jamaica, and other Queens slum areas in 1936, Corona was not on his itinerary (*New York Times*, 14 January 1936). If, as James Weldon Johnson noted of the 1920s, "buying property became a fever" for black New Yorkers, much of this fever was allayed in Queens (1968).

Black Coronaites were also well-educated, showing a median number of school years completed in 1940 slightly higher than their white neighbors and comparing favorably to the city's population as a whole. This well-educated population experienced unemployment rates in 1940 slightly lower than their peers in the borough (24 percent, compared to a borough average of 26 percent for blacks). Although black Corona residents faced the same exclusionary hiring practices as African-Americans elsewhere in the city, a solid core of working-and middle-class people coalesced around the community's rapidly growing institutions.

The "We Seven," after reporting an altercation that occurred outside a Corona nightclub between the members of rival black social clubs, editorialized about Corona's changing population and its implications for the community's reputation:

> It is getting so that desirable respectable families migrating from other parts venture further out on the Island outwardly avoiding Corona. We of Corona used to call it a "dead town." Now our fair town is overrun by undesirous "life" which is coming to a point that the local police are ordered to arrest any person disturbing the peace (in the strictest sense). What has happened to the Corona of old? (12 August 1939)

Corona was no longer a "dead town" socially or politically. And as its population and voting power grew, Black Corona began to flex its political muscle. By 1940 the tactical, guerrilla actions of Walter Reifer's Negro Youth Association were yielding to the development of broader-based political strategies which, stressing solidarity among neighborhood leaders, sought to present a united front before the white political establishment and, in particular, the Queens County Democratic Party.

In March 1940 the *Age* reported on a "unique gathering" at St. Mark AME Church of Corona, the purpose of which was to discuss community problems. The meeting at St. Mark, attended by a mix of clergy, professionals, and civic activists, cross-cut denominational, generational, and, more than likely, ideological boundaries. Hosted by the Reverend Theodore Garrison of St. Mark AME, the meeting was moderated by Charles Taylor (Private "Rough House" who had led the pickets at the Palace Theater), a social worker and former leader of the NYA. Two Corona physicians gave presentations on community health. O. P. Armwood, Corona's "young mortician," spoke on the subject of expanding black businesses. Reverend Father Hamilton, pastor of the Episcopalian Church of the Resurrection, discussed the "spiritual state" of the community. Walter Reifer "urged a united front," and H. Anton Slaughter, a Corona attorney and soon-to-be founder of Corona's NAACP, addressed the problems of youth (*Age*, 12 March 1940).

African-Americans in Corona and in Jamaica's growing black community had already begun to test the political waters, challenging the established political leadership of Queens with the prospect of a black united front. John A. Singleton, "the militant dentist-president" of the Jamaica branch of the NAACP, founded the Colored Temporary Committee for Democratic Unity in

Queens. "The aim of the Committee," the *Age* reported, "will be to seek a square deal in the equation in which the New Deal has operated among members of the Negro Democratic ranks on Long Island" (*Age*, 27 January 1940).

Although it had been reported in the press that Singleton had received the endorsement of County Democratic leader James A. Roe to "reorganize" the Negro vote, a black precinct captain in Jamaica accused Singleton of using the NAACP "to further his own ends" and suggested that independent clubs like Singleton's were "shields for gambling and gamblers." Urging patience, the captain reassured *Age* readers: "The Negroes of Jamaica have an organization, a part of the Democratic organization of Queens County. They are recognized by our Democratic Party executives and we shall be well taken care of as soon as city and county return to the Democratic political columns. We want no Singleton!" (*Age*, 16 March 1940).

Not long after Singleton's challenge, in a symbolically potent gesture of defiance, the newly formed Corona branch of the NAACP, led by H. Anton Slaughter, sent telegrams to J. Edgar Hoover and Attorney General Frank Murphy, requesting that action be taken against "un-American" groups in Queens. The telegrams called for a federal probe of the Klu Klux Klan which, the NAACP charged, Congressman Martin Dies of Texas had refused to investigate (*Age*, 20 January 1940).

Queens County's political machine had shown little interest in extending the spirit of the New Deal across the color line. Only the year before, Queens Borough President George L. Harvey, a conservative Republican, had tried to halt the construction of a low-income housing development in Jamaica which, financed through the New York City Housing Department's slum clearance program, was to provide housing for 456 African-American families. At a meeting of the New York City Board of Estimate, Harvey opined: "Where would we be if we followed this thing out to its logical conclusion, and had one class of people supporting another? That's what these projects are. That kind of thing is all right in Russia, but [it] isn't all right in Queens. It's communistic" (*Age*, 17 June 1939).

Although African-Americans in Corona, still a demographic minority in predominantly white electoral districts, could not hope to elect blacks to political office, as did black majorities in Harlem and Brooklyn's Bedford-Stuyvesant during the 1940s, the organization of black voters could produce political patronage in the form of jobs and support for community projects.

During the 1940s and 1950s African-Americans in Corona began to organize political clubs that could mobilize black constituencies and leverage patronage from white politicians. In 1948 the ever present Walter Reifer founded the Jethro Democratic Club in a ceremony held at Big George's nightclub. James Graham, owner of a popular Corona barbershop and meeting place, was installed as its president, and Daniel J. Hill, one of the founders of the Congregational Church, was inducted as treasurer (*Age*, 18 December 1948). When a second black political club headed by a black postal worker failed to collect petitions for the white Northside Democratic Club, based in heavily Italian Corona Heights and headed by political kingpin "Papa" Joe Lisa, the Queens borough president visited Jake Govan and his associate, George Carol, at their meeting place in back of the Triboro Funeral Home.

Jake Govan recalled:

> So the borough president came over and said to us, would we help Joe Lisa. And Georgie said, "What do you mean help Joe Lisa?" He said, "Joe needs names out of his district here, which he didn't get from Buddy Reid." So Georgie said, "Well, all right, I'll tell you what we'll do. If you give us all the [poll] inspectors, we'll get the names for you." So he gave us all the inspectors, and we got the names.

Govan chuckled at the memory, shaking his head from side to side in a gesture of bemused frustration.

"See," John Booker explained to me, "our nemesis has always been Joe Lisa, or that guy in Flushing, Jim Roe. They were the two kingpins—Lisa and Roe fighting for blacks over here. Walter Reifer got his break out of Jim Roe. He didn't get much out of Joe Lisa."

"Oh no," Govan interjected. "Well, you see Jim Roe gave him cash money and let him do what he wanted to do, so long as he did what Jim Roe said. That's where Reifer went."

However, the days of patron-client black politics in Queens were quickly coming to an end. In 1948 the "militant dentist" of Jamaica, John Singleton, read a report before the executive committee of the Inter-Community Civic League of Queens, heir to the Colored Temporary Committee which demanded the appointment of a black assistant district attorney.

> For too long now the idea has been that if you keep the Negro from organizing, he will not be in a position to demand any of the political plums that fall from the political tree. The Negro areas have been carefully gerrymandered—cutting them up so that there is not a substantial number in any one district to elect a zone leader.
>
> If the leaders of the major political parties fail to see the advantage of a concentrated Negro vote which can easily be the balance of power in any one election, it is about time that organizations such as ours get together and make the average citizen aware of these facts.
>
> It is time to wake up! In Manhattan, Brooklyn and even little Nassau [County], we have Negro Assistant Attorneys . . . Why should Queens County with its vast Negro population and many qualified men for these jobs, not enjoy the same distinction of having an Assistant District Attorney? (*New York Age*, 21 September 1948)

Long Island columnist for the *Age*, Sylvia Bartley, before reporting on a luncheon appearance of Lena Horne, "Queens's most glamourous resident," called for unity and assured her readers that the fight for an African-American district attorney "was civic and not political" and that the hoped-for appointment would be a "step forward for the whole community, not a personal triumph for an individual" (1 October 1948).

Following a meeting of the Inter Community Civic League of Queens with Democratic County Chairman James A. Roe, Westervelt Taylor of St. Albans was sworn in as the first African-American assistant district attorney in Queens (*Age*, 11 December 1948).

After decades of political organizing and struggle, Westervelt Taylor's appointment was a small, if not ephemeral, victory. When Harry Truman appeared at Lost Battalion Hall in Elmhurst on the eve of the 1948 presidential election, no African-Americans appeared on the speaker's platform. "Thirty invitations were sent out we were assured," columnist Sylvia Bartley noted skeptically in the *Age*. "Did you get one? Do you know anyone else who did?" (6 November 1948).

By mid-century, Black Corona had grown to become a thriving working- and middle-class community of nearly nine thousand living within a predominantly white area.[32] Black Corona's borders were not defined by its spatial coordinates on the urban landscape but rather by the complex power relations and practices that excluded its residents, on racial grounds, from fully participating in the political economy and public life of the society. Black identity was "crafted," negotiated, and contested along these ever shifting boundaries of exclusion from the labor market, the polity, and the wider public sphere in which whites produced and exercised their citizenship and national identity (Kondo 1990).

However, black identity and the communal life that produced and sustained it was not a mere reaction to, or "compensation" for, racial exclusion. Like other Americans, black Coronaites pursued the pleasures of building social relationships and families, found fulfillment in education and work, grappled with the social and political quandaries of the day, and some (albeit not many) worked diligently to improve their overhand serves. And, like other Americans, black Coronaites argued and exercised differences rooted in class, gender, ethnicity, and sexuality.

Racial exclusion did not repress these differences as much as shape their meaning and social significance in ways that were particular to the shifting experience of urban black populations. For example, the process of class formation in Black Corona was conditioned by the specific ways in which residents lived their class positions in a political economy that was structured in racial terms. The Great Depression and the New Deal drove home the message that, from the point of view of capital, organized labor, *and* the state, racial identity was as important, if not more so, than class position in determining the livelihood and futures of African-Americans. Consequently, though class distinctions were important to black Coronaites, they were formed and negotiated in a cultural politics of "racial uplift" that celebrated economic mobility *and* the social resources and political power that made it possible. For in a racialized economy where teachers often slipped into domestic service, machinists into unskilled labor, and clerical workers onto the relief rolls, the workplace provided shaky grounds on which to construct social identities and divisions, let alone to organize politically.

The surge of political activism in Black Corona during the late 1930s and 1940s was incited in part by this antagonism between the political economy of racism and the social processes of black class formation—a contradiction that had reached crisis proportions during the Great Depression. And if black residents of Corona rallied more often to the call of "racial uplift" than class struggle, it was not because their struggle had nothing to do with class; indeed, it had everything to do with class in a society in which class had everything to do with race.

Similarly, African-Americans negotiated gender asymmetries that were overdetermined by race. Black women, confined largely to domestic service occupations where they were often supervised by white women, confronted a labor market that was structured in terms of both gender and race. Like white women, black working women were excluded from skilled male occupations in the gendered hierarchy of labor. But unlike white working women, race barred black women from taking advantage of the limited opportunities that were opening for white women in clerical and professional areas, as well as in skilled industrial work during the war.

However, far from subordinating their interests as women to the largely male-led politics of racial uplift, black women established their own "race conscious programs of self-help," working "at times in concert and at times in conflict" with men (Higginbotham 1993:8). Like their sisters elsewhere, black women in Corona organized and directed church-based and other voluntary associations through which they not only provided critical labor, funds, and other forms of institutional support for political and social welfare activities but also pursued their own interests as black women and, in the process, shaped the political culture and agenda of black activism. As a woman who worked intensively with the Missionary Society of the Corona Congregation Church in the 1950s put it: "We all worked together back then. So I don't think that you could say that there was conflict, I mean between men and women. See, we had our own money, and I guess you could say that we did pretty much what we pleased. Because women have always been the backbone of the church, you know."

In the years to come, Black Corona would draw heavily on these social networks and political resources as its residents mobilized to confront the key problems of the 1960s: political powerlessness, urban decline, and black poverty.

CHAPTER THREE

The Movement

The patience of the Negro is virtually at an end. For years,
starting with Franklin Roosevelt's New Deal, the Negro has
looked for his political salvation through the evolution of the
ordinary American party system. New York has been looked
to as the spearhead of this movement. The news of the latest
judicial appointments indicates that the Negro is still regarded as a moron, beast-of-burden, or idiot by the white
top political brass, both Republican and Democratic.
(New York Age editorial, 1951)

IN 1957 Martin Luther King, Jr., spoke at a rally sponsored by the Jamaica
branch of the NAACP held at the same Elmhurst hall where black leaders had
been snubbed during Harry Truman's visit, and only blocks from where
Booker T. Washington had spoken on the subject of Negro progress almost a
half century before. A Queens newspaper reported the next day, "Non-violent
resistance to segregation was urged last night in Queens by the man who persuaded 50,000 Montgomery, Alabama, Negroes to quit riding segregated
buses" (*Long Island Star Journal* 13 November 1957).

For residents of Corona who attended the rally that night, the message
struck home. While the civil rights movement was gathering steam in the
South and winning its first major victories against Jim Crow, African-Americans in Corona were witnessing a hardening of the color line: a consolidation
of de facto forms of segregation that were increasingly penetrating the bedrock
of black working- and middle-class society.

To be sure, black Coronaites had always suffered racial exclusion in employment, housing, politics, as well as in access to education and public services. Nonetheless many had succeeded in negotiating these complex and
shifting barriers and managed to achieve a modicum of social and economic
stability. The material and symbolic expression of this success for black Coronaites, as well as for other Americans, was homeownership (K. T. Jackson
1985; Hayden 1984). And it was homeownership and, more generally, the
political economy of black urban spaces that would increasingly come under
attack after World War II.

Property ownership was a key benchmark in what the *New York Age* called
"the story of progress" of Negroes in Queens, not only embodying accumulated wealth but also symbolizing hard-fought victories over job and housing

discrimination, the depression, and for many the social dislocations of the Great Migration (21 July 1951). For black Coronaites, this story of progress was less a celebration of acceptance by white society than a complex narrative of struggle with that society.

For example, Blanche Hubbert was raised on a farm near Hanover, Virginia, where her parents grew cotton and raised turkeys and chickens. Her mother was a schoolteacher and social activist and had founded a rural school with funding from the Rolls Walst Foundation. "And naturally, being on the farm," Hubbert told me, "she helped with the farming and had her share. The female share of it."

When the farm was destroyed by a hurricane in the 1920s Hubbert's father went North to find work in the Pittsburgh steel mills. Her mother sent the children to Richmond, Virginia, to finish school and then moved to Far Rockaway, Queens, where she found work in domestic service.

> And during the summer months, my mother would bring us, and anybody else's child up [North]. All the young girls that wanted to come up, she got jobs. A lot of times it was domestic jobs, babysitting and whatever. This was in the thirties, I guess. And after I finished high school, I came up and never returned. Started working here and there during the depression years. My mother stayed then, too. She gave up teaching.

During World War II Hubbert renewed her acquaintance ("We weren't courting at the time, you understand") with a man she had known in Virginia, and they married. After losing her wartime job as a machinist in a defense factory at Brooklyn's Bush Terminal, Hubbert and her husband found employment as domestic workers for a wealthy Long Island family to "put together a nest egg."

> So after that, we saved enough money and started to buying property. Through some friends, through my hairdresser really, we met Walter Reifer who had a real estate office up on Northern Boulevard. And my friend the hairdresser had just bought a house out here and gave me Reifer's number. We got in touch with him, and we bought our first house. After that we started investing in rental property. And it just grew from that. We eventually ended up with, I guess it was nine or ten houses in this area. And then I started a catering business, which was pretty successful.

For working- and middle-class residents of Corona like the Hubberts, progress did not simply mean job mobility and the accumulation of wealth but, more fully, the capacity to produce, sustain, and defend the social and political conditions that made such mobility possible. Black middle-class identity, formed through what Drake and Cayton (1945) called the "social rituals" of black society, wedded a celebration of economic security to a consuming preoccupation with exercising the social and political networks that sustained it in the face of racial inequality. It was this dynamic and often tenuous synthesis of economic mobility and social activism that epitomized the race leader and characterized the ideology of racial uplift.[1]

During the 1950s this narrative of black progress, lived and recollected by people such as the Hubberts, would be forcefully disrupted by changes in the U.S. economy and by racist policies of the state.

THE NORTHERN FACE OF JIM CROW

Between the world wars African-Americans in Corona formed a small and dispersed minority of the area's population. As late as 1947 Olivia Frost reported that in contrast to Harlem there was no black belt in Corona: "Negro families live alongside white families and there are only a few blocks . . . that are occupied by people of either race solely" (68). Health Area 6.10, where 60 percent of Corona's 4,381 black residents lived, was only 13.2 percent black in 1940. Sixty-six percent of Corona's population was native-born white in 1940, and the remaining 27.5 percent were foreign-born whites, 60 percent of whom had been born in Italy. In addition, Frost noted twenty additional white ethnic groups living in Corona, including Germans, Irish, Russians, Austrians, Greeks, and British Islanders (1947).

Residence in a racially integrated neighborhood afforded important advantages to residents of Black Corona over life in racially segregated ghettos. The mere presence of whites in significant numbers assured better public services, such as public schools, building code enforcement, and garbage collection, as well as access to mortgages and other banking and commercial services. "Compared with other minority groups," Douglas Massey and Nancy Denton noted, "[African-Americans] are markedly less able to convert their socioeconomic attainments into residential contact with whites, and because of this fact they are unable to gain access to crucial resources and benefits that are distributed through housing markets" (1993:151; see also Oliver and Shapiro 1995; Wilson 1996).

An African-American woman, who ran for State Assembly district leader in 1962 against the favorite of Corona's Northside Democratic Club headed by white political boss "Papa" Joe Lisa, underscored the collateral effects of residential segregation: "I could have lived with Mr. Lisa, if he had lived here in North Corona and was my neighbor, so that when I didn't have garbage picked up, he didn't have his garbage picked up. And when we didn't have enough street lights, and our kids were getting killed, he would experience the same thing. Then he would have to be concerned about it, because it would be affecting him and his family."

Although racial exclusion was a key, if not decisive, factor in the building of a relatively independent sphere of black civil society, the viability of that society rested paradoxically on the ability of African-Americans to blur and contest its spatial, political, and symbolic borders; that is, to disrupt the alignment of black identity with the binary logic of racism, a process that found its realization in the segregated ghetto.

Black activists were careful to point out that demands for racial equality extended beyond the interests of the black community to affect the lives of other groups. For example, in its column "Branch News," the *Crisis* reported on the efforts of the NAACP's Jamaica chapter to stop the closing of a Boys' Club, underscoring the fact that the club had "Negro and white members with the latter forming 70% of the membership" (August 1939:248). Moreover, as impending struggles against school segregation would demonstrate, black Corona activists supported school busing precisely because they recognized that the presence of whites in predominantly black schools ensured the provision of quality educational services for black children.

However, beginning in the late 1940s, the racial demography of Corona drastically changed, registering regional and national redistributions of population. After a depression-era lull, black out-migration from the South intensified during and after the World War II. Between 1930 and 1940, 398,000 African-Americans left the South. By comparison, in each of the three following decades, nearly 1.5 million African-Americans left, roused by the collapse of the southern agricultural labor market and by the prospect of industrial, public sector, and other jobs in the North and West (Farley and Allen 1987:113).

Already congested black areas, such as Harlem, Brooklyn's Bedford-Stuyvesant, and the Morrisania-Mott Haven section of the Bronx, struggled to absorb this postwar surge in migration. During the 1940s the black population of Bedford-Stuyvesant more than doubled, reaching 137,436 by 1950 (Connolly 1977). As housing and neighborhood conditions deteriorated in black areas of Manhattan, Brooklyn, and the Bronx, black settlement in Queens skyrocketed. Between 1950 and 1957 the black population of Queens grew 125 percent to 116,193, or to nearly 7 percent of the borough's population. By 1962 the South Jamaica–St. Albans area in southern Queens had more than 100,000 black residents and had become spatially the largest black section of the city (*New York Times*, 13 March 1962).

The negative effects of this surge in population were heightened by a postwar housing shortage that disproportionately affected low-income people and racial minorities in particular.[2] In the decades following World War II, the overall vacancy rate in New York City averaged about 1 percent, affecting the low- and moderate-income end of the housing scale most severely (Massey and Denton 1993). For African-Americans, and increasingly Puerto Ricans, this housing shortage was exacerbated by not only housing discrimination but also by slum clearance projects funded under Title I of the Federal Housing Act of 1949 (cf. Hirsch 1985). By constricting the number and location of housing units available to African-Americans and other racial minorities, housing discrimination and equally racialized policies of urban renewal played critical roles in promoting the deterioration of Corona and other stable, working- and middle-class communities during the postwar period (see Caro 1975; K. T. Jackson 1985; Logan and Molotch 1987).

In the ten years following the passage of the Federal Housing Act of 1949, New York City's slum clearance program, administered by Robert Moses, had not only failed to reduce the number of substandard housing units in the city but had also resulted in the dislocation of tens of thousands of poor and disproportionately minority persons from urban renewal sites (*New York Times*, 26 July 1959; Caro 1975). Although provisions under Title I required that local authorities ensure the relocation of displaced residents of slum areas in "decent, safe, and sanitary dwellings," the city's Committee on Slum Clearance circumvented these requirements by manipulating relocation statistics and by failing to monitor the compliance of Title I development corporations which, as Robert Caro observed, were often "hastily set up by Democratic clubhouse politicians" (1975:965).

Unable to afford the comparatively high rents charged at "renewed" Title I sites and closed out of already saturated public housing, tens of thousands of low- and moderate-income families evicted from renewal areas were turned out into the tight, postwar housing market. Lawrence Orton, a City Planning Commission official, estimated that 170,000 persons had been evicted from their homes in the seven years following the end of World War II alone. During the next three years Orton projected that 150,000 persons would face a similar fate through slum clearance (Caro 1975). Moreover, for African-Americans and the city's growing Latino population, this tight housing market was racially stratified.

Until 1948, when the United States Supreme Court ruled against their use, restrictive covenants enabled property owners to write legally binding provisions into deeds barring occupancy by African-Americans and other groups deemed "undesirable." Such legal practices reflected widely accepted beliefs and policies in the real estate industry and in government agencies, such as the New Deal–inspired Home Owners Loan Corporation (HOLC) and Federal Housing Administration (FHA), which were grounded in the self-fulfilling appraisal that the investment potential of an area declined when the "social and racial classes" were not kept separated (K. T. Jackson 1985). Even after the city's Fair Housing Practice Law went into effect in 1958, barring discrimination in the rental of most but not all privately owned housing, rental agents and property owners continued to use covert but equally effective strategies to circumvent antidiscrimination laws (*New York Times*, 13 March 1962).[3]

The massive in-migration of African-Americans and Puerto Ricans in the midst of a racially stratified housing crisis and urban renewal program, described by a City Planning Commission report as "an enforced population displacement completely unlike any previous population movement in the City's history," proved devastating for communities such as Corona that bore the brunt of the housing crisis (quoted in Caro 1975:968)

Robert Caro observed:

> Crowd as they would into slums, there would not be enough room in the slums for them. So they would move into areas adjacent to the slums, into areas in which landlords, without incentive to keep up their property anyway because of the slums' proximity, would see an opportunity for financial profit and take it by breaking up large apartments into small and by cutting down on maintenance and repairs. The slums would spill over their boundaries, spreading into blocks as yet untouched by blight. Moreover, some slum dwellers hounded from their homes would flee into "soft" areas of the city such as Brownsville, neighborhoods in which there were a large number of vacancies. These vacancies would now be filled by the dispossessed of the ghetto. (1975:966)

Corona was one of these "soft areas" where racially structured public- and private-sector practices at the macro level interacted with local conditions to transform radically the social, economic, and political base of neighborhood life. During the 1940s Corona's black population doubled in size, accounting for 26 percent of the area's population in 1950. By 1960 this percentage had increased to 50 percent, and black residents of Corona and East Elmhurst numbered 20,793 (Hart, Krivatsy, and Stubee 1970). Housing conditions in Corona and sections of East Elmhurst deteriorated as many single-family homes were converted into rooming houses and multifamily dwellings. This rapid growth in Corona's black population was accompanied by an equally dramatic exodus of whites. During the 1950s, 70 percent of Corona's white population left the area, reflecting a boroughwide wave of panic selling in neighborhoods where blacks were settling and a more general, postwar exodus of whites from the city to Long Island, Westchester, Rockland, and other New York counties (City Planning Commission 1963).

Barbara Coleman, a longtime Corona resident, recalled this transition, underscoring, as did many, the impact of white flight on neighborhood resources and amenities.

> The butcher had gone, the laundromat had gone—Wing's Chinese Laundry had gone, Public Service Supermarket was still there but they served junk. White people started moving away. They moved away to the Island, or they moved to Westchester, or someplace like that. But they moved away from Corona. Because the associations were bad. It was *black*, it was ghetto, people didn't have jobs, and you could walk down the street and see your friends holding up buildings. That's what they did for a living. They held up buildings.

"White flight" was not simply a response to the increasing presence of African-Americans and other racial minorities in the neighborhood. Corona whites not only found that they could afford housing being built in suburban developments, such as Levittown on Long Island, but also that FHA- and Veterans Administration (VA)-insured, fixed rate and long-term mortgages often yielded monthly payments lower than what they were paying for comparable housing in Queens (K. T. Jackson 1985:205–206). In contrast, African-Americans and other racial minorities found this avenue to the suburbs, with their amenities and forms of middle-class symbolic capital, blocked by state-subsidized racism (K. T. Jackson 1985; Sacks 1994).

Created by the National Housing Act of 1934, the Federal Housing Administration was designed to stimulate the depression-crippled housing construction industry by making it easier for home buyers to secure and service mortgages. By insuring mortgages made by private lenders for home construction and sale, the FHA (and later the Veterans Administration) provided a strong incentive to lenders not only to lower down payments but also to reduce monthly payments by extending the repayment period.

FHA regulations established minimum standards for home construction and developed equally standardized criteria and procedures for appraising not only properties and borrowers but neighborhoods as well. As Kenneth Jackson pointed out, FHA appraisal ideology and practice not only favored lending in suburban versus urban areas but also encouraged and actively promoted lending in homogeneous white areas that were free of "inharmonious racial or nationality groups" (1985:208).

Continuing a practice begun by the Home Owners Loan Corporation, FHA appraisers evaluated neighborhoods in terms of mortgage risk, classifying areas with black people a priori in the highest-risk category (K. T. Jackson 1985). As a result, racially integrated areas such as Corona were deemed poor lending risks, and racial segregation was institutionalized as a sine qua non of federally insured suburban development.

As early as 1938 black activists in Queens were calling attention to and protesting the racialized policies of the FHA. The Jamaica branch of the NAACP, headed by Dr. John A. Singleton, investigated numerous complaints that the FHA was systematically refusing to underwrite mortgages for black home buyers. A 1938 *Crisis* article summarized the concerns of the Jamaica branch:

> The N.A.A.C.P. charges that the F.H.A., by the enforcement of this [underwriting] rule, is creating segregation problems where none now exist. Instances were cited where local builders, local banks and local community sentiment were not opposed to Negro home builders, but the F.H.A. refused to guarantee the mortgage. In some cases local banks or finance companies financed the mortgage without the F.H.A., showing that local sentiment was not opposed to Negroes in the neighborhood. (February 1938:55)

Though the FHA did not invent redlining, it made it public policy, creating and systematizing technologies, protocols, and databases that synchronized the machinery of the real estate and banking industries with the mystical calculus of racial, ethnic, and class hierarchies. As the NAACP's protest fore-warned, FHA policies played a critical role in articulating the meanings of racial categories and in shaping the specific institutional and popular forms that racism would take in urban communities. If white homeowners in Corona were worried that an influx of racial minorities would provoke a decline in property values, their worries were well founded.

When Corrine Harris decided to move to Corona in 1951, where many of her coworkers at the Pennsylvania Railroad's Sunnyside Yards were already living, she found getting a home mortgage even more difficult as a divorced, working mother of three. The Discala family, eager to sell to Harris and join their children in Elmont, Long Island, decided to hold the mortgage for Harris, allowing her to circumvent the racist and sexist underwriting practices of the banking industry. When the Discala family's lawyer insisted that the agreement be written into a contract, Mrs. Discala ignored his advice.

Harris remembered:

> She said to me, "Look me in the eye. Are you a Christian?" I said yes. She said, "All right, look me in the eye. If you don't do what we say and what you promised, I'm gonna put a hex on you that will last for all your generations." I was laughing, because I didn't believe in any of that old stuff. But God bless her, 'cause I paid off that mortgage in seven years!

White flight from Corona was a gradual process occurring on Harris's block over a fifteen-year period and drawing on younger and more financially secure whites first. Some older residents like the Discalas remained in Corona after their children had left the neighborhood. Social ties between Corona blacks and their former white neighbors sometimes endured. For example, Harris continued to visit the Discala family on Long Island. Similarly, Jake Govan remained in contact with many of his former neighbors through his ties to the predominantly white Northside Democratic Club. "And a lot of them out there in Suffolk County," Govan once assured me, "are sorry now they left Corona."

In 1958 NYC Superintendent of Schools William Jansen, alarmed by the loss of twenty thousand white pupils from the city's elementary schools, proposed the construction of more affordable, middle-class housing to stem the exodus of whites to the suburbs (*New York Times*, 6 January 1958, 25). The following year, the Tri-Community Council of Queens, which represented fifty civic associations in Rosedale, Laurelton, and Springfield Gardens, appealed to New York's secretary of state, Caroline Simon, to clamp down on real estate agents who engaged in "block busting," that is, urging homeowners to sell when blacks moved into white neighborhoods. "Such chaotic, unsettled conditions," Simon replied in a letter to the Council, "are harmful, if not dangerous to orderly community life" (*New York Times*, 26 July 1959, 58).

Soon afterward, the city's Commission on Intergroup Relations set up a citywide "alarm system" to monitor racial tensions in white neighborhoods that were absorbing African-American and Hispanic newcomers. "When a report of trouble is received," the *New York Times* reported, "the commission plans to dispatch a tension control team to the neighborhood" (*New York Times*, 21 September 1959). One of the first alarms answered by the "tension control team" was in the Glendale-Ridgewood section of Queens where white residents were protesting the transfer of black and Puerto Rican students to local schools.

Such efforts were cosmetic at best and could do little to stem the intensification of racial segregation and neighborhood deterioration that was transforming Corona. As white residents left predominantly black areas, a rigid color line was defined distinguishing North Corona from what was commonly referred to as "Italian Corona," or "Corona Heights," to the south. Between 1950 and 1957 the black population of Corona Heights dropped to three hundred from four thousand, with some of that number resettling in North Corona and East Elmhurst (Community Service Council of Greater New York 1958). White and black youth gangs fought skirmishes along Roosevelt Avenue, the boundary said to separate the two communities. Patricia Corbett, whose family moved to "Italian Corona" in the early 1950s, remembered: "I lived in fear. I lived in fear because the race relationship was so bad there. I mean the white gang, the Dukes, they would be hanging out on the street right in front of my house, harassing people. You know, when you're a little girl and you see that, it's pretty frightening."

Junction Boulevard, the recognized frontier between Black Corona and predominantly white and middle-income Jackson Heights to the west, became known as the "Mason-Dixon line" when white Jackson Heights parents fought against a plan to desegregate the area's schools. White businesses fled African-American sections of Corona leading to the deterioration of Northern Boulevard, a vibrant commercial strip. A white grocer on Northern Boulevard informed one black customer that he was leaving the area because he "didn't want to sell black-eyed peas and grits."

Neighborhood deterioration in black areas of North Corona, tied to overcrowded housing and poor municipal services, fueled a spatial differentiation of the community along class lines. Many black working- and middle-class residents sold or rented their homes in Corona and bought houses in East Elmhurst to the north.

Fronting on Flushing Bay, East Elmhurst had been home to wealthy Long Island farmers, merchants, and professionals at the turn of the century. North Beach, a popular turn of the century amusement park and recreation area, occupied the western end of the shoreline. Ditmars Boulevard, which skirted the north shore, was lined with Spanish-style stucco homes and known as "Doctors' Row" through the 1940s (*Long Island Press*, 31 October 1971).

Dr. George Lopez, a Howard University–trained dentist who lived on Ditmars Boulevard, remembered:

> Over here, on this side, of course, that's where all the rich people lived. And the blacks only came up here to work. I never thought I'd be living in these houses because this is the place we looked up to. 'Cause you've got to realize that there was water all around here. My deed reads "beach front property." Me and my buddy, Charlie, used to come up here [from Corona] as youngsters and raise hell with the white folks; go out on their boats in the water.

Although cut off from the shore by the construction of LaGuardia Airport and the Grand Central Parkway during the 1930s, East Elmhurst remained an exclusive area whose spacious, detached homes and well-manicured lawns and gardens contrasted sharply with the more modest, semidetached row houses in Corona.

During the 1940s black Coronaites began purchasing homes in East Elmhurst along with new black arrivals from other areas of the city and from the South. Doctors, realtors, entertainers, and other members of Corona's black elite bought properties on Ditmars Boulevard, which became known as the "Black Gold Coast." Black veterans purchased their homes using VA-insured mortgages. In 1952 Walter Reifer relocated his real estate firm to East Elmhurst where, the *New York Age* reported, he planned to build six-room, semi-attached homes "on one of the most desirable streets in the neighborhood" (22 March 1952).

Residence in East Elmhurst became associated with elite status a cut above working- and middle-class life in Corona, which many perceived to be "going down the hill." Northern Boulevard, and later Astoria Boulevard, came to be regarded as the boundary separating the low-income and working-class residents of Corona from the more affluent homeowners of East Elmhurst. In an effort to legitimate this distinction, residents of East Elmhurst lobbied the U.S. Postal Service to assign their area a separate zip code.

One of the first African-Americans to move to Ditmars Boulevard highlighted the increasing significance of this class-inflected boundary:

> It changed when they put the East Elmhurst Post Office in, and then you all got—people started saying, "society folks live over here, and niggers live across the tracks." A lot of times people hear me talking and I refer to "Ditmars-Corona." And some people will correct me. But this was *all* Corona when I was a kid. Wasn't no East Elmhurst, that's Johnny-come-lately. They put a post office here and changed the boundaries. This side of Northern Boulevard [became] East Elmhurst, and the other side Corona.

Although this border, like the socioeconomic differences between the two areas, remained fluid and contested, the symbolic distance from "Corona" became increasingly meaningful as a marker of status and economic stability for the working- and middle-class homeowners of East Elmhurst.

One woman who had moved with her family to East Elmhurst from Corona in 1952 told me: "If you didn't have a college degree, [the neighbors] would walk all over you. I was surrounded by people who owned their own businesses, and they got to putting on airs. I told them, 'I pay the same taxes as you all do, I go to the bank just like you, I throw out just as much garbage as you do, and I do just as much for my children as you do.' That stopped them!"

If postwar neighborhood decline sharpened the perception of class differences between the two areas, it also heightened awareness among activists that Corona's escalating problems of housing deterioration, poverty, and poor city services were tied to its lack of political power as a *black* community. Class and status differences, real and imagined, remained crucial factors in reckoning black identities and social relations and in conditioning the specific effects of racial exclusion, but the experience of neighborhood decline exposed the vulnerability of black residents in both neighborhoods to wider structures of racial exclusion and injustice.

"Why, one may ask, was it necessary to form such an organization," began a brochure commemorating the founding of the Julian I. Garfield Democratic Association in 1960.

> The only truthful answer could be, it grew out of the need for political representation, recognition, and consideration. That is, consideration as it pertains to patronage and the other benefits which normally accrue from political participation. Plus consideration of community problems which were brought about due to the lack of political representation. We will not cease to function until we have made our community a better place for all to live regardless of race, creed, color or national origin. (Julian I. Garfield Democratic Association 1962:11)

Denied political power on the basis of race, activists viewed its benefits as undifferentiated by class. Corona had become a black community.

The postwar period was critical in shaping not only the social meanings and political significance of African-American racial and class identities but also in defining the terms of the contests that would take shape in Corona and East Elmhurst during the civil rights period. State-subsidized neighborhood segregation and deterioration served to anchor racial identities to the urban and suburban landscape and, in the case of Corona–East Elmhurst, to invest the notion of "black community" with concrete spatial form. Whereas in the past the borders of Black Corona had been somewhat porous and fluid, marking social more than spatial limits, by the late 1950s these boundaries had become etched into a racialized geography that was enforced by the political economy of the housing industry as much as by the street gangs that fought along Roosevelt Avenue.

The consolidation of this "black belt" in Corona–East Elmhurst, as in other urban areas, led to the deterioration of housing, schools, and other public services as fiscally overdrawn urban authorities, their tax base weakened by the suburban exodus of middle-income whites, directed dwindling resources and revenues unequally to their white constituents (cf. Hirsch 1985). In the minds of urban residents, as in the practices of public authorities, racial and class identities had become firmly conflated with space. And for African-Americans in Corona–East Elmhurst, *where* you lived had become as important as *how* you lived in the figuring of black class identities and opportunities.

It was this conflation of race, class, and urban space in the ideology and practice of public authorities and the private sector that would be the focal point of activism in Corona–East Elmhurst during the civil rights period. "When I was growing up around here," one activist remembered, "there was no such thing as a black area or a white area or a Hispanic area. But then, I guess that must have been in the 1950s; then everybody around here started talking about, 'Corona is a *black* ghetto.' And that's what we went up against, in the movement. Corona becoming a ghetto like over in Harlem."

MOVEMENT POLITICS AND THE BLACK PUBLIC SPHERE

> I remember when they killed that boy, Emmett Till. And we watched on television as those white men were acquitted and walked past his mother and laughed in her face. Well, my husband went off. And he said, "You better tell me something with all the organizations you belong to. Something to channel all this fear and anger that I have." And I said to him, "Go down to the NAACP, O.K.?" So he did. I took him down because I was just full with the kids, and the schools, and the PTA, and everything else. He really threw himself into the NAACP. And it kept us in touch with the movement.
> *(City Councilwoman Helen Marshall)*

During the 1960s and 1970s African-Americans in Corona pursued a wide range of strategies to address the interlocked goals of political empowerment and neighborhood preservation. "Politics," which on the limited playing field of the patronage system was for many black Coronaites synonymous with narrow and elitist interests, came to be seen as critical to the integrity and progress of the black community. What distinguished the era of civil rights activism in Black Corona from earlier periods of social activism was the widespread and deep politicization of the institutions and social relations of black community life.

This process of politicization involved both a widening in the scope of power relations contested and an enlargement of the political space within which such contests occurred. On the one hand, a broad spectrum of issues, ranging from mortgage lending practices and unemployment, to political empowerment and school quality, not only became focal points of activism but also were formulated and publicized as *interrelated* effects of structural racial inequalities. On the other hand, the political landscape on which these issues were elaborated and contested broadened to insinuate a heterogeneous array of institutions, voluntary associations, and social networks.[4]

In 1962 the Julian I. Garfield Democratic Association, successor to the Corona Democratic Association, nominated Corinne K. Harris to run for the position of female district leader in the Fifth Assembly District (A.D.) (Part B) against a candidate supported by the Northside Democratic Club in Corona Heights. A "gang foreman" in charge of a maintenance crew of forty-two men at the Pennsylvania Railroad's Sunnyside Yards, Corrine Harris was the first black candidate ever fielded in Corona.

The viability of Harris's candidacy rested on a number of interrelated factors. By 1960 the black population of Corona–East Elmhurst accounted for approximately 50 percent of the area's population. Although the Fifth A.D. included segments of predominantly white Jackson Heights, Forest Hills, and Elmhurst (distinct from East Elmhurst), which provoked charges of gerrymandering from black activists, mobilized black voters could now sustain a serious bid for political representation.

Equally important were divisions within the Democratic Party between "regular" Democrats, generally associated with the partisan and often corrupt politics of the ruling party machine, and "reform" Democrats, who espoused an ideology of nonpartisan governmental efficiency (see Katznelson 1981).

In 1959 the New York Committee for Democratic Voters, a Manhattan-based reform group of liberal Democrats, announced its reorganization on a citywide level and reaffirmed its commitment to "antibossism" (*New York Times*, 30 December 1959). By 1960 insurgent Democratic associations and clubs were operating in the Fourth, Sixth, and Seventh Assembly Districts surrounding Corona–East Elmhurst and corresponding roughly to Jackson Heights, Flushing, and Forest Hills (*New York Times*, 5 June 1960).

Some African-Americans in Corona–East Elmhurst joined white, insurgent clubs in Flushing and Forest Hills. John Bell, who became the first black member of the reform-oriented North Shore Democratic Association in nearby Flushing, recalled:

> There were no political clubs that I could identity with [in Corona]. Most of the political clubs here at that time were controlled by whites from outside the community. The blacks had their clubs and the county leader or assembly district leader, who was white, controlled those clubs. Even though you supported all of their candidates, you couldn't be a member of their clubs. That was the way it was.

The Garfield Democratic Association of Corona worked closely with the Yellowstone Reform Democratic Club of Jackson Heights establishing ties between black activists in Corona–East Elmhurst and liberal Democrats in Jackson Heights that persisted through the decade of the 1960s. The "regular"

Democrats, based at the Northside Democratic Club in Corona Heights, were perceived to be conservative and not responsive to the needs of the black community. By contrast, white liberal reformers were viewed by some to be supportive of the black community's civil rights agenda, particularly around issues of school desegregation and neighborhood preservation (cf. Shefter 1992).

Corinne Harris, who shared a slate with two white insurgents during her primary run for district leader, recalled: "We felt that the reform Democrats were part of the movement to push for civil rights. That was all tied up together. And we felt that the regular Democrats weren't concerned about blacks, and the welfare of blacks.[5]

Although Harris and the reform slate lost to the regular party candidates in the primary, the defeat was followed by a surge of political mobilization. Inspired by the southern civil rights movement, black activists formed ad hoc political action committees, which, in contrast to the party-affiliated political clubs, drew support from a heterogeneous array of institutions and social networks and articulated an equally complex and far-reaching political program.

In 1963 the Independent Citizens Committee, a coalition of community activists based at the Corona Congregational Church and closely tied to the local NAACP, ran Reverend Robert D. Sherard for the office of city councilman-at-large for Queens County. Reverend Sherard, a veteran civil rights organizer from New Orleans, had been appointed pastor of the Congregational Church in 1958 and soon afterward assumed leadership of the Corona–East Elmhurst NAACP. With the endorsement of the Liberal Party, Reverend Sherard faced Joseph Modugno, running on a Republican-Conservative ticket, for one of two boroughwide seats on the City Council.[6]

The formation of the Independent Citizens Committee not only signaled black disillusionment with clubhouse politics as a privileged route to political power but also heralded a rearticulation of the meaning, terrain, and frontiers of politics within Black Corona. Influenced by the southern civil rights movement and alarmed by the rapid deterioration of the their community, black activists stressed unity across partisan lines and framed local issues in terms of wider demands for civil rights and economic justice. Before the 1960s, John Bell recalled, "You had a few [black] Republicans and a majority of Democrats in Corona who were fighting each other instead of fighting the *system*."

Adopting strategies and tactics developed by the Southern Christian Leadership Conference (SCLC) in its Crusade for Citizenship, the Independent Citizens Committee mobilized residents through existing organizations and social networks within the black community and, most notably, its churches. "All during that time," Reverend Sherard recalled, "we were looking to what was going on in the South, in Montgomery and Birmingham, for examples, for strategies. At our church, Corona Congregational, and at other churches in the community we had people coming in from the SCLC, from CORE [Congress of Racial Equality], and from other groups to speak about organizing, about tactics. We learned from their experience."

Activists emphasized the influence that SCLC tactics, strategies, and concepts, such as "direct action," had on how they interpreted, framed, and responded to local issues. One Corona man, recalling a strategy session before a demonstration for school integration in Jackson Heights, told me: "Some of us felt that we should march across Junction Boulevard into Jackson Heights just like King and them did at the [Edmund] Pettus Bridge in Alabama. Because, you see, Junction Boulevard was our Mason-Dixon line. There was no difference."

Whereas Corona's churches had played a minor role at best in Corinne Harris's 1962 primary campaign for district leader, the Congregational Church provided the institutional base for the Independent Citizens as well as for many other political struggles in Corona during the 1960s.

Aldon Morris's analysis of the close relationship between the Southern Christian Leadership Conference and black churches offers key insights into the role Corona's churches played in 1960s activism:

> The SCLC was anchored in the church and probably could not have been otherwise. For it was these activist ministers who became the leaders and symbols of the mass bus boycotts, controlled the resource-filled churches of the black masses, had economic independence and flexible schedules, were members of ministerial alliances that spoke the same spiritual language whether in Brooklyn or Birmingham, and who came to understand that there is power harnessed in an organized group. (1984:87)

Like the SCLC, the organizers of the Independent Citizens Committee worked to "refocus the cultural content of the church" so as to encourage ministers and their congregations to become directly involved in politics (Morris 1984:109).

"The greatest domestic issue facing our country, our city, and our borough since 1860," the Independent Citizens declared in a letter sent to clergy before the City Council election, "is the moral issue of Civil Rights. We appeal to you, as a moral leader in your community, to join with us in our campaign to rid our city of this dangerous cancer of bigotry and race hatred, with all its explosiveness. We now have the political means of doing something about this moral issue" (Independent Citizens Committee 1963).

Corona's churches were not naturally disposed to play this key role in Corona's civil rights–era struggles. In fact, bitter disputes erupted within and between congregations over not only political strategies and ideologies but also over the degree to which the church should be involved in secular politics. What made black churches key institutions, aside from the resources at the disposal of their ministers, was that they congregated people who collectively possessed a diverse body of political knowledge, experience, and affiliations. For example, the memberships of the Congregational and First Baptist Churches of Corona included cadres of activists from the NAACP, school parents associations, political clubs, voluntary associations, and trade unions. These multiple political links and commitments coalesced in churches like Corona Congregational, making them critical public sites where a variety of political positions and strategies were aired, debated, and acted on.

A campaign flyer defining Reverend Sherard's positions during the 1963 City Council race demonstrates both the range of issues and constituencies that were embraced by the church-based committee and the interweaving of local issues with the national civil rights agenda: "United, the Negro community can attain: Civil rights for all and an end to discrimination and segregation; A full employment economy; Improved and integrated education; Increased housing for low- and middle-income families; A vigorous program to hold down rents; Consumer protection against increased fares, rates, and prices; Honest, efficient, and responsible government."

Although Sherard lost the race for city councilman-at-large, the Independent Citizens continued to function, directing their energies to voter education and registration. In December 1963 the Independent Citizens elected officers, began a newsletter, and rented a storefront office on Northern Boulevard. Proceeds from a cake sale were used to pay the first month's rent, and public meetings were held at the Congregational Church to educate and mobilize voters. Later that month the Independent Citizens' newsletter urged community residents to attend a public hearing on a board of education plan to desegregate neighborhood schools. A second item noting Sherard's defeat stressed the importance of political mobilization:

> Does it matter WHO gets elected to public office? In the last election for Councilman-at-large, Queens had the opportunity of electing Robert D. Sherard to one of the two new position created by the City Council to provide minority representation. Unfortunately not enough people voted, or understood this. As a result, the Republican, conservative-backed Modugno was elected. His first public act will be to introduce a resolution banning cross busing in the N.Y.C. schools. With this kind of action it will be impossible even to start planning to desegregate our de facto segregated schools. This is one small example of how politics affects us every day. (Independent Citizens for Good Government, January 1964)

In the summer of 1964 the Independent Citizens joined with the NAACP, black Republican and Democratic political clubs, and the Sixteen-Square Block Association (a consortium of block clubs) to create the Ad Hoc Committee for Voter Registration, chaired by Leonora Leach of the Independent Citizens. "We have pledged to put aside all individual differences," Leach

TABLE 3.1

Pledges of Money and Labor Received at the Meeting of the
Ad-Hoc Committee for Voter Registration, July 21, 1964

Donation Paid or Pledged ($)	Workers Pledged	Person Present	Organization
16.00	3	Mr. Hammond Alexander	Corona AME Zion Church
		Mr. John Bell	First Baptist Church
25.00	50	Mr. John Booker	Congregational Church
	50	Mr. Edward Fisher	First Baptist Church
		Mr. Charles Howell	Community Action Council
25.00	10	Mrs. Leonora Leach	Independent Citizens
25.00	10	Mrs. Leslie Maddox	Progressive Republican Club
		Mrs. Louise Marion	Congregational Church
		Mrs. Florence Marden	Kennedy Democratic Club
10.00	10	Mr. Edger Mandeville	105th Street Block Association NAACP
25.00	0	Mr.Carl Meikle	16 Square Block Association
		Mr. Irving Merkelson	Independent Citizens
		Mrs. Eva Morris	First Baptist Church
		Mr. N. Nesbitt	Congregational Church
50.00	20	Mrs. Jane W. Robinson	NAACP
		Mrs. Ester Robertson	Interested Citizens
		Mrs. Helen Wolfe	Congregational Church NAACP
	0	Mr. Julian Wolfe	Congregational Church NAACP

wrote in a letter to community residents, "and work as one to achieve our objective" (Ad Hoc Committee for Voter Registration, 7 July 1964).

The Ad Hoc Committee, an "organization of organizations," coordinated voter education and registration drives throughout Corona on the eve of the 1964 presidential election in which Senator Barry Goldwater challenged incumbent Lyndon Johnson, soliciting pledges of financial donations and political workers from member groups to support organization efforts. Table 3.1, which lists pledges received after a July 1964 meeting, illustrates the range of overlapping church, political club, and civic association activists that were mobilized for this effort.

At Ad Hoc Committee meetings, detailed strategies and tactics were discussed and developed for recruiting campaign workers through voluntary associations (such as the Prince Hall Masons, the Elks, and Greek letter societies), for coordinating door-to-door voter registration drives, and for overcoming "the apathy and hopeless feelings of some citizens." Reverend Sherard met with local clergy to map the community into block groups which were then targeted by churches for voter registration and education. The Ad Hoc Committee's publicity chair, Charles Howell, organized a media blitz intended to expose neighborhood residents to "three or more announcements about the coming campaign as preparation for the political worker's visit" (Ad Hoc Committee, 21 July 1964).

In one of its first press releases, the Committee charged that Corona–East Elmhurst had been bypassed in the designation of Voter Registration Centers: the centers selected, the release noted, were all located outside the neighborhood. And before the 1964 election the Independent Citizens acquired two voting machines so that first-time voters could practice casting their vote. "We must decide how to use these machines most effectively," a letter sent to residents noted, "Goldwaterism must be defeated" (Independent Citizens, 17 October 1964).

The 1964 voter registration campaign paralleled and supported other important political struggles in Corona during the 1960s. Empowerment through the electoral system was not pursued as an end in itself but rather as one means among many to mobilize residents around a wide agenda. "A community, which has thousands upon thousands of registered and voting citizens," a letter announcing the registration drive pointed out, "can: (1) Elect public officials, (2) Insure Code Enforcement, re: Housing, Health, Sanitation, Zoning, etc., (3) Insure vigorous law enforcement, (4) Obtain well-planned recreational facilities, i.e. Parks, Playgrounds, Community Centers, etc., and (5) Obtain modern well equipped schools and libraries" (Ad Hoc Committee for Voter Registration n.d.).

This politicization of Black Corona reached deep into the organizational structure of the church, not only reorienting its "cultural content" toward a more militant social gospel (Morris 1984) but also reordering its structure and relations of power. In 1965 the auxiliaries of the Corona Congregational Church were disbanded and replaced with task forces, including Public Education, Politics, Housing, Employment, and Community Service. The previously gender-segregated Laymen's Fellowship and Women's Fellowship were merged to form the Lay, Life, and Work Fellowship. And under Sherard's leadership, the first woman was elected to serve as chair of the Board of Trustees (Easton 1967).

Corona's other churches increasingly served as important sites for organizing and for social activism. Mount Horeb Baptist Church became headquarters to the Corona Coordinating Council, a federation of community-based civic organizations that met during the early 1960s to define and carry out the community's preservation and development agenda. The First Baptist Church, under the leadership of the Reverend Robert Gardner, provided space for a community-organized, alternative school during a 1964 school boycott.

Although the southern civil rights movement played a key role in galvanizing activism in Corona by articulating a national agenda and discourse and by cultivating a wellspring of political networks and expertise, activists in Black Corona drew on experiences rooted in multiple arenas of political life. The hybridity of black political culture and its diverse, temporally layered intellectual and experiential roots is highlighted in the political biographies of activists (cf. Kelley 1994).

John Bell left North Carolina for Brooklyn in 1939 to earn money for college. Falling victim to a robbery, his hopes of attending college were dashed, and he found work in the fur trade and became active in Local 64 of the Furriers Union. As a union activist, Bell worked to organize shops and was elected to the union's executive board in 1942 on which he served for twenty-five years. After moving to Harlem, Bell became involved in electoral politics and participated in many of the marches and demonstrations organized by Adam Clayton Powell, Jr., during the 1940s and 1950s.

Bell remembered:

During those years the unions were very politically active. I wasn't a member of a political club because I didn't have too much faith in either one of the parties. And the reason I embraced the Democratic Party was because of Roosevelt. We [also] had a Congressman by the name of Vito Marcantonio, who was very progressive, and Adam Clayton Powell. You see, during that time, you could elect Communists to the City Council. Because we weren't in that—we weren't in that red-baiting period. So politics was open. So we elected Ben Davis to the City Council. So that's the kind of politics I've been involved in. Progressive politics.[7]

In 1957 John Bell and his family moved to Corona from Harlem where the quality of life was declining. "I wanted to get my children out in the country," Bell recalled, affirming Corona's still suburban reputation. "And I'll tell you the truth, I didn't even know there was such a place. I didn't know anything about Queens when I was in the city."

Like John Bell, many of the people who came to Corona and East Elmhurst after World War II did so to escape deteriorating conditions in increasingly "ghettoized" areas of the city, but they brought with them deeply rooted commitments to social equality, forged in diverse and transnational arena's of black political culture. Helen Marshall, Corona's first black representative to the State Assembly and, later, the City Council, was strongly influenced by her father's political beliefs.

Marshall's father left Guyana for Harlem at the age of seventeen as a stowaway on a Scandinavian steamer. The son of a Scottish anarchist, who was living in exile in Guyana, the young arrival joined the Garvey movement and worked as a merchant seaman before becoming a house painter through the WPA. As a child living in Harlem in the 1930s Marshall was exposed to the political discussions that would take place in her home between her father and his West Indian–born friends and was encouraged to keep abreast of political news and current events. "He would take the prophesies of the Bible," Marshall recalled, "and trace them through the newspapers, and then make little notes in his book. He was very vocal on black liberation and, of course, he was a Garveyite."

After Marshall's Guyanese-born mother died of tuberculosis, her father married an African-American seamstress from the South who was an organizer with the International Ladies Garment Workers Union. During the 1930s her father and stepmother both worked with the American Labor Party (ALP) and brought Marshall with them to rallies and other political events.

In 1937 the family moved to the Bronx and, at age sixteen, Marshall became active in electoral politics, campaigning for Elder Hawkins in his failed bid for the State Assembly on the ALP ticket and later in the successful race of Walter Gladwin, who became the first black State Assembly representative from the Bronx. After her marriage to a native-born New Yorker, Marshall became a Parents Teachers Association (PTA) activist in her Bronx community where the schools were being neglected in the aftermath of white flight.

The diverse political backgrounds of John Bell and Helen Marshall, not atypical among activists who shaped the political history of Corona–East Elmhurst, underscores the heterogeneity of black political culture and the multiple local, national, and international struggles and social movements that informed civil rights activism. It was this hybridity that in part enabled the intensive coalition building across class, ethnic, generational, and, to some extent, racial lines during the 1960s. And nowhere were the challenges of coalition building more salient than in struggles over neighborhood schools.

For many, if not most, African-Americans who settled in Corona and East Elmhurst, access to quality schools was a prime motivation for coming to Queens. And in Queens, as elsewhere, quality schools meant integrated public schools. Before the 1950s black residents of Corona and East Elmhurst had attended racially mixed, if not predominantly white, public and parochial schools. Although those who attended these schools were quick to point to experiences of bigotry and discrimination, school quality was not a salient issue.

However, by the late 1950s schools in Corona and East Elmhurst had become increasingly segregated, reflecting a citywide trend associated with changes in the city's population and the intensification of residential segregation. Only weeks after the Supreme Court's 1954 decision in *Brown v. Board of Education*, Dr. Kenneth Clark, a black psychologist at the City College of New York, charged that the city's school system was racially segregated and was providing black students with an inferior education (Rogers 1969; Ravitch 1974).

Clark's charge, released at an Urban League symposium, prompted Arthur Levitt, president of the New York City Board of Education, to commission an investigation by the Public Education Association (PEA). The PEA study was released in the fall of 1955 and revealed that forty-two elementary schools and nine junior high schools in the city were 90 percent or more black and Puerto Rican. When compared to predominantly white schools, these schools had higher rates of teacher turnover, smaller proportions of tenured teachers, and older and poorly maintained physical plants (Ravitch 1974).

In 1956 and 1957 a commission on integration appointed by the board of education held hearings to develop recommendations for desegregating the city's school system, highlighting in its subsequent report the issues of teacher assignments and zoning. While teachers reacted with hostility to the suggestion of compulsory assignment to minority schools, many white parents objected to re-zoning for integration which they feared would lead to the long-distance busing of their children to "ghetto" schools (Ravitch 1974).

During the late 1950s, as school segregation intensified, the board of education gingerly implemented a voluntary teacher reassignment program and a "permissive zoning" policy, which allowed black and Puerto Rican students in some schools to transfer out of their districts to all-white schools. Whereas the teacher assignment initiative achieved a negligible response (only 25 of the city's 40,000 teachers volunteered for reassignment), the first experiment in permissive zoning incited a school boycott in 1959 when white parents in the conservative white Queens communities of Glendale and Ridgewood resisted the arrival of 302 black elementary students from Brooklyn's Bedford-Stuyvesant (Rogers 1969).

Civil rights activists were outraged by the board's inability to implement an effective desegregation plan and, by 1960, were planning boycotts and other direct actions. Reverend Milton Galamison, president of Brooklyn's NAACP, organized the Parents' Workshop for Equality, which, supported by a coalition of civil rights groups, threatened to organize a citywide boycott and a massive sit-in on the opening day of school in September 1960 (Rogers 1969). Under increasing pressure from civil rights groups, Superintendent John Theobald announced the adoption of Open Enrollment, which offered minority high school, junior high school, and some elementary school students the option of transferring to designated, predominantly white schools in other districts.

Meanwhile, in Corona and East Elmhurst parents had been organizing around school overcrowding and other issues affecting the quality of schools. Helen Marshall, who had been a PTA activist in the Bronx and later Corona, moved to East Elmhurst in 1960 and was impressed by the level of parent activism there.

> Now when I came to East Elmhurst, it was a different story. A lot of people who lived in East Elmhurst had come there from Corona. I went to the PTA there and *parents* were in charge. The place was packed. I had never gone to a PTA meeting where you had to sit in the next to the last row. And you had *fathers* in the PTA, which was rare. I mean, they had an investment in their children's education. See, they were striving. A lot of them were professional and civil service. There was a much more lively kind of thing going on there.

For African-Americans in East Elmhurst and Corona, many of whom were working two jobs to pay home mortgages, education was the linchpin that not only enabled social mobility, especially in the expanding public sector, but also provided "credentialed" security in a racially stratified and unstable job market. If homeownership embodied black progress, educational achievement insured it, shoring and sustaining it through time and across generations.

In 1961 the board of education announced that, because of overcrowding, it was eliminating the seventh and eighth grades at Public School (P.S.) 127 in East Elmhurst. The affected students were to be transferred to Junior High School 141 in Astoria to the west. Parents in East Elmhurst reacted with suspicion and alarm. Although schools in East Elmhurst were overcrowded, this claim had been used elsewhere by the board of education to justify the busing of black students to white areas so as to lessen white resistance to integration plans. Moreover, P.S. 127's students were to be sent to a school in distant Astoria rather than to Junior High School 145 located much closer in Jackson Heights.

Although black parents in Corona–East Elmhurst supported school integration as a method of insuring school quality, most were opposed to "one-way" busing plans that placed the burden of relocation solely on black children and their parents. And, as the relocation plan took effect, their worst fears were confirmed when children reported being harassed and assaulted by whites in Astoria.

Helen Marshall, explaining East Elmhurst's resistance to the transfer, highlighted the concerns and fears that had been expressed by black and Latino parents across the city in relation to one-way busing plans: "A lot of us didn't want to take our kids out and send them on those buses because of the stories we were hearing, coming back. *I* was a lonely black kid in an all-white school. And I *never* forgot that. I *never* forgot that. And I'd be damned if I wanted my kids to go through that, too. No way. No way."

During the summer of 1961 parents at P.S. 127 mobilized, raising funds to hire a lawyer and planning a boycott for the following fall. As the boycott gathered momentum, parents at P.S. 127 enlisted the support of a spectrum of neighborhood groups, including the NAACP, block and civic associations, and the Nation of Islam. Corona's mosque had been founded by Malcolm X, who had taken up residence in Corona in 1959. Reverend Gardner, pastor of Corona's First Baptist Church, provided space for the operation of an alternative school. Using funds raised during the summer, PTA activists hired teachers. Boycott organizers traveled to Harlem to seek the advice of school activists there who were in the process of organizing the influential Harlem Parents Committee under the leadership of Isaiah Robinson.

By the opening day of school, support for the boycott had spread to all three schools in East Elmhurst and Corona, Public Schools 127, 92, and 143. Fire Department inspectors and other city officials confronted black parents at First Baptist Church and threatened arrest and prosecution. "It was a sight to see," Helen Marshall recalled. "Reverend Gardner just stood there and said, 'This is the house of the Lord. And these children are protected by a higher power.'"

When a group of parents were arrested under the state's Compulsory Education Law, activists held a meeting to organize a larger protest and to insure that people "could not be picked off as individuals." Marshall recalled:

> So we had a meeting and we decided who could go to jail and who couldn't go to jail. Who's going to take care of the children. My mother-in-law was going to take care of our children. My husband and I were both going to jail. Some women who were in disputes with their husbands, in divorces, couldn't go because then the husband could take the children. We also had policemen who could not go to jail.

During the three-day boycott, thirty-five parents from Corona and East Elmhurst occupied Superintendent John Theobald's office. When Corona–East Elmhurst's legal bid to end the busing to Astoria was defeated in federal court, activists redirected their efforts to improving the quality of education at Astoria's Junior High School 141, demanding, among other things, that foreign-language classes be offered and that the curriculum be enriched.

The 1961 boycott was a prelude to a second school battle that would galvanize African-Americans in Corona–East Elmhurst across class and political divisions, as well as highlight for many the extent and depth of racism in the North.

By 1963 the number of elementary schools having 90 percent or more minority-group students had risen to 134, more than triple the 1955 figure. In that same year the national director of CORE declared that the integration of New York City's schools would be a prime goal of his organization and joined the NAACP, the New York Urban League, and the Harlem Parents Committee in a coalition represented by Reverend Galamison's City-wide Coordinating Committee for Integrated Schools. The Coordinating Committee began planning a boycott for September 1963 that would follow on the coattails of the March on Washington (Ravitch 1974).

Under pressure from the New York State commissioner of education to produce a desegregation plan and faced with a citywide boycott by civil rights leaders, the city's superintendent of schools, Dr. Calvin Gross, introduced a desegregation plan in September. The new initiative expanded open enrollment, vowed to improve education in minority schools and, among other measures, noted the possible introduction of "school pairing" as outlined in the so-called Princeton Plan in selected schools by September 1964 (*New York Times*, 29 May 1964; Rogers 1969).

The Princeton Plan advocated the "pairing" of closely located black and white schools such that both groups of children attended one school from kindergarten to the third grade and the other school from the fourth through the sixth grades. The pairing plan addressed the demands of civil rights groups for two-way busing and, equally important, for a fair share of educational resources in schools located in majority-minority communities.

Early in 1964 the board of education announced that P.S. 92 in Corona was being considered for pairing with P.S. 149 in Jackson Heights. Although fewer than six blocks apart, the two elementary schools differed in important ways. P.S. 92, built in 1910, was 97 percent black and, though parents had repeatedly asked for improvements, P.S. 92 had been placed below 114 other schools on the board of education priority list for renovations. In contrast P.S. 149, built in 1935, was 87 percent white and had been completely renovated in 1962 (Powledge 1964). Under the pairing plan, children would attend first and second grades at smaller P.S. 92 and the remaining grades at P.S. 149.

Parents and activists in Corona–East Elmhurst greeted the proposal, which was supported by the local school board and the parents associations at both schools, with guarded enthusiasm. "I went and did the research," one East Elmhurst woman recalled, "and found out that everybody [black and white children] moved equal distances. Everybody made the switch." However, white parents in Jackson Heights who would be affected by the pairing plan vehemently opposed it.

Only days after the plan was first leaked to the press in September 1963 white parents in Jackson Heights met in the rumpus room of a co-op building where many of them lived, and they formed Parents and Taxpayers (PAT) which quickly grew into a citywide, antibusing coalition with chapters in Brooklyn, Manhattan, and Nassau County, Long Island (Powledge 1964; Rogers 1969). By May 1964 the Jackson Heights PAT chapter claimed 1,556 dues-paying members and, at a parents association meeting held at P.S. 149, rebelled against the association's pro-integration leadership, voting down the integration plan by 223 to 58 votes (Powledge 1964).

White Jackson Heights residents were split over the school pairing proposal. Pro-integrationists, many of them members of P.S. 149's parents association, were reported to be largely "middle class, upward mobile, college educated, liberal Jews" and were organized and led by Harry Ansorge, an attorney active in reform circles of the Democratic Party (Rogers 1969:78). In contrast, PAT supporters were typically less educated and were lower-middle-class Irish, Italians, Germans, and Jews who, often the children of immigrants, had recently relocated from white ethnic enclaves in Manhattan, Brooklyn, and the Bronx that were undergoing racial transition (Rogers 1969; cf. Rieder 1985).

Judy Grubin, a Jewish resident of the South Ridge Co-ops who supported the plan, recalled the ferocity of the conflict:

I remember going to a number of meetings in rumpus rooms in the different co-ops and people said terrible things, cursing and screaming. And all the prejudice came out. We liberals were willing to go along with the experiment, to see how well it would work. We didn't know how good the education would be, but we were willing to go along. But people who had been friends never talked to one another again. There was a mass exodus of whites from the community. They fled. It was ugly, real ugly.

In 1964 Joan Addabbo, president of the Jackson Heights PAT organization, filed a suit in the state supreme court against the board of education, arguing that the transfer of white students on the basis of their race violated their constitutional rights (Vavruska n.d.). In a *New York Times* feature article, Addabbo gave her reasons for opposing the pairing plan: "We think the academic standards would be hurt if the schools were paired. After all, the Board of Education itself and the so-called civil rights groups all say that the ghetto schools are behind the other schools academically. If we can't believe *them*, who else *can* we believe?" (Powledge 1964:12).

On July 13 the state supreme court upheld the board of education's plan. Justice Charles Margett ruled that although racial integration was an important factor, it was not the only one to be considered and that the pairing plan "will result in many benefits to the students of each school" (quoted in Vavruska n.d.; see *New York Times*, 14 July 1964). When PAT failed to win a stay of Justice Margett's ruling in an appellate court in time for the September opening of school, Addabbo and her supporters vowed to start a private school in the recreation room of the Southridge co-op building, which stockholders had agreed to make available rent free (*Herald Tribune*, 30 July 1964).[8]

White residents opposed to the plan denied that racism was an issue in their statements to the press yet typically appealed to racial stereotypes to explain their reasoning. A forty-four-year-old sales manager and father of two children in P.S. 149, described P.S. 92's black children as "arrogant trouble-makers," and added, "They're different because of their attitude, not their color." A white woman, denying discrimination in the sale of apartments in her FHA-insured co-op building, explained: "There are strict regulations here on the number of people who can live in a four-room apartment. The colored people try to jam half a dozen people into one little apartment. That's what's keeping them out. It isn't prejudice" (*New York Times*, 10 May 1964).

White racism in Jackson Heights, as inarticulate as it was zealous, gave voice to the silent policies of the government and private sector that were reshaping the urban landscape during the postwar period. Corona and East Elmhurst *had* become more black, more poor, and more dilapidated. And when whites in Jackson Heights conflated race with neighborhood decline, tracing paradoxical and paranoid links between black elementary school children and "troublemaking," they registered the policies of a power structure whose racist practices of mortgage underwriting, urban renewal, and subsidized suburban development had made real their best and worst fantasies.

Many whites in Jackson Heights were the children and grandchildren of Irish, German, Italian, and Eastern European immigrants and had left Brooklyn, the Bronx, and Manhattan to settle in the nearby suburbs of

Queens.[9] And, like their peers who settled further out on Long Island, many were first-time home buyers who had taken advantage of Veterans Administration and FHA-insured mortgages to buy homes and cooperative apartments. A *New York Post* feature, "The Old Neighborhood," described Jackson Heights during its postwar heyday as a "poor man's Forest Hills," highlighting in nostalgic prose the symbolic importance of the area for white, working-class ethnics who were striving, as Karen Sacks put it, "to buy into the emerging white suburban life style" (*New York Post*, 29 December 1969; Sacks 1994:97).

For many working-class whites, arrival in Jackson Heights and other racially segregated areas symbolized the simultaneous and related attainment of "whiteness" and entry into the fuzzy category of the middle class. "In the major school integration struggles," one black East Elmhurst parent recalled, "the white ethnics were our toughest customers, because they had left what they felt was a dying community in Brooklyn and they came here to live in Queens. In a co-op. And now you're talking about taking their kids out of this lily-white school and putting them in a black school." Similarly, David Rogers underscored the tenuous hold that many PAT supporters in Jackson Heights had on middle-class identity: "Many of these homeowners are clerical workers, salesmen, or small businessmen, with little to distinguish them from blue-collar workers except their occupational status and residential area" (1969:79).

The degree to which many whites experienced class identity and mobility through the selective interpretation of neighborhood conditions and racial demography is illustrated by a reporter's interview with two white men in a Jackson Heights bar. A construction worker observed, "It used to be very nice. You used to be able to go out for a walk at any time—and there was places to walk, too. Now? Now it's the same as every place else. You work all your life and wind up no better off." The racialized geography underpinning the worker's anxiety about class mobility was highlighted by a second man, a plumber, who protested to a *New York Post* reporter: "Aw, come on. At least there aren't any riots. And you can print that, too" (29 December 1969).

This conflation of race, place, and class identity underscores the critical role that the consumption of publicly subsidized amenities tied to racial segregation played in the formation of white, middle-class identities. For white anti-integrationists in particular, housing and school segregation were key components of what W.E.B. DuBois called the "wages of whiteness" through which they evaluated and experienced class identity and mobility, as well as waged a form of antistate and antiblack "class struggle" (1992).

In white racist discourse, this imaginary link between race and class was typically marked by a propositional gap that elided the socially constructed political links between race and social mobility. A white Jackson Heights woman assured a *New York Times* reporter at the height of the school pairing controversy:

> I'm not a bigot. You have no business even intimating that I'm a bigot. I don't discriminate against colored people and I never have. But I and my husband have worked hard to get what we've got. The only material things we have in this world are a car and a cooperative apartment, and we just aren't going to watch them go down the drain. (Powledge 1964:3)

By the early 1960s this link between white class mobility and racial segregation, institutionalized in government and private sector urban development practices, had become so commonsensical as to not require elaboration. From this vantage point, the school pairing battle was as much a struggle over the wages of whiteness, pitting disparate elements of the emerging white middle class against one another and the state, as one over the racial integration of schools; that is, a struggle over what it meant to be white and middle-class in postwar, racially segregated American society.

In fact many African-Americans in Corona and East Elmhurst were taken aback by the ferocity of controversy, not because they had underestimated its underlying racism but rather because much of the initial enthusiasm and support for the school pairing plan had come from within the white community.[10] George Anderson, a Corona resident and the vice president of P.S. 92's parents association, told *New York Times* reporter Fred Powledge:

> It wasn't our idea. It came from some of the white people at P.S. 149. The local school board had some meetings and we went and I told them that we were only trying to get the same educational facilities for our own children that you're getting for your children. I told them that we didn't want to come to their parties or visit in their homes . . . We felt for once that inasmuch as they had gotten up the plan themselves it would work out well. But it didn't. Things got very tense. It seems as if the P.A.T. people had put up a curtain along Junction Boulevard—a Mason-Dixon Line. (10 May 1964:3)

In September 1964, and despite a PAT boycott, the pairing plan went into effect, splitting Jackson Heights whites between, as a Jewish activist put it, "a diehard group of white liberals, and everybody else." Mary Vavruska, a parents association activist whose children attended the paired schools, remembered: "It was interesting. In [P.S.] 149, you would have these big kindergarten classes. But by first grade, half the kids, the white kids, would disappear into private schools or into Blessed Sacrament [Catholic School]. Because they didn't want to send their kids on the bus to P.S. 92. I mean the school was only six blocks away!"

Liberal supporters of the plan in Jackson Heights organized and formed coalitions with residents of Corona and East Elmhurst. In 1964 the Citizen's Committee for Balanced Schools of Jackson Heights, Corona, and East

Elmhurst was established, claiming a membership of three hundred black and white-area residents (*New York Times*, 10 May 1964). That same year the Neighbors for Coordinated Action from Corona–Jackson Heights (NCA) was formed in Jackson Heights to improve relations between the two communities.

"They found the need to have some kind of a dialogue with the predominantly Negro community of Corona," recalled Reverend Sherard at Corona Congregational, who had been asked to organize black support for the group. Sherard's response, like that of many in Corona–East Elmhurst, was lukewarm at best: "And I told them what we needed in Corona, in the black community, was action and not more 'dialogue.'" Many black activists, like Sherard, felt that integrationists in Jackson Heights evaded the problem of racism. For example, in a press statement, one of NCA's white organizers observed of its members, "They have found that there is little difference between the problems of Negroes and whites. There are people in our organization who were never exposed to people of another race" (*Long Island Post*, 11 February 1965).

This appeal to a race- and power-evasive discourse to frame relations between the two neighborhoods highlights the weakness of integrationist strategies and suggests cause for their lack of political resonance within the black community during the period. Though the two communities did share problems and concerns, their origins and solutions, overdetermined by race, were distinct. In a peculiar celebration of racelessness, a local community newspaper reporter awkwardly opined:

> There are some striking things about the NCA—things which even the casual observer cannot help but notice. Not once at an NCA meeting attended by this reporter last month were the words "Negro," or "white" or "integration" used. The group is so thoroughly natural and spontaneous in its ways that within itself there is no thought of the integration of two essentially ghetto communities which has [already] been accomplished. (*Long Island Post*, 11 February 1965)

However, for residents of Corona–East Elmhurst there was nothing at all natural or spontaneous about race relations and, more important, about the political and economic processes that had transformed the two communities into very distinct ghettos, divided by a "Mason-Dixon line." Activists in Corona and East Elmhurst recognized that what was at stake in struggles over segregated schools was not racial integration but rather the asymmetrical allocation of power and economic resources by the state and private sector along racial lines. Integration, though a cause célèbre among white liberal supporters of the pairing plan, remained insignificant as a discourse and strategy among activists in Corona–East Elmhurst. As one Corona man explained:

> I didn't get involved in that school pairing business because—see those whites over in Jackson Heights were not the real problem as far as I was concerned. What we needed here in Corona was a new school, not white children. And that's what I told them at one of those meetings they had over at [P.S.] 92. I said, "Why don't

you build a new school here. We don't need white kids. We need a new school. We got our own children." But they didn't like that too much, 'cause then you're messing with the real powers that be.

White resistance to school pairing highlighted not only the intensity of white racism but also the degree to which racism cut across class lines. If middle-class identity for whites had come increasingly to be a function of their distance, symbolic as much as physical, from the "black ghetto," for residents of Corona and East Elmhurst black socioeconomic security and mobility came to be seen as requiring the mobilization of an equally coherent concept of black community and "black power." Just as the citywide civil rights movement shifted its emphasis by the mid-1960s from school integration to black "community control" over local schools, activists in Corona–East Elmhurst increasingly stressed unity across class lines toward the goals of black empowerment and self-determination.

Donald Stewart, an activist in the school battles of the 1960s who later became the first black member of the community school board, recalled:

There was a great deal of civic awareness in the community. A lot of the youth, the younger people, were really interested in what was happening. And suddenly, people started hearing about this fellow, Malcolm X, who was having meetings [on Ditmars Boulevard], talking about "blacks" and saying some pretty controversial things. He was dynamic and interesting. And at that time, some of the things he was saying seemed way out. But they were things that a lot of us, particularly the young people, wanted to hear.

In 1968 Corona residents organized a chapter of the Black Panther Party, which opened an office on Northern Boulevard. The Black Panther Party drew its membership in Corona from the youth of working-class families, some of whom had been associated with Corona street gangs such as the Enchanters. Like Black Panther organizations elsewhere, Corona's chapter operated a "liberation school" and a free breakfast program for children.

Activists affiliated with the Nation of Islam and the Black Panther Party worked in concert with middle-income school, NAACP, and block association organizers on a number of projects, ranging from protests over the lack of traffic lights at dangerous school crossings to the founding of a black library and cultural center in Corona in 1969. Young middle-class activists, such as Stewart, attended Black Panther Party and Nation of Islam meetings and were strongly influenced by their political programs and beliefs. Indeed, the much touted binary division between the "children of Malcolm" and the "children of Martin" not only fails to capture the social complexity of 1960s black political culture but the heterogeneity of black political subjectivity as well.

The hybridity of black activism in Corona–East Elmhurst is illustrated by the experience of Elwanda Young whose parents moved to Queens from North Carolina in 1956. Young found her first job in the Congregational Church's

Head Start Program in 1965. After completing high school, Young rented her own apartment in Corona and worked as the secretary of her family's integrated church, the Leverich Memorial Church. While employed at Leverich, Young attended the Nation of Islam's mosque in Corona and worked with the Black Panther Party. "They were slick, as far as I was concerned," Young recalled of the Black Panthers. "They were saying everything that I wanted to hear and say. And that began to attract me. I even worked with the [Black Panther's] breakfast program and for the liberation school. I taught reading and math to small children. It helped me to develop my whole political consciousness."

By the late 1960s Elwanda Young and veteran activists of struggles for better schools, political power, and neighborhood stabilization would find themselves working on a new political landscape created in part by the state's War on Poverty. If the surge of political activism in Corona–East Elmhurst during the civil rights era politicized black civil society, enabling the mobilization of diverse constituencies around a wide range of interrelated and far-reaching political and economic needs, state interventions through the War on Poverty would serve to funnel black activists into a race- and power-evasive arena of poverty politics where the complex relations and practices of racial subordination would be framed and addressed through the depoliticized discourse of "urban blight."

CHAPTER FOUR

The State and the War on Politics

I don't think that we should consider the "modern state"
as an entity which was developed above individuals,
ignoring what they are and even their very existence, but
on the contrary as a very sophisticated structure, in which
individuals can be integrated, under one condition: that
this individuality would be shaped in a new form, and
submitted to a set of very specific patterns.
(Michel Foucault)

In 1961 the City Planning Commission (CPC) of New York launched a study of the community development needs of north-central Queens under the auspices of the city's Community Renewal Program (City Planning Commission 1963). The Federal Housing Act of 1961, a Kennedy administration "New Frontier" initiative, had authorized $2.5 billion for urban renewal, enabling the production of subsidized housing for families with below-median incomes in neighborhoods such as Corona–East Elmhurst (Mollenkopf 1983). In June the CPC designated the northern portion of Corona, north of Northern Boulevard and adjacent to the site planned for the 1964 World's Fair in Flushing Meadows–Corona Park, an urban renewal area. The following year a second survey was commissioned to consider extending the renewal area south of Northern Boulevard to Thirty-seventh Avenue.

Urban renewal designation, a first step toward receiving federal funds, was supported by a broad coalition of community groups in Corona and East Elmhurst that had become alarmed by the decline of the neighborhood's housing stock and commercial areas, particularly along Northern Boulevard. When Corona's urban renewal designation was approved, the City Planning Commission created a Community Action Council composed of local residents that was charged to work with city officials to define community needs and to conduct research.

The Community Action Council's role in the Urban Renewal Study Program was noted in the City Planning Commission's report on the southern extension:

The Council, composed of many local organizations and churches, offered a variety of ready-made lines of communication which were tapped in making broad community contact with tenants and owners. Paving the way for easy and direct contact, the Commission staff maintained an office in a storefront used by the local NAACP Chapter, the space being donated by a local landlord. (City Planning Commission 1963:5)

The notions of "tapping" and "paving," conveying a sense of access through constraint, serve well to capture the increasingly interventionist role that the state would play in the public life of Corona–East Elmhurst during the 1960s; it was a role signaled equally aggressively by the slogans, "New Frontier" and "War on Poverty." For during the decade the state would extend its reach deep into the fabric of black civil society, mapping its hitherto uncharted political spaces, reconnoitering what Michael Harrington called "the invisible land" of the African-American poor (1971 [1962]:1).

Black poverty and its associated social problems would no longer be ignored. Instead, as Michel Foucault observed in an analogous context, there would be "an institutional incitement to speak about it, and to do so more and more; a determination on the part of the agencies of power to hear it spoken about, and to cause *it* to speak through explicit articulation and endlessly accumulated detail" (1990:18).

This chapter investigates the state's role in regulating political dissent and resistance in Corona–East Elmhurst during the civil rights period. I emphasize how the War on Poverty and related government-sponsored experiments in decentralized city governance transformed the institutional and discursive economy of black activism, not only incorporating activists into a "new genre" of state-sponsored institutions and relations but also producing knowledge about neighborhood needs and problems that obscured the origins of urban deterioration and black poverty in practices of racial subordination (Katznelson 1981:135).

THE POLITICS OF BLIGHT

The state's newfound interest in the "renewal" of Corona–East Elmhurst during the decade of the 1960s contrasted sharply with its earlier posture of malignant neglect and had origins, in part, in the Democratic Party's effort to resurrect its New Deal–era electoral majority that had been weakened by a postwar surge of conservatism and by splits within the Democratic Party coalition (Mollenkopf 1983).

Blue-collar, white-ethnic voters, who had been the linchpin of the Democratic Party's political base in cities during the New Deal, experienced unprecedented job mobility after World War II, and taking advantage of VA-and FHA-insured mortgages flocked to the suburbs (K. T. Jackson 1985; Mollenkopf 1983; Sacks 1994). This state-subsidized suburbanization of white male ethnics, their families, and, increasingly, their industrial jobs, weakened their allegiance to the Democratic Party as well as to its costly, urban-based program delivery system.

Under the Republican administration of President Dwight D. Eisenhower, the federal government aggressively promoted suburban development, most notably through the 1956 Interstate and Defense Highway Act, while withdrawing an already equivocal commitment to urban development programs serving low-income and minority constituencies. For example, the 1954 Housing Act, which created the Urban Renewal Administration, decimated the government's already weak public housing program and shifted "urban renewal from a nationally directed program focusing on housing to a locally directed program which allowed downtown businesses, developers, and their political allies, who had little interest in housing, to use federal power to advance their own ends" (Mollenkopf 1983:117; see Piven and Cloward 1971; Hirsch 1985).

In contrast, the Democratic Party had experienced deep divisions in its electoral base during the postwar era. As African-Americans migrated to northern industrial cities, their voting power in national elections grew. In the face of mounting black political pressure, President Truman had urged Congress to act on the recommendations of the President's Committee on Civil Rights during the 1948 campaign—inciting a defection of southern Democrats, particularly in the deep South. This growing North-South split was aggravated by divisions within democratic cities like New York between white conservatives, blacks, and liberal whites (Piven and Cloward 1971). In Corona politics, this schism was expressed and fueled by the "reform" movement's challenge of the "regular" democratic party machine (notably, in the campaigns of Corinne Harris and Robert Sherard), as well as by the citywide battles over integrated schools that pitted regular Democrats and their shrinking white constituencies against "liberal" reformers intent on mustering growing numbers of black and Hispanic voters.

When the Democrats returned to power in 1960 in the midst of the 1959–60 recession, they used federal housing and urban development programs as key policy instruments to shore up their electoral base and stimulate the national economy. Just as the New Dealers had used the PWA, WPA, and other federal programs to mobilize underrepresented constituencies such as urban industrial workers, architects of the Kennedy-era New Frontier and ensuing Great Society initiatives utilized these programs to harness a rapidly growing black and largely urban electorate, which by 1960 numbered more than five million (Mollenkopf 1983). In the 1960 presidential election John F. Kennedy won twenty-seven of the thirty-nine largest U.S. cities, collecting 75 percent of the black vote. And in 1964 Lyndon B. Johnson, vigorously supported in Corona–East Elmhurst and other black communities, received 90 percent of the nation's black vote (Mollenkopf 1983).

To be sure, African-Americans were the weakest and most vulnerable partner in this electoral coalition, which tenuously aligned liberals, pro-growth business interests, white Catholics, blue-collar unionists, and other constituencies. Nonetheless, heightened black activism and civil disturbances in urban areas worked in tandem with the vote-seeking strategies of Democrats at the national and local levels to propel urban renewal and the War on Poverty to the forefront of the 1960s policy-making agenda.

In Corona–East Elmhurst urban renewal designation marked the beginning of a long conversation between African-American activists and a rapidly growing army of state officials charged with implementing a disparate and unstable array of federal and local programs designed to address the urban crisis. A critical result of this engagement, as John Mollenkopf and others pointed out, would be the rearticulation of black activist networks and the incorporation of grass-roots constituencies into state-sponsored bureaucracies (1983).[1] However, equally important would be the increasing role that the state would play in interpreting African-American needs, interests, and identities through the propagation and legitimation of power-evasive discourses about black poverty and "urban blight."

For during the decades of the 1960s and 1970s the state would subject Corona–East Elmhurst to a battery of surveys and studies; these would not only severely tap the political energy and resources of neighborhood activists but would construct and legitimate a narrative of poverty and urban decline that would systematically and with remarkable consistency obscure their origins in structures of racial and economic subordination.

The template for this race- and power-evasive narrative of urban decline was the city's 1961–62 urban renewal study which, according to the chief of the City Planning Commission's Queens office, provided official recognition that "Corona was in trouble" (*Long Island Press*, 24 April 1968). The cornerstone of the renewal study was a survey of fourteen hundred residential structures in Corona–East Elmhurst which revealed that the majority of the area's housing stock showed "deficiencies resulting from neglect of maintenance" (City Planning Commission 1963:4). To supplement these building survey data, the Commission's staff, assisted by the Community Action Council and local churches, interviewed residents, eliciting data on size and composition of households, income, rents, and mortgage arrangements.

After noting deterioration of the area's housing stock and commercial buildings, particularly along Northern Boulevard, the Planning Commission report concluded its description of the area with a statement that comes closer than any other to offering an explanation for the neighborhood's problems.

The section has experienced a recent transition in population. It was basically developed and settled in the first quarter of the century, primarily by families of Italian extraction who had close ties to the Corona Area to the south. Census figures show that in the decade from 1950–1970, 70 percent of the white families in the area moved away while Negro families moved in to take their place. The area's 12,000 residents constitute a younger population group having many more pre-school age and fewer high school age children than the former residents. To many of the Negro families, living in this neighborhood presented the opportunity to own a home, as well as to leave older, densely populated tenement sections of the City. To a large degree, the new residents brought with them a pioneering spirit determined to live and bring up their children in a better environment. However, many of the efforts by families to improve their structures have been frustrated because of difficulties in obtaining financing at other than exorbitant rates. Signs of blight are visible and the area is generally deteriorating. Existing community facilities are over-taxed. Many of the new residents fear that the blight they left behind may overtake them unless substantial improvement is undertaken soon. (City Planning Commission 1963:4)

Here, as in subsequent studies of the area's problems and renewal needs, the impact of institutional racism on neighborhood conditions would be systematically elided. In this depoliticized narrative of racial succession, it is the age distribution of the black newcomers that bears responsibility for the "overtaxing" of community facilities, revealing in its wake the telltale signs of urban blight. Though the report highlighted financing problems experienced by black homeowners and called for a "broadening" of federal mortgage insurance programs and the "fullest" involvement of banks in providing mortgage capital, it did not relate these problems to practices of racial discrimination.

The Planning Commission's silence on the issue of race at the high point of civil rights activism should not be viewed as a mere elision, yielding an incomplete but nonetheless "workable" perspective on the renewal needs of Corona–East Elmhurst. As Foucault has pointed out, "Silence . . . is less the absolute limit of discourse, the other side from which it is separated by a strict boundary, than an element that functions *alongside* the things said, with them and in relation to them within over-all strategies" (1990:27; emphasis added). Rather, the Commission's silence on racism operated to enable the construction of other claims about the roots of urban decline; claims which, circulated within the expanding networks of bureaucratic problem solving, would invest urban "blight" with a peculiar agency of its own.

In its urban renewal designation report, the City Planning Commission recommended a comprehensive program of rehabilitation, city-service coordination, code enforcement, and the "spot clearance" of buildings beyond repair. The report also underscored the need to develop recreational facilities, improve library services, and rehabilitate Northern Boulevard's commercial strip whose "vacant stores, poorly maintained buildings, unattractive signs, and second-floor flats in poor condition" were said to be adversely affecting the neighborhood (City Planning Commission 1963:7). However, in 1966 the city's Survey and Planning Application for Corona–East Elmhurst's urban renewal program was rejected by the federal government because of limitations in funding (Hart, Krivatsy, and Stubee n.d.).

The following summer, as city officials became increasingly alarmed by rioting and civil unrest in black communities, Queens Borough President Mario Cariello toured Northern Boulevard in Corona.[2] "The tour had an unspoken, although understood aim," the *Long Island Press* reported the next day, "to keep the 'cool' that has prevailed so far during this hot summer" (1 August 1967). Vowing to do something about Corona's unemployment and lack of recreational facilities, Cariello visited the Walter White Neighborhood Manpower Center, a city-funded, multiservice agency. "We need a boys club in the area," Cariello told a group of Neighborhood Youth Corps workers at the center. "In the meantime," he added, "take advantage of Flushing Meadows–Corona Park. It's a beautiful park" (*Long Island Press*, 1 August 1967).

With no prospect of funding from the federal urban renewal program the City Planning Commission awarded a contract to a San Francisco–based group of planning consultants to conduct another study in 1967, this time extending the study area to include the nearby white communities of Jackson Heights and Elmhurst. The Hart, Krivatsy, and Stubee report, completed the following spring, relied heavily on the data and recommendations presented in the earlier renewal study and advanced an even more depoliticized perspective on racial succession and neighborhood deterioration.

Hart, Krivatsy, and Stubee described the study areas as "aging suburbs," which, given the "rising standards and changing tastes" of the middle class, are at risk of becoming obsolete: "They offer a unique combination of convenience and modest cost, and still represent, as they did fifty years ago, a vast improvement over the old slums. However, as they age and grow more obsolete they face the danger of blight. The old original residents are moving away; the old buildings, facilities and improvements deteriorate" (Hart, Krivatsy, and Stubee n.d.:1)

In this race- and power-evasive narrative, neighborhoods, like living organisms, experience a natural aging process and become susceptible to blight. Moreover, the authors reasoned, the future of Corona–East Elmhurst and surrounding communities depended on property owners and residents or, more to the point, on their *perception* of neighborhood stability:

> Will people invest in property here, improve it, build anew? Will money be spent on maintenance; will time be spent on demanding better public services? The answers to these questions depend on the psychological quality of the neighborhood. Would an investor feel secure here? Is this area on the way up or on the way down? Will a banker make a loan? Will the neighbors stay and make other improvements?
>
> In these circumstances what can the City do? Priorities for public funds and energy are low in relation to other more demanding, more glaring problems. What

can be started with the limited means at hand, and how can it all be made to add up to real improvement of the neighborhood, especially its "psychological quality" [*sic*]. (Hart, Krivatsy, and Stubee n.d.:1–2)

With this introduction to the problem, the report went on to provide standard profiles of the five neighborhoods (North Corona, South Corona, East Elmhurst, Jackson Heights, and Elmhurst) and reached the conclusion that the "primary problem is the creeping blight of the Northern Boulevard area." Although the authors conceded that there were problems in the areas surrounding the roughly twenty-block Northern Boulevard area (problems associated with aging), it was the "isolated slum" that posed the real threat (Hart, Krivatsy, and Stubee n.d.:53).

The Hart, Krivatsy, and Stubee report, by locating the source of urban blight in the Northern Boulevard strip where the effects of decline were at once most visible and most racialized, served to obscure its origins in the deliberate policies and practices of the public sector and private capital, thereby reconfirming popular and professionalized discourses about poverty that located its roots in the race-specific behaviors and cultural dispositions of the poor (cf. Smith 1988).

This conflation of race and neighborhood condition becomes apparent when Hart, Krivatsy, and Stubee expressed their approval of the city's 1968 decision to designate Roosevelt Avenue as the boundary assigning North Corona and South Corona to two separate Community Planning Districts (CPDs).

And there is justification for this definition. Since 1950, the northern area of Corona, between Roosevelt Avenue and Northern Boulevard, has absorbed a large percentage of Negroes with serious problems of social disorder. The area south of Roosevelt Avenue remains stable—solidly white and predominantly Italian. Roosevelt Avenue defines these two significantly different areas. On the other hand, the boundary between northern Corona and East Elmhurst is not clear. (n.d.:25)

Whiteness speaks for itself; its stability goes without saying. By contrast, the class-inflected boundary between predominantly black neighborhoods of North Corona and East Elmhurst remained fuzzy.

The significance of these City Planning Commission studies reaches beyond what they reveal about the strategic biases of bureaucratic knowledge. Of greater interest is the manner in which these and other power-evasive constructions of poverty and urban decline were insinuated into the discourses and everyday practices of neighborhood activists through the state's efforts to harness and reshape local political networks and encourage "community participation to insure the fullest possible understanding . . . of the renewal problems involved" (City Planning Commission 1963:9).

Through public hearings, community meetings, the media, and an assortment of newly formed and state-sponsored citizens advisory boards, federal and local officials disseminated and legitimated bureaucratic formulations of neighborhood problems while enlisting the participation of local activists in "top-down" urban development strategies.

For example, while Hart, Krivatsy, and Stubee were doing their ninety-day survey of the area, Community Planning Board 14A, representing Corona–East Elmhurst and parts of Jackson Heights, was conducting its own parallel study (*Long Island Press*, 24 April 1968). Board 14A, like others that were operating in the city, had been authorized by the 1961 City Charter which mandated that the city be divided into Community District Planning Boards. "The districts will become," the City Planning Commission wrote in 1968, "the units for the collection of new data and analysis. As partners in the planning process, the boards can bridge the gap between a centralized government and the City's neighborhoods. The boards can provide an effective means for the local citizen to participate in the development of his community and city" (City Planning Commission 1968:1). As stipulated in the 1961 Charter, each Community Planning Board consisted of five to nine local-area residents appointed by the borough president and serving as unpaid volunteers.

Planning Board 14A's report, "Corona and East Elmhurst: Chance for Change," zeroed in on the Northern Boulevard "strip," described in the study's opening paragraph as a "pernicious cancer" and a "blighted, festering area" threatening surrounding communities. Although the Community Planning Board's mapping of the socioeconomic topography of the area contrasted in significant ways with the Hart, Krivatsy, and Stubee report, both studies constructed the Northern Boulevard "strip" as the epicenter of urban blight: "Corona and East Elmhurst are, basically, substantial, middle-income areas of light population density, comprised mainly of small homeowners, both white and negro. The communities are now neither slums nor deteriorating. If it weren't for the creeping tentacles of "The Strip," neither would be susceptible to being labeled incipient social slums" (Community Planning Board 14A 1968:1).

Planning Board 14A's report appropriated the naturalized and power-evasive language of "blight" typical of urban renewal narratives as well as much earlier discourses about poverty in which the "aetiology of epidemics was . . . linked to the pauperising conditions of the labouring classes" (Dean 1991:205). In this discourse of urban blight, the agency and practices of political and economic elites were masked by the imagery of an isolated cancer, festering in neglect.[3]

Reverend Robert Sherard told me:

When that Planning Board report came out suddenly everybody started talking about the blight up on Northern Boulevard—the Northern Boulevard strip, they called it. But Northern Boulevard wasn't the real problem. It was only a symptom of the problem. The real problem was the absentee landlords who were letting their properties go down. And *jobs*. People in Corona needed jobs. And the city wasn't doing nothing about that. They promised us [building] code enforcement when they did their studies, but they never got us the money for it.

However, community activists and their representatives on the Community Planning Board were not passive receivers of this discourse of blight; rather, they appropriated its metaphors in an effort to address local interests and concerns. On the one hand, given the urban renewal program's past emphasis on "slum clearance" rather than on housing development, activists feared that highlighting wider, structural problems in the community would lead to the indiscriminate razing of housing. "Simply bulldozing a large part of the blighted 'Strip,'" Board 14A warned, "dislocating many families, overcrowding other parts of the community, could cause a general undermining of the stable Corona–East Elmhurst neighborhoods" (Community Planning Board 14A 1968:4).

On the other hand, having been denied renewal funding in the past, activists highlighted, if not exaggerated, the threat of social disorder on "the strip" so as to incite government attention and action. Although the report briefly summarized housing, education, employment, and other issues, it placed overwhelming stress on crime: "Window breaking and looting of merchandise are almost a sport," Board 14A noted. "From time to time motorists are stopped and attacked in the streets by groups of hoodlums" (Community Planning Board 14A 1968:2).

No doubt aware of the relationship between civil disorder and antipoverty funding, Board 14A underscored the strip's riot potential:

The police practice a "containment" policy, occasionally employing a "tactical" police force when minor riots result in skirmishes between area youths and patrolmen. One of the ironies of the situation is that there has never been a full-scale riot in "The Strip," even during the "long, hot summers." Thus, there has been no dramatic pinpointing of the area as a socially explosive neighborhood. But the potential persists. (Community Planning Board 14A 1968:2–3)

If, as John Mollenkopf argued, the War on Poverty constituted an attempt to incorporate and shape neighborhood-based networks of political leadership, given the intensity of the community's needs many activists felt they had little choice (1983). Planning Board 14A concluded its report with just such an invitation:

During the course of our six-month investigation of the area, one single factor impressed us most: the reservoir of available, willing and dedicated people ready to aid in *any* program of community betterment. Despite some natural inhibition by the small, lawless "Strip" element, and despite a sense of frustration engendered by long-time bureaucratic neglect, a substantial leadership cadre exists. More than any other reason, this untapped capacity for self-help strengthens our resolve to *persuade the City to bring to bear, in a coordinated manner, all of the available resources that can assist these communities to regain full stability and fulfillment.* (Community Planning Board 14A 1968:7)

Planning Board 14A's report did not represent the views of the entire community or, more than likely, of all its members. Activists in Corona–East Elmhurst mobilized in multiple political arenas where they formulated and publicized definitions of community need and constructions of black identity that clashed with and challenged bureaucratic models of urban reform. Nevertheless, as the state increasingly channeled its resources, political as much as economic, into the community, the War on Poverty and its decentralized apparatus of institutions would absorb an ever increasing share of political commitment and resources.

On April 23, 1968, Community Planning Board 14A and Corona–East Elmhurst's Urban Action Task Force convened a meeting at the Walter White Manpower Center on Northern Boulevard to present the recommendations of the Hart, Krivatsy, and Stubee report and the results of Board 14A's own study, "Chance for Change."

The *Long Island Press* announced the next day: "The Brakes are being applied today to Corona's years of social and economic decline. Together and separately, and with a great deal of harmony, community and governmental organizations have given Corona and its adjacent communities a fine-tooth-comb inspection to determine its assets, its shortcomings, its aspirations and how best to fulfill them" (24 April 1968).

Corona's Urban Action Task Force was part of a newly formed "riot prevention system," implemented by Mayor John V. Lindsay in ghetto communities across the city (Katznelson 1981:137).[4] Each local task force, composed of a high-level representative of the mayor, local city bureaucrats, and community leaders, held weekly meetings intended to open channels of communication between city government and residents in order to facilitate the coordination of city services and the voicing of grievances. "While such services and activities were in fact provided," Katznelson observed, "their principal purpose was not the solution of substantive programs, but the maintenance of social order" (1981:139).

The April meeting was attended by community leaders, task force and CPC officials, and about seventy-five residents. Charles Smith, director of the Planning Commission's Queens office, told residents that the CPC would work with local leaders to explore possibilities for developing low-income "vest pocket" housing on vacant lots on the strip. J. Bruce Llewellyn, deputy commissioner of the city's Housing and Development Administration, informed residents that his agency had applied for federal funding to support a code enforcement program to arrest housing deterioration on the strip. And CPC officials affirmed their commitment to increase recreational and cultual resources in the area, notably through the creation of a library and community center on Northern Boulevard (*Long Island Press* 26 April 1968).

Housing development, code enforcement, and improved school, library, and recreational facilities had long been on the agenda of activists in Corona–East Elmhurst. These specific issues had been targeted in the voter empowerment drives of the Independent Citizens for Good Government, as well as in earlier neighborhood-based political forums. However, through the state's efforts to cultivate, reform, and harness grass-roots political networks and constituencies, these issues were disengaged from their broader political contexts and reframed as local quality-of-life issues that could be resolved by "opening channels of communication" and improving the coordination of services.

For example, whereas housing and education had earlier been addressed as civil rights issues, implicating racially stratified political and economic relations, these and other issues were now embedded in an institutional apparatus and discourse that located their origins in "the creeping tentacles of 'The Strip.'" NAACP, church, and other activists found these commitments increasingly taxed as they were called on to participate in a bewilderingly complicated and often redundant battery of local and federally sponsored studies, public forums, and institutions.

"There were so many meetings going on around here," one woman recalled, "it was enough to make your head spin. One day there would be the mayor's task force on something or the other. Then the next day there would be something at Walter White over on Northern Boulevard with some other group. And then later on at night they'd have something over at, I don't know, somewhere else. It got so—well, I just stopped going."

At the April public meeting on "the strip," the Corona–East Elmhurst Development Committee was formed under the aegis of the Urban Action Task Force. The Committee's purpose "was to work for the implementation of the program that had been outlined and to carry forward detailed planning for the community" (Hart, Krivatsy, and Stubee 1970:3). The membership of the Development Committee, which was further divided into six subcommittees, constituted a "who's who" in grass-roots activism in Corona and East Elmhurst, including John Bell (code enforcement), Helen Marshall (housing), and Donald Stewart (education). The Committee also included block association activists such as Jerome Hardeman and Edward Fisher, long-time NAACP organizers such as Edger Mandeville, and youth advocates such as Cecil Watkins. Joseph Bostic, director of the Walter White Manpower Center, was appointed to chair the Development Committee.

Later that year a plan to create a community development corporation in Corona–East Elmhurst was approved by the New York City Council Against Poverty, clearing the way for direct antipoverty funding through the federal government's Office of Economic Opportunity (OEO) (*Long Island Press*, 12 November 1968).[5] The Corona–East Elmhurst Development Corporation, formed as a result, was funded to operate satellite antipoverty programs throughout the community.

This influx of state resources did yield significant benefits. On the one hand, the mobilization of public officials in support of selected neighborhood goals worked to expedite, if not enable, the implementation of projects that had long been on the agenda of community activists. By 1970 the Langston Hughes Community Library and Cultural Center had opened on "the strip" and plans were underway to construct a regular branch library in East Elmhurst. In that same year the Corona–East Elmhurst Development Committee was involved in selecting a site for a new intermediate school in North Corona (Hart, Krivatsy, and Stubee 1970). And in 1973 the Corona Congregational Church celebrated the opening of Meadow Manor, a 132-unit housing complex in Corona. Sponsored by the church's housing task force, Meadow Manor was the first middle-income apartment building constructed in Queens through New York State's Mitchell-Lama Act, which provided low-interest, construction financing (*Long Island Press*, 1 November 1973).

On the other hand, funding for direct services through city agencies, such as the Department of Social Services and the Youth Board and the federal government's Office of Economic Opportunity, provided desperately needed youth counseling, job training, recreation, and day care services. With increased funding, the Walter White Manpower Center expanded its adult education and counseling services and developed a job-training and job-placement program for machine tool operators. Publicly subsidized day care centers were established by the Church of the Resurrection, the East Elmhurst–Corona Civic Association, and the NAACP. And a variety of other direct services were provided by the Elmcor Youth and Adult Center and by other community-based agencies operating under the umbrella of the Corona–East Elmhurst Development Corporation.

Moreover, although state intervention absorbed much of the energy of grass-roots politics, incorporating neighborhood activists and their demands into bureaucratic arenas of problem solving, it did not exhaust it. Activists continued to define and address neighborhood needs and interests through relatively "state-free" institutions, such as the NAACP, the Black Panther Party, and civic associations. And in Corona, as elsewhere, activists appropriated the federal rhetoric of citizen participation and the institutional resources provided by the War on Poverty to press demands against local governing agencies and elites (see Lipsitz 1988; Piven and Cloward 1971). In so doing they extended the concept of "maximum feasible participation" to goals and arenas of activism that reached beyond the service coordination focus of the War on Poverty (cf. Fainstein and Fainstein 1974; 1983).

For example, the need for a community-controlled library and cultural center addressing the African-American experience had been a persistent concern of neighborhood activists and resulted, in 1961, in the formation of the Library Action Committee of Corona–East Elmhurst. The Action Committee, composed of residents "from all age levels, economic strata, educational backgrounds, religious and political persuasions," pressed their demand for a black library and cultural center through state-sponsored forums such as the Urban Action Task Force and the Corona–East Elmhurst Community Development Corporation (A. Jackson 1985:1). As a result, the Langston Hughes Library and Cultural Center was targeted as a key objective in the City Planning Commission's development agenda for "the strip" and, with the sponsorship of the Queens Borough Public Library, was funded by the New York State Board of Education.

However, when the Library Action Committee selected the site of a former Woolworth's Department Store on Northern Boulevard to house the library, they encountered resistance: the building's owner, who was renting the boarded-up site to a toy company as warehouse space, refused to lease the building to the community. In response, the Action Committee organized daily pickets at the Woolworth's site, drawing on support from parent, youth, and senior citizen groups and from local chapters of the Black Panther Party and Nation of Islam (A. Jackson 1985). The East Elmhurst–Corona Civic Association, based in East Elmhurst, and block associations held fund-raising events to create a bail fund for jailed protesters. Faced with widespread neighborhood protest, the building's owner relented and the Langston Hughes Library and Cultural Center was dedicated in 1969.

The library struggle highlights not only the heterogeneity of grass-roots activism in Corona–East Elmhurst during the 1960s but also the degree to which the realization of civil rights–era gains through War on Poverty programs depended on the exercise of political power by relatively independent political forces in the black community. As Thomas F. Jackson has pointed out, with respect to the impact of OEO's Community Action Program, "federal sponsorship did provide needed resources and legitimacy, but the driving force of social change in these instances was independent and strong black leadership and organization, not community action" (1993:420). The founding of the Langston Hughes Library and Cultural Center, like other civil rights–era gains in Corona–East Elmhurst, was less the consequence of state largess than of the mobilization of black political power. And it was precisely this political capacity, nurtured through decades of struggle and institution building, rather than neighborhood deterioration that would fall victim to the state's War on Poverty.

The War on Poverty in Corona led to the creation of highly specialized community service organizations, bureaucratically tied to a tangled assortment of city, state, and federal agencies. These service organizations were not only dependent on government agencies for funding but were also constrained to formulate and address neighborhood needs in ways that complied with the narrow program priorities, guidelines, and service delivery strategies of their sponsors (see Reed 1979; Fraser 1989). Moreover, the viability of these organizations depended less on the political mobilization of residents than on the tactical support of local political elites.

Reverend Robert Sherard, who served as president of the NAACP during the period, recalled:

> I'll tell you what happened. The loyalty of the people went to Borough Hall, rather than to the church and what it was doing, and to the people. The antipoverty program—the funds that were appropriated to lift up the so-called fallen very seldom got down to them. In Corona, for the most part, it got as far as the administrative staff. And you can't do this kind of work with a paid staff. The troops have to be volunteers. You can't pay them off. Because the people, the political organizers who have these rare kinds of protest experiences with other people—that's psychic income. It doesn't have cash value.

In fact, after 1967 federal regulations governing OEO's Community Action Program, sponsor of the Corona–East Elmhurst Development Corporation, expressly forbid voter registration and other forms of political mobilization through federal-funded programs (see Mollenkopf 1983; Jackson 1993). In 1974, under the Nixon administration's new federalism policy, the Community Development Block Grant Program was established, which further weakened federal requirements for citizen participation by relegating decisions concerning community participation to local officials (Fainstein and Fainstein 1983).

An equally important effect of this process was to remove the issue of poverty—and, by extension, the interests of the poor—from the purview of community-based institutions which, like the NAACP, churches, and civic associations, had hitherto played prominent roles in addressing the needs of the poor and in conceptualizing the political significance of black poverty. It was not that the membership and leaders of these groups had lost interest in the plight of the poor; rather, their roles in both defining and mobilizing residents to act on the issue of poverty was superseded by the antipoverty program. As an NAACP activist who served on the Community Corporation's Board of Directors put it, "Our loyalty to the community became transcended by our loyalty to the people who were responsible for getting the money to us. And it shouldn't be that way."

Elwanda Young, highlighting this shift, contrasted her experience directing an antipoverty youth program in the early 1970s with her earlier experiences working with Corona youth through the Congregational Church and Black

Panther Party: "We were still working with poor kids from Northern Boulevard but there was all this separatism: 'You work with them, you keep them over there. That's what you get money for.' See, there was no longer a lot of interaction with other groups in the community. So you had to develop resources on your own. There wasn't any support system to help you work with them."

If the War on Poverty tended to isolate the black poor as clients in government service bureaucracies, the opening of new mainstream channels of political participation tended to funnel African-American activists into arenas of bureaucratic problem solving where interrelated neighborhood issues were fragmented and restricted to the purview of specialized citizens bodies.

In the wake of the decentralization, for example, housing, zoning, and other quality-of-life issues fell under the jurisdiction of a politically appointed Community Board. Matters pertaining to the schools became the concern of the local community school board. And after 1979 the power to advise the city on the awarding of community development block grants was delegated to an Area Policy Board (APB). Each of these local governing bodies had its own appointment process, catchment area, meeting schedule, and decision-making protocol.

This complex structure of decentralized city government rendered the mechanics of political participation confusing, if not incomprehensible, to many neighborhood residents. Moreover, by fracturing interrelated needs and issues, these new arenas of participation committed African-American activists to political strategies and discourses that obscured the links between neighborhood problems and broader structures of economic and racial subordination.

As Ira Katznelson has pointed out:

At issue was the attempt to take the radical impulse away from the politics of race by the creation of mechanisms of participation at the community level that had the capability to limit conflicts to a community orientation, to separate issues from each other, and to stress a politics of distribution—in short, to reduce race to ethnicity in the traditional community bounded sense. The new institutions of decentralized schools, neighborhood government, local planning, and the like were developed to perform the functions for blacks and their political blocs that party machines had performed for white ethnics. (1981:177)

Under the city's 1969 decentralization plan, East Elmhurst and North Corona were included, along with Jackson Heights, in Community Planning District 3, successor to CPD 14A. The resulting district was 75 percent white, 20 percent black, and 5 percent Asian and Latino (Columbia University 1973). Although CPD 3's boundaries preserved the integrity of its three subcommunities, African-Americans in Corona–East Elmhurst were incorporated as a minority into a larger political constituency which was hardly representative of their needs and priorities.

A 1972 study of CPD 3, conducted by Columbia University's Bureau of Applied Social Research, warned: "The high degree of subcommunity identification within these geographically and demographically distinct areas raises questions about attempts to implement a decentralization plan using the Community Planning District as the administrative (or political) unit" (Columbia University 1973:1–2). The Columbia study surveyed community residents and leaders in CPD 3 about neighborhood problems, the quality of municipal services, and their attitudes toward city government. In summarizing the results of the survey, the authors underscored the disparity between the problems and needs identified by African-Americans in Corona–East Elmhurst and those stressed by the board's white majority in Jackson Heights:

> Overall, it appears that the people of CPD #3 assign greater priority to environmental and recreational or school problems than to poverty related problems such as housing, unemployment and low pay. Interestingly, however, preliminary analysis of the "great problems" question by *sub*community suggests that residents of East Elmhurst and North Corona are indeed concerned with basic survival problems. Fully 90% of those who cite housing, 75% who designate unemployment, and 50% who report low pay as their "most important" problem come from these two sections of the CPD (residents from these two areas constitute only 25% of the total CPD #3 sample; the remaining 75% come from Jackson Heights proper). These subcommunity differences in problem priorities signal the danger of viewing the CPD as a unified whole. (1973:9)

These differences in problem priorities between the two areas would seriously limit the effectiveness of the Community Board as a public forum for addressing the needs and problems of African-Americans in Corona and East Elmhurst. The economic and political impact of racial inequality, illustrated by the school battles along the "Mason-Dixon line" during the 1960s, gave rise to not only distinct problems and concerns in the two areas but also to disparate and conflicting strategies for resolving them.

Moreover, Community Planning Boards were not intended to address "basic survival problems," let alone provide residents with a political forum for mobilizing around issues of racial and economic injustice. Like earlier "riot-prevention" experiments in neighborhood government, Community Planning Boards were designed to provide mechanisms for improving communication between city officials and local communities and for coordinating the delivery of city services. And, like the antipoverty program, the Community Planning Board system would draw African-American activists into arenas of political participation where issues of racial and economic inequality were fragmented and reformulated as administrative problems of bureaucratic service coordination.

"HIROSHIMA OF THE WELFARE STATE"[6]

You know, there are some people, the ideologues, who
believe it's a sin to make a buck, that somehow or other
the government should own all the property. I am not one
of those people.
(Mayor Edward Koch)

I find that there was a backlash. We thought that to pressure
the government would change the hearts of people. But the
more advancement we got, it seems to me, the more
resistance we got from the white man. I came from where
you had to get off the sidewalk when you met a white
woman. Obviously, there's been a lot of gains for us. But
then there's been a lot of gains on the other side—on
the white man's side. He's always on top. But I'll tell
you one thing, Gregory. You'll never get me to
say "the good old days."
(Floyd Ramsey, East Elmhurst activist)

By the mid-1970s Corona–East Elmhurst's infrastructure of antipoverty agencies was under attack at the national and local levels of government. Under the
Nixon and Ford administrations the federal government, supported by neocon-
servative critics of Great Society programs and state activism, implemented a
policy of New Federalism, which dismantled many War on Poverty programs
(such as Head Start and Model Cities) and introduced revenue-sharing proposals that provided states and localities with nontargeted block grants over which
they could exercise considerable discretionary control (Logan and Molotch
1987). As Michael Smith pointed out, this shift to revenue-sharing grants enabled local political elites to divert federal revenues away from programs
benefiting low-income communities:

> Revenue sharing lacked the limited redistributional requirements imposed on lo-
> cal political elites by Great Society human resource programs targeted to benefit
> "the poor" as a categorical group. Therefore, national, state, and local public
> officials facing spiraling inflation in the general economy were free to respond to
> the policy priorities of more fiscally conservative, general service oriented seg-
> ments of society rather than to the anti-poverty agenda of the 1960s. (1988:95)

In New York City this assault on the 1960s antipoverty agenda in the name
of the conservative fiscal politics of "retrenchment" was accelerated by the
1975 fiscal crisis. The recession of the early 1970s, aggravated by an out-
migration of key sectors of the city's manufacturing economy and by the ongo-

ing suburbanization of middle-income taxpayers, contributed to an imbalance between city revenues and expenditures (Pecorella 1994). As tax revenues waned during the 1960s and 1970s the city relied increasingly on borrowing money from New York banks to finance municipal services and social welfare services that had skyrocketed during the same period. By 1975 the city had amassed an operating deficit exceeding $3 billion and needed to sell an average of $750 million in short-term notes each month to meet its financial obligations (Shefter 1992).

In February 1975 the Bankers Trust refused the city's bid to issue new securities, as credit markets closed to the city and refused to purchase additional debt. Alarmed by the prospect of default, New York State officials seized fiscal control from the city government and created the Municipal Assistance Corporation (MAC), a quasi-public agency composed largely of representatives of finance capital and empowered to issue bonds and to oversee the city's expense budgets and short-term borrowing plans (Pecorella 1994). In September the fiscal control and political leverage of business and financial elites over the city was buttressed by the Financial Emergency Act of 1975, which established the Emergency Financial Control Board (EFCB). The EFCB, composed of the mayor, the governor, the state and city controllers, and three members of the private sector, centralized fiscal policy making and operated as the lead retrenchment organ of the city.

The creation of MAC and EFCB, as well as the appointment of Kenneth Axelson (from Lazard Freres and J.C. Penny) as deputy mayor in charge of finance, greatly expanded the institutional role of financial elites in the city's governance, enabling them to exercise, as Martin Shefter put it, "something close to financial blackmail" (1992:129). The years following the 1975 crisis and the restructuring of fiscal power in the city witnessed a dismantling of the public sector and the social welfare system. More than sixty thousand city workers were laid off, wages were frozen, and pension funds were invested in the municipal debt. Municipal services such as sanitation, transit, education, police, and fire protection were severely cut and, in some cases, redeployed from politically weaker "outer boroughs" like Queens and the Bronx to Manhattan. Low- and moderate-income communities such as Corona–East Elmhurst typically bore the brunt of cuts both in municipal services and in funding for welfare payments and social programs. "When that fiscal crisis came along," a Corona block association president recalled, "they took everything right back again. The programs, the jobs, the day care, all the things we fought so hard for around here. They pulled the rug out."

Retrenchment continued into the administration of Mayor Edward Koch, beginning in 1977, when there were already signs that the city was on the road to fiscal recovery. In 1981 the city balanced its budget, marking the beginning of a period of rapid growth. Between 1981 and 1988 more than 300,000 jobs were added to the economy, and during the period from 1983 to 1989 real spending in the city budget grew by 26 percent (Mollenkopf 1992). However, despite the economic boon of the 1980s the Koch administration allocated few resources to public services and social programs benefiting low- and moderate-income communities. Instead, postfiscal-crisis spending increases were dis-proportionately directed to promoting private development.

Through the use of tax-incentive programs, developer-friendly zoning poli-cies, direct public subsidies, and other policy instruments, the postfiscal crisis Koch administration promoted the land use interests of private developers and the advanced corporate sector. The administration's strategy was to promote private development in support of central business district functions while minimizing opposition from residential communities and displaced sectors of manufacturing industries. "It accomplished this end," Mollenkopf observed, "by narrowing the parameters of public discourse on planning, by ensuring that regulatory and development officials were firmly supportive of growth, and by adopting symbolic mitigating measures where expedient" (1992:143).[7]

While aggressively promoting the interests of a "growth coalition" of public officials and private sector elites, the Koch administration launched an attack on the already weakened influence and autonomy of community-based organi-zations and service providers. As his first executive order after taking office in January 1978 Koch initiated a three-year restructuring of the Community Ac-tion Program, which eliminated the New York City Council Against Poverty and the community-based corporations it funded (Fuentes 1984; Mollenkopf 1992). Arguing that the Council Against Poverty "lacked fiscal accountability and programmatic credibility" and vowing to get rid of the "poverty pimps," Koch centralized administrative and fiscal control of the antipoverty program in the newly formed Community Development Agency (CDA) which, unlike the Council Against Poverty, was directly accountable to the mayor's office.[8]

Under the new program, described in the 1979 *Final Plan for the Restruc-turing and Reorganization of New York City's Community Action Program*, thirty-three Neighborhood Development Areas (NDAs), roughly coterminous with Community Planning Districts, were formed in low-income neighbor-hoods such as Corona. Although the Community Development Agency re-tained control over funding, local Area Policy Boards, as mentioned above, were formed in each area and charged with the tasks of defining program priorities, evaluating funding proposals, and recommending programs to the Community Development Agency for support (Fuentes 1984).

Community activists protested the reorganization plan which weakened community-based control not only by concentrating fiscal and administrative authority in the Community Development Agency but also by increasing the power of elected officials and private sector interests in the newly created Area Policy Boards. Each APB was to consist of eleven elected representatives of the poor, three elected members from the private sector, and seven elected officials or their representatives (Fuentes 1984). In addition, a citywide Community Action Board was formed to advise the CDA "with stronger representation from public officials and private social welfare groups" (Mollenkopf 1992:159).

An important effect of this restructuring process was to weaken the power of community-based groups while expanding the control and influence of the mayor and allied elected officials over the city's antipoverty program. "Mayor Koch was able to use this process to his advantage," Mollenkopf argued, "and prevent the networks of city-funded, community-based organizations from becoming an independent base for political mobilization (1992:160).

Consequently, although spending on "third-party" nonprofit service providers increased in a number of areas during the postfiscal crisis of the 1980s despite federal cutbacks, the restructuring of New York City's antipoverty program served to subordinate community-based organizations involved in formulating service needs and priorities to a governing coalition composed of the Koch administration, its allied elected officials, and leading financial and development interests serving the Manhattan-oriented advanced corporate sector.

One night in 1988, after an awards dinner sponsored by the Frederick Douglas Democratic Club, an officer and lifetime member of the Corona–East Elmhurst chapter of the NAACP told me that the "civil rights movement was the worst thing that ever happened to black people." Mr. Bullard explained that civil rights–era gains "divided the black community—it destroyed our unity. It made us dependent on the powers that be." Although Mr. Bullard's way of expressing this point was extreme in comparison to what many activists voiced, the latter conveyed a similar ambivalence about civil rights–era gains and the legacy of the Great Society.

In Corona–East Elmhurst the civil rights period witnessed the deep politicization of neighborhood life. Through existing institutions, such as the church and NAACP, as well as newly created ad hoc groups and coalitions, activists contested a broad spectrum of social injustices, ranging from local school problems to wider issues of political empowerment and employment. The proliferation of these *counterpublics*, to use Nancy Fraser's term, enlarged the public sphere of community politics, enabling activists with diverse political backgrounds and commitments to "formulate oppositional interpretations of their identities, interests, and needs" (Fraser 1992:123).

The state's response to this heightened activism in Corona and elsewhere was to extend its reach into the infrastructure of black political life and reshape the associational networks and relations of community activism. Through the antipoverty program and newly created institutions of decentralized city government, activists were incorporated into state-managed and state-funded arenas of civic participation where interrelated social and economic problems were addressed as discrete and depoliticized categories of bureaucratic service provision.

To be sure, activists held views that stretched beyond and frequently conflicted with these power-evasive constructions of neighborhood problems—political views and commitments that had been honed over time across a range of social and institutional settings and struggles. Moreover, the War on Poverty, far from a coherent and functionally integrated system of social control, was rife with contradictions and jerry-built policy compromises which were themselves, as Linda Gordon put it, "the artifacts of political and social conflict" (1990:23). As a result, activists in Corona–East Elmhurst were able to appropriate and exercise the resources and rhetoric of the War on Poverty to address critical needs and goals that sometimes pushed beyond the administrative frontiers of its planners.

Nevertheless, within the new institutional spaces created through the state's War on Poverty activism, eminently political issues concerning racial and class inequality were subordinated to the "riot prevention" strategies and tactics of governing elites and the power-evasive discourses of urban blight on which they relied. And although these institutional power arrangements and discourses enabled certain forms of agency, they both privileged and elicited ways of thinking about, and acting on, urban poverty and decline that elided their roots in racialized hierarchies of political and economic power. Far more than simply constraining black activists, the state's war incited the articulation of new forms of political subjectivity and action.

The effects of the state's war on politics projected far beyond the rhetorical limits of the inner city. For by framing urban poverty and decline as a black problem and as an issue "of needy places rather than faulty labor market structures" (Smith 1988), War on Poverty discourse and practice served to conflate poverty, urban space, and black identity in the consciousness of many Americans, not only limiting its political base of support but also rendering programs and strategies for addressing urban poverty and related social problems particularly vulnerable to conservative and neoliberal attacks on the welfare state and on the "special interests" to which it was said to cater.[9] Indeed, both the Reagan-Bush presidencies and the Koch administration in New York City aggressively cultivated pro-market and antistatist ideologies and policies that constructed the needs, interests, and political demands of "inner-city" African-American and Latino populations as diametrically opposed to those of the hard-working and tacitly white American middle class.

If the state's war on politics weakened the political resources of black communities such as Corona–East Elmhurst, undermining many of the gains of civil rights–era struggles, changes in the U.S. economy since 1970 have wrought havoc on the social and economic well-being of their populations. The deindustrialization of the U.S. economy, capital flight from cities, and the attack on the wages, benefits, and collective bargaining power of workers by private corporations and their political allies have led to a deterioration of the employment opportunities and working conditions for African-Americans and other politically and economically vulnerable social groups (see Wilson 1996). Economic restructuring, coupled with drastic cuts in the social welfare system would lead to an intensification of joblessness and poverty in Black Corona in the closing decades of the twentieth century, challenging activists to bring their political experiences, resources, and commitments to bear on a daunting array of neighborhood problems and issues.

This historical perspective on activism within the context of a changing U.S. political economy proves critical not only to understanding the power relations and struggles that constituted people in Black Corona as political subjects; it is also crucial to appreciating the temporally structured social and discursive fields in which they exercised their political interests, identities, and commitments during the 1980s and 1990s. For power relations and discourses, like the social agents who inhabit and shape them, have complex and layered histories that project social meanings and relations through time, contouring the political and cultural spaces in which people act in their "presents."

In parts 2 and 3 I examine how neighborhood activists in Corona and East Elmhurst negotiated this complex institutional and symbolic landscape in struggles over the destiny of the urban environment and the quality of neighborhood life: struggles that engaged activists in conflicts with the state, with capital, and with one another over the meanings and interrelation of race, class, and place in the aftermath of the civil rights era. Some of the people who appear in the ethnographic chapters to follow were veterans of the social movements discussed earlier. Others, like the women of Lefrak City who are the subjects of chapter 5, were relative newcomers to Corona and East Elmhurst but nevertheless acted on a political landscape that had been shaped by its past.

PART TWO

CHAPTER FIVE

Race and the Politics of Place

ON A February evening in 1987 Community Board 4's Neighborhood Stabilization Committee met in the basement of a co-op apartment building on the southern border of Corona, one block from the massive and predominantly black Lefrak City housing development. Helma Goldmark, chair of the all-white committee and a resident of the well-kept Sherwood Village co-ops, took her place alongside three other committee members at a folding table that had been set up in the back of the brightly lit community room. A handful of white and black residents, two uniformed police officers, and other invited guests chatted among themselves as they waited for the meeting to begin.

Goldmark invited Judith Shapiro, a Sherwood Village resident, to open the meeting and address the first item on the agenda: the problem of security at the Lefrak City library, a public library located next to the black housing development. Shapiro complained that the library was being used as an after-school "baby-sitting service" by Lefrak City parents. These "latchkey kids," she claimed, were disruptive and making it difficult for others to use the library appropriately. She called for increased library security so that "the problem kids can be identified and removed by force if necessary."

Joseph Sardegna, chief of investigation and security for the Queens Borough Public Library, interrupted. Sardegna, invited by the committee to attend the meeting, argued that Shapiro was exaggerating the threat posed by the Lefrak City kids, remarking cryptically: "The mind conceives and the eyes perceive. Lefrak isn't so bad."

The official's comments provoked an outburst of protests. Rose Rothschild, Community Board 4's manager, retorted, "Lefrak security *is* bad. These kids are ten going on forty. They have no respect for authority." She went on to argue that people in Corona were afraid to use the Lefrak City library and for that reason wanted a library of their own. Goldmark agreed. She asked Sardegna to station a security guard in the library from 3:30 in the afternoon until closing.

"We don't want to have a library under siege," Sardegna responded, insisting that the security problem was not serious enough to justify stationing a uniformed guard. He reached into the pocket of his powder blue blazer and pulled out a pager. "We are only a beep away," Sardegna declared, holding up the device. "We already have plainclothes guards a beep away."

Rothschild stood, pressing her palms against the table: "You know, you've already repeated the same thing in a million different ways. Lefrak City is an entity in itself—a city in a city. I don't care what you say, security is bad in Lefrak." When Sardegna reiterated his point that more security would not solve the Lefrak library problem, Rothschild threatened to call his supervisor. Indignant, the library official, trailed by his assistant and two librarians, walked out.

The Neighborhood Stabilization Committee turned to the next issue on its agenda: drug dealing on Fifty-seventh Avenue, a commercial strip bordering Lefrak City. New York City Police Officer Sharpner, assigned to the 110th Precinct in Elmhurst, reported on his department's efforts to arrest drug dealers. Ken Daniels, a white Lefrak City resident and member of the committee, testified that he could see drug dealers flagging down cars from the window of his apartment.

"You know, when I moved to this neighborhood," Rothschild remarked, "there was no crime. I met with [District Attorney] Santucci and for some reason they don't want to face the fact that we need more policemen."

Phil Clark, chief of Lefrak City's private security force, responded. "Lefrak City has a lower-than-average crime rate," he said, adding that there had been a decrease in violent crime in the housing complex in the past few years. What crime there was, the Lefrak official opined, was owing to a lack of "parental guidance." Rose Rothschild agreed. "No father around, single mothers. Isn't it a shame that people have to live in fear?"

Edna Baskin and two other black residents of Lefrak City remained relatively silent as committee members and security officials discussed the problem of the latchkey kids, drug dealing, and the lack of "parental guidance" in Lefrak City, offering only their confirmation that there were real security problems in the library and housing complex. As African-American tenants of the complex, they were excluded from this discourse of neighborhood stabilization that linked crime to family disorder in a racialized topography of urban space. It was their children and neighbors who were being described as "disruptive," as drug dealers, and as objects of surveillance and law enforcement.

Although race was never explicitly referred to, the issues of crime, drugs, and parental discipline bore racial connotations that remained precariously close to the surface of discourse. For example, when Officer Sharpner reported an incident involving two "white girls from Forest Hills" who were mugged after a drug buy in Lefrak City, Rothschild quickly interjected, "We're not talking about race." Later, when the committee's chair described a mugger who was robbing people in her co-op building, she avoided explicit reference to his race: "He is about thirty-five, has bushy hair, and is Jamaican." Ethnicity served in this latter case both to signal and to deflect race within a discourse of "stabilization" that was overdetermined by an ideology of black crime.

This chapter examines the struggle of black Lefrak City residents to disrupt this conflation of race, crime, and space in the discourse and practice of everyday politics. In public forums ranging from the monthly meetings of the Neighborhood Stabilization Committee and Community Board 4 to the mass-mediated reports of journalists, Lefrak City was viewed as a threat to the quality of life of surrounding neighborhoods; a potent symbol linking anxieties about urban decline and crime to ideologies of black welfare dependency and family pathology.

At stake in this politics of representation was more than the perpetuation of racial stereotypes: the all too familiar tropes of the deviant welfare mother and her "fatherless," crime-prone progeny. More important, by constructing Lefrak City and its residents as objects of surveillance and law enforcement, this discourse of black crime and family pathology hindered, if not precluded, their participation as subjects in the process of neighborhood stabilization. In presenting this case study I emphasize the close interplay between struggles over the representation of identity and the meaning of place, and those over the distribution of political power and resources.

In mobilizing to address the needs of the latchkey kids, Lefrak City activists would contest and subvert the discourse of black crime and family disorder underpinning the "stabilization" strategies of local governing institutions such as the community board. Moreover, they would create new political networks and spaces from which to construct alternative interpretations of the identities, needs, and interests of black youth.

LEFRAK CITY: "CRUCIBLE OF RACIAL CHANGE"

Lefrak City's twenty high-rise apartment buildings occupy an entire census tract, roughly nine blocks in size, adjacent to the eight-lane Long Island Expressway that forms Corona's southern border with Rego Park, a predominantly white middle-class neighborhood across the expressway (Figure 5.1). The rental and co-op apartment buildings, office buildings, and bustling commercial strips in the Lefrak City area contrast sharply with the lower density single-family homes and storefront businesses typically found in Corona Heights and North Corona to the northeast.

In 1990 Lefrak City's population of nearly twelve thousand was 73 percent black and formed a population of African-Americans and people of diverse Caribbean and African origin in northern Queens second only in size to Corona–East Elmhurst to the north. Hispanics of equally diverse origins accounted for 19 percent of the complex's population in 1990, and whites and Asians, 5 and 2 percent, respectively.

Lefrak City was constructed on a forty-acre tract of swampy land that had served throughout much of Corona's history as a dump.[1] In 1960 Samuel J. Lefrak, one of New York City's most prolific developers of middle-income housing, purchased "Mary's Dump" from Lord William Waldorf Astor. Be-

Figure 5.1. Schoolchildren crossing the Long Island Expressway
on their return home to Lefrak City.

tween 1945 and 1960 Lefrak's development company built nearly 20 percent
of the new housing in Queens County (*New York Daily News*, 14 February
1982). In 1973 Samuel Lefrak was reported to be landlord to a quarter of a
million, largely middle-income New Yorkers (Tobias 1973).

Completed in 1964 the six-thousand-unit Lefrak City apartment complex
was envisioned by its planners to be a self-contained "city within a city" for the
middle classes: a "magic world of total living" that would offer shopping,
recreation, security, and other services and amenities within easy walking distance (*New York Times*, 24 October 1971).

Until the early 1970s Lefrak City's tenants were predominantly white and
middle-class, reflecting the racial, if not socioeconomic, composition of the
nearby and largely working-class neighborhood of Corona Heights (Cuomo
1983). In 1970, 69.8 percent of Lefrak City's 11,501 residents were non-
Spanish-speaking whites, 14 percent were Hispanic, 7.7 percent Asian, and 8.6
percent black. Neighborhoods surrounding the complex shared a similar demographic profile. Corona Heights, a predominantly Italian-American neighborhood adjacent to Lefrak City, was 81.5 percent non-Spanish-speaking
white in 1970 and 1.2 percent black. Elmhurst (not to be confused with East
Elmhurst), west of Lefrak City, was 74.3 percent white in 1970, with blacks
accounting for only 0.4 percent of the remaining population.

But in 1972 the U.S. Justice Department filed a housing discrimination suit
against the Lefrak organization charging that it had discriminated against

blacks in the renting of apartments owned by the company in Brooklyn and Queens. The discrimination suit was settled by a consent decree: the Justice Department agreed to drop the suit if the Lefrak organization would end discrimination in apartment rentals and give a month's free rent to fifty black families as well as assist them in moving into predominantly white buildings.

Although the suit was not directed specifically at Lefrak City, the Lefrak organization by some accounts relaxed tenant screening procedures and income criteria and began aggressively recruiting black tenants for the twenty-building complex. A former Lefrak City tenant leader reported to me that the Lefrak organization had concentrated black tenants in Lefrak City so as to comply with the terms of the consent decree without affecting the racial composition of other Lefrak-owned properties.

As a result, the black population of Lefrak City increased dramatically from 25 percent in 1972 to nearly 80 percent in 1976. Many tenants and other area residents complained that the new arrivals were disruptive and were threatening the community with crime, drugs, and "urban blight." A white Lefrak City resident who witnessed the transformation while serving as a tenant leader told me:

> All of a sudden we just saw different people coming in. And I keep saying to you that it has nothing to do with the color. There were always black people here when I moved in. They were friendly people. They were very high-class people here when I moved in. They were very high-class people—rich people, some of them. And you would never think anything of seeing another black person move in—or another—or another—nothing to do with it. But when you saw these people coming in—in their *undershirts*, and their *hair*, and their *staggering*. It really was the most *horrible* thing you ever saw. There were some good people too—but it was just such a drastic change. It was such a *shock*—it was the shock value. It was just unbelievable. That's what *really* did it.

Not all white residents were prone to conserve this tenuous distinction between race and social class. The rapid increase in black tenants, coinciding with a precipitous decline in building maintenance and security services, fueled perceptions that Lefrak City had become a "welfare haven," a black ghetto enclave which, like the Northern Boulevard "strip" in Corona, menaced nearby white neighborhoods with poverty, crime, and drugs. "If you bleed in Lefrak, you bleed in Corona and Elmhurst," a white activist warned at a 1975 public hearing in Corona, invoking the image of the spread of violent crime from Lefrak City to surrounding areas (*Long Island Press*, 21 November 1975).

Despite the findings of a 1976 city-sponsored report that only 3 percent of Lefrak City tenants were receiving public assistance, blacks, crime, and "welfare" were conflated in the political discourse of white community activists.[2] These images and anxieties were enlivened by two political conflicts that had been brewing in Corona and nearby Forest Hills since the mid-1960s involving the construction of low-income, "scatter-site" housing for minorities. White civic groups in both communities had opposed the New York City Housing Department's housing integration plan, and in 1972 (the year of the Lefrak City suit) the controversy in Forest Hills was coming to a head and receiving nationwide media coverage.[3] In fact the Forest Hills housing controversy was an important factor in inducing the Nixon administration to abandon the scatter-site housing concept in 1973 (Cuomo 1983:149).

Mario Cuomo, appointed by Mayor John Lindsay in 1972 to mediate the Forest Hills dispute, described the attitudes he encountered while working with white anti-integration activists in Forest Hills.

> I'm inclined to think that no matter what statistics and evidence we're able to marshal, this community's fear will not be totally dissipated. One story of a mugging at a project—whether or not true—will overcome in their minds any array of statistics. The syllogism is simple: Welfare and Blacks are generally responsible for a great deal of crime; there are Welfare and Blacks in projects; there will be a great deal of crime in and around the project. And then, too, there is a quick projection from the problem of crime—however real, fancied, or exaggerated—to all other middle-class complaints: taxes, education, etc. All of these may be legitimate, but this coupling of them with the crime problem results eventually in an indictment of the project for all the sins against the middle class (1983:49).

This conflation of race, poverty, and social pathology was also encoded in media coverage of the Lefrak City "crisis." A 1976 *New York Times* article noted that the "principal issue within Lefrak City is not one of race but of standards of behavior," yet carried the headline, "Lefrak City Crucible of Racial Change" (1 February 1976). Complaints of poor building maintenance, inadequate security, and "undesirable tenants" were often reported as problems of *racial balance* as in "Lefrak Moves to Correct Racial Makeup at Project" in the *Long Island Press* (31 March 1976). In an effort to "stabilize" the complex and to allay neighborhood fears, the Lefrak organization pressured city officials for federal Section 8 rent subsidies which local community leaders were assured would make it possible to rent vacant apartments to low-income, elderly whites. An infusion of elderly white tenants was presented as a strategy for restoring the "racial balance," offsetting the threat symbolized by the welfare mother and her offspring.

A white member of Community Board 4 recalled the visit of a Lefrak organization official to one of its meetings to win the board's support for the rent subsidy plan. His account provides a good example of the complex and shifting entanglements of race and class in white activist ideology.

> [The Lefrak official] came to the Community Board and- and he wanted *us* to fill his vacant apartments. So we got Section 8 approved. And he claimed—well in Section 8, that he would put 90 percent senior citizens in. You know, in order to . . . uh . . . stabilize the area. And also he claimed that the . . . the Section 8 would

be used mostly for elderly *white* people. You know, because they were the ones being displaced and whatever. So we went along and he got the approval. And then of course it turned out that—you know, he gave all the Section 8 to the *big* minority families and *not* to the senior citizens he promised to. And even the senior citizens he promised—the security was so *bad* that they . . . they were . . . that they would run for their *lives*, 'cause they couldn't survive with the kind of people he was letting in. But *again*, it was nothing to do with the color of the black people. We had Indians, we had Chinese, we had *all* kinds of people here. But they was—it was a different *class* of people.

The counterposed images of "big minority families" and "senior [white] citizens" fused race, class, and age differences in a symbolic shorthand that encoded complex and at times conflicting ideologies and social forces. White opposition to black welfare families converged symbolically and in practice with local resistance to the exercise of power by big government and big business. On the one hand, white residents felt that their neighborhood was being victimized by city officials because of its political weakness as a "middle-class" community: low-income housing and other undesirable projects were "dumped" on Corona because, as one resident put it, "we were a soft touch." On the other hand, many residents attributed the decline of Lefrak City to the greed and opportunism of the Lefrak organization which some held was resolving its lawsuit at their expense while failing to provide proper maintenance services.

For example, in response to the *New York Times* article, "Lefrak City Crucible of Racial Change," a Queens reader wrote to the editor: "It was sad to read about what is happening at Lefrak City. Yet an unhappy thought keeps nagging at my mind. Those young hoodlums, the modern-day Visigoths who are ripping doors off their moorings may not be bringing any new techniques to that high rise mausoleum. Perhaps they are merely continuing the ripoff policies of the management" (21 March 1976). Opposition to black "undesirables" in Lefrak City was entangled in white activist ideology with resistance to the power of big government and corporate greed.

This perception that the middle class is being squeezed "betwixt and between the impoverished and the affluent," as Jonathan Rieder put it (1985:98), has been tied by Sidney Plotkin to the development of an "enclave consciousness," an ideological stance weaving together a diverse assortment of perceived threats to the local community. "Working- and middle-class urbanites," Plotkin wrote, "understandably feel that their enclaves are squeezed between the economic depredations of the corporate and political elite and the random street attacks of drug users. For the enclave consciousness, the city is manipulated by greedy forces from above and beset by uncontrollable violence from below. It is an external arena of predatory interests, a conflict-ridden system aimed at controlling, exploiting, and destroying the enclave" (1990:228). Within the span of a few years the "city within a city" for the middle class had been transformed in the minds of many residents into a predatory beachhead within a rapidly shrinking white enclave.

By the early 1980s the worst of the Lefrak City crisis appeared to be over. Community activists, supported by local politicians, city officials, and the local press, succeeded in their effort to pressure the Lefrak organization to evict "undesirable" tenants and embark on an extensive renovation program. Strict tenant screening procedures were enacted and minimum-income criteria were reinstated to reduce the number of low-income tenants. In "Troubled Lefrak City Turning the Corner," a *New York Times* article pronouncing the recovery, Samuel J. Lefrak praised his rehabilitated tenantry: "They're decent, hard-working, middle-class people who pay their rent and pay their full share of taxes. What's happened is the best kind of gentrification" (11 March 1984).

Despite such assertions, many white residents continued to regard Lefrak City as a site of black crime and poverty symbolizing the vulnerability of the community to violence, decay, and the arbitrary exercise of elite power. These perceptions were institutionalized in part with the founding of Community Board 4's Neighborhood Stabilization Committee. Created in 1973 under the auspices of the city's Commission on Human Rights, Corona's Neighborhood Stabilization Committee defined its purpose as the promotion of "understanding and cooperation between different ethnic groups."[4]

Although the committee's initial efforts focused on integrating Corona's rapidly growing Spanish-speaking population into neighborhood affairs, by 1976 the committee had turned its attention to Lefrak City where its on-site office coordinated the stabilization efforts of city officials, community groups, and the Lefrak organization. By 1987, when the Neighborhood Stabilization Committee met to address the problem of the Lefrak library's "latchkey kids," it was functioning as a subcommittee of Community Board 4. Unlike the board's other committees (e.g., Traffic, Public Safety, and Youth Services), the purview of the Neighborhood Stabilization Committee was limited to Lefrak City and its environs, thereby institutionalizing the perception that the black housing complex represented a peculiar threat to the stability of the community. Before the formation of Concerned Community Adults to which I now turn, black participation in neighborhood politics within Community Board 4 had been limited to, if not contained by, this committee.

"RUBBING AGAINST THE GRAIN"

Concerned Community Adults (CCA) was organized largely through the efforts of Edna Baskin, an African-American woman who moved to Lefrak City with her husband and two children in 1979. Raised in Buffalo, New York, Baskin had been active in community politics and Buffalo's antipoverty program as well as in a local Baptist church founded by her grandfather.

Although Baskin had been employed earlier as a medical lab technician, on her arrival in Queens she began working in her home as a "sitter" or child care provider for women living in her four-building section. Since the few licensed child care centers in the Lefrak City area were expensive, many parents used unlicensed sitters located within the apartment complex.[5] Baskin estimated that twelve of the eighteen floors in her building had sitters caring for pre-school children.

Through her child care work, Baskin developed a network of relationships with Lefrak City women. Each evening, when these women, whom Edna referred to as her "mothers," came to pick up their children they would gather in her apartment to socialize and exchange information about community services and issues. Baskin also endeavored to welcome and orient new tenants to the apartment complex and the surrounding community, a consideration she found lacking when she arrived in Lefrak City.

> When I moved here, I had to try to learn about the community by myself, because there was nobody to help me or to tell me where things were. And when people move in now, I tell them where the best places are to shop and, if they have children, which schools I think are the best. Even people on my floor—like when new people move on this floor, I immediately go and introduce myself, tell them who I am, and give them a voter registration form—because the first couple of weeks we were here, I was like, "Well, will somebody come and tell us where we go to vote?"

These everyday networks of child care, communication, and exchange among women, linking households, floors, and buildings within the complex, would provide the social base for the mobilization of Lefrak City tenants as a political force within the community. Not long after Baskin arrived, her "mothers" and other neighbors elected her to be a representative to the Tenants Association.

The Lefrak City Tenants Association was organized during the 1970s crisis and was instrumental in pressuring the Lefrak organization to renovate the complex and tighten security. However, by the 1980s some tenants had come to feel that the association had sold out to management and become little more than a "social club." Moreover, though community leaders regarded the Tenants Association as the institutional voice of Lefrak City, its leadership played a relatively minor role in neighborhood affairs. The Tenants Association's lack of involvement in local politics, coupled with the perception of many that it was working in concert with Lefrak management, contributed to the political isolation of Lefrak City's black tenants. In 1987, for example, few if any Tenants Association members attended meetings of Community Board 4, the most important governing body in the community. However, two former presidents of the Tenants Association sat on the board: a white man and a black man, both of whom had had a falling-out with the Tenants Association's leadership.

These personal animosities more than likely reinforced the perception that Lefrak City, a "city within a city," constituted a distinct political entity.

This sense of political isolation can be gleaned from the spatial language used in a statement written by the African-American president of the Tenants Association on the occasion of its 1988 annual awards dinner.

> Looking at our neighborhood and its outer perimeters over the past ten years there has been a subtle change. We must take a survey of our community but most importantly we must take a survey of ourselves. Do we knock the establishment or do we work within the system? Positive self-motivation and positive self-awareness will bring about a drastic upward change. Apathy will cause community deterioration. A convergence between all the serving agencies (Police, Sanitation, Politicians, Lefrak organization, merchants, outer perimeter groups, local community board) and our community is important to the continual upgrading process (Lefrak City Tenants Association 1988:1).

When Tenants Association leaders did not support her proposal to register voters during the 1984 presidential election, Edna Baskin organized her own voter registration drive using the opportunity to inform tenants about other neighborhood issues. After the election Baskin began attending meetings of Community Board 4, bypassing the Tenants Association leadership. After each meeting she would meet with tenants in the lobby of her building to explain how the board's actions would affect Lefrak City tenants.

"They told me that they wanted something more than what they were getting from the Tenants Association," Baskin recalled. "They came and said, 'Edna, you know, we need somebody out here looking out for our political status.' They said, 'There's nobody looking out after us politically. We have people on the Community Board, but we never get a report as to what the board is doing.'" However, Baskin stopped holding these meetings when the president of the association objected and informed her that she was "rubbing against the grain." Such encounters with the association's leaders convinced Baskin of the need to develop an alternative base of political power within Lefrak City, one that would be more responsive to the needs of its tenants.

In 1986 Baskin was encouraged by Rose Rothschild, Community Board 4's district manager, to participate in the Neighborhood Stabilization Committee. Rothschild and the board's chairperson, also a white woman, had made significant efforts to increase the involvement of people of color on the board. Under their leadership Korean, Chinese, and Latino persons had been seated on the predominantly white-American board, reflecting the changing demography of the community. However, despite Lefrak City's large black population, only one African-American sat on the thirty-four member Community Board in 1987. Rothschild, the board's manager, often complained that the Tenants Association's leadership (in particular, its male president) blocked her efforts to involve Lefrak City residents in the Community Board's activities.

Whatever the case, the Community Board's leaders perceived Baskin and her social networks to be a resource for expanding relations between Lefrak City and the surrounding community.

Meetings of the Stabilization Committee generally focused on crime, drug sales, and other "quality-of-life" issues in the Lefrak City vicinity, such as traffic congestion and price gouging by merchants. Agenda items frequently targeted threats posed by Lefrak City residents (primarily black youth) to the surrounding area rather than to the problems faced by residents within the complex. Similarly, problem-solving strategies emphasized law enforcement rather than the mobilization of Lefrak City tenants around shared concerns.

After attending a number of Stabilization Committee meetings, Baskin came to feel that the committee was not addressing the needs of Lefrak City residents and, in particular, those of its youth. Her participation on the committee waned as she began to form her own group, organizing her "mothers" to that purpose. In June 1987, in her apartment, Baskin convened the first meeting of Concerned Community Adults.

I arrived early at Edna Baskin's apartment on the twelfth floor of the Ceylon building overlooking the Long Island Expressway. Baskin had just returned from Borough Hall where she was taking a leadership training course sponsored by the borough president's office. Rose Rothschild, manager of Community Board 4, had nominated Baskin to the board, and the course was preparation for her expected appointment.

The kitchen table was covered with notepads, flyers announcing community events, and an assortment of booklets and other materials from the leadership course. In the adjacent living room, neatly stacked children's toys and a yellow plastic play table with chairs occupied one corner along with a Soloflex exercise machine. A sliding door led from the living room to a small terrace with a view of the expressway and the squat, red-brick apartment buildings of Rego Park and Forest Hills beyond.

Baskin lived in the two-bedroom apartment with her husband, Ron, a television news writer, and their teenage son, Previn. Her husband's brother, Duane, a Wall Street paralegal, had been sharing the apartment since his arrival from Buffalo the year before. During the week Edna took care of about six children ranging in age from three to seven years. Two school-age children attended Public School 206 across the expressway in Rego Park. On a typical weekday Baskin would take the preschoolers for a morning walk (running errands along the way), return home for lunch, naps, and playtime, and then pick up the older children from school, pulling the preschoolers behind her in a large red wagon.

Baskin was excited about the leadership training course and, in particular, the sections addressing the definition of objectives and the development of strategies. "You know women do this kind of thing naturally," she told me. "They have to plan how to spend money and send their kids to school. All those kinds of things." Baskin and her "mothers" had drafted a statement of purpose for the new group and adopted the bylaws of a not-for-profit agency in Harlem. "The purpose of Concerned Community Adults," read the statement of purpose, "is to provide a wide range of youth advocacy, education, and development services to young people and their parents residing in Lefrak City and the surrounding area." At the meeting that evening members of CCA's newly formed board of directors were to review both documents and plan activities for the summer.

Carol Willins and Firdasha Jami were the first to arrive. Willins, an administrator at Harlem Hospital, had been born in the Albany Projects in Brooklyn and moved to St. Albans, Queens, when her parents bought their first home. After entering City College's nursing program in 1972, Willins rented a studio apartment in Lefrak City. Willins's husband, also a graduate of City College, was an architect and, like Carol, had been born in Brooklyn and raised in south Queens. In contrast, Firdasha Jami had lived in Lefrak City for only a few months. A single parent, she had moved to New York from Indiana to study communications. Baskin took care of Firdasha's preschool daughter and the Willins's two school-age children. Contrary to the stereotypes held by many residents in surrounding areas, the majority of Lefrak City's black tenants were working and middle class.

CCA's first meeting began at 7:00 in the evening with a discussion of the bylaws. Two other women who had also been invited to attend called to cancel: one could not find a babysitter for her newborn; the other had concert tickets. Baskin's brother-in-law, Duane, wandered in and out of the kitchen between innings of the baseball game that he and his brother were watching in the bedroom. He looked on with curiosity as the three women discussed each point of the bylaws. When a debate arose over the issue of membership dues, Duane took a seat at the table and joined in.

The group turned next to defining the needs of young people within Lefrak City. A problem underscored by all was the lack of a community center and, more generally, the lack of recreational public spaces for youths and adults alike to congregate. Despite its population of twelve thousand, Lefrak City had scant indoor or outdoor public facilities. An empty, apartment-size space located in the basement of one building served as an all-purpose meeting room for the entire development. Little playground space was located on the complex's grounds, and its two outdoor swimming pools were no longer in use. Much of the open space between buildings was taken up by parking lots.

"We have a lot of children here, and there is nothing for them to do," Baskin declared. "To me, those children are kept like prisoners because the sitters don't have any place to take them. And those kids are stuck in those hot apartments all day. It's like my son said to me—he said, 'Mama, there's no place to go just to sit down and cool out and talk to other kids.'"

This lack of public space, Baskin and others pointed out, also limited interaction among adults and made organizing tenants particularly difficult. Carol

Willins, contrasting Lefrak City to St. Albans where she was raised, observed: "A missing aspect of this place is a mutual meeting ground—a community center. If we had one local place where tenants could meet, that would solve a lot of our problems because you would get the sense that you lived in a community even with this massive amount of people."

For an hour, the board members discussed strategies for creating this "mutual meeting ground" at Lefrak City and for mobilizing its tenants. Baskin suggested pressuring the Lefrak organization to build a community center at the site of one of the abandoned pools. Duane, her brother-in-law, replied that zoning laws would probably not allow this and advocated an immediate, if less ambitious, solution. He suggested that CCA organize a Lefrak City block party that would, as he put it, "occupy" the disused public areas for the benefit of residents.

In the midst of this discussion Jonathan Bates arrived. A student in communications at Long Island University, Bates had attempted to form a youth organization in Lefrak City the year before. When he approached the Tenants Association with the idea, they invited him to head a youth committee within the association but provided little support. Moreover, the Tenants Association would not give the youth committee control over its budget, which Bates felt set limits on its effectiveness as well as its autonomy. When Jonathan heard that Baskin was forming a new organization, he telephoned her.

Dressed in a dark gray suit and red silk tie, Bates told the group about his organizing experiences in Lefrak City and stressed the importance of involving youth in decision making. Baskin and the others agreed and resolved that the goals and activities of the new organization should be defined by the young people themselves. To ensure this "youth viewpoint," the board decided that the first activity of Concerned Community Adults would be a public forum where Lefrak City youth could voice their concerns and set the group's agenda. Jonathan volunteered to make flyers for the event and said he would spread the word among youth in the complex. In the meantime Firdasha Jami would develop a "needs assessment survey" that would be passed out to parents in the complex before the meeting.

The first Lefrak City Youth Forum was held two weeks later in the Continental Room, Lefrak City's all-purpose community room in the basement of the Rome Building facing troubled Fifty-seventh Avenue. About fifty Lefrak City youth, a dozen parents, Boy Scout and Girl Scout troop leaders, and three members of Community Board 4 gathered in the dimly lit, narrow room. The Community Board representatives included its chairperson, Miriam Levenson, and Daok Lee Pak, a Korean-born woman who worked closely with business groups that represented Korean merchants in the Lefrak area. Baskin and her board had chosen Jonathan Bates to chair the meeting as a means of stressing youth involvement in the group and countering, as she put it, "negative images of black males."

Figure 5.2. Lefrak City teenagers speak out at the
Concerned Community Adults Youth Forum.

A long, folding table had been set up at one end of the room for the members of CCA and the Community Board. Behind the table a large American flag had been tacked to the wood-paneled wall. Flanked by Baskin and three women members of her board, the youthful chair of the forum described CCA's purpose and then invited the young people present to speak about their needs and problems. The teenagers remained silent, but a few adults stood and made statements concerning the need for tutoring and recreational programs.

For some thirty minutes the forum dragged on, alternating between parents' appeals for more youth services and Jonathan's inspired lectures on career planning, positive thinking, and the "new world of computers." After an adult Scout leader asked about the possibility of getting funding for bus trips, a young man sitting in the back of the room stood to speak. He was the first teenager to do so that night (Figure 5.2).

Um . . . all this time people been talkin' about "let's go on this trip and let's go on that trip." Why get away from the community? We should concentrate on having more fun *in* the community. They run us out—you know, like from the park or whatever. I . . . I mean they say it's late at night, but *think* about it. I recall last week Thursday, they ran us out of the park at 2:30 in the afternoon. You see, now there was only five of us. I mean sittin' on a *bench*—[they] said we couldn't sit on the bench. They run us out of Lefrak altogether. I don't understand that. Now you talkin' about "oh, let's go out, do this trip here, and have fun there." Why can't we have fun where we live?

The young audience erupted in wild applause. Baskin, who had not yet spoken, stood, nodding her head and motioning with her hand to the back of the room. The audience settled down.

> The young man who just made that comment—thank you very much. I did not *realize* there was a problem with Lefrak security running the youth *out*. See, that's another reason for us getting together—so that we, the *other* adults here who *don't* know what's going on, can be made aware.

In fact Baskin *did* know of this problem with Lefrak security, and she often complained about the harassment that her teenage son received from Lefrak security guards, as well as from city police officers. Her comments were directed to "the *other* adults" present, particularly to the members of Community Board 4 who, unlike those who were living in Lefrak City, had not yet heard this side of the story. This intervention, like many of CCA's activities to follow, served to contest and rework the discursive field within which Lefrak City was constructed as a racialized and pathological place.

The discussion, now animated and dominated by the young people, moved to the topic of the security services. A young man in his late twenties linked the harassment by Lefrak security to media representations of black teenagers as drug dealers. His comments are interesting because they mark the reduction of black teenagers to drug dealers and then expand the category at issue to include a broader "us"—an adult and employed "us": "They done blamed these young people as all drug pushers. That's what they doing. And they want to clear us *all* out. Every teenager is bad in their eyes. And the guys—you be comin' home from work and go to the park, and they push us out 'cause they suspect you to be a drug pusher."

This eruption of frustration and criticism over how black youth were stereotyped and harassed by Lefrak City's security services and the police challenged a central theme in white activist ideology and practice. By inverting the familiar relation between black teenagers and security, so central to the ideology of black crime, the testimony (and Edna's marking of its significance) raised the possibility that black teenagers who were often the targets of police action could play a constructive role in neighborhood stabilization. This novel prospect was given further support, ironically, when the forum's chair, intent on being a source of useful information, suggested that the teenagers voice their grievances about Lefrak security at the next meeting of the Neighborhood Stabilization Committee (Figure 5.3).

The Youth Forum, which ended with the planning of a youth and adult "march against crack," established CCA as a grass-roots force in the eyes of Lefrak City residents and representatives of Community Board 4 from its

Figure 5.3. Jonathan Bates (*center*), chair of the Youth Forum, and Edna Baskin (*right*) listen to complaints about police harassment.

"outer perimeter." The importance of this event can be judged in part by the reaction of the Lefrak City Tenants Association. A few days after the Youth Forum, the president of the Tenants Association approached Baskin and asked her to place her organization under his "umbrella." When Baskin refused, the association's president warned that CCA would never get off the ground without his support. Nonetheless, the forum had legitimated Concerned Community Adults and encouraged the leadership of the Community Board to deal directly with Baskin on youth issues without the mediation of the Tenants Association.

Equally important, the mobilizing efforts of Baskin and CCA created new political spaces and ways of envisioning neighborhood stabilization that not only invited the involvement of residents who had been marginalized in local political institutions and discourses but also created public forums where alternative interpretations of the identities, interests, and needs of black residents could be publicly formulated.

CONTESTING THE POLITICS OF "URBAN BLIGHT"

A few weeks after the Youth Forum, CCA became involved in a neighborhood "cleanup" competition that further increased the organization's visibility and influence in neighborhood politics. Community boards in Queens were invited by the office of the Queens Borough president to organize teams of youth to clean sidewalks and educate merchants about sanitation codes. The winning team would go to Disneyland.

Again mobilizing her network of women, Baskin organized a team of twelve youth, many of whom she had "sat" for at one time or another. Since no other organization in the community had been able to organize a group, CCA's cleanup team, composed entirely of black Lefrak City youth, became the official representative of Community Board 4. CCA also gained the support of the area's Korean merchants through Daok Lee Pak, the Korean-born woman who had attended the Youth Forum representing the Community Board and the Mid-Queens Korean Association, an organization of Korean businesspersons. Because relations between Korean merchants and African-Americans in New York City had often been strained, this linkage was politically important.

The cleanup team's activities received considerable attention from community leaders and the press. Community Board members visited the cleanup team at work in the Lefrak City area. Merchants donated refreshments, free haircuts, and school supplies, and posed with team members during picture-taking sessions (Figure 5.4). The Korean owner of a local grocery store offered to hire two cleanup team members when business picked up. Lefrak City management informed Baskin that Samuel J. Lefrak himself had noticed that the neighborhood looked cleaner. Viewed within the context of Lefrak City's history as a political issue and object of discourse, the cleanup campaign was extremely significant.

The image of black Lefrak City youth removing rubbish from the streets surrounding the housing complex undermined the construction of Lefrak City as a site of danger and urban blight—images tied symbolically to pollution and disorder (Douglas 1966) as well as to "blackness" and poverty (Gilman 1985; cf. Conquergood 1992).[6]

The potency of garbage as a polysemous symbol of disorder and threat to community was intensified during the summer of 1987 by a highly publicized political brawl concerning the disposition of a garbage barge. A seagoing barge containing more than three thousand tons of New York area garbage had been turned away by officials in Louisiana where it was to be dumped. After wandering around the Gulf of Mexico for a few days, the barge returned to New York City where it triggered a crisis of sorts. City officials refused to allow the barge to dock until it could be tested for environmentally hazardous materials. A supreme court judge in Queens ordered the barge to be put under "24-hour surveillance" while city officials and politicians debated the origin and content of the garbage (*New York Newsday*, 21 May 1987).

"It's nothing but 100 percent, all-American garbage," a New York State inspector assured the public, responding to fears raised by some politicians that it might contain "vermin," carrying diseases from Mexico or Belize (*New York Newsday*, 19 May 1987). When the town of Islip, Long Island, agreed to accept the garbage for its landfill, the borough president of Queens refused to allow it to be transported across her borough until more testing was done. The town supervisor of Islip accused the Queens official of using the garbage as an issue to mask her "image problems," alluding to a political corruption scandal that had rocked Queens the year before. "I heard her say Islip's garbage will never travel the streets of Queens," he declared. "And she presides over the corruption capital of the universe" (*New York Newsday*, 20 May 1987).

The complex meanings associated with garbage, manipulated by Queens politicians to represent corruption and violations of turf, resonated with local symbolic deployments of such notions as "vermin" and "garbage" to signify the threat posed by Lefrak City. For example, a Community Board 4 member once reported to the board after a Lefrak "tour" sponsored by the Stabilization Committee that the inspection team had encountered the "smell of rats," a claim that was duly recorded in the minutes.

Baskin was well aware of the potency of the "garbage barge" as a mass-mediated symbol framing the activities of her clean-up crew.[7] I asked, "Do you think the fact that it was a cleanup campaign, as opposed to something else, had something to do with its success?"

> Of course. Because, all during the summer—you know—the garbage barge sitting out there—okay?—only emphasized the problem the whole country is having with *garbage*. You understand? And that *our children* could *see* that this is really a problem. See, we have to make our children aware that there's a problem today. So that when *they* become adults, *they* have some . . . some knowledge to draw on, as to how to *deal* with problems like this. You have to *learn* this. This is nothing that somebody . . . that you could read in a book and do. It's something you have to get out here and do.

Of interest here is less the symbolic investments of garbage per se than the manner in which Baskin and her organization deliberately engaged in a politics of representation that drew on and reworked deeply historical and mass-mediated discourses about the interrelation of race, place, and urban blight. The practice of constructing black identity was an integral component of CCA's strategy and tactics of community mobilization.

Although the CCA's team did not win the boroughwide cleanup competition, Baskin was able to strengthen support for her group among politicians, Community Board members, local merchants, and representatives of a major new immigrant community in Queens. The Mid-Queens Korean Association, noted above, invited Baskin, her team members, and representatives of Community Board 4 to a dinner party at a Korean restaurant to "honor" the young people. Although black-Korean relations were not the explicit focus of the event the topic surfaced repeatedly, suggesting that race and ethnic relations were being negotiated through activities surrounding the cleanup competition.

Figure 5.4. Edna Baskin (*far right*) poses with members of the cleanup team and "Leo the Greek," a local merchant who donated refreshments during the summer campaign. Rose Rothschild, district manager of Community Board 4, stands at the far left next to Miriam Levinson, the board's chairperson.

During a brief speech Edna remarked that relations between Korean merchants and Lefrak City had been good during the summer. "The most important thing for our group," she continued, "is our children. When we brought our children to you, you helped." Daok Lee Pak, the Korean-born member of the Community Board who had attended the Youth Forum, responded: "Our body is just a rented car. Sometimes you are driven by a back-seat driver but the real driver is colorless." The dinner was reported in the *Korean Times*, a Korean-language newspaper.

The cleanup competition, like the Youth Forum, undermined key ideological themes that had been articulated in activist and mass-mediated discourses since the desegregation of Lefrak City. Through cultural practices ranging from the cleaning up of streets and public spaces to everyday interactions with merchants, city officials, and neighborhood residents, CCA and its cleanup team challenged and reworked the racialized economy of space and its underlying power relations that had constructed Lefrak City as a threat to middle-class stability.

By summer's end CCA activities had attracted the attention of local politicians. An awards dinner held to honor members of the cleanup team was attended by Helen Marshall, the area's state assemblywoman, and by an aid to the local city councilman. Both officials had begun to explore ways to provide CCA with public funding in order to support a tutorial program that the group had begun in the Lefrak library. CCA awarded certificates of merit to merchants, supporters on Community Board 4, and to cleanup team members. Rose Rothschild, district manager of the board, described CCA's activities (and her certificate) at the Community Board's next meeting and redoubled her efforts to have Baskin seated on the board. Already active on the board's Youth Services Committee, Baskin was appointed co-chair of its Day Care Committee.

However, the most telling translation of the summer's organizing work into political power involved CCA's participation in the election of the local Area Policy Board. As discussed in chapter 4, the Area Policy Board, or APB, is a locally based, elected body that defines local funding priorities and makes recommendations to the city concerning the allocation of community development block grants. Area Policy Board members serve as volunteers and, at least in theory, are "representatives of the poor" insofar as candidates are required to live in designated "poverty areas."

Procedurally, candidates must submit petitions to the New York City Community Development Agency (CDA) in order to appear on the ballot. Once formed, the Area Policy Board holds public hearings to assess neighborhood service needs and then meets to review proposals for funding received from local service providers. Although the APB is only empowered to make recommendations for funding, the city generally supports their decisions. For this reason, APBs wield considerable power over local resources, particularly in the wake of the national and local retrenchment policies of the 1970s and 1980s.

After concluding that Lefrak City needed better access to community development funds for youth service programs, Baskin and her board decided to field candidates in the APB elections. To that end, CCA invited representatives from the city to speak to residents in Lefrak City about the Area Policy Board and election process. After the orientation Baskin encouraged a number of Lefrak City residents to begin the process of collecting petition signatures.

Most of these candidates were members of social networks that had been mobilized by CCA during the summer. For example, six of the eight candidates who qualified for the APB election in Lefrak City were women: three were among Baskin's child care mothers (one of these women was co-leader of the cleanup team), two served as volunteer tutors in CCA's Lefrak library tutorial program, and the sixth was a senior citizen activist and former director of the Lefrak City Senior Center. Of the two male candidates, one was the husband of a "mother" on CCA's board of directors, and the second was a retired civil servant who lived in Baskin's building. Since the retired civil servant would serve on a citywide advisory board, Baskin decided to select, as she put it, "a man of experience, familiar with the way government bureaucracies work."

Baskin's increasing visibility and clout as a grass-roots leader in Lefrak City was demonstrated when Assemblywoman Helen Marshall contacted her about the APB elections. Aware of CCA's growing influence in Lefrak City, Marshall wanted Baskin to support six candidates from Corona–East Elmhurst along with CCA's Lefrak City slate. However, Baskin declined on the grounds that she did not know Marshall's candidates. Moreover, since Marshall's APB candidates would be competing for votes with those in Lefrak City, supporting the former would draw votes away from CCA's slate.

Before the election, the Community Development Agency sponsored separate "Candidates Nights" in Lefrak City and Corona–East Elmhurst. The purpose of the meetings was to inform the public about the election process and provide APB candidates with a platform to present their thoughts about the community's development needs. Baskin and her board made flyers publicizing the meeting and held a luncheon for CCA's candidates to develop a platform stressing day care and educational services.

On Candidates Night I met Edna and Ron Baskin at their apartment. Ron had become increasingly involved in CCA during the course of the summer and had been delegated to handle the group's public relations. Together with his brother, who served as corresponding secretary, Ron was planning a newsletter.

"People here don't support anything that has to do with the education of our kids," Ron remarked, as Edna gathered an assortment of informational material to hand out at the meeting. Ron lit a Kool 100 and pursued his point, referring to a television program he had seen in which a member of the Klu Klux Klan was interviewed at a "survivalist" training camp. "Now this KKK guy said, 'We're going to teach our kids how to survive, not play basketball.'"

Duane, standing by the refrigerator, raised his eyebrows. "Hello! Tell me about it."

Ron continued. "Now, I could relate to what that cracker was saying because they're teaching their kids how to survive against what they perceive to be the enemy."

Duane closed the refrigerator door. "Thank you! They use our bodies and abuse our minds."

The importance of providing young people with educational services, rather than just recreational activities, was a major theme at CCA's biweekly meetings. Ron, Edna, and other members of the organization frequently criticized the "sports mentality" that they felt dominated the youth programs provided by schools and by the city's community development programs. Ron and Duane, who had both worked with War on Poverty programs in Buffalo, argued that current programs, like those of the 1960s, were developed to keep "black people off the streets" rather than to equip them with the necessary tools to survive in the modern economy. CCA's board meetings often digressed into discussions of the global economy, junk bond trading on Wall Street, and the impact of information technologies on the educational needs of black youth.

When the Wall Street stock market crashed in the fall of 1987, these discussions reached a crescendo, influencing CCA's strategies for providing youth services. Concern about the job market for African-American youth had led Baskin and her board to explore ways of utilizing the Lefrak City library to provide educational services. After a librarian informed her that the Lefrak library's small auditorium was not being used, Baskin organized an after-school tutorial program and recruited two volunteer tutors from Lefrak City.

Riding down in the elevator, Baskin told me that her brother-in-law, Duane, would soon be meeting with Queens Borough Public Library officials to discuss other ways of using the Lefrak library for CCA's activities. "We want to do just like they did at Langston Hughes," Baskin remarked, referring to the Langston Hughes Community Library and Black Cultural Center on Northern Boulevard in Corona–East Elmhurst (see chapter 4).

As we negotiated the maze of underground tunnels linking Lefrak City's twenty buildings, Baskin pointed out broken lightbulbs and unlocked security doors along the way, jotting down the location of each in a pocket-sized spiral notebook. When we arrived at the Lefrak Senior Center in the basement of the Rome building, Baskin greeted CCA's six candidates and introduced herself to the seven candidates who had come from North Corona. Not counting the candidates, about thirty neighborhood residents attended the meeting.

By the time the forum was scheduled to begin, the city's representatives who were to lead it had still not arrived. In fact an earlier forum in Lefrak City had been canceled when the same officials simply did not show up. Baskin felt that the last-minute cancellation of the first forum, which had been widely publicized by CCA, had turned off many residents to the APB election process. After waiting fifteen minutes, she began the meeting herself.

Baskin described the purpose of the Area Policy Board and suggested that the candidates and audience join in a discussion of the community's development needs. One of the priorities of Concerned Community Adults, she said, was to ensure that public libraries serve the educational needs of children and not function merely as "babysitting services." One of the candidates from Corona–East Elmhurst asked, "Are you talking about Lefrak City or about the *entire* community?" Baskin responded that people in Lefrak City looked to the Langston Hughes library in Corona–East Elmhurst as a model.

A second candidate, a member of Corona–East Elmhurst's NAACP, declared: "That library only exists because the community fought for it and fought to make it work. That's what we have to do here with this Area Policy Board."

The audience applauded.

"That's right," Ron Baskin remarked, "and do you want to know why? Because as soon as white folks know that you want to educate your kids, that money will dry up."

Just as the NAACP activist had begun to elaborate on the efforts of his branch to improve early childhood education in Corona–East Elmhurst, the officials from the city's Community Development Agency arrived and took over the meeting. The two CDA officials repeated the APB orientation that Edna had given and then asked each candidate to give a brief summary of their reasons for wanting to be elected.

All the candidates stressed the need for day care services and tutoring programs for youth. "We need educational programs," one of Baskin's "mothers" stated, "because we are losing our children. We have 'recreationalized' our kids to death." A man from North Corona stressed the importance of providing math and computer skills training. A PTA president and church activist from North Corona complained that her children had to commute to Queens College for tutoring in math and reading. "We should put things into this community," she continued, "instead of always going somewhere else."

Despite the Community Development Agency's poor planning of the event, Candidates Night provided an important opportunity for African-American tenants and activists in Lefrak City to meet with their counterparts in Corona–East Elmhurst in order to discuss common needs, compare organizing experiences, and define priorities for public funding. Because Corona–East Elmhurst and the Lefrak City area were represented by different Community Boards (Boards 3 and 4, respectively), there were few public forums that brought black activists from the two neighborhoods together to deliberate about neighborhood needs and problems.

This widening of the public sphere of community activism was enabled in part by the city's assignment of the two communities to the same Neighborhood Development Area—one that linked "poverty areas" in the two Community Boards. However, equally significant were the efforts of activists themselves not only to mobilize residents to participate in the election process but also to renegotiate bureaucratic definitions of space, political identity, and community interest. On the one hand, CCA's ability to marshal rapidly a Lefrak City slate for the Area Policy Board elections depended on the existence of activist networks that had been cultivated through the summer cleanup campaign and other activities. The mobilization of these grass-roots constituencies in turn prompted politicians and officials, such as Helen Marshall, to pursue strategies for coordinating CCA's activities in Lefrak City with those of black activists and groups in Corona–East Elmhurst, such as Elmcor Youth and Adult Services, the community's largest Community Development Agency.

Moreover, Baskin and CCA members endeavored to overstep the administrative and symbolic boundaries that had politically isolated Lefrak City and its residents from wider circuits of power and influence. For example, Baskin visited the Langston Hughes Community Library and Cultural Center in Corona–East Elmhurst and met with its director, Andrew Jackson, to gain support and expertise for CCA's programs in the Lefrak library. And later, during Black History Month, CCA organized bus trips to the Langston Hughes library for Lefrak City youth. Baskin's reference to the Hughes library as a "model" for Lefrak City residents not only flagged this transneighborhood tie but also linked CCA and its black constituency in Lefrak City to one of the most powerful symbols of Corona–East Elmhurst's civil rights–era struggles. In claiming this legacy Baskin and her group appealed to a notion of community that transgressed bureaucratic boundaries and appealed instead to a common interpretation of black needs, identity, and historical experience.

Although voter turnout for elections to the Area Policy Board was light, three of the candidates fielded by Concerned Community Adults were elected.

NEGOTIATING THE SPACE OF POLITICS

Shortly after the APB election Baskin's organization was incorporated. Status as a not-for-profit corporation would enable CCA to receive public funds and corporate donations. However, Baskin and her board members were wary of applying for public funds: it was felt that such funding might compromise CCA's ability to act independently. "Public sector funding is a trap," Ron Baskin argued at a CCA board meeting in September. "If you want to take money from the city, you have to hire people who are acceptable to the very same people who failed us already." Edna and others expressed similar apprehensions.

Ron Baskin and his brother often disagreed with Edna about strategy. After a dispute over accepting donations from Lefrak management, the two brothers contended that Edna had "stacked the board" with her "mothers" to offset their voting power. When a subsequent meeting led to the reversal of the earlier decision to accept the Lefrak donation, Edna remarked that she had lost the vote because "her people didn't show up," referring to two women board members.

Ron and Duane often appealed to "professional," workplace-based expertise when structuring arguments in opposition to Edna and her supporters on the board. And although Edna tended to discount the significance of gender relations when explaining the internal dynamics of the organization, she frequently emphasized the role that gender identity played in her dealings with outside agencies.

For example, when CCA held meetings with officials of government agencies and private corporations, Edna often encouraged her husband or brother-in-law to serve as the group's representative because, as she put it, "men get more respect—they take you more seriously." Before a meeting with Lefrak management that was to be conducted by her husband, Edna explained: "This is a white man's world. It's much easier to deal with corporate America if you are a black male. Women act as backup." She went on to say that it was also important for black men to be seen in leadership positions and "as positive role models for our youth." This dual purpose stood behind her decisions to appoint Jonathan Bates to chair the Youth Forum, to invite her husband to take charge of CCA's "public relations," and to insist that her teenage son (much against his wishes) participate in the cleanup campaign.

Edna's tactical appropriation of patriarchal ideology to present a strong face to institutional power *and* to disrupt negative images of black masculinity illustrates not only the complex manner in which racial and gender ideologies crosscut in the construction of political subjects and space; it also illustrates, as Lila Abu-Lughod put it, that "intersecting and often conflicting structures of power work together," sometimes positioning women in the equivocal situation of both resisting and supporting existing power relations (1989:42).

The distinction drawn by Edna and her "mothers" between the public face of masculine political authority and women's roles as organizers or "backup" resonates with Karen Sacks's description of women union activists at Duke University (1988). Sacks found that some women activists expressed the view that women are organizers and men are leaders. "They suggested," Sacks wrote, "that women created the organization, made people feel part of it, and did the routine work upon which most things depended, whereas men made public pronouncements and confronted and negotiated with management" (1988:78–79). Contrasting the movement's "spokes*men*" with what she called its "centerwomen," Sacks observed that the latter played key leadership roles in constructing social networks at the workplace and transforming them into a social force. Centerwomen politicized notions about work, adulthood, and responsibility, first learned in a household context, by bringing them to bear in the workplace in the form of an oppositional working-class culture (cf. Westwood 1985).

The concept of the centerwoman and the attention it draws to the politicization of everyday social ties and networks prove helpful in understanding how gendered relations and forms of resistance inscribe the political terrain on which racial meanings and identities are contested and rearticulated. Just as Edna used a gendered ideology of leadership to negotiate institutional power and to undermine racial stereotypes, so, too, did she appropriate a rhetoric of "family" and "family values" to signal political unity and a broadening of the public sphere of political participation.

When asked why, given his marginal involvement, she had paid special tribute to the husband of one of her "mothers" at the cleanup competition's closing, Baskin replied:

> I wanted people to see that there were families involved. Not just my family, but other families like [this] family where we had mother, daughter, father, smaller daughter—you know. That was our whole point—to show we had *family* involvement, which of course makes you a stronger group—when families can see what you doin'. And of course this would encourage other families to become involved with us.

Like women organizers at Duke University, Edna often explained her strategy, her political relations, or, more generally, her political philosophy in terms of a conception of women's political power and collectivity rooted in "familistic" values and—in her case—tied to household and church.

> STEVEN GREGORY: Now that your organization is established, would you consider getting involved in politics? I mean, let's say, running for political office?
>
> EDNA BASKIN: I always want to be just where I'm at right now—right in my own home, working to organize an extended group. But see—
>
> SG: A what?
>
> EB: An *extended* group. Just like the Area Policy Board—that's an extension of what our committee [i.e., CCA] is. We're just extending ourselves outward, you know. Because that's the problem. We have nothing. And a long time ago, of course, coming from this good church background, I learned that women are the key. And as a woman, *you* set the tone in your household—*I* set the tone. I set the rhythm in here. You know what I'm saying? And so do other women in their households. *You* set the tone. You set the *rhythm*, you know. You determine how we're gonna make this work, and how we're gonna make this flow. You know when you want your husband to do something and he's not agreeable, you just work around him, find another *way*, you know. Find *another* way to deal. And it's the same thing here.
>
> SG: How would a political role be different from this—from what you called before "grassroots"?
>
> EB: Because you're dealing—as a politician you're dealing with *other* people's ideas and how you have to implement those ideas—versus me in this setting. We're dealing with our ideas and *we* wanna do it collectively, as a group, without any input from outside. Whereas when you're a politician, you have other influences that are paramount to what you're doing.

The household serves here as a *political* model not only for grass-roots autonomy but also for negotiating relations of power. This is not a "family ideology" that reduces black political, economic, and social conditions to the "stability" of the African-American family. Rather, Baskin's deployment of

"family" and "household" speaks to a wider conception of political mobilization, accountability, and power that, although anchored in part in the household, is not contained by domestic ideology.

Indeed, the efficacy of Concerned Community Adults rested precisely in its
ability to cultivate and sustain what Alberto Melucci called the "submerged
networks" of everyday political life where actors produce and practice alternative frameworks of meaning, social relations, and collective identity below the
horizon of established or officially recognized institutions (1989:70). The
Youth Forum, cleanup campaign, and the everyday meetings of "mothers" and
tenants in Lefrak City apartments and public areas laid the groundwork for
new modes of collective action by producing new forms and alignments of
political identity, and by creating relatively autonomous public spaces where
the needs and demands of residents could be interpreted and communicated in
alternative and, often, oppositional ways.

Melucci, referring to the work of these submerged networks, captures a
paradox that is key to understanding CCA's strategy and, in particular, the
resistance its organizers showed toward participation in "regular" politics:

> The forms of action I am referring to are at one and the same time prior to and
> beyond politics: they are prepolitical because they are rooted in everyday life
> experiences; and meta-political because political forces can never represent them
> completely. Paradoxically, unless collective action is represented it becomes frag-
> mented and dispersed; at the same time, because it is never fully capable of repre-
> sentation it reappears later on new ground, with changed objects and altered strat-
> egies (1989:72).

Edna Baskin's reluctance to place her organization under the "umbrella"
of the Lefrak City Tenants Association or to link CCA's slate in the Area
Policy Board elections to that of the area's state assemblywoman was an effort to remain rooted in this paradoxical space before and beyond representational politics in Melucci's sense. For to succumb to the "trap" of representational politics (recall Ron Baskin's concerns about accepting public funding)
would risk exposing CCA's submerged and "nomadic" activist networks to
the disciplinary pressures and interests of political elites. Indeed Baskin's
concept of an "extended group," one that, based in grass-roots social networks, extends itself outward onto the truncated field of electoral politics,
captures concisely the strategic impulse to check the conceit of power with
the unruliness of the everyday, to juggle rather than reconcile the terms of
Melucci's paradox.

This strategy of resisting political incorporation and the severing of links to
the undisciplined social spaces and networks of grass-roots activism was demonstrated in CCA's relationship to the Community Board. In January 1988
Edna Baskin was officially seated on Community Board 4 and soon afterward

appointed to co-chair its Youth Services Committee. Concerned that this heightened participation on the Community Board would weaken her ties to Lefrak City residents, Baskin created a "joint" Youth Services Committee representing *both* Community Board 4 and Concerned Community Adults.

Meetings of this ad hoc, joint committee, held in the Lefrak City library, blurred the administrative identity and spatial jurisdiction of the Community Board's Youth Services Committee, creating in its place a hybrid and structurally amorphous political entity and public forum, one that enabled the participation and cooperation of a heterogeneous cast of political actors. For example, a February 1988 meeting of the joint committee, chaired by Edna Baskin, was attended by officers of Community Board 4, CCA's board members, Assemblywoman Helen Marshall, members of the newly elected Area Policy Board, Scout leaders, librarians, and an assortment of "invited guests" specializing in the field of day care. At a March joint committee meeting, which also focused on the need for day care services, a PTA activist and a youth organizer from Forest Hills (Community Board 6) were invited by CCA to share their experiences, as Baskin put it, "from the other side of the [Long Island] Expressway." Alberta Ridgeway-Brown, one of Lefrak City's representatives on the Area Policy Board and a volunteer tutor in CCA's library program, also gave a presentation on the availability of city funding for day care and youth services.

This widening and diversification of the public sphere of community politics enabled activists to construct neighborhood needs, strategies, and alliances in ways that stretched beyond the rigid functional and territorial jurisdictions of officially sanctioned political bodies such as the Community Board, the Area Policy Board, and the offices of elected officials.

Like the fluid joint committee, CCA's newsletter, the *Clarion*, provided an important public forum for coordinating the organizing work of neighborhood activists and for publicizing local and national political issues. Produced on the Baskins' home computer, the *Clarion* served as a clearinghouse, informing Lefrak-area residents about community resources and programs, public hearings, and about the structure and functioning of neighborhood government. Editorial features often interpreted the local significance of national economic and political news.

For example, in an editorial entitled "Duck You Suckers," the *Clarion* warned its readers of the possible impact of the 1987 Wall Street crash on youth services in the city, citing the 1974 fiscal crisis as a historical precedent:

> Mayor Koch has recently unveiled a proposed City Budget which should be sending chills up and down the spines of parents in the five boroughs. Only in terminology does this surprise package differ from the draconian documents of the fiscal crisis. Only now, instead of the fiscal crisis getting the blame (you know about the subways and highways and bridges and everything else that couldn't be

maintained because of the "fiscal crisis"), it's the stock market crash. Many people who never benefited from the bull market of the past few years will nevertheless pay the price for Wall Street's greed and folly, and those people are likely to be our children.

The editorial ended with a call to political mobilization: "One of the ways to halt the crisis is to remain vigilant. Time will not permit us the luxury of sitting back and waiting for someone else to do it, for this crisis is truly our own. We must be prepared to identify and challenge ANY person or body which attempts to reduce services to our youth . . . There is no mystery to organization. There is only organization and hard work" (*The Clarion* 1, no. 2 (1988): 1).

For Edna Baskin and Concerned Community Adults, the "hard work" of community organizing rested less in mobilizing ready-made subjects in response to fixed grievances and ideologies than in constructing an alternative political space or public sphere in which the needs, interests, and identities of Lefrak City residents could be collectively contested, negotiated, and recast in empowering ways.[8]

CCA's Youth Forum, cleanup campaign, and other youth-oriented activities challenged and reworked politically disabling discourses about Lefrak City that had obscured and depoliticized the needs of black youth by constructing them as threats to neighborhood stability and by locating the origins of this criminal deviance in the disorder of the black family. As in the case of the "latchkey kids" and the teenage drug dealers, this ideology of black crime and family pathology interpellated black youth as subjects in need of discipline and policing rather than community services. By subverting this racialized ideology of space and identity, CCA established the educational and empowerment needs of black youth as legitimate subjects of political discourse and action within a more inclusive construction of community.

Subsequent activities, such as the Area Policy Board campaign, the creation of the Joint Youth Services Committee, and the publication of the *Clarion*, expanded and deepened this public sphere of neighborhood activism creating alternative and more inclusive arenas of political participation and deliberation. In mobilizing black "families" and households, Baskin and CCA not only contested ideologies of black family pathology but also disrupted and manipulated gendered constructions of political space and agency that privileged formal, officially recognized modes of political activism over the more fluid, "submerged," and sometimes household-based networks of everyday politics.

If an important legacy of the state's response to civil rights—era activism has been a harnessing of the black public sphere and a depoliticizing of racial inequalities, the case of Edna Baskin and Concerned Community Adults demonstrates that these processes of subjugation are recognized and challenged through the everyday practices of neighborhood activists. CCA's success in mobilizing Lefrak City residents and in mustering the support of neighborhood institutions and political elites rested on the constitution of a heterogeneous and relatively autonomous public sphere through which the needs of residents could be publicly articulated in ways that yielded new and sometimes oppositional forms of collective action and identity.

CHAPTER SIX

A Piece of the Rock

"I THINK blacks missed the boat," George Lopez said wryly, rattling the ice in his tumbler and then glancing up at John Booker. "Right in front of my office," he continued, "the Koreans are all opening up businesses. And blacks only have a numbers drop. We're still waiting for the last figure to come out. That's the way I put it. Next door, the Korean's got his store fixed up stacking oranges."

Booker slid to the edge of the leather sofa, eyes flashing with interest. George Lopez, a Howard University–trained dentist and state assembly district leader, was one of the "old crowd," as Booker put it. The son of a merchant seaman from Jamaica, West Indies, Lopez's roots reached deep into the history of Corona, tracing the rugged terrain of black progress.

"But we're not enterprising, George," Booker responded. "We've got a dependency syndrome ingrained in us. We like to be hangers-on."

"That slave mentality," Lopez continued. "We're waiting for the welfare check. And waiting for the last number to come out. And it never comes out."

Booker half grinned, sensing controversy. "But there was a strong, organized determination after they brought the blacks here to America. Our spirits were broken way back then."

"But I mean, John. When is it going to change?"

"I don't know," Booker replied, shaking his head wearily, eyes glazed over in thought. "The thing the young blacks clamor for is to be a corporate officer. They want to put on a Brooks Brothers suit. That's all they want."

Lopez nodded briskly, raising his eyebrows. "They're making so much money in those corporate setups—far more than professionals like us."

"But I'm afraid the rug is going to get pulled out from under them," Booker said, looking to me for agreement.

Lopez laughed. "I don't know, boy. Some of those guys that hang out with my daughter, those buppies. Man, they make megabucks." He leaned back into a story. "Last week my daughter gave a political fund-raiser. Man, that was some beautiful affair. And John, I looked at those buppies. They were something. One gal leases Lear jets to companies. A person's a damn fool to go into medicine or dentistry now, with those kinds of things open. They're not gonna make *that* kind of money. I tell you if I had it to do all over again, I'd take the corporate route."

Between leasing Lear jets and "waiting for the last number to come out" is a broad spectrum of black class identities which, like all social identities, are shaped by diverse and often incongruous readings of the past, present, and future. Lopez's conversation with Booker not only highlights the ambiguities and fissures present in narratives of black progress but also underscores the degree to which evaluations of class mobility and identity for African-Americans remain fastened to questions of political power. John Booker's concern that "the rug is going to get pulled out" tempers both the celebration of victory and the condemnation of defeat and constitutes a "we" that continues to be entangled with the experience of racism in America.

Recent discussions of the changing significance of race and class for African-Americans have, on the whole, failed to capture the complex manner in which people such as John Booker and George Lopez conceptualize and negotiate these categories in their everyday lives and politics. In many accounts, binary and, typically, androcentric models of African-American identity, are used to draw out under-theorized contrasts between the "middle class" and the "ghetto underclass," "old heads" and rowdy teenagers, and, more recently, "respectable" men and men who are not (Wilson 1987; Anderson 1990; Duneier 1992). In narratives of the bifurcation of black class structure, the notion of class, loosely defined as income-earning capacity, is often called into service to plot the imagined frontiers between a morally isolated ghetto and the "greater order" of mainstream American society.[1]

This tendency to conceptualize black class identities as transparent and as fundamentally moral reflexes of occupational status not only obscures the heterogeneity of African-American identities and communities, but it also depoliticizes the concept of class by treating it as a static category, unmediated by power relations, political struggles, and cultural practices.

Classes are neither given by occupational status nor, as in some dogmatic Marxist approaches, inevitably determined by their position in the social rela- tions of production. Rather, class identities and their constituent social meanings and relationships are produced and reformed through power relations and practices that implicate a multiplicity of social locations, struggles, and relations both at the workplace and beyond (see Laclau and Mouffe 1985; Hall 1985; Aronowitz 1990).

In this chapter I examine the construction of black class identities through the political culture of grass-roots activism. On the one hand, I stress the role that neighborhood-based power relations and social processes play in the articulation of black class identities. Against static and binary treatments of black class structure, I highlight the fluid, composite, and contested quality of class identities and of the meanings and social relations that inform them. In Corona–East Elmhurst, as in other urban communities, class dispositions are produced and practiced in a range of social and institutional settings and in relation to disparate readings of neighborhood needs and interests.[2] In these settings—ranging from political meetings to church services to the annual dinner dances given by community groups—activists interpret, debate, and publicly "perform" the present meanings of black class divisions and racial identity and bring those meanings to bear on the recollected past. Thus the process of black class formation occurs within a political and cultural field that is both heterogeneous and deeply historical.

On the other hand, I stress the role played by the state in configuring the political and discursive terrain on which activists negotiate the meanings of race, class, and community. I argue that the state's harnessing of the black public sphere through War on Poverty politics and practices of decentralized community governance has played a pivotal role in conditioning the *political* effects of black divisions during the post–civil rights period. Specifically, the mechanisms for political participation created in the wake of 1960s activism have proven to be disproportionately responsive to black middle-income constituencies and, equally significant, to formulations of neighborhood problems and needs that obscure their origins in wider processes of racial and economic subordination.

SIGNS OF PROGRESS

Arthur Hayes was weeding a triangle-shaped lot across the street from his home in middle-class East Elmhurst when I arrived. He shook the soil from a huge clump of weeds and then topped off the last of three Hefty trash bags.

"I decided to make a garden in this lot twenty years ago," he declared, wiping the sweat from his brow and smiling. "That was after a neighbor almost ran over a drunk who was sleeping in here with all the weeds." He took off his canvas work gloves and raised them to shoulder level to show me how high the overgrowth had reached.

A tall, big-framed man, Hayes was president of the East Elmhurst–Corona Civic Association, the largest and most powerful homeowner association in the neighborhood. Founded in 1952, when Corona and East Elmhurst were experiencing the brunt of postwar urban decline, the Civic Association has emerged in the post–civil rights period as the area's most influential black civic association, eclipsing the NAACP, the churches, and other community groups in its capacity to muster and sustain a broad-based, though largely homeowning, constituency. As the pastor of a Corona church once put it: "If you want to be a mover and shaker in this community, if you want to get anything done, you begin with the Civic Association."

In recent months neighborhood residents had complained about receiving parking tickets on blocks where the "No Parking" signs were missing or unreadable. To address this problem, Hayes had decided to conduct a block-by-block "inspection" of the neighborhood to document the location and condition of its parking signs. The completed survey would be presented to a Traffic Department official at the next Civic Association meeting (Figure 6.1).

Figure 6.1. Arthur Hayes, president of the East
Elmhurst–Corona Civic Association, stands before a
vacant lot in Corona during neighborhood inspection.

Born in Louisiana, Hayes grew up in a small oil town in Texas. In the 1930s
he moved to Harlem and, after serving in World War II, became a seaman on
a passenger ship. In the mid-1950s Hayes and his family bought a house in
East Elmhurst, using a Veterans Administration-insured mortgage.

"Was mostly Italian and Irish and some Germans, too, when we first got
here," Hayes told me, waving his hand at the houses surrounding his detached
home and landscaped garden. "They were all pretty nice, but they were leaving. At the time they were going out to Long Island—Levittown and places
like that. See, we used to have the GI Bill back then."

We began the tour at Astoria Boulevard and Ninety-third Street, which
marked East Elmhurst's border with predominantly white and Latino Jackson
Heights to the west. I checked the readability of the signs, and Mr. Hayes noted
the location and condition of each on a clipboard. Many of the signs had been

weathered by wind and acid rain, leaving only a bleached white surface with traces of pink lettering.

Between signs, Hayes told stories about his experiences growing up in the South, underscoring the race pride his family had instilled in him. As we zigzagged our way south into North Corona, Hayes pointed out important places in the community's past. When we reached the Refuge Baptist Church on tree-lined Thirty-fourth Avenue, he told me that the modest red-brick building had been an early home of the First Baptist Church.

"See, the church has always been a sanctuary for blacks," he said. "It was the only place where we could be complete men for a few hours a day." To stress this point, he explained that most of Corona's congregations had been organized by small groups of people who mortgaged their homes to finance their churches. He then called my attention to a vacant lot next to the church that was being used as a dump for car tires. The narrow lot was littered with a motley assortment of bald tires. A pink refrigerator door, its corners eaten away by rust, rested awkwardly against a jagged chunk of brick and mortar. Hayes told me he had been monitoring the situation for some time and believed that repair shops, operating illegally in residential-zoned buildings, were dumping their tires in the lot. He made a note on his clipboard.

When we reached the Corona Congregational Church farther along Thirty-fourth Avenue, Hayes returned to the topic of the black church, noting its former pastor's role in the struggles of the civil rights era: "Reverend Sherard was a strong leader in this community. You see, ministers can say things that other people can't because they wear the collar." He pointed to his neck and smiled ironically. "Our problem has always been unity," he continued. "A lot of people up in East Elmhurst look down on people in Corona today, even though their churches are still here." As we turned on to 103rd Street and headed back toward Astoria Boulevard, Hayes discussed the leadership potential of the community's ministers, assessing the ability of each to bring together various segments of the community.

For the remainder of the inspection Hayes continued his commentary, reading the signs of the present against the multilayered histories of space. For Hayes and other activists, an illegal dump or an effaced parking sign were not simply eyesores, mere violations of the spatial economy of the present. Rather, embedded in the recollected meanings of place, such threats to the built environment were also assaults on shared memories of the past that formed the bedrock of the community's political culture and identity (cf. Negt and Kluge 1993).

Writing of these "invisible" spacial identities, Michel de Certeau observed:

It is striking here that the places people live are like the presences of diverse absences. What can be seen designates what is no longer there: "you *see*, here there used to be . . .," but it can no longer be seen. Demonstratives indicate the invisible identities of the visible: it is the very definition of a place, in fact, that it is composed by these series of displacements and effects among the fragmented strata that form it and that it plays on these moving layers. (1984:108)

Arthur Hayes's inspection, like other everyday negotiations of the neighborhood landscape, was thus an act of recapitulation: a looking into and recovery of the multiple meanings of place and of its inhabitants' identities (see Rosaldo 1980). For in reading the signs of neighborhood—the sites of struggle, sacrifice, achievement, and defeat—Hayes was also constructing a community identity: a *we* who organized to get *this public school*, who fought for traffic lights at *this crossing*, who mortgaged our homes to build *this church*.

In the post–civil rights period this sense of a collective black identity, forged through the political culture of organizing and struggle, has become increasingly tenuous for many. Although class distinctions tied to occupation, wealth, and evaluations of social status had always differentiated African-American society in Corona–East Elmhurst, in the wake of civil rights–era activism and state-sponsored reforms, these class divisions hardened and became politically more significant.

The weakening of overt practices of racial discrimination provided many working- and middle-class African-Americans with unprecedented access to education and employment opportunities (Wilson 1978). In stark contrast to their parents, Corona–East Elmhurst's postwar generations have had access to a wide range of secondary and postsecondary schools, as well as jobs in the public and private sectors. For example, Calvin Wynter, born in East Elmhurst in 1960, attended Intermediate School (I.S.) 145 in predominantly white Jackson Heights and the Bronx High School of Science, an elite public school. After graduating from Colgate University in 1984, Wynter found employment as a stockbroker with Merrill Lynch. Michael Howell, who also attended I.S. 145 and the Bronx High School of Science, received degrees from Cornell University and the University of Michigan. After taking a Ph.D. in marine geology from the University of South Carolina, Howell found work as a geochemist with the Mobil Research and Development Corporation. During my fieldwork Wynter and Howell were often lauded at public events as examples of the new generation of professionals who were the "hope of the future."

These civil rights–era gains in education and employment buttressed and enlarged the neighborhood's black middle class, which, during the post–World War II period, had become increasingly concentrated in East Elmhurst. Socioeconomic differences between East Elmhurst and North Corona can be gleaned from data from the 1980 federal census. Calvin Wynter was raised on Ninety-ninth Street in East Elmhurst within a census tract that is representative of the area. Census Tract 355, a fifteen-block area of East Elmhurst on the North Shore, had a population of 2,156 persons in 1980, 85 percent of whom were black. Whites constituted 11 percent of the area's population, and Asians (nine Chinese people in all) about .5 percent. Persons of "Spanish origin," primarily Puerto Ricans and Cubans, comprised 8 percent of the area's population and were counted in the "black," "white," and "other" racial categories (United States Bureau of the Census 1980a).[3]

Residents of Wynter's census tract were solidly middle-class in 1980, showing a median household income of $17,451 in 1979, which was higher than the median of $15,219 reported for Community District 3 as a whole.[4] Only 9 percent of the people in Wynter's tract lived in households with incomes falling below the poverty level; more than 75 percent lived in households with incomes that were at least twice the poverty level.

Like Wynter, 22 percent of the area's workers were employed in managerial and professional specialty occupations (compared to 20 percent for Community District 3), and an additional 37 percent were employed in technical, sales, and administrative support occupations. Illustrating the importance of public-sector employment for the black working and middle classes, 32 percent of Census Tract 355's workforce was employed by the federal, state, and local governments, compared to 17.6 percent for the city as a whole.

East Elmhurst's solidly middle-income population contrasted sharply in 1980 with the population of North Corona. Of its 2,262 residents, Census Tract 377, where Jake Govan was raised, was 83 percent black and 6 percent white in 1980, with "others" accounting for 10 percent. Ten percent of Govan's neighbors were of Spanish origin, many of whom were counted in the racial categories "white" and "other." The median income of Govan's area was $8,112 in 1979, less than half that of Wynter's area. Thirty-two percent of Govan's neighbors lived in households with incomes below the poverty level. Only 13 percent of the area's workers were employed in managerial and professional occupations, and 50 percent were employed in service jobs and as "operators, fabricators, and laborers," compared to 30 percent in Wynter's neighborhood.[5] In short, when contrasted with their neighbors in East Elmhurst, residents of North Corona had lower incomes and occupied a lower percentage of managerial, professional, and other white-collar jobs.

The sharpening of class divisions in Corona–East Elmhurst, however, was not an unmediated effect of gains in education and occupational opportunities experienced by middle-income persons relative to lower-income and less educated groups. Rather, the process of class formation was shaped by the state's structuring of the political arena of neighborhood life in ways that incited the production and exercise of particular forms of black "middle-class" identity and disproportionately empowered middle-income, largely homeowning residents of East Elmhurst. Upward mobility did not translate neatly or mechanically into a black "middle-class" identity with transparent interests, beliefs, and attitudes; instead, black class divisions and identities were constructed and given their meanings through political processes and struggles in which the state played a leading role.

On the one hand, state intervention through the War on Poverty politically isolated the black poor in Corona, situating them as clients in bureaucratic service agencies, while enclaving deliberation and debate about poverty and its related social inequalities within specialized networks of community service professionals. This bureaucratization of the community's service infrastructure increased the social, political, and ideological distance between low- and middle-income residents by differentiating the institutional settings in which the needs and interests of the two groups were defined and addressed. This sense of difference was heightened by the discourse of urban blight which, by locating the origins of complex neighborhood problems in the behavioral traits of residents of the "strip," exaggerated spatial and ontological distinctions between the "blighted" areas of the poor and the stable environs of the middle class. The antipoverty program thus served as a kind of institutional wedge between the middle classes and the poor, tying the latter as clients to external service bureaucracies rather than to wider, cross-class constituencies and social institutions within the community.

Elwanda Young, who served as executive director of Elmcor during the 1980s, spoke to how this client-based service strategy restricted social and political interaction across class lines: "I'm thinking about the clients we serve and how they might even begin to interact with the upper-class blacks, and there's no type of connection. Their paths never cross anymore. The only possible connection might be in the church where you might have this grass-roots person still attending this church. But other than that there's little opportunity for them to meet."

On the other hand, the channels of political participation that were made accessible to African-Americans in the post–civil rights era (notably the institutions of decentralized municipal government, such as the Community Board, and electoral politics) have proven to be disproportionately responsive to the largely middle-class homeowners of East Elmhurst who were organized into tightly knit networks of block and civic associations.

QUALITY OF LIFE POLITICS

Block associations, referred to as the "building blocks of the community" by State Assemblywoman Helen Marshall, crisscross East Elmhurst and, to a lesser extent, North Corona. Of the sixty or so block associations active in East Elmhurst and North Corona during the late 1980s, the vast majority were based in middle-class East Elmhurst. Whereas 24 percent of East Elmhurst's block faces were organized by such associations, the same was true for only 12 percent of the block faces in North Corona. The East Elmhurst–Corona Civic Association, which serves as a federation of block clubs, is also based in East

Elmhurst and draws its membership largely from among its middle-income homeowners.[6]

The differing roles played by block associations in the two areas can be correlated to differences in housing tenure. Block data from the 1980 federal census disclose higher rates of owner-occupied housing in East Elmhurst than in North Corona. For example, 74 percent of the blocks listed in East Elmhurst census tracts showed owner-occupancy rates of 50 percent or more; that is, at least 50 percent of the housing units on those blocks were occupied by their owners. In contrast, only 15 percent of North Corona's blocks exhibited owner-occupancy rates of 50 percent or more (U.S. Bureau of the Census 1980b).[7]

A number of researchers have pointed to the relationship between home-ownership and neighborhood activism (Cox 1982; Harvey 1978; Logan and Molotch 1987). In contrast to renters, homeowners have "exchange-value interests" in their homes, which are crucial components of their lifetime wealth strategies (Logan and Molotch 1987:20). As a block association president in East Elmhurst put it: "Over on the other side, there are less homeowners and more tenants than we have here. When you have your nest egg in your home, you're willing to fight for it. And economic differences are another factor. We have some tenants on this side that are just as active as homeowners, but generally they are homeowners."

Moreover, as Philip Cox pointed out, relocation presents peculiar and formidable obstacles to homeowners.

> The option of relocation as opposed to activism affects homeowners rather differently from the way it does renters. For the homeowner, transaction costs may be considerable. Selling a house is often a lengthy, tedious and costly process involving making the house available for viewing, negotiating with would-be buyers, carrying out small repairs regarded as necessary to clinch the sale, as well as a substantial commission for the realtor. (1982:117–118)

To be sure, apartment renters have important investments in neighborhood quality of life and often organize effectively to address problems (see chapter 5). Nevertheless, differences in tenure not only affect how renters and homeowners variously formulate their interests and organize to address them; it also conditions the ways in which government authorities and private-sector groups respond to their demands.

The block associations of East Elmhurst serve as skirmish lines on the field of community politics: front lines of defense against threats to the neighborhood's quality of life. Block associations provide interlocking networks of communication for disseminating neighborhood news and information and for alerting residents to problems. As tightly knit and territorially based micro-constituencies, they are effective in pressuring community leaders and public officials to respond to their interests and concerns. Generally these concerns focus on the block and its environs: potholes in the street, poor garbage collection, and an outbreak of car break-ins are typical of the issues that incite block association activism. In other cases, a more organized threat, such as a public agency's plan to locate an undesirable business or facility in the neighborhood, will catalyze block association activism.

For example, only days after it was formed in 1988, the Ninety-ninth Street Block Association of East Elmhurst was faced with a crisis. Members of the association had learned that a not-for-profit corporation planned to open a diagnostic center for foster care children in a two-family building on their street. The association called a public meeting at the local office of the area's state assemblywoman, Helen Marshall. Representatives of the not-for-profit sponsor and the New York City Human Resources Administration, which would fund and monitor the facility, were invited to attend.

About thirty-five residents of Ninety-ninth Street gathered at Assemblywoman Marshall's storefront office on the evening of the meeting. Some had come directly from work. Others had walked the short distance to the office in small groups of friends, family, and neighbors. Folding chairs were brought out to seat the overflow crowd. A few latecomers stood in the open doorway waiting with arms folded for the meeting to begin. "No way they're gonna put that thing here," one woman said. "And right there next to the school?" added a second, raising her eyebrows. Most of the residents were middle-aged, and women were a clear majority. They eyed with suspicion the three representatives of the foster care agency whose business suits and briefcases, more than their race, disclosed their identity.

With awkward solemnity, the block association's officers took seats at a folding table facing the restless audience. The association's president, a West Indian–born man in his mid-forties, convened the meeting and introduced the association's "chaplain," who was to give the invocation. Those present were asked to rise and bow their heads as the chaplain gave thanks for "the large turnout and the unity of our association." He asked that God continue to protect the neighborhood and its residents.

Next, one of the sponsors was asked to describe the proposed facility. The diagnostic center, she reported, would house about twelve children between the ages of eight and twelve for a period of three months. Once the three-month period of diagnostic evaluation was concluded, the children would be referred elsewhere for additional services. Anticipating the concerns and anxieties of the association's members, she concluded: "The children staying at our facility will be compatible with the children already in the neighborhood. There will be no drug abusers, retarded, or antisocial types."

After her presentation, members of the association posed a battery of questions: "How many supervisors will there be?" "Will the supervisors be qualified?" "What about the parents who abandoned the children—will they be allowed to visit?" "Where will the children who stay in the home play?" "How can these children be normal after all they've been through?" The agency representatives skillfully parried each question with assurances drawn from well-prepared notes. One man, apparently frustrated by the direction the meeting was taking, stood and declared: "These are problem children. We as a block of people don't want this type of building on our block. This is a private neighborhood; there are no public buildings. What happens when your kids meet our kids?"

"That's very sad," a representative responded glibly, "because what we do keeps neighborhoods together." She then alluded to the insensitivity of the not-in-my-backyard, or NIMBY, attitude, concluding: "These kids are the kids who become problems if they are not helped." The allusion to NIMBY called to mind similar controversies, many of which involved middle-class white communities opposing the location of low-income housing, homeless shelters, and other facilities in their communities. Since the beneficiaries of such projects are sometimes African-Americans or members of other "minority groups," the accusation of insensitivity carried with it an ironic twist that resonated as a subtext throughout the meeting: how could a "black community" oppose a facility intended to serve a minority population?

Elwanda Young, the executive director of Elmcor, the city-funded community development agency, stood to address the issue of insensitivity. "This community *is* very sensitive to the needs of people," she began. Members of the block association nodded their heads in agreement. "That's demonstrated by the number of facilities we already have. This community is already oversaturated. Do we want another?" she asked, surveying the audience with a quick glance. "No, we've had enough!" a young woman declared. Elmcor's director then turned back toward the agency representatives. "This is not a NIMBY. Our backyard is already full."

When the meeting was about to end, the block association's president rose and addressed the three representatives. "Enough has been said," he concluded, slapping the palm of his hand against the table. "The neighborhood is infested enough. We would like you to find somewhere else for the home."

The Ninety-ninth Street Block Association's opposition to the group home highlights the key organizing role that block associations play in neighborhood political life. As territorially organized interest groups and "voting blocks," these associations are able to leverage the tactical support of public officials and exercise considerable influence in defining the neighborhood's interests, political agenda, and, indeed, collective identity.

Equally important, the association's resistance to the foster care facility illustrates how the state's harnessing of the discourse and politics of urban poverty has sharpened the perception and impact of class divisions within Corona–East Elmhurst by framing poverty and its related social issues as bureaucratic problems imposed on the neighborhood by *outside* agencies. In opposing "your kids" to "our kids" and *private* neighborhood" to "*public* buildings," block association members were constructing the poor and disadvantaged as outsiders to the "community" and recognizing a transformation of the field of politics that situated issues of social inequality beyond the horizon of grass-roots activism and beyond the purview of the institutions of local governance.

Although the power and influence that block associations wield in these micropolitical contexts are considerable, their importance within the larger framework of neighborhood politics should not be minimized. Involvement in a block association is often a resident's first experience in community activism. Not only are the interests addressed through such associations "closest to home," but participation in a block club requires less travel and inconvenience than involvement in other local institutions. This is especially significant in the case of older, often retired people, who form a large percentage of the membership of neighborhood-based organizations.

Block associations are therefore key recruiting bases for activists and are also places where residents learn the nuts and bolts of local politics and the often bewildering procedural mechanics of municipal service bureaucracies. Many residents who hold positions in other, more broadly based neighborhood groups began their activist careers in block associations. Frequently such community leaders remain active in their block clubs long after assuming positions of greater responsibility.

For example, Floyd Ramsey moved from Harlem to East Elmhurst in 1961 where he bought a two-family, detached home on Ninety-ninth Street. As the owner of a Medallion taxi cab and the leader of an association of black cab owners, Ramsey found little time to participate in neighborhood affairs. "And then," he recalled, "I started to lighten up on my cab business and began thinking about retiring. That's when I decided to join up with some of the organizations around here, like the block association and the Civic [Association]." Following his retirement, Ramsey became an officer of his block club and the Civic Association, an activist with the Frederick Douglas Democratic Association, and City Councilwoman Julia Harrison's liaison to Corona–East Elmhurst.

However, involvement in a block association is not only basic training for participation in community politics. Equally important, such involvement integrates residents into the informal social networks that constitute the fabric of local politics (see Stone 1989). These informal ties, which Avery Guest and R. S. Oropesa have called "localized friendships," motivate people to act collectively: "Due to their integration into social networks, individuals with localized friendships are likely to be influenced by others arguing for collective action. In this sense individuals with highly localized friendships may be mobilized because they are part of a two-step flow of communication, involving the transmission of ideas from opinion leaders to the rest of the population" (1986:567).

This exchange of information is especially pronounced—or, perhaps better, "block-focused"—in the case of homeowners. Topics such as property taxes, home contractors, tenants, and the maintenance of streets, sidewalks, and other amenities by municipal authorities are central to the discourse of homeowners because of the latter's investment in the physical environment—a symbolic as well as material relation to the block in particular and the neighborhood in general.

Homeowners tend to experience the boundary between the home and the neighborhood as porous and vulnerable. The sense that the community is a vulnerable extension of the private sphere of the home ("This is a private neighborhood, there are no public buildings") attunes property owners to signs of decay in the urban landscape. Poor garbage collection, abandoned cars, and potholes in the street are not simply inconveniences but highly charged signifiers of disorder that speak to the social, economic, and moral well-being of the family and the community. Homeowners, in particular, become adept at reading such signs of the community's quality of life, and, through participation in block associations, they share the information gleaned.

The political power of individual block associations is strengthened through their participation in the East Elmhurst–Corona Civic Association, which translates local block issues into quality-of-life concerns of the community as a whole. As Floyd Ramsey put it: "The block associations are like the states in the United States. Each state operates on its own and reports back to Washington, which is our Civic Association. People here tend to look out for their own blocks. But when they have a problem they can't handle, they go to the Civic." In this way, the Civic Association is able to link the mobilizing efficiency of its constituent block clubs to an institutional structure sufficient in size and visibility to bring pressure to bear on local politicians and city officials and get results.

The East Elmhurst–Corona Civic Association has proven to be the most powerful neighborhood interest group in the black community and, with an average meeting attendance of fifty to seventy-five persons, is strongly supported by residents. And since many of the members of the Civic Association are block club presidents, ministers, and other community leaders, the association's social base is much greater than meeting attendance indicates.

Like the block clubs, the Civic Association focuses primarily on quality-of-life issues. Over the years it has fought the Port Authority of New York and New Jersey over the expansion of LaGuardia Airport, won concessions from hotel developers in the airport area, lobbied with civic associations in surrounding white communities for the cleanup of Flushing Bay, and resolved numerous quality-of-life problems brought before it by its constituent block associations. Civic Association meetings were held at the LaGuardia Airport Holiday Inn on the northern fringe of East Elmhurst. The right to hold meetings at the hotel was one of the concessions granted to the Civic Association by the Holiday Inn Corporation in return for support of a zoning variance required to build on the site.

The popular support enjoyed by the Civic Association rests on its ability to exert pressure on public officials and members of the business community to resolve neighborhood problems, such as poor garbage collection and inadequate police protection. In return, these officials use the Civic Association as a public forum for assembling and negotiating community support for public policies and business initiatives. Through the Civic Association and its block clubs, controversial policies and issues can be micromanaged and contained at the local, block-focused level. Both the recognition and use of the Civic Association as a public forum by public and private authorities tend to bolster the former's influence and power, relative to other neighborhood-based institutions.

Perhaps the best way to disclose how the Civic Association works with city officials, businesspeople, and local politicians is to describe a meeting held in April 1989. The meeting was attended by about sixty women and men, most if not all of whom were East Elmhurst homeowners. Many Civic Association members are also active in other neighborhood institutions; in general, the tendency for community activism to overlap with Civic Association membership is strong. Community leaders, whether elected officials or members of the clergy, are often evaluated by the frequency with which they are seen at meetings of the Civic Association.

The April meeting opened with a prayer asking for protection of the community. After minutes of the previous meeting had been read and approved, Arthur Hayes, president of the association, made a report summarizing developments in the neighborhood since the last meeting. First on his list were ongoing negotiations with Field Associates, a hotel development firm that had recently purchased the Holiday Inn and was in the process of constructing a new luxury hotel in East Elmhurst to service LaGuardia Airport passengers. As with the Holiday Inn Corporation, the Civic Association had demanded that the development firm provide amenities in return for the right to "come into our community." Although the Civic Association had no authority to sanction development, let alone deny or approve zoning variances, its capacity to enlist the support of elected officials, Community Board 3, and other public officials made it an effective lobbying group. Moreover, the overlapping memberships that Civic Association activists held in institutions such as the NAACP, the Frederick Douglas Democratic Club, and community churches further bolstered its clout.

Representatives from Field Associates had attended a number of Civic Association meetings in the past to answer complaints about hazardous and unsightly conditions resulting from construction at the new hotel site. Many of these complaints had been brought to the attention of the civic association by the Ditmars Boulevard Block Association (the hotel was being constructed in its vicinity) whose president was a member of both the Civic Association and the Community Board. Monthly meetings between the development company and a Civic Association committee had culminated in agreement on a number of concessions to be granted to the community: the developer would give preference to residents of North Corona, East Elmhurst, and Jackson Heights (the neighborhoods included in Community Board 3) when hiring staff for the new hotel, and Field Associates would establish a scholarship fund for residents interested in studying hotel-related subjects.

After the president's report, an official from the Department of Sanitation was invited to respond to complaints about services that residents felt were inferior to those provided in neighboring white communities. The Sanitation Department's community liaison addressed his agency's efforts to better serve the neighborhood. The official's presentation exemplifies not only how expert knowledge is bureaucratically deployed to fragment and depoliticize community issues but also how officially sanctioned ideologies penetrate local contexts, in this case to redefine a problem of political weakness as one of moral crisis. In response to complaints about erratic garbage collection, the Sanitation Department official cited statistics on the number of summonses that been issued in the area for "behavioral incidents"; that is, for the failure of residents to sweep the fronts of their homes and businesses. Continuing in a more philosophical vein, he observed: "Garbage is no longer out of sight, out of mind. There is a moral breakdown in our society that includes crime, drugs, garbage, and everything. It is the young kids who don't care about your houses and don't have values and morals."

The next speaker was a young African-American police officer from the local precinct's crime prevention squad. He discussed the precinct's attempts to stop drug use in a residential building in North Corona that was being used as a "crack den." A number of arrests had been made, but since the building was privately owned, the police could not legally close it. He suggested that the block club and the Civic Association pressure the Community Board to have the building closed by the city. The chairman of the board of the League for Better Community Life complained that his group had done everything it could and nothing had worked (the crack house was located next to the League's day care center). The police officer responded by repeating that arrests had been made and that the community had to apply more pressure. "Arresting people is no panacea," he remarked. "We have to change the attitude of people. Society has to do something." The woman whose prayer had opened the meeting responded, "Yeah, you can shoot them all!"

The April meeting underscores not only the considerable power and influence that the block and civic associations of East Elmhurst were able to exert on municipal authorities, politicians, and private sector interest groups (an influence far exceeding that of other community organizations); it also highlights the increasingly pivotal role that homeowner activism and its associated quality-of-life discourse has come to play in defining the needs, interests, and political identities of Corona–East Elmhurst residents. In this quality-of-life discourse, crime, drugs, and poor city services were not spoken about as *social* problems tied to poverty, racial discrimination, and economic injustice; rather, within the political arena of homeowner activism, these issues were disarticulated from their broader structural context and framed as local and, typically, episodic violations of the rights of individuals to maintain a "middle-class" lifestyle. And since homeownership constitutes an important symbolic and material base on which black middle-class identity is constructed and exercised, these rights were often defended in the name of "property values."

For example, not long after the Ninety-ninth Street Block Association rejected the state's plan to locate a foster care facility on its block, the Civic Association convened a public hearing to review the proposal. Once again, Assemblywoman Marshall invited representatives from the not-for-profit sponsor to present their plan to the community. After the presentation the audience of about eighty was invited to ask questions.

"Shouldn't you come to the community first before you go into contract [to buy the house]?" asked one resident.

The representative responded with a question: "Do you ask permission from neighbors when you move into a new neighborhood? We see our home as one big family."

This response provoked an angry outburst from the audience since it seemed to conflate the establishment of the group home with the experience of black families moving into segregated white neighborhoods. Marshall tried to restore calm, assuring the audience that the area's Community Board would hold a public hearing later in the month.

"What guarantee does the community have that the residents won't be a problem?" a middle-aged woman asked.

"They will not be a detriment to the community," the representative responded curtly.

"Will there be drug testing?" a young woman asked.

"The residents will be mentally retarded adolescents, not drug addicts," came the response.

The audience again erupted in anger: "No way! We have enough problems with our own families," one man stated. A second shouted: "I don't want them. I live two doors away. They should be institutionalized." And he added menacingly, "I'm a pretty good shotgun artist." A woman stood. "How can you force this on us when we don't want it? Why don't you put it next to where you live? You put it in the heart of the community instead of outside. Our property values will go down." Another woman agreed: "There will be twenty outsiders in the middle of the block with our kids. How do you expect us to accept the tearing apart of the fabric of our community? This is basically a business and a quality-of-life decision for us."

Marshall, again trying to calm the audience, stood and addressed the official. "You see, Mr. Farnum, this is a *black* community and everyone has put their life investments into this community. We care so much [about disadvantaged people] that we already have 481 beds [for special populations]. We did our share but the city did not do *its* share." The audience applauded with enthusiasm.

Twenty minutes later, after the representatives from the home's sponsor had left, Arthur Hayes stood solemnly to address the audience, as if to explain to the association's members why they themselves had opposed the group home. "We do care," he said earnestly, "but we have to care about the whole community."

If the appeal to "property values" highlights the prominent role that the defense of the quality-of-life interests of middle-class homeowners has come to play in block and civic association activism, Marshall's remarks suggest that, for African-Americans in Corona–East Elmhurst, class identities continue to be cross-cut by questions of race and power. On the one hand, her appeal to the area's identity as a *black* community contextualized the rhetoric of property values within a wider and deeply historical discourse of "life investments" in which African-American social mobility has been, and remains, tied to struggles against racial injustice. On the other hand, Marshall's assertion that "we did our share, but the city did not do its share," called attention to the lack of parity in decisions concerning the siting of social services for "special populations": poor, minority, and other politically vulnerable communities are typically forced to bear a disproportionate part of the burden of accommodating facilities for special populations, as well as for environmentally hazardous urban functions, such as sewage treatment and toxic waste storage (see Dear and Wolch 1989; Bullard 1990).

In short, East Elmhurst's opposition to the group home and its appeal to property values in the last instance cannot be read as a transparent, unambiguous reflex of their interests as "middle-class" homeowners. For though the block and civic associational networks of East Elmhurst tended to privilege a narrow and space-bound set of quality-of-life interests linked, in part, to their status as middle-income property owners, those interests and the political commitments they insinuated remained complex, unstable, and subject to dispute and rearticulation. On the one hand, most activists participated in a variety of social institutions where the needs, interests, and identity of the community were often constructed in ways that transgressed the ideological and territorial frontiers of block and civic association politics. For example, while the NAACP drew on deeply historical and translocal discourses and traditions of black civil rights activism, community churches evoked notions of "Christian fellowship" that explicitly challenged parochial and elitist expressions of social thought and action. Far from being stable and monolithic political subjects, activists held complex and often conflicting social and political commitments that registered the variety of their experience and the heterogeneity of their social and political milieus.

On the other hand, the quality-of-life issues pursued by East Elmhurst's block and civic associations cannot be readily disarticulated from the broader political economy in which they were embedded. As the conflict over the "group home" and other issues illustrates, activists were well aware that local, block-focused problems were intimately linked to racially structured patterns in the distribution of social resources and burdens, even though they were quick to deploy a bottom-line rhetoric of property values when confronting representatives of the state and private sector. Indeed, as I will show in part 3, both the state and private capital actively worked to encourage East Elmhurst activists to experience and represent their interests and identities as local and as racelessly "middle-class" so as to hinder the formation of coalitions around wider economic and political interests.

This account of civic activism does not lead to an easy conclusion as to whether East Elmhurst's activists are essentially "middle-class" homeowners, committed to protecting their property values and quality of life or, alternatively, working people engaged in a long-standing struggle against racial injustice. For although such portrayals provide tidy sound bites for discussions and debates about the "state of black America" in the mass media and the academy, they fail to reveal not only the complexity of black identity but also the social processes through which that heterogeneity has been produced, negotiated, and contested in the everyday lives of African-Americans.

In the next section I explore these processes through an analysis of an emergent social group's efforts to formulate and address Corona–East Elmhurst's empowerment needs.

REVISITING THE PAST, REINVENTING THE FUTURE

"We have the perception of power. We don't
have real power."
(John Bell, community activist)

In 1988 a multiethnic committee of neighborhood activists met in the basement of the Corona Congregational Church. The committee, calling itself the Cultural Awareness Council, had been formed two years earlier in the wake of the racist attack on three black men by whites in Howard Beach, Queens that resulted in the death of Michael Griffith. Most of the members of the council, which included Jews, Asians, and Latinos, were from the neighboring community of Jackson Heights and had been invited to the church by its new pastor, the Reverend Irvine Bryer.

For the five church members who attended, all well over sixty, the dimly lit and sparsely furnished church basement was steeped in community history. During the 1960s, voter registration drives, school desegregation strategies, and political campaigns had been discussed and planned there. The basement had also served as a classroom for after-school tutorial programs and, beginning in 1965, had housed the church's Head Start Program. Square wooden cupboards that once held the preschoolers' lunch boxes and book bags still lined one of the walls.

Most of the church members present that evening had participated in one way or another in those activities. John Booker had served on the Board of Trustees of the Congregational Church during the 1960s and played a key role in organizing church-based employment training, the Neighborhood Youth Corps, and other Great Society programs. When the former pastor of the church ran for political office, challenging Corona's white Democratic party machine, Booker had worked to form alliances with reform Democrats in predominantly white Jackson Heights. Out of respect for his decades of activism, many in the neighborhood called him the "Governor."

In fact it was the memory of this coalition building during the 1960s that framed the opening of the discussion. Judy Grubin, the Jewish founder of the Cultural Awareness Council, began the meeting by recalling the longtime relationship that activists in Jackson Heights had with African-Americans in Corona. With the assembly seated in a wide circle, she recounted the long struggle twenty years before over the desegregation of the community's schools through the Princeton Plan, a controversial arrangement that paired a white elementary school in Jackson Heights with its counterpart in Corona. "We've been here," she said. "We're not just reacting to Howard Beach."

Grubin went on to describe the council's purpose. "We were formed to discuss the cultures and traditions of different groups and to open up a dialogue." The African-American church members listened attentively, some jotting down notes on the backs of flyers announcing the meeting. "Sharing diverse ethnic backgrounds," she continued, "is just the first step toward promoting harmony among people."

Glancing at her clipboard, Grubin explained the format of the council's meetings held monthly at various locations in the area. "Each person in the circle talks personally about their particular ethnic background and the experiences they've had in the neighborhood." Blanche Hubbert, a church member and part-time caterer in her seventies, frowned and peered over her glasses at John Booker. "What do I want to be talkin' about my ethnic background for?" she asked him. Booker shrugged and then focused his attention on Zakallah Prasada, a slender man from Pakistan who was to be the first speaker.

Prasada described how during the Iranian hostage crisis he and his wife and children had been harassed by people because they are Muslims. "Two times they burned our mosque in Corona," he reported. "For me, religious freedom is the most important issue." Frank Weinstein, the director of a coalition of Jewish organizations in Jackson Heights, spoke next. He told the group that he was a child of Holocaust survivors and reported that a swastika had been painted on his synagogue during Passover.

Next in the clockwise rotation was Nayibe Nunez Berger, who described her migration to the United States from Columbia in 1963 and her marriage to a Jew. "Nothing's changed in the past twenty years!" she exclaimed. "People here still misinterpret and condemn Hispanic street behavior." Yanghee Hahn, a woman from Korea, described cultural misunderstandings between Korean merchants and African-Americans and emphasized the importance of communication. An elderly Jewish man described growing up on the Lower East Side of Manhattan in the 1920s and encountering anti-Semitism when he moved to the Jewish "ghetto" in Middle Village, Queens, in the 1940s.

When Blanche Hubbert's turn came, she hesitated and fidgeted with her notepad. After an awkward silence, she spoke about food stereotypes people have, suggesting this was a form of prejudice. "I'm a caterer," she said, "and people always assume I'm going to serve collard greens." Everyone smiled. John Bell, who was next, looked annoyed. Just turning seventy, Bell had been a labor organizer in the furriers union and active in Harlem politics during the 1930s and 1940s. When he moved to Corona in 1957, he worked with John Booker to establish the Frederick Douglass Democratic Club, the first major black club in the area. Youthful in appearance and debonair, Bell stood, striking a pose that betrayed decades of political speaking.

"John Booker and I are the only ones here who have been active in both communities," he began, motioning to Booker at his side. "It seems like history is repeating itself!" Pausing for effect, he described how Corona and Jackson Heights were once divided by a "Mason-Dixon line" that black children could not cross. "The Princeton Plan was a chance for Jackson Heights to get to know who we were. And we don't have that anymore." John Booker nodded in agreement. "All that you have experienced here," Bell continued, gesturing to the group from Jackson Heights, "we already experienced. We have to become a *political* force, not a social one."

Howard Cuff, an African-American resident of Corona since 1924, shook his head wearily. "This is a new world, John. People are disillusioned! We need *new* ideas, not old ones."

Bryer, the minister, intervened. The discussion was quickly turning into a familiar debate among his congregation, pitting those advocating grass-roots political activism against those stressing "moral regeneration." Many, like Cuff, had come to feel that only a renewal of church and family values could resolve the apathy, despair, and hopelessness that some believed rested at the heart of community problems.

"The past is a teacher for the future," Bryer said. And then, turning to the visitors: "Most of you benefited from the civil rights movement. But those of us who have been here the longest have not. We have to get angry enough to *change* the system—not just talk about it."

Judy Grubin nodded in agreement. "We got a lot done when we worked together in the sixties but it only lasted ten years."

After the meeting Booker, Bell, and I accompanied the minister to his small office upstairs. He was anxious to find out what we thought about the meeting. As a newcomer to the community, Bryer relied on the "Governor" for political advice, and he asked Booker whether he thought the Cultural Awareness Council could be useful and whether a second, more publicized meeting should be arranged in Corona. Booker hesitated, as if to gauge the minister's thoughts. "No, I don't think so, Reverend. We've been down this road already."

For John Booker, as for many African-Americans in Corona and East Elmhurst, the end of the civil rights era marked less a political victory than a rupture with politics. The sense that history is repeating itself registers not merely the awareness that the struggle for racial equality is not yet over but, more profoundly, the perception that its conditions of possibility, both political and discursive, have been weakened, if not undermined. Blanche Hubbert's choice of a story about catering and collard greens was intended neither to be humorous nor to trivialize the issue of racism. Rather, it was a strained attempt to transpose the complex politics of race in the United States into the reductive logic of "cultural misunderstanding."

When I began my fieldwork in 1987 many veteran activists expressed frustration and grave concerns about the economic and political future of Black Corona. Nearly a decade of Reagan-era budget cuts had weakened, if not crippled, the area's community-based social service providers, leaving organizations such as Elmcor to compete in a zero-sum game with other, often neighboring groups for an ever dwindling supply of community development funds (See Logan and Molotch 1987). Perhaps more troubling for many than this politics of scarcity was the sense that the neighborhood's institutions and networks, which had sustained generations of struggles for social justice, were no longer capable of mobilizing a broad social base.

Paramount among the concerns of veteran activists such as John Booker and John Bell was the fear that there would not be a younger generation of activists willing and able to carry on their work. The active members of neighborhood groups such as the NAACP, the Civic Association, and the Frederick Douglass Democratic Association tended to be older people, frequently well over sixty. Although the rosters of block and civic associations include many middle-aged persons, older residents tend to dominate their leadership cadres and shoulder much of the responsibility for organizational work.

The reasons for this skewing of activist networks toward prewar generations are complex and have to do with the temporal demands of neighborhood activism and its political culture. On the one hand, activists must not only have considerable time to devote to the day-to-day tasks of organizing but must also have flexible schedules. For these reasons retired or semi-retired persons, those who no longer have fixed and demanding employment schedules and have relatively few familial obligations associated with child-rearing, tended to be more available for activist work than young and middle-aged persons with commitments to full-time employment, school, or family-related responsibilities.

On the other hand, the political culture of neighborhood activism gravitated around social networks, cultural practices, and lifestyle dispositions which, though far from static, tended to resonate with the experience of people who were raised before the civil rights period. Not only did these activist cohorts share political experiences and, very often, work and migration histories, but they also shared generation-specific cultural symbols and referents, forms of sociality, and notions of black progress and identity. As Karl Mannheim pointed out, generation-based affinities do not result from mere co-presence in time and space but rather are melded through participation in the "common destiny" of a social-historical group.

> [A] generation as an actuality is constituted when similarly "located" contemporaries participate in a common destiny and in the ideas and concepts which are in some way bound up with its unfolding. Within this community of people with a common destiny there can then arise particular *generation-units*. These are characterized by the fact that they do not merely involve a loose participation by a number of individuals in a pattern of events shared by all alike though interpreted by the different individuals differently, but an identity of responses, a certain affinity in the way in which all move with and are formed by their common experiences. (1952:306)

The notion of an affinity in the ways in which people "move with and are formed by" common experiences proves helpful in both capturing the historically informed specificity of black activist culture in Corona–East Elmhurst and the difficulty activists encountered when attempting to mobilize "younger" constituencies. For example, as I discuss in more detail below, the sense of shared "southern roots" loomed large in the reckoning and public elaboration of black community identity, values, and commitments among many activists. Although this political culture did not exclude younger participants or others with varying experiences (such as the area's Latin American and West Indian populations), it nonetheless tied activist work to cultural practices, symbols, and patterns of sociality that did not always resonate with alternative formations of identity and experience.

A second area of concern for many activists was the sense that the social base of the community's leading institutions had narrowed in the post–civil rights period and had become increasingly monopolized by the social networks and homeowner associations of East Elmhurst. Many residents of Corona and East Elmhurst alike expressed the opinion that this political infrastructure was not responsive to the needs and interests of lower-income people "on the other side" in Corona.

For example, an activist recalled her neighbors' reactions when their block in North Corona suffered a crime spree:

> When they stole us all blind around here—stole all the flowers and plants, and even stole my stone lions out here in front [of the house]—my neighbors said, "If we lived in East Elmhurst, we wouldn't have that. See, the rich people in East Elmhurst, they could put anything out. They must all have guns or something. Nobody steals from them." And I said, "I got news for you. They steal over there, too." And they said, "Yeah, well, they don't worry. They don't even care what happens to us. They're hoping that it happens to us."

Though residents rarely articulated this sense of political alienation publicly in terms of social class, activists in Corona and East Elmhurst often expressed the concern that organizations such as the Civic Association, the NAACP, and the Frederick Douglass Democratic Association, as well as the community's churches, were not effectively responding to the problems and needs of the wider black community and, in particular, to those of the poor. As a black stockbroker once put it, contrasting East Elmhurst to black areas of southern Queens, "Southeast Queens is a black community. It has a black consciousness. We in East Elmhurst are people who live with blacks but in a white community. We think outside our community."

During the summer of 1987 a group of activists began meeting for the purpose of establishing a social action committee in Corona–East Elmhurst to define the community's political and socioeconomic needs and to develop strategies for addressing them. The committee, calling itself the Social Action Volunteers for Empowerment (SAVE), was organized by the Reverend Irvine Bryer, the newly appointed pastor of the Corona Congregational Church, and two senior church members and longtime activists, John Booker and John Bell.

Booker and Bell had worked together in voter registration, school desegregation, and antipoverty struggles during the civil rights era. In the 1960s John Bell, a former union organizer, had served as vice president of the Independent Citizens for Good Government (see chapter 3) and was vice president of the NAACP. John Booker had served as president of the Corona–East Elmhurst

Development Corporation, the community's federally funded antipoverty program, and was active in civic association and church politics. Booker and Bell had also worked together in the Frederick Douglass Democratic Association and the short-lived Martin Luther King Democratic Club.

Before his appointment at the Congregational Church, Reverend Irvine Bryer had served as pastor of a church in south Queens and as vice president of the Southeast Queens Clergy, a coalition of activist ministers. After the racial attack by whites on three black men in Howard Beach, Queens, in 1986, Bryer co-founded Concerned Citizens of South Queens, a multiracial coalition of thirty-five religious, civic, and political organizations committed to combating racism in the city (*New York Times*, 3 January 1987).

For Booker, Bell, and other church members, Bryer's arrival at Corona Congregational presented an opportunity to reengage the church in a social activist agenda and, as Booker put it, "bring some new blood into the old business as usual." Although Bryer's appointment was contested, his supporters felt that his political and ministerial links to black neighborhoods in southeast Queens would enhance the organizing efforts of activists in Corona–East Elmhurst, particularly around issues of economic development and political empowerment.

By examining the discussions, debates, and organizational practices surrounding the formation of SAVE, I want to shed light on the ways in which activists struggled to interpret and address the complex and interrelated issues of racial identity, class divisions, and community empowerment through the everyday practices of cultural politics.

IMAGINING BLACK EMPOWERMENT

Reverend Bryer and Cal Wynter picked me up at the Woodside Avenue train station on the elevated Flushing line. They had just come from Elmhurst Hospital where they had been visiting a member of the congregation who was suffering from an AIDS-related illness. Just turned forty and youthful in appearance, Bryer pointed out the former Bulova watch factory on Astoria Boulevard, which had been bought by British Airways. Wynter glanced back over his shoulder at me: "See, Bulova is the Columbia University of East Elmhurst. They've been buying up real estate all around here. The community is pretty upset," he added, loosening his bright red necktie with a sharp tug.

At twenty-six, Calvin Wynter was about to begin a job as a stockbroker at Merrill Lynch. A Colgate University MBA, Wynter had returned to East Elmhurst the year before from Los Angeles where he had been working in international trade. During the interim he had been running an executive search business out of the basement of his mother's split-level house. Known to be a political protégé of John Booker, the young and aspiring stockbroker represented for many the best and the brightest of the new, corporate-tested black middle class now returned to the community to make a contribution. Wynter's matter-of-fact style, brash mannerisms, and dress-for-success sensibilities often drew admiring comments from older activists.

When we arrived at Wynter's house in East Elmhurst, John Booker, John Bell, and other members of the SAVE committee were waiting in the basement. The teak-paneled basement was set up as a 1960s-style "playroom." A fully equipped bar with stools occupied one wall. A couch and director's chairs were arranged around a pool table at the other end of the room. Booker and Bell were watching the baseball game on a television that had been built into the mirrored wall behind the bar.

Four other members of SAVE were gathered around the pool table: Melanie Witherspoon, an assistant to Congressman Floyd H. Flake in southeast Queens; Michael Valentine and Frank Pollard, also from south Queens and affiliated with Concerned Citizens of South Queens, the antiracism group; and Deborah Nesbitt, chair of the Congregational Church's Youth Ministry. All but Booker, Bell, and Reverend Bryer were younger than thirty.

Bryer opened the meeting by providing an overview of the purpose of SAVE: "This community needs to be stabilized, and what we have to begin to do here tonight is identify community institutions and people who can play a role in achieving this stability." The Corona Congregational Church, he continued, needed to take a more active role in promoting this development by reaching out to young people and to newcomer groups, such as Latin American immigrants, and including them in the empowerment process.[8] Bryer went on to describe the church as a power base in the black community that had given rise to such leaders as Martin Luther King, Malcolm X, and Marcus Garvey. "See, the common fiber of black communities," he explained, clasping his hands together in a gesture of unity, "is church attendance."

Wynter, whose organizing experience had been largely in electoral politics and the private sector, looked impatient: "What about political action?" Taking issue with Bryer's statement about the pivotal role of the church, Wynter argued that the political significance of the church had been undermined by the gains of black elected officials.

Melanie Witherspoon, whose boss, Congressman Floyd Flake, served as pastor of the powerful Allen AME Church, raised her eyebrows in alarm: "Without the church there would *be* no elected black officials. I think we should recognize that fact and not try to model what we do after what other ethnic groups are doing." She then suggested that the Congregational Church organize a church revival that would bring together all the churches in the community.

Wynter argued that a revival would be divisive since it would not muster all denominations, and, more important, it would obscure SAVE's political agenda. Moreover, he contended, it had been the domination of Corona–East

Elmhurst politics by Reverend Sherard, the Congregational Church's former pastor, that had led to his downfall and to the splitting of the community and church along factional lines.

John Bell, who had worked closely with Sherard, disagreed. "He did a lot for this community," Bell argued. "The mistake he made was that he did not develop community support for all of his plans."

People often talked about the Congregational Church and the community as being "split." In the church this division was often explained in terms of conflicts among the congregation over Reverend Sherard's "militant" political stance during the 1960s and 1970s. Some felt that Sherard had taken the church too far into secular politics by standing for elected office and, more generally, by stressing community work over the pastoral needs of his congregation. Others viewed this split as dividing "progressive" supporters of Sherard from more conservative and elite factions within the church.

These schisms, tempered by personal and other institutional grievances within the church, were also related to long-standing conflicts between church factions and other political formations within the community. For example, a 1970s power struggle in the Frederick Douglass Democratic Association had led to the establishment of an opposing political club, the Martin Luther King Democratic Club, by John Booker and John Bell. Not long after, the King Club, supported by Sherard, had challenged candidates from the Frederick Douglass Association in key elections, most notably Helen Marshall's 1978 bid for the State Assembly. Although some of these conflicts had been reconciled, Bell and Booker, along with former Sherard supporters at Corona Congregational, were viewed by some as insurgents intent on using the church as a power base to upset the community's elected officials. This political history of internal and external discord rendered SAVE's negotiation of the fuzzy boundary between religion and politics a delicate and contentious matter.

Following the discussion of church politics under Sherard, Bryer returned to the issue of the church. "Black people need to be empowered through the word of God," he began. "I just had an argument yesterday with two members of my congregation who were saying that the primary mission of the church is to save souls. And I told them that before you can help others you must first be empowered. It is this belief in oneself that gives power to the faith statement."

Frank Pollard, who had until now kept out of the discussion on the role of the church in politics, spoke up: "I think that what we need to do now is to define what we as a group have to offer the community. We need to define what we are about, what our purpose is."

"To remove fear, blight, and social degradation from this community!" Booker declared. "That's what we need to do. That's the only way we can keep our young people here." To emphasize his point, Booker spoke of a neighbor's daughter who had just moved to a white neighborhood in New Jersey to get away from the "neighborhood blight."

John Bell took up this theme: "The gap between the young and the old is the result of a loss in Christian spirit. People work in the church as though it were a political club. Everybody wants to be a big 'I.' The neighborhood is declining. What can we do to get people to care? That's my question."

"We live in a materialist world," Booker responded, shaking his head. "These young people haven't suffered. We've suffered for them."

"You see," Bell continued, glancing at Wynter and the young members of the committee. "We have the perception of power, not real power. We have to organize people—do like the Koreans and Jews. Collectively we have the money to do things. Next year I will be seventy. I want to see a better community before I leave."

Booker agreed: "I'm seriously concerned about the plight of the entire black community. Economically, they can pull the rug right out from under us."

"That's right," Bryer said. "We have to get a piece of the rock. We have to use our collective power, the power of our Lord Jesus Christ. Look at us here. This group ranges from people in their twenties to people in their eighties. This is the right place, the right time, and we are the right people. I see this group as a tool, and the church is pivotal."

"What areas should we target for change?" Bell asked.

Wynter suggested forming a youth division within the NAACP, that would cooperate with similar divisions in other branches.

Pollard leaned into the discussion: "The idea of a youth wing of the NAACP is great, but we still need to step back and say, 'What are we going to do to help Corona–East Elmhurst.'"

Wynter replied that a young adult division would provide a pool of young black professionals on which the community may draw.

"Yeah," Pollard continued, "but we need to put a mechanism in place to make sure that we don't exclude nonprofessionals."

Melanie Witherspoon, who had argued with Wynter regarding the role of the black church, agreed: "My main concern is with those who have no professional aspirations." She cut her eyes toward Wynter. "The real question is how do we organize the *whole* black community and not just people who have already gotten theirs."

"Everyone has a valid role," Bryer intervened, opening his extended arms in a gesture of inclusion. "It's not just the grassroots, it's all groups. Professionals, too."

John Bell shook his head. "There's no question that we have the talent in this community. But people are disillusioned. We have to organize to get services. That's what we need to do."

"What's missing here," Booker said, "is the justification—the moral aspect of the whole thing."

"That's right," Bryer declared. "And if we start thinking too much about getting funding, an office—if we think just about being another political club we won't have anything. We have to stay a grass-roots group because we have a lot this way. We have commitment to the community. That's the moral element of what we're doing—the faith statement. That's our purpose."

"To ensure the survival of black people!" Booker declared, darting forward to the edge of his seat.

"Right, and I'm going to lift this to another level," Bryer continued, standing. "I'm going to say our *community*, because if we just espouse blackness in our struggle—we know that we're black. But I think—let me give you an example. Last week someone called about a wedding. A Dominican woman. Now we've been saying that we need to get involved with Hispanics. But I said to her, 'Well, as a rule, we don't do that here.' See, we haven't had a wedding or a baptism from outside the church [i.e., for a nonchurch member] for fifteen years. But after I got off the phone I wanted to kick myself. I turned right around and called the lady back and told her, 'Come on over so I can show you the church. Sure you can use it for your wedding.' The next day I got another call from a Haitian lady. A baptism. I didn't ask her what church she went to or what denomination."

"That's how you build alliances!" Booker interrupted.

"There you go," Bryer replied. "That's how you bring the community together."

The meeting continued for another two hours. Mrs. Wynter, Cal's mother, served coffee and an assortment of Pepperidge Farm cookies. Questions concerning the goals of political organizing, the social base of activism, and the black community's relations with other ethnic groups remained topics of debate.

Wynter, supported by Booker, pressed for an agenda that would pave the way toward participation in electoral politics. Citing his corporate experience, he stressed the importance of organizing black professionals and described church-based activism as "passé." In contrast, Witherspoon, Pollard, and Bell advocated broader-based community organizing that would educate and mobilize residents across class and ethnic lines. "We're not going back to the talented tenth," Witherspoon told the committee. "I'm not about that. Those days are over."

Bryer, although acknowledging the importance of electoral politics (particularly in light of Jesse Jackson's expected bid for the presidency in 1988), continued to stress the importance of the black church as a social arena in which to construct and mobilize political constituencies. As the SAVE meeting drew to a close, the committee outlined its plans for the future.

First, SAVE would sponsor a series of public events at the Corona Congregational Church to signal its social activist agenda and its commitment to building coalitions. The first event would be a reception to applaud the appointment of Haywood Burns, a civil rights activist, as dean of the Queens College law school. The Haywood Burns reception would be followed by Reverend Bryer's installation service, a welcoming ceremony at the church for its new pastor. Second, SAVE would begin planning long-term initiatives, such as mobilizing the community for Jesse Jackson's presidential bid and organizing a campaign to provide services to homeless persons housed in a neighborhood hotel.

In response to Wynter's concern that organizing within the church would mute SAVE's political agenda, Bryer referred to his coming installation as the second of two "statements" that would serve the committee's goals:

> The second statement will come when we do the installation. This is when we're really going to pull the Sixth and Seventh Congressional Districts together. And here there will be a political statement being made. We're bringing two important black theologians together who make political statements. And they are Ben Chavis and also Jeremiah Wright, who is beginning to make some statements other than just preaching. And they've both been charged with an agenda that's similar to the one we're talking about. They're talking about economic empowerment and issues of justice.

SAVE's discussion and debate underscored not only the range of positions within the African-American community concerning the goals, methods, and social base of political empowerment but also the multiple and conflicting interpretations of black experience, needs, and identity that informs them. For at stake in the dispute about the role of the black church was more than the relationship between church and state or "spiritual" and political empowerment. More fully, the discussion brought to light historically formed and class-inflected differences in how people conceptualized the social process of political mobilization. For Calvin Wynter and, to a lesser extent, John Booker, black professionals would play the leading role in the empowerment process, providing expertise and organizational resources for top-down strategies aimed at assembling voters for electoral contests. In contrast, Melanie Witherspoon and John Bell stressed a politics of inclusion that would construct broad-based constituencies around a spectrum of social needs and interests. For the latter the church offered a social space that was potentially more expansive and diverse than the narrow networks cultivated through electoral politics.

"In the church," Witherspoon commented after the meeting, "you have a lot of different types of people, grass-roots people, professionals, youth and senior citizens, even immigrants. You can get your message across to a large community. You can bring people along with you to where you want to go. If you just go the way of the political club, you are always going to have a small clique of people who are basically out for themselves."

Witherspoon's notion of "bringing people along with you" highlights the interrelation between collective action and everyday cultural practices that build and communicate shared interpretations of political interests and identities. For it is in everyday practices of sociality and cultural production, ranging from barbecues and dinner dances to political meetings and rituals, that the social networks of neighborhood activism are articulated and reworked and their political commitments expressed, contested, and subjected to the scrutiny of public culture and memory.

CULTURE, MEMORY, AND THE PRACTICE OF IDENTITY

Calvin Wynter and I arrived at Carmichael's Bar and Grill in East Elmhurst on Sunday afternoon for the annual Curtis Street Block Association barbecue and fund-raiser. Debra Nesbitt, chair of the Youth Ministry, had sold us tickets to the event at the SAVE meeting. About one hundred people, dressed in a bright assortment of Bermuda shorts, polo shirts, and designer running suits, filled the picnic tables behind Carmichael's. Some wandered from table to table, greeting friends and exchanging news. Others had formed a long line in front of two enormous grills crafted from fifty-gallon drums and attended by two middle-aged men dressed in jeans, block association T-shirts, and crisp, white chef's hats. With a quick flip of the wrist one of the cooks turned over a full rack of spareribs, setting off a blast of flames and white smoke. He leaned back to avoid the fumes, tongs suspended in the air, and grinned.

Wynter and I sat at a table with Deborah Nesbitt and her sister, a Special Education teacher at a local school. Nesbitt had been born in Corona and had "moved up to the 'hurst" with her family in the 1960s, when their economic situation improved. When her parents died, she kept the family home in East Elmhurst and went to work with British Airways. Her roommate, Janice, also at the table, had just taken a job as the manager of a Pepsi Cola plant in Brooklyn.

Wynter, dressed in a blue Brooks Brothers suit, red tie, and red suspenders, took off his jacket, folded it, lining out, with quick turns of his wrists, and lay it over his knee. Pivoting straight-backed in his chair, he surveyed the crowd, nodding to an attractive, gray-haired woman sitting at another table. "President of Overlook," he reported, referring to the Overlook Park Block Association to which he belonged.

"There are a lot of people here from Overlook," he continued. "You know I should tell the president to make an announcement supporting Curtis Street, but then she would ask me to do it. And I don't want to call attention to myself." Wynter, like Bryer, was concerned that assuming too visible a profile at such public events would draw gossip and criticism branding him as a "Johnny-come-lately" out to usurp the authority of seasoned community leaders.

A local disc jockey, hired by the block association, began playing a mix of jazz, calypso, and 1960s soul music, a standard musical program at social events in East Elmhurst. A few couples danced to a Mighty Sparrow calypso. Wynter began pointing out block association constituencies to me. Most associations had bought blocks of the twenty-dollar tickets and were clustered together at tables. "They're from Ninety-ninth Street," he remarked, pointing to a table at the opposite end of the yard. "Ninety-ninth Street has the strongest block association in East Elmhurst. "You can tell because all the houses have the same lampposts on their front lawns."

Blanche Hubbert, looking radiant, sat at our table along with John Booker. Hubbert and Booker were both from Richmond, Virginia, and had come north to Harlem during the 1920s. Hubbert and her husband moved to East Elmhurst in 1953 and were soon followed by John Booker and his family. Calvin introduced me to Mrs. Hubbert and then began a conversation with Booker about the Rainbow Coalition convention that would be held in Raleigh, North Carolina, in October.

Mrs. Hubbert owned real estate in Corona and East Elmhurst and, as mentioned above, operated "a little business" as a part-time caterer. Many of the smaller community affairs, particularly those held at the Congregational Church, were catered by her crew. Seen at almost all community functions and renowned for her youthful fashion sensibilities, Hubbert edited "Community Lights," a weekly gossip column in the Queens-based and black-oriented *New York Voice* in which she profiled "outstanding achievers." Like its predecessor "Corona Chatter" in the *New York Age*, Hubbert's column provided lively commentary on social events, successful careers, and political issues, publicizing the community's subtle and sometimes not-so-subtle shifts in social relations, alliances, and political fortunes. Mrs. Hubbert had recently profiled Reverend Bryer, provoking a wave of intense speculation about events unfolding at the Congregational Church. Wynter, ever alert to compromising publicity, had declined her invitation to be "profiled."

Midway through the barbecue, Bryer arrived, briskly navigating the maze of picnic tables to shake hands, exchange pleasantries, and receive introductions. John Booker stood and waved him over to our table. Bryer took a seat just as the president of Curtis Street began introducing the block association's officers. Each woman stood in turn and waved to the crowd. Bryer turned to Hubbert, raising his eyebrows and smiling: "They're all women!"

"Naturally," Mrs. Hubbert replied. "It's just like in the church. Who do you think does all the work?"

Bryer laughed. "But Blanche, what about those men over there doing all the cooking, sweating bullets, and all covered with barbecue sauce?" He looked to Booker for support.

Hubbert glared at him, slapping her hand on the table in mock irritation. "Cooking's not work. Besides, anybody can burn a chicken."

Booker laughed. "Oh, she's got you there, Reverend. What you say, Blanche? Don't take nothin' to burn a chicken!"

Bryer pursued the topic of women in the church and told us that one of the key goals of his ministry was to bring young men into church activities and committees. He pointed to SAVE as an example of one such attempt. Hubbert looked over her rhinestone-trimmed eyeglasses and took notes in a small spiral notebook.

The conversation turned to the issue of black economic development. Debra Nesbitt expressed concerns about the Korean-owned businesses that were opening all along Northern Boulevard. "They could at least have signs written in English so that people could read them," she declared. Reverend Bryer said that he had been praying on this issue and had come up with an idea for a project that would involve black professionals in the community investing money in a cooperative business. He offered the example of the First Baptist Church's credit union.

"You know," Mrs. Hubbert said pensively, "sometimes I think that it's not in us as black people to be entrepreneurs."

Booker nodded his head in agreement. "The young people today all want to be managers—to pursue the corporate path. Nobody wants to be owners." He looked toward Wynter, chair of SAVE's newly formed economic development committee, for a response.

Wynter suggested that SAVE focus on service industries that would require little start-up capital. He gave the example of a valet dry cleaning service that would pick up and deliver clothes "like Federal Express." Deborah Nesbitt argued that there wasn't a big enough market and that the idea was one more example of Wynter's narrow focus on the needs of the black middle class. Nesbitt's comments led to a general debate about the role of the middle class in black empowerment. Midway through the discussion, Mrs. Hubbert called for silence: the president of Curtis Street had begun announcing the winning numbers in the ticket raffle.

Curtis Street's annual barbecue and fund-raiser was one of a manifold array of social events that produced the political culture of activism in Corona–East Elmhurst. At these public functions, ranging from block parties and political luncheons to the frenetic itinerary of awards dinners sponsored by groups such as the NAACP, Elmcor, and the East Elmhurst–Corona Civic Association, political identities and commitments are publicly negotiated and performed. These social events, always well attended, are important venues through which activist networks communicate with one another, with public officials, and with wider constituencies that are not directly involved in the day-to-day activities of neighborhood groups (cf. Kaplan 1992). Through this public culture residents learn about the structure of local governance and the issues and agenda of groups, as well as participate in the elaboration of a shared political language. Moreover, at such events, residents enjoy direct access to public officials and community leaders, seldom afforded in more official settings.

Such occasions are important performative events through which activists organize and display social networks and allegiances and convey their potential for collective action. Like Wynter, activists read the "turnout" at public

Figure 6.2. Fashion show held during the Ericsson Street Block Association's
annual block party in East Elmhurst.

events such as Curtis Street's barbecue in order to measure the strength of
specific constituencies and chart their allegiances and commitments. It is common to hear people at such affairs methodically assessing "who showed up"
and interpreting the implications of the "no shows." For example, the large
turnout at the barbecue and the range of community groups represented (e.g.,
the NAACP, Elmcor, the Frederick Douglass Democratic Association, and the
East Elmhurst–Corona Civic Association) not only communicated Curtis
Street's influence and capacity for social mobilization but also the social
power of the area's block associations as a whole, most of which were represented and ceremonially recognized. The cameo appearance of State Assemblywoman Helen Marshall confirmed the event's political importance.

Like other neighborhood events (for example, see Figure 6.2), Curtis
Street's barbecue provided the opportunity for residents to articulate issues of
racial, gender, class, and ethnic identities and relations within everyday contexts of social interaction. For example, Reverend Bryer's comment about the
block association women, broadened by Mrs. Hubbert to the issue of women's
role in the church, provoked a discussion and clarification of Bryer's program
for addressing gender disparities in the church—a public position that eventually found its way into "Community Lights" before a boroughwide reading
public. Similarly, the discussion about black business development not only
marked the importance of black entrepreneurship as a key component of the
empowerment agenda envisioned by activists but also aired deep ambiva-

lences in how activists thought about the health of what Franklin Frazier called "black business culture" (see Hodge and Feagin 1995). In fact, following the announcement of the winning raffle tickets, Wynter did rise and declare his block association's support for Curtis Street's event and, perhaps more important, for SAVE's agenda to promote black entrepreneurship and "black business confidence."

For activists such as Wynter, Bryer, and the organizers of SAVE, attendance of these myriad and densely scheduled functions is critical to assembling constituencies, communicating agendas, and, indeed, achieving recognition and legitimacy as "movers and shakers" in the neighborhood. Activists regularly speak of the need to be seen at specific events as a means of conveying the importance of a particular constituency or of publicizing their commitment to a particular issue. For example, when explaining his reasons for attending the annual NAACP dinner dance, Wynter remarked, "I just need to show my face there to check-in on the education issues," referring to the NAACP's protracted campaign for a new elementary school in Corona. Reverend Bryer once complained to me that his modest salary as a minister did not provide him with sufficient means to cover the rigorous but obligatory cycle of awards dinners and fund-raisers which can cost as much as sixty dollars to attend.

Being seen is especially important for political newcomers like Bryer, who must publicly demonstrate a deeply rooted commitment to the neighborhood and an intimate knowledge of both its social history and the discourses and symbolic forms through which that history is communicated. In part, this social history is one of prominent people, places, and events: an "official transcript," as James Scott put it, of the neighborhood's past (1990). But at a deeper level, this history, performed and reworked through everyday cultural practices, implicates individual and shared narratives of social sacrifice and achievement and of important experiences and relationships that give meaning to or "frame" the present (McAdam 1994).

Public events provide occasions for conveying these intergenerational narratives and for bringing their assorted meanings to bear on the present. For example, a funeral service held at the Congregational Church gave pause not only to reflect on the life of Lillian Clark but also to link the meanings of her life to the experiences and struggles of the wider community.

Although Lillian and her husband, William, were not members of Corona Congregational, the latter decided to hold his wife's funeral services there where many of their friends and neighbors worshiped.[9] A wake had been held earlier in the basement of the church, and food, prepared by Assemblywoman Marshall's staff, was served. A college graduation photograph of Lillian Clark, who had completed her degree four years before, rested on top of the closed casket. The spacious chapel was filled to capacity with church members, visiting friends and family of the Clarks, and representatives of civic and political organizations.

Accompanied by the organ, Reverend Bryer led a slow procession of deacons and deaconesses down the center aisle toward the altar, reciting a prayer along the way. When they reached the altar, a deacon read from the Scriptures. Next, a woman in the choir sang two verses of *Amazing Grace*. With a subtle lift of her arms she invited the congregation to join her, and their voices filled the chapel.

Next, Assemblywoman Marshall described Mrs. Clark as a woman who had stayed behind the scenes, supporting and enabling her husband's activist work with the Civic Association. She said that both were neighborhood leaders and that now was the time for the community, gathered together in the church, to stand behind Mr. Clark. A chorus of "amens" rose from the community.

Marshall's tribute was followed by Reverend Bryer's sermon on the topic of "the foundation." Bryer described the family and church as rooted in southern life and culture, and as the social and moral foundation of the black community. William and Lillian Clark, he declared, had shown the world this foundation building through their community work and through their raising of three surrogate children. "That's right," the middle-aged woman sitting next to me said quietly.

"Nowadays, this foundation building is disappearing among the youth of our community," Bryer continued. "Our young people, raised on this foundation, are leaving the community. Suddenly they've become too busy for their parents--too busy to celebrate holidays together with their families. Now they want to take vacations--go off to Martha's Vineyard or somewhere!" He pointed to somewhere out beyond the chapel door and raised his eyebrows to a look of loftiness. Quiet chuckles rose from the congregation.

Bryer continued, highlighting the Clarks' community work and linking their activism to the values and "old ways" of the South. Older people in the congregation nodded their heads in approval. After describing Lillian Clark's college graduation as an example for youth to follow, he acknowledged the presence of other "role models" in the audience. First to be recognized were State Assemblywoman Marshall and City Councilwoman Julia Harrison. Bryer then called on the members of the East Elmhurst–Corona Civic Association, to which the Clarks belonged, to stand. About thirty people scattered throughout the congregation rose from their seats. "You know," the woman sitting next to me said to no one in particular, "I can almost see Lillian up there, too."

Lillian Clark's funeral highlights the range of social issues and concerns that residents address and negotiate through everyday cultural practices. Questions of class and generational schisms, political empowerment, racial inequality, and gender and family relations are formulated and reworked before heterogeneous and multigenerational publics. In these settings individual and collective histories are recollected, brought to bear on present conditions, and projected into possible futures through the social production of public memory (Bodnar 1992).

Through the fashioning and refashioning of public memory, activists selectively construct narratives about the past that lend new meanings to present circumstances and serve as idioms for articulating shared experiences, identities, and commitments in the present (Thelen 1990). For example, Reverend Bryer's appeals to the "old ways" of southern life to account for the Clarks' activism and to challenge the class pretensions of the younger generation highlights not only the continued salience of the South in the reckoning of black identities; it also points to the central role that the themes of sacrifice and commitment to community, linked for many to the experiences of the Great Migration and the civil rights movement, continue to play in the production of political culture in Corona–East Elmhurst.

Older residents continue to sustain social and symbolic ties both to their pre-migration communities in the South and to networks of persons in the North who share common origins and migration histories. Kinship and friendship networks are often conceptualized and activated in relation to these pre-migration roots. For example, when asked by a neighbor who would be attending a crab bake in East Elmhurst, a man in his sixties replied, "That's that Lynchburg [Virginia] crowd." Similarly, Blanche Hubbert's column "Community Lights" seldom fails to note where the family of the week's celebrity "hails from."

Souvenir booklets, produced and distributed at annual awards dinners, church celebrations, and other community events, include long listings of "dedications" which, purchased by groups and individuals, record and publicize support for the event's sponsor. Such dedications, frequently purchased by kinship, workplace, and friendship networks, are often made in the name of a pre-migration place of origin. For example, in a booklet celebrating the seventy-fourth anniversary of the Congregational Church, "The friends of the Tar Heel State" expressed their congratulations, listing in their dedication ad the names of seventeen former North Carolinians. And in a booklet commemorating an annual Civic Association awards dinner and dance, eleven "Daughters of Virginia" conveyed their "compliments and best wishes."

Not only do residents sustain these social ties, but many spend vacations in their hometowns and many return to the South after retirement. When I asked a resident of Corona why, after forty years, he was returning with his wife to Raleigh, North Carolina, he replied, "Well, people tend to go back to where the [umbilical] cord was cut."

Equally important is the role that this discourse of "southernness" plays in the cultural elaboration and reproduction of social and political commitments. "Southern values" and "old ways" are often constructed as the foundation of not only kinship and church-based loyalties but of political struggle and self-sacrifice as well. Older residents frequently narrate their experiences in the Jim Crow South and their post-migration struggles against discrimination in the

North as a means both of lending cultural authority to certain values and beliefs and of critiquing, through historical comparison, social conditions in the present. The idea of "southernness" operates as a countertradition, contrasting sharply with what many regard to be the individualism, political apathy, and forgetfulness of the dominant, mass-mediated culture.

For example, at the 1989 annual "public meeting" sponsored by the Corona–East Elmhurst NAACP, the Reverend Congressman Floyd Flake, the rally's keynote speaker, invoked his experiences growing up in the segregated South to emphasize the continued importance of traditions of black resistance and self-help and to mock attitudes of complacency. Having been "raised by Jim Crow," Flake told the audience of nearly four hundred, "can't nobody tell me about racism or about hard work." He went on to recount his experiences picking cotton in Texas, describing in detail the various methods used by black workers to artificially inflate the weight of the cotton sacks. "Now some of you *know* what I'm talking about," he continued, smiling. "But sometimes people get a little comfortable and start going around telling everybody they're from New York when they're really from somewhere down South." Laughter and declarations of "That's right!" and "Tell it like it is" rose from the audience.

The social construction of "southernness" as public memory, as a tradition invented and reinvented in everyday life, cuts across generational and, to some extent, ethnic lines (see Hobsbawn and Ranger 1983). Less an essentialist view of cultural origins than a culturally exercised recollection of shared trajectories of struggle, this countertradition and its symbols and tropes are appropriated and practiced by northern-born, as well as foreign-born, black residents. For example, when Reverend Bryer's turn came to speak at the NAACP meeting, he began his comments with a narrative about his experiences picking apples as a teenager in upstate New York, stressing the continuities and parallels between black life in the North and South.

West Indian and southern-born residents often compare and contrast "back home" values, beliefs, and experiences. For example, at a political dinner I attended, a Jamaican-born woman struck up a conversation with me about the lack of a work ethic among neighborhood youth. She went on to contrast the attitudes about work and education among "the youth of today" with those she had encountered growing up in Jamaica. Midway through her story, a Virginia-born man interrupted: "Why, he wouldn't know nothing about that, Hyacinth. He was born up here." Laughing, she replied, "That's what I'm telling you!"

The permeability of these black ethnic boundaries is shown or, better, performed in everyday civic culture. Bands and deejays performing at neighborhood events typically play a complex mix of African-American music (ranging from 1940s fox trots to the latest contemporary beats), calypso, soca, reggae, and, to a lesser extent, Latin music. The food served at neighborhood affairs also reflects this diversity and often includes barbecued ribs and collard greens along with curried goat and rice and peas, as well as the obligatory Swedish meatballs. Calvin Wynter, pointing to a table of food at a family barbecue, which included dishes prepared by a Jamaican-born aunt, a Haitian cousin by marriage, and his Florida-born mother, explained to me that his Jamaican side (e.g., his father's relations) had become "southernized" through intermarriage with African-Americans.

It is through these everyday cultural practices and forms of sociality that the social networks of community activism are forged and their political commitments constructed, negotiated, and communicated. In these multiple settings issues of racial, class, ethnic, and gender identities and differences are articulated and subjected to varied interpretations of the past as well as expectations for the future. The heterogeneity of this political culture and its discourses and symbolic forms highlights the complexity and fluidity of black identity and the degree to which the formation and mobilization of constituencies relies on what Stuart Hall has described as the "winning of identification" through the production and exercise of shared interpretations of the world (Hall 1992).

However, despite this heterogeneity, the civic networks and forms of cultural politics discussed in this chapter are not "all inclusive," nor do they represent the social processes and venues through which *all* residents of Corona and East Elmhurst construct their identities and practice their political activism. As noted above, the block and civic associations that form the social base for many of the neighborhood's formal or "officially recognized" institutions are composed of largely middle-income homeowners in East Elmhurst. And although their income and social status do not translate into a coherent and uniform set of class interests and ideologies, homeowners tend to privilege certain quality-of-life concerns, while de-emphasizing others—for example, issues concerning the rights of tenants and immigrants, unemployment, police brutality, and cuts in social welfare spending.

Moreover, participation in this homeowner-focused political culture presupposes access to social resources that are generally not available to low-income persons. Both membership and meaningful participation in groups such as the block and civic associations, the Democratic Club, and the NAACP require considerable financial resources and leisure time that are often not available to low-income persons. For example, although yearly NAACP membership dues are as low as $20, attendance at the NAACP annual awards dinner and the myriad ticketed events sponsored by other, collateral civic groups can add up to as much as $750. Consequently, although financial constraints do not necessarily exclude low-income residents from membership, they do bar many from intense participation in the overlapping social networks and organizations that not only leads to positions of influence and leadership but also lend these latter legitimacy. In the political culture of Corona–East Elmhurst, as elsewhere, being heard depends very much on being seen.

Low-income persons, apartment renters, as well as migrants from Latin America, all of whom are not well represented in the homeowner—based activist networks of Corona–East Elmhurst, do, of course, organize and act collectively in other social arenas. Block and tenants associations, for example, operate in lower-income areas of Corona. But these groups are generally not active in the powerful East Elmhurst–Corona Civic Association or integrated into its extensive spheres of influence. Consequently, these Corona-based organizations do not enjoy the same political clout that the East Elmhurst–Corona Civic Association leverages for its member clubs from public authorities and the private sector.

New and old migrants from Latin American, concentrated in southern areas of North Corona, participate in a variety of churches with Spanish-speaking congregations and in community-based social clubs, voluntary associations, and publicly funded community service organizations (see Ricourt 1995). Though these groups are exerting increasing influence on public authorities, often through boroughwide and citywide advocacy groups and elected officials, people of Latin American descent play a minor role at best in the predominantly black civic institutions of Corona–East Elmhurst.

For the organizers of SAVE, participation in the multiple social arenas of black political culture proved key to building neighborhood support for the committee's political initiatives. In the summer of 1987, as had been planned, SAVE sponsored a reception and rally for civil rights activist and Queens College dean Haywood Burns at the Corona Congregational Church. The well-attended reception and public forum drew activists from southern Queens and other areas of the city to discuss empowerment needs and strategies (see Figure 6.3). In October SAVE organized a delegation to the National Rainbow Coalition convention in Raleigh, which laid important groundwork for mobilizing grass-roots support in Corona and East Elmhurst for Jesse Jackson's 1988 presidential campaign as well as for David Dinkins's successful mayoral bid in 1989.

SAVE's organizing efforts, and those of the other activist networks and associations discussed in this chapter, defy ready portrayal as oppositional or accommodationist or as challenging or not challenging "basic" structures of political and economic inequality in American society. People and the power relations in which they are embedded are much too complex to sustain such categorical neatness at any but the most general, abstract, and oftentimes ahistorical levels of analysis.

The political commitments and practices of residents of Corona and East Elmhurst have been shaped by a variety of social forces acting in a range of social locations over time. Through struggles over schools, urban decline, political empowerment, and other issues affecting the quality of black urban life, activists negotiated and contested crosscutting hierarchies of race, class, gender, and ethnicity, casting and recasting their interests and identities in mani-

Figure 6.3. Calvin Wynter (*left*) and John Bell of SAVE oversee final preparations
for the reception of Queens College dean Hayward Burns at the
Corona Congregational Church.

fold and frequently conflicting ways. Public authorities, often operating in the
interests of private capital, participated in this process of fashioning collective
identities, configuring the topography of neighborhood politics in ways that
enabled some forms of identity and activism, and disabled others. It is to this
political struggle with the state and capital over the social construction of identity and place that I now turn.

PART THREE

CHAPTER SEVEN

Up Against the Authority

The new professional-managerial class colonizes exclusive
spatial segments that connect with one another across
the city, the country, and the world; they isolate themselves
from the fragments of local societies, which in consequence
become destructured in the process of selective reorganization of work and residence. The new state, asserting its
sources of power in the control and strategic guidance of
knowledge, fosters the development of an advanced
technological infrastructure that scatters its elements
across undifferentiated locations and
interconnected secretive spaces.
(Manuel Castells)

We're gonna get dumped on, have this goddamn monorail
twenty feet up in the air, have to look at it every goddamn
day. And we're not gonna be able to use it!
(Rosemary Poveromo, community activist)

ON MARCH 2, 1994, a Continental jetliner skidded off Runway 13-31 at
LaGuardia Airport, dipping its massive, cone-shaped nose into Flushing Bay.
Although there were no injuries, the incident followed a U.S. Air accident two
years earlier that resulted in the deaths of twenty-seven people. The mishap in
March increased political pressure to expedite plans already under way to construct a runway safety overrun on land reclaimed from Flushing Bay. The
proposed overrun would add 460 feet of landfill to Runway 13-31, inciting
alarm and opposition among the people of East Elmhurst.

LaGuardia Airport, operated by the Port Authority of New York and New
Jersey (PANYNJ), has been an ongoing target of neighborhood activism.
Civic and block associations in East Elmhurst and nearby communities have
repeatedly skirmished with the Port Authority over the expansion of airport
facilities (such as airline terminals, parking lots, and airport service industries),
noise pollution, and, most recently, the Authority's plans to build a high-tech
Automated Guideway Transit system that would provide an elevated, light rail
connection between Manhattan's central business district and Queens
County's two airports, LaGuardia and JFK. For residents of East Elmhurst and
their representatives, the expansion of LaGuardia Airport has resulted in what

some have termed the *colonization* of their community and the deterioration of its quality of life. "The Port Authority and the city," City Councilwoman Helen Marshall told a *New York Times* reporter, "are more concerned about a land grab than they are about safety" (24 April 1994).[1]

Opposition to the safety overrun drew on a complex set of issues, concerns, and anxieties embedded in the social history of Corona–East Elmhurst. Residents were concerned about the impact that the safety overrun and other expansion projects would have on Flushing Bay and, in particular, on the quality of life in residential areas along its shores. The North Shore, which includes Ditmars Boulevard, an affluent black residential strip, has been a potent symbol of black upward mobility throughout the community's history. Residence on the North Shore signaled elite status, eliciting images of littoral leisure and opulence tied to its turn-of-the-century status as a resort area and its later development as "Doctors Row," an exclusive residential enclave for the professional and powerful. For contemporary residents, many of whom had lived through its pre-depression heyday, Ditmars Boulevard and the North Shore symbolized the delicate frontiers of black middle-class progress, a place in which a "past sleeps," as Michel de Certeau put it (1984).

This landscape of progress and achievement had been threatened since the early days of black settlement in East Elmhurst. The building of LaGuardia Airport and the construction of the Grand Central Parkway on landfill, displacing the shoreline one hundred yards into the bay, undermined the social capital of the North Shore just as African-Americans were making inroads into affluent and white East Elmhurst during the 1940s (see chapter 3). Subsequent development activities at LaGuardia Airport and in the bay area have similarly threatened the quality of black homeowners' lives, inflaming memories of the past and anxieties about the future.

In 1963 the New York City Parks Department, along with the World's Fair Corporation headed by Robert Moses, constructed an earthen dike extending twenty-eight hundred feet into Flushing Bay from the eastern end of LaGuardia Airport. The dike's purpose was to serve as a breakwater that would protect small craft docked at the newly constructed World's Fair Marina (City Planning Commission 1994). The dike, which came to be known as the "finger" by activists in East Elmhurst and surrounding areas, obstructed the tidal circulation of water in Flushing Bay, adding to an already severe problem of water pollution.

Though government authorities contested the finger's influence on the tidal flushing of the bay, it became a potent metaphor for East Elmhurst's struggles with the Port Authority over airport expansion issues. A *Newsday* reporter, attuned to this local symbolism, began his account of the battle over the runway safety overrun in this way: "Thirty years ago, legendary powerbroker Robert Moses gave Flushing Bay the finger" (20 April 1994). Beyond its metaphoric potential, the issue of the dike would provide a venue to activists for framing problems of airport expansion as questions of environmental justice.

Local residents were alarmed by the power and resources the Port Authority was able to wield to implement planning decisions that would affect the quality of their lives. Of all the public and private agencies with which activists negotiated land-use decisions, the Port Authority was perceived to be the least responsive to community pressure. "After years of working with the Port Authority," a black activist remarked at a Civic Association meeting in East Elmhurst, "I've seen their *arrogant* attitude with regard to community needs and their refusal to accept anything except the plan that *they've* offered. It's impossible to get them to change their minds, regardless of the problem."

Created by a treaty between the states of New York and New Jersey in 1921, the Port Authority of New York and New Jersey is relatively immune to political pressures and controls (Danielson and Doig 1982). PANYNJ, like the Metropolitan Transit Authority (MTA) and other public authorities, is a corporate subsidiary of government and, having a legal identity distinct from municipal government, is not subject to the direct control of the city's oversight agencies. Most authorities, for example, are not subject to the city's budget processes and can raise and spend money free of many of the city's administrative rules and laws governing personnel management, procurement activities, and project approvals. "For decades," Annemarie Hauck Walsh pointed out, "authorities have had considerably more influence over the physical and economic shape of the city than the City Planning Commission, the city council, and the line departments of city government" (1990:197).

Self-supporting and directed by twelve commissioners appointed by the governors of the two states, the Port Authority of New York and New Jersey has been a leading urban development instrument with far-reaching authority over the creation and operation of transportation and commerce-related facilities in the bistate region.

For residents of East Elmhurst, the Port Authority embodied power that was not only unaccountable and elusive but was also in the service of urban development policies that promoted the "outside" interests of Manhattan-based elites. Port Authority initiatives, such as the runway 13-31 safety overrun and futuristic Automated Ground Transit (AGT) system, were interpreted by residents as efforts to enhance the mobility of business and other Manhattan-based elite travelers or, as a PANYNJ booster publication put it, "the international movement of people and goods" (1994a:1).

During the summer of 1994 the Port Authority's plans to build the runway safety overrun and AGT system, as well as the continued presence of the finger would become flash points of neighborhood activism. Residents of East Elmhurst, Corona, and nearby communities would be faced with the challenge not only of resisting a form of authority that was relatively immune to local pressures but also of mobilizing against projects which, driven by regional economic and political forces, transgressed the place-bound interests and identities of local communities.

SCREAMING BLOODY MURDER

Plans to build a runway safety overrun were already under way when the Continental jet aborted takeoff and skidded off the end of runway 13-31 in March. The existing hundred-foot overrun, intended to provide a margin of safety for such emergencies, was far out of compliance with Federal Aviation Administration (FAA) guidelines which, after 1970, recommended safety areas of one thousand feet where feasible (City Planning Commission 1994).

The Port Authority's proposal for the overrun, submitted to the U.S. Army Corps of Engineers for review in 1992, called for the addition of a 690-foot safety zone at the eastern end of the runway. The twenty-acre safety area would be constructed on landfill, hydraulically pumped in from hopper barges temporarily moored in Flushing Bay. Linked to the overrun project in the Port Authority's plan was the partial removal of the 2,800-foot earthen dike, the finger, that had been built in 1963 to serve as a breakwater for the World's Fair Marina. In the proposal the 12-foot-high finger was to be shaved down to 3.2 feet above mean low-water level (that is, low tide), which would bring it down to the level of the adjacent mudflats. Lowering the breakwater to the level of the mudflats would serve to offset or mitigate the loss of tidal wetlands resulting from the construction of the safety overrun. And material removed from the finger was to be used as fill for constructing the overrun (U.S. Army Corps of Engineers 1992).

As early as 1985 Community Board 3 and activists in East Elmhurst voiced opposition to the construction of a safety overrun using landfill. A landfill overrun, they argued, would aggravate the water pollution problem in Flushing Bay by further restricting the circulation of water, particularly in the inner bay area. Instead, Community Board 3 and East Elmhurst civic leaders had asked the Port Authority to explore the possibility of constructing the safety overrun on pylons which, they argued, would reduce the problem of silt buildup and lessen the impact of the overrun on the flushing of the inner bay.

Activists argued that shaving the finger down to 3.2 feet *above* the mean low-water line, as the Port Authority proposed, would not adequately address the water circulation problem, since the earthen dike would remain above the water's surface at low tide. Instead, neighborhood activists proposed reducing the finger to six feet *below* the mean low-water line (City Planning Commission 1994).

Port Authority officials argued that building the overrun on pylons would be too expensive and would result in the closing of runway 13-31 for more than a year. On the finger issue, Port Authority officials contended that there was no evidence to suggest that dredging the finger down to the six-foot level recommended by the community would improve the tidal flushing of the bay.

Following the near disaster in March Mayor Rudolph Giuliani gave orders to expedite the overrun application's journey through the complex, bureaucratic approval process (*New York Times*, 24 April 1994). On March 8 the Port Authority's application was approved by the New York State Department of Environmental Conservation which determined that the overrun proposal posed no negative environmental impact. On March 14 the Port Authority's application was submitted to the New York City Department of Business Services in accordance with the rules of the city's Uniform Land Use Review Procedure (ULURP). ULURP approval, required for any project involving the disposition of city-owned lands, was needed by the Port Authority because the underwater land on which the safety overrun was to be constructed was owned by the City of New York. The approximately twenty-acre site would have to be leased by the city to the Port Authority as an addition to its LaGuardia Airport leasehold.

Through the ULURP procedure, the Port Authority's proposal would be subject to review by the community boards of the three neighborhoods affected by the project, a borough board composed of the chairpersons of three boards and their representatives on the City Council, the borough president of Queens, and, finally, the City Planning Commission. At the end of the process, the recommendations of the reviewing agencies would be submitted to the City Council, which would then vote on the application. Although the ULURP procedure enables community participation at public hearings held by the reviewing agencies and through the offices of the community boards, the reviewing agencies in the ULURP process play only an advisory role. The City Council ultimately approves or disapproves land-use decisions.

Under pressure from Mayor Giuliani and Queens Borough President Claire Shulman, the Port Authority's application for the safety overrun was expedited through the usually prolonged ULURP process. "We were very impressed by the speed of the application," a member of the City Planning Commission later told me. "The Giuliani people said that they wanted this application approved immediately. And that cut back on our ability to get all the information we were asking for from the Port Authority. And I think it also cut back on the public's ability to review that information and to make comments."

Community activists in East Elmhurst were also impressed by the accelerated review process. Less than a month after the Port Authority's ULURP application was filed, Community Board 3 held a public hearing on the overrun project. "What they have done this time is despicable," observed Barbara Coleman, an African-American member of the board. "Normally we have sixty days to make a decision. They shortened that to something like thirty days. And during that time a letter was sent to all board members [from the borough president], urging that we approve the airport overrun. And of course we all screamed bloody murder on the grounds that we are a volunteer agency, designed to serve the community and not the needs of the borough president or the mayor."

By a vote of 31 to 1, with one abstention, Community Board 3 adopted a resolution disapproving the Port Authority's ULURP application and noted that "the Port Authority has failed to give the Community Board rational alternatives to a landfill safety overrun and no specific information regarding the use of pilings" (City Planning Commission 1994:6). Furthermore, the board charged that the Port Authority had ignored its earlier recommendations to reduce the breakwater, or finger, to six feet below the mean low-water level. In addition to the environmental concerns expressed by the Community Board and activists in East Elmhurst, many perceived the runway safety overrun project to be part of a broader, long-term process of airport expansion that threatened not only to engulf the bay and adjacent neighborhoods but also to increase airplane traffic at LaGuardia. The Port Authority's apparent lack of responsiveness to community concerns, coupled with the speed with which the overrun project was being ferried through the complex ULURP approval process, exacerbated these fears.

"We've had to fight the Port Authority to help them understand that we're partners in this effort," Councilwoman Helen Marshall told *New York Newsday* as the controversy reached the press. "We have watched this bay shrink and shrink as the airport continues to grow" (16 April 1994). While Port Authority officials offered assurances that the overrun was a safety measure and not an *extension* of the runway, city officials evoked the issue of safety to thwart community opposition.

"We're doing what we can to address the issue of the bay," a spokesperson for the deputy mayor told the *New York Times*, "but the runway construction should not be held hostage while that's being determined" (24 April 1994).

"I would call anyone wrong who suggests that we're trying to put our community needs ahead of airport safety," Councilwoman Marshall retorted in the same *Times* article. "We use the airport, too. All we're saying here is 'Let's be fair and talk frankly with one another.'"

On April 18, and with the support of two of the three community boards in the bay area, Borough President Shulman recommended approval of the Port Authority's plan. "The critical public safety issues associated with the action," the recommendation read, "demand an expeditious review and approval." As a proviso, Shulman called for a "comprehensive analysis that identifies all possible options allowing for total removal of the dike and mud flat be completed" (City Planning Commission 1994, Appendix 1). Soon afterward Shulman, with the support of Queens Congressman Thomas Manton, made a request to Congress for $500,000 to fund an Army Corps of Engineers study exploring the "feasibility of dredging Flushing Bay to historic levels" (*Queens Chronicle*, 28 April 1994).

On April 20, two days after the borough president issued her recommendation, the City Planning Commission held a public hearing on the overrun application, the last step in the ULURP review process before its consideration by the City Council. Councilwoman Helen Marshall, who had played a leading role in organizing opposition to the overrun and other Port Authority projects, mobilized a group of activists from East Elmhurst to attend the hearing.

"They were certainly very well organized," Analisa Torres, a member of the City Planning Commission, remembered. "And they came in numbers. Generally we don't see a large group of people at Planning Commission matters. But in this case we had a group of mostly middle-aged to elderly, black middle-class and educated people, who made it clear that the Port Authority had ignored their need to have a clean, functioning bay.

"It was very impressive because, for one, they had all the technical know-how. You know, they were very well versed in the type of remedial action that needed to be taken—the dredging of the dike, the flushing actions [laughter] necessary. In other words, they came well prepared and well versed and were very persuasive."

The delegation from Corona–East Elmhurst, which included Councilwoman Marshall, Community Board 3 member Barbara Coleman, and representatives from the East Elmhurst Clergy Association and block and civic associations, testified against the Port Authority plan, renewing their demand that the overrun be built on pylons and that the earthen dike be excavated to six feet below mean low-water level. Residents also raised broader issues concerning the negative environmental impact of airport operation on noise levels and air quality, and charged that the community was being ignored in the planning of projects affecting the bay and surrounding communities.

The spokesperson from the Port Authority assured the Commission that there was no "master plan" to fill in Flushing Bay and that the landfill method of constructing the overrun would be cheaper and require less of a disruption of airport operations. On the question of the finger, the Port Authority official contended that reducing the finger to six feet below mean low-water level, as requested by the community, would have a significant impact on the bay and therefore would require a complete study by the New York State Department of Environmental Conservation and the U.S. Army Corps of Engineers.

Although the City Planning Commission supported the Port Authority's positions on the overrun and the finger, approving the application on May 16, commissioners voiced reservations about the project during their deliberations. One commissioner remembered: "Generally, there were remarks made about what seemed to be the callousness of the Port Authority. Most of us thought that it was typical that a huge, wealthy state agency would ignore, for so many years, the cries of this community. We did not think they had acted in good faith. Overwhelmingly, the Commission found the testimony of the public to be completely credible and the testimony of the Port Authority to be less credible."

On June 14, 1994, following the City Planning Commission's approval of the Port Authority's ULURP application, the City Council voted to approve the safety overrun project at LaGuardia Airport. Although community pressure had failed to modify the Port Authority's proposal for the safety overrun and removal of the finger, the opposition mobilized by activists, Councilwoman Marshall, and the Community Board educated residents and publicized complex concerns about airport expansion and the environmental integrity of Flushing Bay.

This widening of publicity, particularly in the print media, persuaded elected officials and the Port Authority to recognize and address some community concerns. Queens Borough President Shulman and Congressman Manton made commitments to pursue congressional funding for a study that would investigate ways of improving water quality in Flushing Bay. Moreover, the executive director of the Port Authority gave assurances to the speaker and majority leader of the City Council, Peter Vallone, that the Port Authority would take specific actions to improve the environmental quality of Flushing Bay (City Planning Commission 1994).

Equally important, mobilization against the overrun and the publicity that ensued educated residents, politicizing a range of interrelated environmental issues linked to airport operation and expansion. Questions concerning the impact of airport operation on air and water quality and noise levels, as well as on the ability of residents to influence land-use decisions, became subjects of discussion and debate in block and civic association networks and in other informal neighborhood settings.

"Their interpretation of the year 2000," a member of an East Elmhurst block association told me, not long after the overrun's approval, "is to have a large jet airport. And it was never meant to be that. It's too close to residential areas to have that kind of noise, air pollution, and everything. They're conjuring up one process after another. They come up with plan after plan, and we have to get after them. And it seems to have worked this time."

The frustration felt by activists in their attempts to hold the Port Authority accountable undermined their confidence in the established mechanisms of citizen participation, such as the community board system, the City Planning Commission, and other agencies and officials involved in the land review process. A block association activist, who would play a central role in East Elmhurst's next confrontation with the Port Authority over the AGT light rail system, questioned the ability of community boards to act effectively in the interests of local communities:

> My sense of community boards is that they are a part of the bigger picture, because they are part of the system. They're a part of the borough president's office, and I think that they perceive themselves as maintaining a relationship with the power structure. So, therefore, I don't believe that they can be effective as neutral agencies to deal with many of the community's complaints. I really don't. I think that they're all connected. It's like any other bureaucratic organization. You know, they get bogged down.

In their next encounter with the Port Authority, activists in East Elmhurst and Corona would work to constitute alternative political forums beyond the bureaucratic horizon of the "system." By sidestepping the official channels of political participation, this organizing effort not only expanded debate and deliberation concerning airport issues but also created alliances that stretched beyond the borders of "local community."

"IT AIN'T OVER TILL THE FAT LADY SINGS"

> You wanna know about the AGT? You know it's like you
> don't get hit by one car, you get hit by four, because they're
> following *right* behind each other.
> *(Barbara Coleman, community activist)*

On June 16 a public meeting jointly sponsored by the Ninety-sixth/Ninety-seventh Street Block Association and the East Elmhurst–Corona Civic Association was held at La Detente Restaurant, located on the outskirts of LaGuardia Airport. By 7:30 in the evening the spacious ballroom, ordinarily host to elegant wedding receptions and private parties, was filled to capacity with residents of East Elmhurst, Corona, and neighboring communities.

Near the entrance two women, representatives of the Ninety-sixth/Ninety-seventh Street Block Association, handed out information packets about the safety overrun project and the proposed Automated Guideway Transit system. A third distributed flyers announcing the public meeting. "It Ain't Over Till the Fat Lady Sings," it read. A member of the Overlook Block Association smirked and passed a newspaper clipping around to her neighbors reporting the City Council's almost unanimous approval of the Port Authority's safety overrun proposal the week before.

The assembly, numbering about sixty persons, was predominantly African-American, middle-aged, and female. Most were block association activists and many, like Shirley Clarke, Pat Beckles, and Arthur Hayes, were also active in the East Elmhurst–Corona Civic Association. Some represented public agencies and political organizations, such as Barbara Coleman, a member of Community Board 3 from Corona, and George Lopez, state assembly district leader and resident of Ditmars Boulevard. A handful of whites had come from nearby Jackson Heights and Astoria, where opposition to the airport projects was also gathering steam.

The La Detente meeting was organized by Joyce Cumberbatch, a retired deputy superintendent of schools and active member of East Elmhurst's Ninety-sixth/Ninety-seventh Street Block Association. With a membership roll of more than forty households, this block association had come to be known as the "pit bulls" for its aggressive stand on quality-of-life issues, particularly those relating to the airport.

In 1988, for example, the block association challenged the plans of a nearby, airport-area hotel to operate as a shelter for the homeless. Though opposition to the conversion of the Travelers Inn, triggered by a rash of home burglaries, focused initially on the presence of "undesirables" in the community, Cumberbatch and others succeeded in forging a new consensus among residents that directed attention to the homeless residents' living conditions at the hotel.

Cumberbatch explained:

> We forced [the owners] to put a cap on the number of people they could have at the hotel. And we said, "Okay, if you're going to have them there, you've got to treat them like human beings. You have to give them refrigerators. You have to make sure that the children are taken care of and that their education is not disturbed." We put those criteria in because we felt it wasn't fair to say, "We don't want it." 'Cause who are we to judge? After all, we could be in their situation one day.

Born in Jamaica, Cumberbatch moved to East Elmhurst from Harlem in 1958 where she had attended Harlem Hospital's school of nursing. "When I came here East Elmhurst was like an oasis," she told me in her living room, as jet engines roared overhead. "Slowly but surely the airport has encroached on us." Before getting involved in her block association, Cumberbatch had been active in school politics and community affairs in Brooklyn and in Laurelton and Springfield Gardens in south Queens. After retiring from her job and assuming additional responsibilities in the care of her ninety-eight-year-old mother, Cumberbatch directed her energies to community issues in East Elmhurst. "This area has been very good to me. So I said, 'The only way I can pay back what I've received is to get involved with the AGT issue.'"

As the Port Authority's plans to build the safety overrun and AGT system drew increasing publicity in the spring of 1994, Cumberbatch began discussing the airport issues informally with her neighbors. She also began to investigate reports from neighbors of elevated cancer rates in areas adjacent to the airport. In May the president of the Ninety-sixth/Ninety-seventh Street Block Association suggested that Cumberbatch convene a meeting in her house to address the airport problems.

The meeting's purpose, she later told me, was not only to build a consensus of opinion among her neighbors concerning the airport issues but also to articulate a position that would present the community's opposition to the Port Authority's plans as an issue of environmental justice, rather than as a reactive, "not-in-my-backyard" response to neighborhood change:

> I heard this same rhetoric going over and over again: "We don't need this; we don't want this." But nothing to support why it shouldn't be. I thought that we needed some hard evidence of why it should not be, rather than simply taking an emotional stand. I felt that the Port Authority would listen to that more carefully than neighborhoods just saying, "Not in my backyard," as an emotional issue. Because that's how the Port Authority would interpret it, although it's more than that. If we just say, "Hey, it's our neighborhood, we don't want this," it becomes a NIMBY thing—that communities don't want anything new in their neighborhood. And that's not true. It's true in one sense, but it's also the hazard that it's going to bring into the area—the change of our lifestyle—that we're against.

Key to the strategy pursued by Cumberbatch and the newly formed block association subcommittee were the goals of technical empowerment and coalition building. Familiarity with the "hard evidence" of urban development and its environmental effects, the subcommittee believed, would be crucial both to comprehending the Port Authority's plan and to developing, as Cumberbatch put it, a "proactive" position, rooted in an informed and critical analysis of its complex technical features and environmental implications. On the recommendation of her daughter, Stacy, a program officer with the Joyce Mertz–Gilmore Foundation in Manhattan, Cumberbatch contacted the New York Public Interest Research Group (NYPIRG), a not-for-profit public watchdog and advocacy organization, and the New York City Environmental Justice Alliance, a coalition of environmental justice organizations directed by Michelle Depasse.

At the committee's first meeting, held on May 26, 1994, at Cumberbatch's home, block association members met with Depasse and George Haikalis, a Manhattan-based transportation consultant and advocate for "auto-free" rail development. Also at the meeting was NYPIRG environmental justice advocate Steven Romalewski, a specialist on water pollution. While Depasse and Romalewski discussed the possible environmental impact that the safety overrun could have on Flushing Bay and the surrounding neighborhood, Haikalis provided a critical analysis of the Port Authority's AGT proposal, highlighting, in particular, its lack of integration into existing rail transportation systems.

The block association's outreach to organizations that were addressing environmental and transportation questions not only in the context of the regional political economy but also as issues of environmental justice provided ways of rearticulating local, "backyard" interests in the technical and systems-focused jargon of urban planning and as issues of regional fairness.

Cumberbatch later emphasized the empowering quality of this technical competence and regional perspective: "I know that the Port Authority wasn't very happy with us having those people in, our technical assistants. Because it escalated the issue. You know, it gave it a new dimension, which I don't think they were really expecting to have. They thought it was gonna be the same old N-I-M-B-Y."

The committee's second emphasis was on coalition building. Both the safety overrun plan and the AGT would affect a number of Queens communities. In the case of the latter, the proposed path or "alignment" of the AGT would affect areas of northern and southern Queens, as well as Manhattan's Upper East Side. Although, in the case of the AGT, the Port Authority's Airport Access Program had outreached to elected officials and community boards and held "scoping," or community orientation, hearings in certain areas, many felt that these processes had been poorly publicized and, more to the point, funneled information and debate into official, bureaucratic enclaves, thereby hindering communication and coalition building among neighborhoods.

Cumberbatch highlighted the Port Authority's divisive practices of community outreach, which would remain a central theme in activist critique during the airport struggle:

> I don't know if the Port Authority's approach to us was to separate and conquer. Everybody's done that throughout history. But I saw this. They worked with Community Board 3 but not with Community Board 1 (Astoria), nor with the people down in Jamaica. So we weren't in communication and I think that's terrible, because we all have the same issues. And if we had a collective voice we would be heard. I then decided, since I saw what they were doing—I decided that this piece was missing and I organized the meeting at La Detente to get the communities at least communicating, getting to know one another.

Before the June 16 meeting at La Detente, Cumberbatch began networking with activists from other communities that would be affected by the Port Authority's projects. A friend in Jamaica gave her the names of two women who led civic groups in predominantly black southern Queens. Cumberbatch later visited these groups to provide them with information about the AGT. "They had been kept in the dark by their community boards," she later said, adding that their community boards had declined to meet with officials of PANYNJ's Airport Access Program. Again, working through informal channels, Cumberbatch contacted Rose Marie Poveromo, president of the powerful United Community Civic Association (UCCA) of Astoria, through a visiting nurse attending her mother. "I knew she was from Astoria. So I asked her who should I contact there. That's how I found Rose Marie."

Poveromo, along with community activists from Jamaica and Jackson Heights, attended the La Detente meeting. They were joined by Lou Blain, a NYPIRG advocate, Michelle Depasse, the executive director of the New York State Environmental Justice Alliance, and George Haikalis, transportation advocate, all of whom were to give presentations on the Port Authority projects.

Cumberbatch opened the meeting, emphasizing the importance of being informed about technical matters pertaining to the Port Authority's plans for the safety overrun and for the AGT system: "The reason for this meeting tonight is that it's necessary for you to have information of a technical nature. Statistics on what is happening at the airport—the toxicity levels. All these things are imperative in making up one's mind as to how we should approach this Automatic Guided Train that will be coming into our area in—I think the year is 2004."

Some nodded in agreement. Others scrutinized the Port Authority's undecipherable plans for the safety overrun project, mulling over technical drawings and debating the meaning of such engineering terms as *turbidity curtain* and *rip rap*.

"If you look at the data they gave us," Cumberbatch continued, "and the timetable, they're starting to make inroads now. So rather than wait until they have done their planning, and their planning hasn't included us, it is very important that we be on it and be educated consumers so that we'll know exactly what they're planning to do in our community. And it's also important that the Port Authority take us *all* into consideration. And that means Long Island City, Astoria, Jackson Heights, East Elmhurst, Corona, and going down to Jamaica."

The themes of empowerment through access to information and coalition building across neighborhood lines remained focal points of discussion and debate during the two-hour meeting. The complexity and magnitude of the proposed AGT system challenged residents to decipher and appraise the multitude of technical, engineering decisions underwriting the plan, for example, the Port Authority's decision to build an elevated and automated or "pilotless" system. It also forced them to consider the AGT's impact on the regional economy and environment.

Port Authority officials and boosters of the AGT project typically expressed its importance and urgency in terms of the impact that passenger access to the Queens airports has on the city's ability to compete as a "world city" in an increasingly global economy. A key theme in this discourse of regional and global competitiveness, as Logan and Molotch have noted, "is the assertion that local growth 'makes jobs'" (1987:88).[2]

In *Access*, a PANYNJ newsletter, Port Authority Executive Director Stanley Brezenoff recalled an anecdote that linked the corporate "stress" resulting from problems of airport access to the flight of capital from the city:

> An executive from a national architectural firm was complaining the other day about the traffic-clogged highways around New York's airports. She travels two or three times a week for her company, which is headquartered in New York. Her single biggest complaint and source of stress is that travel time to and from the airport is completely unpredictable. She has missed flights, costing her company business. So she now schedules twice as much time to get to the airport as she thinks should be necessary. She doesn't miss flights, but she wastes valuable time in a slow boil of irritation. (1994a:1)

"Such frustrations," Brezenoff continued, "can be an important force in persuading businesses to leave the area and in keeping away businesses considering a move."

> Firms that have relocated from the New York area have said that poor access to airports is the second most important reason for leaving. Conventions and tourism suffer without convenient, dependable and safe links to the airports. The ripple effect from such losses hurts hotels, restaurants, shops and, in the end, virtually everyone who lives and works here. The airports alone contribute between three and four percent of the annual Gross Regional Product. Everyone agrees that airport access must be improved. (1994a:2)

Claims of the importance of airport access to checking the flight of capital from New York City and, in turn, stimulating economic development and "job growth," provided the AGT proposal with a form of macroeconomic authority which local activists, as we shall see, struggled to penetrate and contest. With varying degrees of success, activists challenged both the economic logic and fairness of this mode of world city development (implied in the "ripple effect" narrative) and specific technical aspects of the Port Authority's plan to realize it.

Their ability to challenge this ideology of global economic development and mobilize local opposition to its processes rested in part on their ability to critically evaluate these claims and their legitimating narratives. It also required that they recast their political interests, identities, and allegiances in a manner reflecting the new alignments of power that were being formed through processes of global economic restructuring, alignments of power being facilitated or, better, "greased" through developments in the region's transportation infrastructure.

For residents of East Elmhurst and Corona, this recasting of identity involved a double, seemingly contradictory, movement. Mobilization required in part an affirmation of community-based interests, identities, and political relationships. However, opposition to the Port Authority's regional growth strategy and "deterritorialized" ideology of global competitiveness required activists to recognize and formulate their needs, interests, and allegiances in ways that projected beyond the frontiers of neighborhood-based politics. Place-based identities, bound by administrative designations of "community" and by historically significant constructions of racial, class and ethnic identities, offered politically ineffective positions from which to oppose the regional and global development strategies and discourses of the Port Authority's growth machine (see Harvey 1989).

Manuel Castells has highlighted the dilemma confronted by grass-roots activists in the "space of flows," a concept he uses to describe the increasingly mobile circuits of power and capital linked to postindustrial modes of capital accumulation:

> At the cultural level, local societies, territorially defined, must preserve their identities, and build upon their historical roots, regardless of their economic and functional dependence upon the space of flows. The symbolic marking of places, the presentation of symbols of recognition, the expression of collective memory in actual practices of communication, are fundamental means by which places may continue to exist as such, without having to justify their existence by the fulfillment of their functional performance. However, to avert the danger of over-affirmation of a local identity without reference to any broader social framework of reference at least two additional strategies are required: on the one hand, they must build communication codes with other identities, codes that require the definition of communities as sub-cultures; and on the other they must link the affirmation and symbolic practice of cultural identity to economic policy and political practice. They may thereby overcome the dangers of tribalism and fundamentalism. (1989:351)

This problem of linking or aligning the symbolic practice of identity to increasingly deterritorialized networks or "flows" of power constitutes a formidable challenge for activists in the postindustrial, post–civil rights era. In returning now to the mobilizing efforts of activists in East Elmhurst, I want to highlight this dilemma by exploring how it is experienced and negotiated by people in local communities. I also suggest that the possibilities for addressing it, for articulating links between symbolic practice of identity at the local level and the wider political economy, are structured in important ways by the configuration of the public sphere, the public spaces where people, through their collective actions, render power visible and, in turn, recognize themselves as political subjects.

The efforts of the Ninety-sixth/Ninety-seventh Street Block Association and their supporters to gain access to technical information, to form coalitions, and to create public forums for publicizing the environmental impact of the Port

Authority's projects served to widen the scope of public deliberation and debate, thus enabling a rearticulation of localized, place-based identities within the broader context of regional political and economic processes (cf. Fraser 1989).

"Let me say first," began Lou Blain, a NYPIRG environmental organizer, "I am an environmentalist, but I want it to be clear that that does not mean I think differently than anyone else. I just want to make sure that I have a healthy city to live in."

Blain paused briefly, surveyed the restless audience, and continued: "I think that we all share a concern for our personal space, our family space, our neighborhood space. And we want to protect that, not by hurting other neighborhoods—by putting it over there. We want to protect all our neighborhoods because we want to live in a safe and healthy city. Sometimes *environmentalism* is an alienating term and I want to make sure that it is not."

Like the speakers who would follow, Blain stressed the importance of addressing quality-of-life, environmental issues within a regional framework and encouraged residents to understand the impact of the runway overrun within the broader context of Flushing Bay's pollution problem. After handing out maps plotting sewage treatment facilities in the bay area, Blain detailed the city's plans for cleaning up the bay, including the Environmental Protection Agency's controversial plan to construct sewage storage tanks in Flushing Meadows–Corona Park.

Joyce Cumberbatch then introduced the next speaker, George Haikalis, an advocate of rail transportation systems. "Good," a black woman blurted. "But where the hell were you when we were fighting them about the overrun?"

The audience listened attentively as Haikalis described the Port Authority's plan for the Automated Guideway Transit system in detail. The proposal called for elevated, computer-operated trains that would originate at a central terminal on the Upper East Side of Manhattan, cross the Queensboro Bridge, and follow railroad and highway routes or "right of ways" to LaGuardia and Kennedy airports (Figure 7.1).

Haikalis and other critics of the AGT system were opposed to the construction of a discrete and high-tech airport access system that would not be compatible with the city's mass transit infrastructure. Instead, Haikalis contended, an airport access system should make use of and, where necessary, extend existing subway lines and roadbeds. This, he argued, would make the system accessible to users traveling to and from a wider range of locations. The Port Authority's proposed system would provide relatively few links or transfer points between subway lines and the AGT and would restrict ridership de facto to airport passengers and employees.

This latter restriction, a particular bone of contention among Queens residents, was the result of the funding mechanism that would be used to finance the project. The estimated $2.6 billion cost of the AGT system would be

Figure 7.1. Edward J. O'Sullivan, director of the Port Authority's airport access
program, poses with a model of the AGT light rail train.

financed by a Passenger Facility Charge (PFC). Under this federally authorized program, the Port Authority is empowered by the FAA to collect a PFC
tax on airline tickets to finance improvements in airport facilities, such as the
renovation or expansion of terminals. However, FAA regulations governing
the program stipulated that PFC funds must benefit airport passengers only. By
proposing to finance the AGT with PFC funds, the Port Authority was "dedi-
cating" the system to airport passengers. Although nonairport travelers would
not be excluded from riding the system, they would pay fares well beyond
those of the public transit system and as high as ten dollars.

When Haikalis finished, a woman from East Elmhurst called out, "I'm not
gonna take no train to the airport. The people who are going to benefit are the
people from Manhattan." A chorus of grumbles echoed her sentiment. Many
felt that the Port Authority was again running roughshod over the neighborhood, in this case privileging the needs of Manhattan-based airport travelers
over the quality-of-life concerns of local Queens communities. People were
well aware that construction activities related to a project of this magnitude
would involve a disruption of neighborhood life for a period of years.

Barbara Coleman, an African-American member of Community Board 3,
you'll recall, asked Haikalis, "What can we do to change this? It's impossible
to get them to change their minds. They don't live in East Elmhurst. They
don't see out their window, a thirty-foot train hanging over them. This is ridic-
ulous. And I want from you some ideas to get them to change their minds."

Haikalis, who had worked with community boards and civic groups in Manhattan also opposed to the AGT, responded:

> The fact is we need to work together to build a collaboration to beat this project. And the question is whether we should defeat all airport access or come up with a constructive solution that will make us happy as well. And I say that for an important reason. The airports are major employers, and the largest proportion of workers at the two airports in Queens come from Queens. And we don't want these people to pack up and go to New Jersey.

Many in the audience were skeptical of such propositions, which seemed to call on them to sacrifice their quality-of-life in the interest of an abstract concept of regional competition.

Rose Marie Poveromo, Astoria's UCCA president, had been listening attentively to the comments of Coleman and others from East Elmhurst and raised her hand to speak. "The [PANYNJ] airport access people have contacted us in Astoria," she began. "And my membership is *not* happy with it."

"That's right," exclaimed Barbara Coleman, sitting behind her. Poveromo had been invited to the meeting by Joyce Cumberbatch but had never met any of the other black activists at the meeting. During the course of Poveromo's comments, Coleman and others from Corona–East Elmhurst punctuated her statements with declarations of support. Encouraged, Poveromo stood and continued.

> ROSE POVEROMO: So . . . um, we're not unique. I think all of us together have indicated, not only to the Port Authority but also to the mayor and his very inept Department of City Planning—
>
> BARBARA COLEMAN: Yes—
>
> RP: —that we in Queens County have *had* it!
>
> BC: That's right!
>
> RP: We are *sick*—sick and tired of being dumped on.
>
> BC: And tired—
>
> RP: The airport access, the monorail, right where we— they can give it any fancy name they want. The people of Queens County *will* not benefit from the air— from the monorail. It will not be for our use unless we travel from Manhattan to the airport every *day* and go on a plane. We as residents of Queens County, who are going to have to live with this—this *monster* twenty feet up in the air—and all the pylons, and the graffiti, and the dirt up underneath these . . . uh . . . this so-called high railing, will not be able to use this access train. It will only be for the use of an airline traveler or personnel at the airports. This is a disgrace. The City of New York—the system is down. It's not only down with the Port Authority. It's down with every system. The left hand doesn't know what the right hand is doing. Foster care, child welfare, the City of New York, the Department of City Planning, the mayor's office, the governors office, the

state—this system is down. And unless we all band together, all of us—community boards, civic associations—

BC: That's right!

RP: —block associations, all of us, we will not accomplish anything in Queens County. We all must stand together, fight together, be vocal and militant, in order for these people who *we* put in office . . . ah. . . understand that we will not reelect them unless *they* come back and *do what we want. We're* payin' the goddamn *taxes* here!

When the applause died down, Haikalis continued, nodding his head in sympathy:

HAIKALIS: Well, I . . . I just wanted to say one thing about—I live in Manhattan. But, basically, people who live in Nassau and Suffolk Counties and work in Manhattan take the Long Island Railroad through Queens during rush hour— and if those people were to drive through Queens, it would be a mess. I think you have to look at this from a systems point of view. We *do* need a way for people to get to—

RP: Yeah, but you misunderstand—excuse me, sir, with all due respect, the people who live in Nassau and Suffolk Counties—unless they're goin' to the airport and getting on a plane, they will not be able to use the monorail—

BC: Thank you!

RP:If they're working in Manhattan they cannot use the monorail. If they're working in Queens County, they cannot use the monorail—

BC: Thank you!

RP: If we residents live here, we cannot use the monorail—

BC: We can't use the monorail.

RP: We're gonna get dumped on, have this goddamn thing twenty feet up in the air, have to look at it every goddamn day, but we're not gonna be able to use it.

BC: Right!

Haikalis *had* misunderstood. Poveromo's comments were not to be read as a reactive, NIMBY response to change, pitting the interests of local communities against the greater good of the region. In fact Poveromo, Cumberbatch, and others *were* thinking globally and raising important questions about the fairness or evenness of regional development policies, procedures, and their legitimating discourses. As Joyce Cumberbatch later put it: "My community is New York City. It's Corona, Astoria, Manhattan, and everywhere else."

Following Haikalis's presentation, residents asked a barrage of questions about specific design features of the proposed AGT system. An East Elmhurst woman asked about luggage space on the trains. She had heard that AGT trains would only have room for light, carry-on bags which she felt was evidence that the system was being developed exclusively for business travelers. Another challenged the claim that airport employees would have access to the system:

"No matter where you get on, you have to have a plane ticket." An elderly man asked what effect train vibration would have on the stability of homes.

Shirley Clark, president of the Ninety-sixth/Ninety-seventh Street Block Association, asked, "How will it affect our property values if it does go through."

Coleman turned in her seat to respond: "You're kidding. You have a house, and out in front of your window is a thirty-foot train!" Coleman asked Haikalis to provide a list of organizations people could contact to lend their support to an alternative airport access plan.

City Councilwoman Helen Marshall, who had arrived late, asked Haikalis detailed questions about the alternative route supported by his organization. "I don't want any goddamn trains in front of the houses on Ditmars Boulevard," she declared. The audience applauded. "We've done everything to protect that view corridor and Flushing Bay. And now, to put a train across there is problematic." Marshall agreed that the AGT was being designed to serve Manhattan business travelers. Further, she pointed out, the airlines were opposed to the use of the Passenger Facilities Charge for the AGT system. Instead, they wanted PFC funds to be used for improving the airport terminals.

As more people spoke, providing new information and new grounds for opposing the AGT, the audience became increasingly boisterous. Hamlet Wallace, the African-American chair of Community Board 3's Aviation Committee, testified that the Port Authority had come to the board and made "a fictitious presentation playing on people's intelligence—the works." He stood and faced the audience:

> One group gets one bit of information, which is not correct, or only half-baked. Another gets another bit of information. The Port Authority is hoping that we will not come together and that we won't understand what the other person is doing, which is their method of approach. All of us have to get together. This way we can make an impact. Otherwise, we're not gonna get anywhere.

Wallace's appeal sparked a thunder of applause. Latecomers to the meeting peered into the packed room through the doorway, raising themselves on tiptoes to get a better view. When the applause subsided, Cumberbatch stepped forward:

> This was my purpose—to get us together so we could communicate and be in alignment with one another. Because if we're not, they're gonna shoot us all down. And it's so important. Each one of you represents about thirty other people, so this is great, this is a good working group. Now what we have to do is plan precisely what our next moves will be.

Cumberbatch's suggestion led to a flurry of conversations across the room. Rose Marie Poveromo announced that her group, the United Community Civic Association of Astoria, would hold a public meeting in late September, which would bring community boards and civic associations in northern Queens together to discuss community concerns. She reiterated the charge made earlier that the Port Authority was carrying out a strategy of "divide and conquer" to contain and fragment community opposition to the project:

> What the Port Authority has done, and they are notorious for this, is to go to you and speak to you, go to me and speak to my association. What they're trying to do is divide and conquer. They're very smart. They're calling it "airport access" and "reaching out to the community." But what they should have done, and what they should do, is call *one* huge meeting at LaGuardia and involve us all, bring us all together, and tell one story. They haven't done that.

Like the speakers before her, Poveromo stressed the link between coalition building and the widening of the political space of community activism. The Port Authority's practices of divide and conquer served to fragment and constrict community participation and opposition, as well as to regulate access to information—information concerning the wider, systemic impact of the AGT project and, as Wallace pointed out, about "what the other person is doing." In this way PANYNJ's Airport Access strategy tended to interpellate and buttress place-bound constructions of identity, interests, and needs by channeling access to information and citizen participation through existing political formations and procedures.

In contrast, activist appeals to "get together," to "be in alignment with one another" (a telling appropriation of the Port Authority's technical jargon), and to confront the Port Authority in "one huge meeting" expressed the need to transgress these static, bureaucratic frontiers and construct a broader and more heterogeneous political space.

Barbara Coleman, raising her voice against the escalating din, turned to Poveromo and told her that community groups from Jamaica in the south should also be invited to the public forum in Astoria, which was planned for mid-September. Poveromo, turning around in her chair to face Coleman, replied: "Yes. And what we need from you is names and addresses of those organizations that *we* don't know how to reach out to."

"Yes, a list," Coleman said.

Phil Secone, president of the Jackson Heights Neighborhood Association, which worked closely with Community Board 3 and the East Elmhurst–Corona Civic Association, said to Poveromo that he would provide her with a mailing list. Cumberbatch gestured to the representatives from Jamaica, reiterating the invitation to attend the Astoria meeting and participate in the coalition.

One of the three African-American women from Jamaica stood to respond. The audience settled down.

> I'm the former president of the United Neighborhood Association and this . . . ah . . . has been rich and very informative. We were not aware of the impact that this kind of thing would have on our community. And now that I've been made aware

tonight of all the things that are going on, I certainly will be bringing it up with my community people. Also, with *our* community board. Community Board 12 represents us, and I don't really know where they stand at this point.

Her testimony provoked a new round of applause and animated cross-talking. Activists from Jamaica and other neighborhoods in southeast Queens were seldom seen and heard at civic meetings in the north. City Councilwoman Marshall stressed the importance of understanding the AGT's impact on Jamaica. Coleman agreed: "The Airport Access people should go down there to Jamaica and make a presentation," she declared, tightening her brow and jabbing her index finger in the air. "And let's see what *they* think!"

The public meeting at La Detente not only underscores the fluidity of political and place-based identities but also sheds light on the social practices and relations through which those positions are socially constructed and negotiated. For during the course of the three-hour meeting, activists advanced various interpretations of their identities and interests vis-à-vis the Port Authority's plans, ranging from narrow, homeowner anxieties about property values and "train vibration" to more systemic and generalized concerns about the environmental impact and social equity of elite-driven urban growth strategies.

The articulation of these broader, alliance-producing conceptions of interest and identity by activists was enabled in part by the character of their opponent: not only did the PANYNJ projects threaten to affect many communities, but its corporate-focused discourse of "global competitiveness" also pit the needs of a formless and nomadic "business community" against those of, what Port Authority officials called, "the neighborhoods." However, equally important were the deliberate efforts of Joyce Cumberbatch and others to collaborate with activists from other community groups and citywide advocacy organizations, and create a political forum outside the territorially based, officially sanctioned institutions of neighborhood government. As activists repeatedly stated, participation through these venues had impeded communication and coalition building across neighborhood borders, enabling PANYNJ to pursue its strategy of divide and conquer.

In following the Port Authority's efforts to win approval of the Automated Guideway Transit system, I direct attention to this practice of divide and conquer and to the opposing efforts of activists in Corona and East Elmhurst to forge alliances and construct their political identities in transneighborhood terms. I stress the degree to which political mobilization and, indeed, demobilization depend on the capacity to mediate and govern the social practices and relations through which identities and differences are produced. "Hegemonic power," Edward Soja and Barbara Hooper note, "does not simply manipulate naively given differences between individuals and social groups, it actively *produces and reproduces difference* as a key strategy to create and maintain modes of social and spatial division that are advantageous to its continued empowerment" (1993:184). As we shall see, this cultivation of social and spatial division by the Port Authority and its allies was the key to its strategy of undermining resistance to the AGT from "the neighborhoods."

Joyce Cumberbatch's charge to the audience at the end of the meeting both warned of the danger of these divisions and named the possibility of a transneighborhood alliance:

> So where do we go from here? Now we have to decide. "Can we align under one program so that we're united? Because if we're not united, we're not gonna get nothing but pylons up in the air. See that's why Astoria is here, Jackson Heights and Corona are here. East Elmhurst is here, and Jamaica. Two of the largest civic associations in Jamaica are recognized right here. So now we've got to get together with a name and move.

"MORE BOUNCE FOR THE OUNCE"

On June 28, almost two weeks after the public meeting at La Detente, officials of PANYNJ's Airport Access Program met at LaGuardia Airport with activists representing Corona and East Elmhurst. The committee, composed largely of members of the Aviation Committee of Community Board 3, had met with PANYNJ officials on a number of occasions in the past weeks. Although neither the committee nor Community Board 3 had the power to veto the AGT proposal, their opposition could influence public officials and the media, particularly during key phases of the AGT project's development and public review. The mission of the Port Authority's Airport Access Program was, in large part, to assemble public support for the project and quell community opposition.

At earlier meetings with the Port Authority, the committee had voiced concerns about the AGT's impact in the area of Ditmars Boulevard where its planned route along the Grand Central Parkway would obstruct residents' "view corridors" of Flushing Bay. In response, the Port Authority had developed alternative alignments for the AGT that were to be presented at the LaGuardia Airport meeting by PANYNJ consultants.

However, the public meeting at La Detente had changed the playing field by widening the scope of community concerns about the AGT and thus including new players in the game. The meeting had provided a forum where local activists were exposed to regional transportation and environmental justice issues and to planning alternatives. Residents had raised questions about the overall design and impact of the AGT and, in particular, its preferential accommodation of elite business travelers at the expense of the needs and concerns of Queens residents. This widening of debate and proliferation of contested issues stretched the concerns of activists beyond the narrow issue of the "view corridor," which had been the focus of earlier negotiations with PANYNJ.

The La Detente meeting had also provided residents of East Elmhurst and Corona, including members of the Aviation Committee of Community Board 3, with the opportunity to network with civic activists from other areas and, in the process, rearticulate place-bound, local identities and interests in transneighborhood terms. To the surprise and chagrin of Port Authority officials, Corona–East Elmhurst's meeting with the Airport Access Program team was also attended by activists from Astoria (Community Board 1) and by the environmental justice and public transportation advocates who had spoken at the La Detente meeting. Also attending were Joyce Cumberbatch and members of the Ninety-sixth/Ninety-seventh Street Block Association.

PANYNJ's response to this broadening of representation and debate was to funnel deliberation about the AGT into enclaved areas of technological expertise and problem solving, which, as Nancy Fraser has noted in a similar context, operates to "shield such matters from generalized contestation and from widely disseminated conflicts of interpretation" (1989:168). This technocratic management of deliberation about the AGT served not only to depoliticize the project by shielding broader and more complex questions of social justice from contestation, it also interpellated and affirmed narrow, place-bound constructions of identity, needs, and interests.

First the community outreach strategy of PANYNJ's Airport Access Program emphasized links with community boards and local elected officials, which encouraged activists to formulate their concerns and interests within administratively defined political and neighborhood boundaries. Second, in their negotiations with activists, Port Authority officials and their consultants would direct discussion and debate to issues that focused narrowly on the AGT's impact on East Elmhurst, thus shielding wider regional environmental and urban development concerns from contestation.

Community activists filed into the small meeting room, set back from the art deco lobby of LaGuardia's Marine Air Terminal, once home to Pan American Airlines "clipper" service. A team of Port Authority officials and consultants greeted people as they arrived. A PANYNJ employee served refreshments. The conference table at the center of the room could not seat the unexpectedly large group of twenty. Extra chairs were provided for Poveromo and the other activists from Astoria, and for Joyce Cumberbatch and two other members of the Ninety-sixth/Ninety-seventh Street Block Association. George Haikalis and the representatives from NYPIRG and the New York City Environmental Justice Alliance sat on a leather couch set against the wall.

Helen Sears, an outreach specialist with PANYNJ's Airport Access Program, opened the meeting, stressing the evolution and durability of PANYNJ's negotiations with "the community." This narrative of orderly step-by-step pro-

progress toward the resolution of disputes would often be invoked by PA-NYNJ officials to keep the discussion on track:

> Needless to say, the community worked very closely with the Airport Access, and the Airport Access with the community, to come to some agreement. I can tell you it's a very arduous past, because we went back to the drawing board time and time again. It wasn't something that could happen overnight, and it wasn't something that could be done in one short meeting or with one design. We turned out developing many, many designs that we presented to this committee. And at the last meeting we presented several options to the committee. One of the options was very acceptable to the committee. We went back and, as a result, that particular option is something that is going to be discussed tonight and I think the committee will find it very suitable.

Then, as if to give public authority to this seamless narrative of dialogue and compromise, the PANYNJ official held up a newspaper article that had been published three days earlier. "And certainly," she began, "you're all familiar with the article that was in the paper. If not, I did bring copies just in case some of you did not see it. It was in Saturday's *Newsday*, talking about how the Airport Access has worked in the community, exactly what the plan is, how that concession has been made, and how the alignment has changed somewhat to keep most of your community and the vision intact."

The article, entitled "E[ast] Elmhurst Gets Way on Airport Rail," reported that the Port Authority had agreed to construct the East Elmhurst section of the AGT system below ground to preserve homeowners' views of Flushing Bay. To the surprise of those at the meeting, it continued: "The move, cheered by East Elmhurst residents and politicians, is expected to add $10 million to the planned $2.6 billion rail project." Queens borough President Claire Shulman was cited as crediting Port Authority officials with "responding to community concerns." Congressman Thomas Manton added that the agreement "represents some progress to satisfy the community so [the Port Authority] can get along with the bigger picture of linking the two airports" (*Newsday*, 27 June 1994).

The *Newsday* article announced East Elmhurst's acceptance of the Port Authority's compromise proposal three days before it had been presented to the community. This incident of manufacturing consent would not go unchallenged for long.

While residents were ruminating over the *Newsday* article, Helen Sears introduced Peter, the Port Authority consultant who was to discuss the routing alternatives that had been considered for the East Elmhurst section of the AGT. Supported by aerial photographs mapping the different alignments in myriad colors and by an assortment of technical drawings, Peter explained the strengths and weaknesses of the routes considered and presented the Port Authority's compromise proposal.

In response to community concerns that the AGT's elevated alignment along the Grand Central Parkway would block the view of Flushing Bay, the Port Authority had agreed to construct the East Elmhurst portion of the AGT below ground level. The AGT, Peter explained, would be "in an elevated condition" from the Queensboro Bridge to LaGuardia Airport. After leaving the airport, the AGT would drop below ground level as it passed along Flushing Bay in East Elmhurst, and then rise once more as it turned south to Kennedy Airport.

"Excuse me," interrupted Rose Marie Poveromo, motioning with her hand. "For those of us who are uneducated here . . . ah . . . what streets are we talking about? I mean you're showing me drawings but you're not mentioning street names." Faltering at first, the PANYNJ consultant gave names to the anonymous streets in the aerial photograph, pointing out where the AGT would meet the Grand Central Parkway in Astoria, skirt along the parkway to LaGuardia, and, on leaving the airport, drop down just below ground level as it passed through East Elmhurst. Poveromo shook her head in defiance and exchanged censuring glances with Joan DaCorta, president of the Astoria Heights Homeowners and Tenants Association. A flurry of questions followed.

Pat Beckles, a civil engineer and president of East Elmhurst's powerful Ditmars Boulevard Block Association, asked the consultant how the revised "below grade" alignment of the AGT would affect the view of the bay for homeowners living on Ditmars Boulevard. The PANYNJ consultant responded by displaying a series of drawings on large poster boards, depicting the AGT's new "depressed" alignment in relation to the homes on Ditmars Boulevard overlooking the bay.

In the illustration the AGT tracks were enclosed in a tube, partially depressed below ground level. The top of the tube, which protruded about six feet above ground, was capped by a concrete ceiling. The ground next to the tunnel had been built up, forming a landscaped slope, or berm, from the tunnel's roof to the parkland fronting on Flushing Bay. Dotted "sight lines" in the drawing traced unobstructed "visual corridors" from the homes on Ditmars Boulevard, over the depressed tunnel, and down to Flushing Bay. The consultant passed the awkward poster boards around the room for people to examine.

Rose Marie Poveromo waved her hand to speak. "I don't understand," she began, raising her voice precipitously. "If you could accommodate one community so it would have a view of the bay, why couldn't you bury the entire thing so every community would be accommodated?" (The *Newsday* article had in fact registered this alarm on the part of Astoria activists, who felt that PANYNJ was using a strategy of divide and conquer. Joan DaCorta, who worked closely with Rose Marie Poveromo in Astoria, was quoted in the article as saying: "If they're going to work with one community and not another, there is going to be a lot of hell raised on the west side.")

"Right, absolutely," Councilwoman Marshall agreed. The PANYNJ consultant replied that it would be too expensive, citing the $10 million in added costs that would be incurred by the East Elmhurst depression. But before he could elaborate on the technical details, Poveromo interrupted again:

> But you have to understand where the working people from Queens County are coming from. They're not gonna *benefit* from this. The only people that are gonna benefit from this are the airline travelers and the people who work at the airports. But those of us who live in these communities are going to be impacted adversely by this monorail, or whatever you want to call it.

Invoking "the working people of Queens County," Poveromo directed attention to the broader, regional implications of the AGT plan and, in particular, to issues of fairness in urban development planning. Her comments provoked disgruntled remarks from residents and a new round of site-specific questions about the elevated route of the AGT system in Astoria, Jackson Heights, and East Elmhurst.

Helen Sears, chairing the meeting for the Port Authority, held up her hands to quiet the audience. "If we are going to accomplish anything here tonight, we will have to agree on some ground rules." The PANYNJ consultant, still waiting to go on with his presentation, informed the gathering that many of the issues now being raised had already been addressed at previous committee meetings. "It would probably take me only a few minutes," he added, "to address what we have discussed in past meetings. Now why don't I do that."

The audience, only half of whom had attended the earlier outreach meetings of the Airport Access Program, resisted the consultant's appeal to a narrative of negotiated, step-by-step progress to the present. Joyce Cumberbatch asked what impact the revised AGT alignment would have on the yet-to-be-built park and promenade along the shore of Flushing Bay which had been promised by the Queens borough president.

Again trying to steer the discussion back on track, Sears intervened: "Well, that's why we've got to finish this first, to address [the questions] the committee has already raised, and then we can go on from there."

The activists settled down and the consultant continued his presentation. Focusing on the East Elmhurst portion of the AGT alignment, Peter explained how the landscaped slope, abutting the AGT tube, would serve as a "visual and acoustic wall," shielding the promised park and promenade from the sights and sounds of the eight-lane Grand Central Parkway, only yards away. He then uncovered a large poster board depicting the portion of the AGT route that would skirt Flushing Bay between the expressway and the parkland. The board displayed a photo blowup of the area. An illustration showing the depressed AGT alignment, the landscaped berm, and the yet-to-be-built promenade had been airbrushed on the photograph.

"This is a view," he began haltingly, holding up the large board. "If you were in a park, and the park were built and . . . ah . . . and the . . . ah—" Caught between the real and the imaginary, the consultant groped for an appropriate tense to describe the image:

> I think that one should imagine a promenade there. I think you can see here—this, by the way is a mechanically drawn, very accurate perspective, using all the dimensions and plans and profiles that are there. It's a very accurate representation because we don't want to fool ourselves, and we don't want to fool you. If you build this, you're gonna have a screen for the Grand Central Parkway. I think that this shows clearly that you're going to have a visual screen. And if you have a visual screen, you've got a noise screen. And the park itself is something that's going to come along when the promenade is designed. Basically what you're going to have is a landscaped backdrop for the project. And the beauty of the berm is—for instance, if you look at the grass along there now, it's sort of wimpy looking. But if you tilt that up toward you [i.e., by constructing the berm], all of a sudden, you're presented with much more green. And you get much more bounce for the ounce out of the landscaping.

While residents were puzzling over the photo-illustration, a Port Authority official added: "I think the point is, really—a number of people have raised the issue, what does [the AGT] do for Queens in general? *I* think it provides a nice space that all the people of Queens can enjoy. It provides the opportunity—"

Before he could finish the consultant interrupted: "It is a setup for the promenade that the promenade does not now have. It's a setup. And it gives you insulation from the parkway."

In short, residents were being asked to view the depressed AGT alignment as a visual and noise screen for a promenade that did not yet exist. Cumberbatch asked the consultant whether the Port Authority would uphold a commitment to landscape the park and promenade. City Councilwoman Marshall intervened, explaining that funding for the future park and promenade had been committed by another source: the New York City Department of Environmental Protection (DEP) would fund the park and promenade as mitigation for locating a sewage storage facility in nearby Flushing Meadows Corona Park. PANYNJ, the consultant added, would only landscape the berm: it was "gravy," he declared.

Councilwoman Marshall, addressing the PANYNJ officials, stressed the importance of coordinating the building of the AGT and the berm with the construction of the Flushing Bay park and promenade by the New York City Department of Parks. As we shall see, the Port Authority's failure to coordinate its planning of the AGT with the Parks Department would end in the abandonment of the depressed alignment plan for East Elmhurst. Marshall also charged the Port Authority officials to commit to enhancing the park, rather than limiting their involvement to landscaping the berm. She then returned to the issue of the Astoria end of the AGT alignment.

Marshall's comments were quickly followed by a flurry of critical comments by activists from Astoria—they wanted their end of the AGT "buried," too.

Rose Marie Poveromo interrupted:

> Excuse me, sir, may I just indicate along with Joan DaCorta—we do live in Community Board 1, we are also members of Community Board 1, and we are also civic activists in the community. And I would just like to indicate to you that we will not go along with an elevated structure. And, certainly, what you have managed to do here is be divisive—divide one community against another, which is very, very bad—because Queens County will suffer no matter what plans you come up with here. This will not benefit the people of Queens County. As I said at the outset, it will benefit the airline traveler, the tourist, and the people who work at the airports. *We*, down the line, will not benefit from this thing.

Arthur Hayes, president of the East Elmhurst–Corona Civic Association and member of Community Board 3's Airport Committee, protested: "At no time did *this* [Airport] Committee attempt to exclude the Astoria Homeowners Association or any other group."

"Not you, Arthur," Poveromo interjected. "We're not saying that. In fact, we appreciate that you people have invited us to this meeting. We thank you." Joan DaCorta added: "You see, the people of Manhattan—I want you to know I spoke with the groups in Manhattan—they're under the assumption that Queens is 100 percent for it. The Port Authority has made them believe that *we're* 100 percent for it!"

Community activists in Manhattan had indeed been led to believe that building the AGT system in Queens had received widespread, if not unanimous, support—an issue I will address in the next chapter. Before the consultant could return to his aerial photographs, DaCorta interrupted again: "Go back to the drawing board, Peter, this is not going to fly in Astoria Heights. I appreciate your presentation. I know you worked very hard at it, and to you it looks great. But to me it *stinks*. Go back to the drawing board. That's all. And I think we'll get enough communities united with us—you're gonna have a tough fight on your hands."

The Port Authority officials and consultants responded by detailing the technical difficulties associated with depressing the AGT along its Astoria route.

"How about you giving us the money to get our own engineers?" DaCorta asked. I guarantee we'll find the answer. But the Port Authority wants the fastest and the cheapest way without showing concern for communities. And we're not gonna let you do it."

The debate between the Astoria activists and Port Authority officials continued. After fifteen minutes Barbara Coleman, Corona resident and member of Community Board 3's Aviation Committee, intervened, recalling the meeting that had been held two weeks earlier at La Detente.

> We had a meeting and a consortium of Queens people, not only from Community Board 3, which may have been the loudest, but also from Community Board 1, and I do feel that their concerns are perfectly acceptable. Go back and come up with a better AGT. Because although what you're telling the East Elmhurst area would appear to meet the needs of most of the people in East Elmhurst, we are concerned about people in *other* communities. And I don't like the idea of you pitting one against the other. Besides, you're going to catch hell from Community Board 12 when you get into Jamaica.

Coleman went on to question the need for a link between LaGuardia and JFK and asked why the AGT planners had not made use of existing rail lines and rights of way—points that had been stressed by the independent transportation advocates who had attended the meeting at La Detente.

Ed O'Sullivan, director of the Airport Access Program, responded cryptically: "Because there have been wars fought over every single one of them." O'Sullivan was referring to the earlier unsuccessful attempts of the Metropolitan Transportation Authority (MTA) to reactivate defunct Long Island Railroad lines in southern Queens. These failed attempts had encountered stiff community opposition.

"Could you tell me about the wars?" Joyce Cumberbatch asked. "I'd like to hear it. What were the wars about?"

Hamlet Wallace, the chair of Community Board 3's Aviation Committee, interjected, "See, those are alignments that have not been used for years. And the people in those communities don't want them, because they don't want to see a train going through their backyards."

"Thank you." Cumberbatch responded. "That's just what I wanted to hear. That's just what I wanted to hear."

Trying again to keep the discussion focused on the plan for the East Elmhurst depression, Sears proposed that Community Board 1 form its own aviation committee, which would then meet with Port Authority officials to address the specific questions and concerns of Astoria residents. Grudgingly, the activists from Astoria and East Elmhurst consented.

Sears continued: "Now maybe we should go back to what was shown to you earlier, which was the depression in East Elmhurst, and the promenade. Can we have a comment from the chair of the committee on exactly what your sentiments are about what has been presented tonight?"

Hamlett Wallace stood to address the gathering:

> At this particular time I'm pleased with the result. Hopefully this will be carried out. I think that this is a positive effort on the part of the Port Authority. As everybody knows realistically this AGT doesn't do anything for us. We want the [Port Authority] to be sensitive to our needs across the board. As far as this committee is concerned we are pleased with the semi-submerged effort, along with the beautification of our promenade. And I think that it will be an enhancement.

A grumble of discontent spread throughout the room. Joyce Cumberbatch cut her eyes to the members of her block association and raised her eyebrows in alarm. Poveromo and DaCorta stood and noisily collected their belongings. Arthur Hayes, president of the East Elmhurst–Corona Civic Association, addressed Ed O'Sullivan, director of the Port Authority's Airport Access Program:

"Just one question," he began quietly, holding up a photocopy of the *Newsday* article foretelling the agreement that had just been reached. "Why was this information released to the press *before* we had an opportunity to meet?" The group settled back into their chairs and awaited O'Sullivan's response.

"We had prepared a press release," O'Sullivan replied, "in anticipation of your accepting this. We did not release it. However, an elected official—the press officer of an elected official—somebody jumped the gun and released it on Friday. It was not the Port Authority. We had no intention whatsoever because all we would do by that is alienate people. So we did not release it."[3]

People in the room snarled when O'Sullivan declined to reveal the identity of the political official involved.

"Let me ask another question," Hayes continued. "I suspect that, since some time ago, you were meeting with elected officials, prior to coming to this committee. Now we come here to discuss a point and you've already agreed on this thing. I think that it should be fair, that any information you discuss with elected officials should be supplied to the chairman of our committee, so that we're aware of what's goin' on behind the scenes. Because we came here in good faith and made these recommendations and I think that we should be aware of everything."

Hamlett Wallace agreed, noting that he had found out about the "agreement" only when a reporter from the New York *Daily News* called him for his comments, and then read the *Newsday* article to him over the telephone.

O'Sullivan repeated his assertion that the story had been leaked by an elected official. "To benefit whom?" Joan DaCorta asked. "Him," Sullivan replied, declining to be more specific.

Sears assured Hayes that although the elected officials of Queens had been briefed by the Port Authority, "the work that has been done has been in this committee. It has not been done in secret briefings with elected officials."

Pat Beckles, president of the Ditmars Boulevard Block Association, stood to speak: "Selfishly, I must say that the promenade is my baby. I don't want to see anything happen to it. Is it going to stay that way?" he asked, nodding at the photo-illustration on the easel, "As the committee wishes?" Beckles peered at the Port Authority officials, smiling skeptically. "I think it's going to change."

Just as the meeting was coming to a close Ed O'Sullivan, director of the Airport Access Program, announced: "There are people in this room who have been making comments who are not part of this committee, and not a part of this community—people who have an idea to extend the N train along Ditmars Boulevard. Maybe you ought to hear from them?"

"Why not?" Barbara Coleman responded. Bewildered, the committee looked around the room, and then to O'Sullivan for clarification.

"George Haikalis," O'Sullivan explained. He nodded toward Haikalis, the transportation advocate whom Joyce Cumberbatch had invited to the meeting.

Nonplused, Haikalis stood: "That's not *my* idea."

"But you've been advocating it."

"No," Haikalis countered. "What we've been advocating is a separate system to Kennedy and a separate one to LaGuardia—and not having this full system sweeping all around Queens. Then we could afford to put the below-grade sections where they're really needed—in sensitive areas. That's the main message—that's the transit advocacy's point of view—"

"Well," O'Sullivan interrupted, "I have a letter from George suggesting that we extend the N train along Ditmars Boulevard to LaGuardia Airport."

Joan DaCorta looked up: "You mean between Thirty-first and—"

O'Sullivan continued. "I think that George—I think that he ought to fully disclose his plan."

"Well, I'd like to see that letter," Haikalis replied. "I would be interested in seeing that letter, if you could make it available to me."

Puzzled, residents questioned Haikalis on his proposed alternative route for the AGT. Haikalis repeated the planning alternatives he had presented at the earlier meeting at La Detente, advocating the reactivation of existing rights-of-way and rail lines.

"George," O'Sullivan continued. "In your publication did you, or did you not, advocate extending the N train along Ditmars Boulevard to LaGuardia Airport?"

"I don't have my attorney here to answer these questions—I mean, is this a cross-examination?"

O'Sullivan pressed on, speaking over the escalating clamor in the room: "This man has been talking to the community, two weeks ago at a seminar," he charged, alluding to the meeting at La Detente. "And he's been in here, at this meeting, passing comments. Yet he hasn't come forward in the forum to tell you that one of his plans is to extend the N train along Ditmars. And I just want to be sure that everybody understands—"

Joan DaCorta interrupted: "What I'm thinking is that this is irrelevant to what we're talking about here, now. That seems to be an issue you two have, and I don't think it should be addressed here."

There was a of murmur of agreement as people collected their belongings to leave.

"May I just say," Poveromo said, standing, "I don't want you in my backyard, I don't want you in my frontyard. We would appreciate it if you would come to Community Board 1 with different renderings. And take into consideration that you will not see a community that's going to roll over and play dead. We *will* be here, and we are here now."

Although Poveromo and the activists from Astoria left the meeting pledging continued resistance, an uneasy settlement had been reached with East Elmhurst—an agreement whose conditions of possibility relied on the construction of neighborhood needs, identities, and interests in fragmented and place-bound terms.

The Port Authority's practices of community outreach and negotiation privileged and indeed reinforced, local, place-bound constructions of neighborhood identity and interests by shielding broader questions about the AGT from deliberation and debate, and by responding assertively to statements of need and interest formulated in narrow, localized terms.

The efforts of PANYNJ officials to keep the discussion on track and narrowly focused on the proposal for the East Elmhurst "depression" rendered questions regarding the appropriateness and fairness of the AGT as a whole beside the point and diversionary. This governing of deliberation had the effect of undermining the attempts of activists to articulate claims of common interests across community boundaries. For example, when Coleman and others argued that the concerns of Astoria residents were not addressed by the compromise plan, thereby questioning the AGT's design and impact in regional terms, PANYNJ officials insisted that Astoria's issues be addressed by its own community board. Activists were well aware of the limitations of this community-based venue for political participation. After the LaGuardia meeting, Barbara Coleman highlighted the difficulty of pursuing transneighborhood issues through the community board system: "Community Boards are set up to deal specifically with their *own* communities and generally not to pay too much attention to other community boards, unless they infringe on their area, because they have too much work to do on their own. There should have been a big meeting with the people from Community Board 12 [Jamaica], our people from Board 3, the people from Board 1 [Astoria], and the groups in Manhattan, but there never was."

The Port Authority employed other less subtle tactics to fragment opposition and anchor resistance to a bureaucratic construction of local community. For example, O'Sullivan's attempt to discredit Haikalis by painting him as an outsider to the community and an advocate of an unpopular subway construction plan constituted an effort to undermine a regional perspective on the problem of airport access by provoking a NIMBY-like response from activists. Similarly, the premature announcement of East Elmhurst's agreement with the Port Authority, leaked to the news media, was read by activists as a deliberate attempt to divide and conquer the AGT's opponents along the administrative frontiers of local community.

If the Port Authority's outreach practices hindered coalition building, they also encouraged activists to experience, frame, and pursue broader and potentially generalizable interests within the context of the immediate environment. By responding aggressively and, to some degree, positively to demands focusing on the preservation of "view corridors" and other local quality-of-life concerns, Port Authority officials prompted activists to formulate and represent their interests and concerns as a defense of private property and of the rights to enjoy it.

Barbara Coleman, explaining why she did not argue against the East Elmhurst compromise at the LaGuardia meeting, gave voice to the resulting paradox:

> The idea of putting the train in a trench is fantastic. Of course the community doesn't want the train. I didn't speak out, simply because there wasn't anything to say at that time. We don't want it, and I personally feel it would be a waste of money, like the "tunnel to nowhere."[4] But they gave us the trench, so in deference to them for giving us that, I didn't say anything. What would I have said? I would have said, "We need a train like I need a hole in my toe."

Why *do* people defer to power—to what they don't want? Why do social groups frequently fail to articulate and act on common interests across differences? And why, when confronted with the "systemic imperatives of power," as S. White put it, do the participants in urban social movements often fall back on place-bound or NIMBY-like formulations of identity and interests? (1991:102)

East Elmhurst's struggle with the Port Authority suggests that this defensive response, this appeal to view corridors and property values in the last instance was neither an unmediated expression of a transparent middle-class political identity nor simply the result of the difficulty activists experience by thinking globally from the grassroots. During the course of the struggle, activists articulated a complex range of opinions and positions regarding the AGT, sometimes emphasizing the structural inequities of the PANYNJ proposal as an issue of environmental justice shaped by power differentials and, at other times, falling back on localized, or "backyard," claims to individual property rights and the quality-of-life prerogatives of black homeowners.

What *moved* East Elmhurst's activists to compromise, to the fantastic idea of the "trench," were an ensemble of practices that, although contested, served to constrict possibilities for recognizing and articulating collective commitments to wider-based struggles for economic and political justice. These practices, ranging from PANYNJ's divisive outreach practices to its policing of debate to its discourse of techno-possibility and to its outright manipulation of the mass media, served to govern the political arena of neighborhood activism, enabling the formation of certain collective positions and allegiances while disabling others.

Barbara Coleman's comment, "I didn't speak out, simply because there wasn't anything to say at that time," conveys the sense not that there was nothing to be said but rather that what could be said *at that time* would not muster the efficacy or "illocutionary force" needed to realign the opponents of the "people mover" in support of a shared critique of its systemic impact (Bourdieu 1991:100). "What would I have said?" Coleman asked rhetorically. "We need the train like I need a whole in my toe."

Coleman's reading of the situational constraints brought to bear on the politically sayable by the Port Authority's practices of governing public debate and deliberation underscores not only the malleability of political subjectivity but also the extent to which the latter endures as a "constantly recreated unity depending on the whole relation of forces in a society at a given moment" (Laclau and Mouffe 1982:100).[5]

Activists from East Elmhurst and surrounding communities accurately perceived that PANYNJ officials were being divisive: they were conducting a war of position within these relations of force to recast opposition along the bureaucratically defined frontiers of local community and on the optical field of what Mike Davis has called "homestead exclusivism" (1990:159). And on this field, the Port Authority's appeal to residents to imagine a landscaped promenade and unobstructed view corridor of the North Shore enabled, if only provisionally, a formulation of community concerns that interpellated their identity as black "middle-class homeowners" committed to a particular quality of life and experience of urban space.

In stressing the Port Authority's role in inciting these situationally bound class dispositions, I do not minimize their heterogeneity or the degree to which they are contested and reshaped in everyday practice. To be sure, the meeting at La Detente Restaurant demonstrated that activists constituted themselves in a variety of ways and in relation to myriad readings of the interrelation of space, identity, and power: as working people of Queens County (versus Manhattan corporate elites), as subjects of "inept" and unjust structures of urban governance, and as members of a transneighborhood alliance mobilized to oppose a discourse and strategy of global competition.

In fact many activists remained opposed to the project and were critical of the arguments made by PANYNJ officials and Borough President Shulman which supported the view that the AGT system was key to promoting the region's global competitiveness and to stimulating job growth in Queens. Barbara Coleman, for example, reflected:

> I don't know how many businesses would be coming into Queens even under the best of circumstances. Whether businesses need access to the airport through a train system, I don't know. I listen to [Borough President] Claire Shulman, and she says she's interested in businesses and the new jobs, and so on. Maybe her foresight is better than mine, but I don't see that many new jobs coming in as a result [of the AGT]. But that's the story they always tell to get what they want.

Similarly, Joyce Cumberbatch criticized the manner in which appeals to global competitiveness were used to undermine community concerns: "I think the [AGT] is great for the world economy but I also think that [the borough president] should be more aware of how her constituents are living and the adjustments that have to be made in their lifestyles. After all, we're part of the global economy, too. And I think she should have been more aware and sensitive to *our* issues and should have addressed them with the Port Authority."

East Elmhurst's acceptance of the compromise proposal was less the result of the activation of class interests grounded in an essential, a priori black middle-class identity than that of a struggle over the social and political meanings of space, the definition of "community," and the interpretation of the city's economic development needs and priorities. And it was precisely the Port Authority's capacity to organize and govern the public sphere of neighborhood activism that enabled PANYNJ officials to spur the consolidation of a parochial, homeowner-centered stance on the AGT, thereby weakening options for constructing broader-based alignments of political interests and identities.

However, the agreement reached with the Port Authority was viewed by most activists as a tactical compromise which, although exhausting possibilities for contesting the AGT through PANYNJ's Airport Access Program, did not prevent them from pursuing other avenues of resistance. For neighborhood activists faced with a daunting array of issues and problems at disparate institutional sites, political struggles are not "won" and "lost" in momentous confrontations between neatly arrayed adversaries. "You have to compromise," Barbara Coleman explained to me after the LaGuardia meeting. "You have to learn to look at a situation and recognize that you've pushed about as far as you can, and that this is all you're gonna get. Then you come back and fight the next day."

Following the acceptance of the compromise plan, activists in East Elmhurst would pursue two additional venues for opposing the AGT system. The first would be to challenge the AGT proposal at public hearings jointly sponsored by the FAA and the New York State Department of Transportation (DOT). The FAA-DOT hearings, mandated by law, were held to solicit public comment on the AGT's Draft Environmental Impact Statement, an impact study of the Port Authority's proposal that had been prepared by FAA consultants.

The second avenue for continuing the fight against the AGT would be through coalition building with activists in Astoria and other communities that were affected by PANYNJ's activities. At the La Detente meeting, activists from Astoria had invited Joyce Cumberbatch and others from Corona–East Elmhurst to participate in an open Town Hall Meeting to voice their opposition to airport expansion and the AGT proposal. The mass meeting, organized by Rose Marie Poveromo's United Community Civic Association, would be held in September and provide residents the opportunity to confront politicians and city officials with their concerns. A broad-based coalition, Cumberbatch and others believed, would have the resources to stage demonstrations and other collective actions as well as pursue legal remedies.

In the next chapter I demonstrate how the efforts of black activists in East Elmhurst and Corona to oppose the AGT and build alliances with white activists in nearby communities were impeded not only by the Port Authority's practices of managing debate and dissent but also by race-inflected constructions of neighborhood stability. In this discourse of community stability, promoted by city authorities, the quality of neighborhood life is imagined to rest on the policing and exclusion of racialized categories of "outsiders" rather than on structural relations of political and economic subordination. By analyzing UCCA's Town Hall meeting I show how these racialized constructions of neighborhood stability and disorder are produced through the governing practices of city officials, and I demonstrate how they serve to deflect critique and opposition from wider and potentially generalizable problems and issues such as the AGT.

CHAPTER EIGHT

The Politics of Hearing and Telling

For some reason the people in Manhattan think the people in
Queens are in favor of it. And the people in Queens think the
people in Manhattan are in favor of it. But *nobody* is
really in favor of it.
(*Barbara Coleman, Community Board 3*)

ON THURSDAY, July 28, at three o'clock in the afternoon, the Federal Aviation
Administration (FAA) and the New York State Department of Transportation
(NYSDOT) convened the second of two public hearing on the AGT's Draft
Environmental Impact Statement (DEIS). The DEIS, a two-thousand-page re-
port assessing the environmental impact of the Port Authority's airport access
proposal, was prepared by FAA consultants in compliance with the National
Environmental Policy Act of 1969 (NEPA) and the New York State Environ-
mental Quality Review Act (SEQRA). The hearing was held at Saint Peter's
Church on Manhattan's Upper East Side, not far from the East Fifty-ninth
Street corridor where the Port Authority planned to build the AGT's Manhattan terminal.

Three representatives from FAA and NYSDOT were seated at a folding
table that had been set up on the chapel's altar, a projection screen hovering
over their heads. To the right of the officials, a darkroom timer had been con-
spicuously stationed on a small stand with its long luminescent hands set to
five minutes, the time that would be allotted to each speaker. A stenographer
equipped with a steno machine and tape recorder sat at a desk between the
platform and the audience.

The hearing's format was the same as that followed at the Queens public
hearing held two days earlier. A representative of the consulting firm that had
conducted the DEIS study presented an overview of the Port Authority's AGT
plan and summarized the findings of the environmental review. After the presentation an FAA official described the procedure for public comment: speakers
would be required to fill out "speaker cards" in advance, restrict their comments to the DEIS report, and observe a five-minute time limit. Public comments, the audience was told, would be reviewed by FAA and NYSDOT officials and incorporated when appropriate into the final version of the AGT's
environmental impact statement.

"Our format does not permit responses to questions or comments during this hearing," the FAA official added. "Should you have specific questions regarding the Draft Environmental Impact Statement, please direct them to the representatives of the [Port Authority] consulting team in the hall." PA-NYNJ officials and their consultants had taken up stations in the hallway outside the chapel amid a hodgepodge of technical drawings and artistic renderings on large poster boards of the AGT, its terminals, and its proposed routes.

Midway through the opening presentation an elderly white man in a gray business suit began grumbling. Distracted, the FAA consultant paused and then continued his presentation. Again the man interrupted, this time speaking loud enough for the audience of more than two hundred to hear.

"This is a *hearing*?" he blurted. "I thought we were here for a public hearing, not for a presentation. Who is this gentleman?" he asked, standing and pointing his finger at the consultant. "And who is he to us?"

"Sir," the FAA official intervened. "I introduced him before this presentation. This is part of the process. And at its conclusion you will be given the opportunity to comment."

The old man, an attorney, waved a handful of papers in the air in a gesture of defiance. "How long is this going to go on? And when is the so-called public going to get a chance to speak about this thing?"

"It will be over shortly," the FAA official replied. "It will be over. Thank you."

The attorney's disruption of the public hearing captured the sense of frustration, powerlessness, and anger that activists opposed to the Port Authority's AGT plan experienced through the course of their efforts to participate in its review. Although the FAA/NYSDOT hearings provided the first opportunity for activists to respond to a detailed disclosure of the proposal, their format severely constrained public discussion and debate. By disallowing the public any questioning of Port Authority officials and by limiting comment to the DEIS report, the hearing screened critical issues concerning the people mover's design, operation, and environmental impact, thus eliminating debate.

This governing of public scrutiny, illustrated by the review procedures for the DEIS, proved to be significantly more disempowering for activists in East Elmhurst and other Queens communities than for their counterparts on Manhattan's Upper East Side. Disparities in political power and resources available to residents of the two areas influenced their respective abilities to shape the outcome of the Port Authority's airport access plan. By examining this process of public hearing, I show how power differentials linked to race, class, and residential location condition the capacity of activists to participate in the process of urban development.

RACE, CLASS, AND POLITICAL CAPITAL

Activists in East Elmhurst and other Queens communities had eagerly awaited the release of the Draft Environmental Impact Statement. The DEIS report was the first document made publicly available that disclosed the details of the Port Authority's $2.6 billion project and evaluated its environmental consequences for neighborhoods in Queens and Manhattan. Critical questions concerning the AGT system's route, expected ridership, terminal and station locations, and design features, which had remained unanswered during earlier negotiations with Port Authority officials, were addressed in the DEIS report. For example, the DEIS confirmed suspicions voiced earlier by activists that the AGT system would "serve only trips to and from the airports by air passengers, workers, and visitors, and exclude use for other trips"(FAA/NYSDOT 1994:ES-1).

Many believed that the FAA/NYSDOT hearings would provide the opportunity to voice publicly their objections to the AGT and to grill PANYNJ officials about alternative solutions to the airport access problem in the presence of federal and state authorities, authorities to whom the Port Authority was, in theory, accountable. "We couldn't stop them in East Elmhurst," Barbara Coleman said to me before the Queens hearing, "but when we get them up there in front of the feds, they won't get away with the double-talk they used on us."

Though the DEIS was dated June 1994 copies of the five-volume, two-thousand-page report were not received by community boards and public libraries (where they were accessible to the public) until mid-July. Activists testifying at the public hearing in Queens pointed out that the short period between the release of the DEIS and the holding of hearings less than two weeks later had hampered their ability to review and evaluate the lengthy and technically sophisticated report, let alone prepare testimony.

"Why might such a short response time in the middle of summer for such a large and complex project be a flaw in its environmental review?" an Astoria activist asked state officials at the Queens hearing. "Such an abbreviated comment period discourages comments," he answered. "Organized groups, such as neighborhood associations and community boards, operate through committees and act through resolutions. So short a period precludes authoritative comment."

For activists in East Elmhurst, the short response period and the timing of the public hearings were also critical issues. The East Elmhurst–Corona Civic Association, Community Board 3, and most block associations suspended meetings during the summer when many residents were away on vacation. Organizing during the summer "off-session," as had been necessary during negotiations with PANYNJ over the East Elmhurst "depression," was logistically difficult and required extraordinary effort and planning. The compressed review period was especially disabling for grass-roots activists who had to coordinate their civic activities with often inflexible job-related, household, and other commitments.

Pat Beckles, president of the Ditmars Boulevard Block Association and a member of Community Board 3, underscored this issue in his testimony before the FAA/NYSDOT panel: "We, the people," he began, speaking slowly and gesturing to the audience with a sweep of his hand, "are once again faced with the dilemma of holding off-session meetings to research and debate—an exercise that would ordinarily be conducted during our normal session. This limits our resources and taxes our ability to undertake the task—an unfair position." Pausing briefly, he peered quizzically at the officials seated at the table next to the podium. "Is this intentional?"

Although the FAA/NYSDOT rules for public comment allowed for the submission of written comments until September 30, 1994, this venue foreclosed the possibility not only of publicizing key issues and questions before a boroughwide assembly of activists, public officials, and the media but also of publicly confronting and questioning Port Authority representatives.

Yet despite restrictions placed on public comment by the short review period and by the hearing's format, some activists raised questions and contested issues that stretched beyond the narrow scope of the DEIS. For example, Stephen Dubrow, a resident of Woodside Queens and president of the Committee for Better Transit, opened the public commentary portion of the Queens hearing by raising a barrage of regional policy issues which had only been marginally addressed in the DEIS:

> Should the Port Authority be allowed to build a special transit facility through communities, without these communities getting some transit benefits from the construction? Should the Port Authority be allowed to use city rights-of-way for a special-purpose transit system, preempting them from other transit uses? Should the Port Authority be spending $2.5 billion to build a segregated system when enhancing the existing regional rail system would provide much higher benefits for the cost expended?

Other neighborhood activists raised key questions about the long-term financing of the people mover, about the desirability of building an elevated rail line when existing "els" were being torn down, and about the AGT system's impact on parklands, noise pollution, "electromagnetic fields," and crime. These latter environmental concerns, addressed in the DEIS, were elaborated on in the testimony of Queens elected officials.

Borough President Claire Shulman, citing the benefits that Queens would realize in economic development and reduced traffic and air pollution, noted the importance of taking such steps as using rubber wheels to minimize noise and vibration, preserving "sight lines" in residential neighborhoods, employing "recessed lighting" to reduce nighttime glare effects, and ensuring that construction activities would have a minimum impact on Flushing Bay, parklands, and other environmental resources.

However, in contrast to the comments of activists that situated environmental concerns within the context of a broader critique and questioning of the AGT system's design, economic feasibility, and accessibility to nonairport travelers, the testimony of Borough President Shulman and other Queens officials constructed the environmental impact of the AGT as a set of local and disconnected problems that could be resolved technologically.

This narrow framing of the AGT system's impact obscured regional environmental and social justice concerns that were shared by different Queens communities. It also depoliticized discussion and debate about the AGT by taking, as Dreyfus and Rabinow put it, "what is essentially a political problem, removing it from the realm of political discourse, and recasting it in the neutral language of science" (1983:196).

For residents of Corona and East Elmhurst who attended the hearing, this framing of interrelated environmental concerns as discrete, technical problems that could be resolved through the deployment of rubber wheels, no-glare recessed lighting, and vegetative screens, undermined alternative interpretations of the AGT system's impact that situated the latter in the wider regional and historical context of airport expansion. As Barbara Coleman put it during Borough President Shulman's testimony, "How are rubber wheels going to get me on the train?" And although five activists from Corona–East Elmhurst attended the hearing, only Pat Beckles gave testimony. Like their counterparts from other areas of Queens, few in Corona and East Elmhurst had had the time or resources to review the DEIS report and analyze its technically abstruse data and conclusions.

The FAA/NYSDOT hearings, like the Port Authority's airport access meeting held earlier, served both to limit and to discipline public debate on the AGT plan by shielding wider issues of urban development and environmental justice from public disclosure and scrutiny while funneling opposition into insulated pockets of technical expertise and problem solving. These practices, ranging from managing the timing and protocol of public hearings to controlling the direction, content, and rules for negotiation, set important limits on the scope of public dissent and, in so doing, undermined the discursive foundation on which activists could form transneighborhood alliances—alliances that are enabled and constructed through the articulation of shared interpretations of political interests and identity. After the public hearing, I asked Joyce Cumberbatch what would become of the coalition with the activists in Astoria: "Well, now I don't know," she replied. "I think everybody is going to be pretty much focused on seeing that the Port Authority delivers on all their promises about the noise levels and the upkeep of the parklands" [i.e., the areas underneath and adjacent to the elevated AGT tracks].

In contrast, neighborhood activists on Manhattan's Upper East Side were more successful at both building coalitions and leveraging public- and private-sector power in support of a critique of the AGT system that underscored its engineering and economic faults in regional terms. Political resources tied to class position enabled Manhattan activists to shore up claims of local, quality-of-life interests not only with the support of public- and private-sector elites but also with the authority of discourses about the city's economic development needs; in short, access to class-based, political resources empowered Manhattan activists to speak in the name of the region's general well-being and economic future.

In Manhattan, opposition to the Port Authority's airport access proposal focused on the siting of the AGT's central terminal at the intersection of East Fifty-ninth Street and Lexington Avenue on the Upper East Side. East Side residents argued that locating the underground terminal at Fifty-ninth Street would not only increase traffic congestion and air pollution in an already congested area but would also limit its accessibility to airport travelers departing from other locations in the city's business district. "Does anyone really think Bloomingdale's is the Central Business District?" an East Side activist asked FAA officials at the Manhattan public hearing.

Activists in Manhattan found support among transportation advocates, urban planners, and an assortment of public and private officials who held that locating the AGT's only Manhattan terminal at Fifty-ninth Street would make it relatively inaccessible to the business community and other travelers living and working in other parts of the borough, such as the West Side of Manhattan and the Wall Street area. For example, representatives of the powerful Regional Plan Association (RPA) and the Environmental Defense Fund argued that the terminal should be located at Grand Central Station where it would be more easily accessible to Pennsylvania Station and West Side rail networks, as well as to passengers transferring from Metro North, an MTA rail link with Grand Central Station serving Westchester County and Connecticut.

Residents of Corona and East Elmhurst had made overtures to some Manhattan-based groups in June. Joyce Cumberbatch and her block association had learned of the escalating opposition to the AGT in Manhattan from George Haikalis, the rail transportation advocate who had spoken at their meeting. Haikalis had been working closely with civic associations and community boards on the Upper East Side. Before the meeting at La Detente in East Elmhurst, Haikalis invited Cumberbatch and other members of the Ninety-sixth/Ninety-seventh Street Block Association to Manhattan to attend a meeting of the Community Board Task Force, a coalition of civic activists representing Manhattan Community Boards 5, 6 and 8.

"They thought we came from Mars," Cumberbatch told me after the visit. "It was so funny. We got there a little late. And we were the only three black people in the room. Everyone else was white. And they really didn't know who the hell we were and why we were there. I don't know if it was because we were black or because we lived in Queens or both, but they gave us the cold shoulder."

Adding to the perplexity of the Community Board Task Force was the belief shared by many Manhattan activists that residents of Queens were unanimously in support of the AGT. In public statements, Borough President Shulman and other boosters of the project frequently pointed to the decrease in automobile traffic and air pollution that would occur if the AGT were built, thereby emphasizing the benefits of the project to Queens residents. And although few Queens activists shared this view, publicized in the media, it was regarded by many as the official Queens position on the AGT. Moreover, activists in Manhattan and Queens reported to me that PANYNJ officials had cultivated the impression that there was solid support for the AGT in Queens—an impression no doubt bolstered by the Port Authority's premature announcement to the press of the East Elmhurst compromise. Whatever the case, Cumberbatch's meeting with Manhattan activists was unproductive:

> They were astounded that we weren't for the AGT. They assumed that they were the only ones that were interested in getting it changed from Fifty-ninth Street to Grand Central. They had their own provincial reasons for getting involved. But they were not aware that any groups in Queens were against the AGT. So that's how parochial they were. I extended an invitation to them to get involved with us and not to be so provincial. And I said that I was shocked to see New Yorkers—Manhattanites—so provincial in their thinking.

Manhattan activists had reason to be provincial. At the meeting, Cumberbatch recalled, members of the Community Board Task Force had been preoccupied with the chore of hiring consultants to study the Port Authority's proposal and the DEIS report. The Manhattan task force had succeeded in securing a grant of $60,000 from the Port Authority to fund an independent evaluation of the AGT proposal. However, no such funds had been made available to community groups in Queens.

Joyce Cumberbatch's meeting with the Manhattan task force was the first and last meeting between opponents of the AGT in the two boroughs. When FAA/NYSDOT held its public hearing on the DEIS at Saint Peter's Church in Manhattan, no residents of Corona–East Elmhurst attended. The audience of about two hundred at Saint Peter's was almost exclusively white and, when compared with those attending the Queens hearing, was more professional in appearance. Many men and women were dressed in business suits, carried briefcases, and sported other accoutrements of the professional classes. Young, exuberant aides of elected officials took up positions near the entrances, distributing copies of prepared testimony, greeting members of the audience, and every so often withdrawing to a quiet nook in the chapel to parley on a cellular phone.

More important than appearances, activists in Manhattan had access to resources or "political capital" that empowered them to participate more effectively in the processes of being heard than did their counterparts in Queens
(Bourdieu 1991).[1] The affluence and class-based power and prestige of the
Upper East Side placed more material and symbolic resources at the disposal
of its civic associations and merchants groups than were available to less
affluent Queens communities in what city officials often referred to as the
"outer boroughs" of the city. For example, this wealth enabled the East Side
Coalition for Airport Access (a consortium of civic and merchants associations) to retain the services of a law firm that represented the coalition at the
hearing.

More generally, East Side residents were able to support a powerful and
highly visible infrastructure of civic and business groups, such as the East
Sixtieth Street Property Owners Association, Civitas (a zoning advocacy
group), the Sutton Area Community Association, and the fifteen-hundred-
member Turtle Bay Association, all of which delivered prepared comments at
the Manhattan DEIS hearing. The affluence of residents of the Upper East Side
also provided them with more flexibility in scheduling, if not leisure time, to
organize, attend meetings, and conduct research than that enjoyed by working
and middle-income activists in East Elmhurst and other areas of Queens (see
Bourdieu 1991:192).

Furthermore, because of the Manhattan-focused bias in the city's political
culture, influential public- and private-sector organizations that had not testified at the Queens DEIS hearing chose to make public their opposition to the
AGT in Manhattan. Included among these groups were the Environmental
Defense Fund, the Airline Pilots Association, the New York Sierra Club, and
the Regional Plan Association. Although these advocacy groups raised many
of the same issues that had been argued by Queens activists, their well-re-
searched comments not only carried more clout but also lent authority to the
oppositional positions taken by Upper East Side civic groups. The result was
a largely Manhattan-centered critique of the AGT, one that stressed traffic
congestion and air pollution problems in Manhattan and elided the AGT's
environmental impact on Queens neighborhoods.

A *New York Times* report on the DEIS hearings in Manhattan illustrated and
advanced this process whereby the local concerns of Manhattan neighborhoods were conflated with the more regional interests of private industry. In
this case, Upper East Side opponents of the AGT system were constructed as
"natural allies" of the airline industry:

Neighborhood residents fear those idling taxis, in combination with the loss of
two lanes on the [Queensboro] bridge would make their streets permanently im-
passable. Wealthy and well-organized, they have already begun to enlist their
politicians and mount a strong campaign against the plan. In this effort, they have

found natural allies in the airlines, which want to see the $3 ticket fee used exclusively for improvements at the airports themselves and are working with some of the neighborhood groups (31 July 1994:33).

The influential Regional Plan Association, which submitted written comments on the Draft Environmental Impact Statement to the FAA in August, also flagged the environmental concerns of Upper East Side residents within the context of its broader critique of the Port Authority's proposal. Like other opponents of the PANYNJ plan, the RPA argued that the proposed terminal at Fifty-ninth Street was "largely disconnected from the regional transportation system" and would present considerable inconvenience to passengers arriving from the West Side, lower Manhattan, and from northern areas, such as Westchester County and Connecticut.

"Second," the RPA statement noted, "because such a large share of midtown customers will require a taxicab ride to reach the AGT, a heavy burden will be placed on nearby streets and an unacceptable burden will be placed on the area's air quality" (Regional Plan Association 1994). Similarly, the testimony of James Tripp, Counsel to the Environmental Defense Fund, at the FAA/NYSDOT hearing highlighted the "enormous traffic burden" that East Side communities would suffer if the Port Authority plan were implemented (Environmental Defense Fund 1994).

The greater class-based political capital at the disposal of residents of the East Side provided them with the capacity not only to formulate their interests more effectively but to bring those interests to bear in public with greater authority than their counterparts in Corona and East Elmhurst. Simply put, Manhattan residents had more money, time, and political clout.

This interrelation of class and political capital was nowhere more apparent than in the testimony of Edward Wallace, an attorney representing the East Side Coalition on Airport Access for the firm of Phillips, Nizer, Benhamin, Krim, and Ballon.

Wallace's testimony at the Manhattan hearing, distributed to the audience and members of the press in written form, began with a summary of the coalition's legal objections to the DEIS:

> One, the DEIS is based on insufficient information as a matter of law; two, the proposed alternatives [to the AGT proposal] are not adequately considered under the standards set forth in NEPA and SEQRA; three, the proposed [environmental] mitigations are implausible, they cannot be implemented, if implemented they will not be effective and they require the violation of the mitigations for other projects now in place; four, the DEIS fails to address the impacts of closing two lanes of the Queensboro Bridge, and the impacts on other river crossings; five, the costs of the project were not properly analyzed.

The attorney went on to develop each point, stressing the failure of both the Port Authority and state officials to comply with federal and state regulations for environmental review. Each actionable point was supported by citations from government regulations and case law, as well as the DEIS. For example, the DEIS acknowledged that the Port Authority's plan to site the AGT terminal at Fifty-ninth Street would increase vehicular traffic in the area and elevate air pollution levels well beyond those set by the Environmental Protection Agency. After noting this pollution threat, Wallace highlighted the inadequacy of the mitigation measures proposed in the DEIS.

A key component of the Port Authority's mitigation strategy was to *discourage* airport travelers from boarding the AGT at the Manhattan terminal during busy times by charging a "peak period fare differential." In effect, the Port Authority proposed to reduce air pollution problems by reducing ridership. "Not only is it highly unlikely," the attorney quipped with irony, "that a discriminatory fare would discourage riders at peak periods, but such a plan would defeat the viability of the AGT by increasing traffic and thus pollution on Queens arterial highways." (East Side Coalition on Airport Access 1994:7).

This class-based capacity to formulate and authoritatively present neighborhood interests, demonstrated by the attorney's testimony, was not available to activists in Queens. Their lack of access to legal representation, research support, and other "instruments of perception and expression" impeded their ability to present their claims to environmental justice with authority and to articulate their specific, place-bound interests within the framework of a systems-level evaluation and critique of the AGT proposal (Bourdieu 1991).

Whereas Upper East Side activists, concerned with traffic congestion and air pollution in their community, were perceived to be "natural allies" of the airline industry and other influential public- and private-sector critics of the AGT, the environmental concerns of East Elmhurst and other Queens neighborhoods were represented as being "local" and therefore not implicating basic issues about the financing and overall design of the AGT system.

This tendency to construct the interests of Queens neighborhoods as local, in contrast to the more regional, systems-wide concerns of Manhattan, is clearly illustrated in a report on the DEIS hearings held in July, published in the fall issue of *Access*, the Port Authority's airport access newsletter. "Many supporters," PANYNJ's cheerful account began, "spoke at the hearings about the positive economic impact the AGT would have on the city. However, several speakers expressed concerns and misconceptions."

The report then outlined, in question form, the concerns raised at both hearings. Each question was followed by a brief response. The Port Authority's representation of issues raised at the Queens hearing highlighted local, quality-of-life issues that could be solved through technology. For example, in response to the question, "Will there be visual intrusion in any neighborhoods?" *Access* reported:

The AGT would be built primarily at or above ground level throughout Queens. The elevated guideway would not resemble the elevated subway structures built almost a century ago. It would be designed to reduce visual bulk and to minimize the creation of shadows. The proposed route was selected to be sensitive to view corridors. The Airport Access Program has worked with and will continue to work with local communities and their elected representatives to mitigate any potential impacts on neighborhoods (*Access* 1994b).

Other questions posed and addressed in the newsletter similarly targeted local quality-of-life issues: "Will there be an impact on parklands?" "Will the AGT cause any additional noise in the communities?" "What will be the impact of the AGT on the region's air quality?" "How will the AGT handle security and safety issues?" "How will the AGT handle luggage?" "What about the landscaping along the route?" And, lastly, "What will the AGT's lighting be like?" (*Access* 1994b:2–3).

As we have seen, all these issues had in fact been raised by activists in Queens and underscored by their elected officials. Indeed, PANYNJ's inventory of issues closely follows the concerns expressed by Borough President Shulman at the Queens hearing, suggesting that the DEIS hearing process was more attentive to the testimonies of elected officials than to those of their constituents. In stressing place-bound concerns, the Port Authority's reconstruction of neighborhood opposition elided the systems-wide issues and criticisms that had been voiced by Queens activists: issues concerning the AGT's overall design, accessibility to nonairport travelers, long-term financing, and integration within existing transportation networks.

In contrast, the Port Authority's representation of the concerns of Manhattan neighborhoods stressed, with few exceptions, basic questions concerning the overall design of the AGT system: "Why not have an AGT stop at Grand Central Terminal?" "What will the fare structure be for the system?" "Will there be any change on the Queensboro Bridge Bike Lane?" "What will the impact be on traffic at the East 59th Street Station?" "Why not extend the Long Island Rail Road (LIRR) to the airports?" "Why not extend the subway to the airports?" "Should the 63rd Street tunnel be explored?" (*Access* 1994b:3–4).

The Port Authority's reinscription of the opposition of Corona–East Elmhurst and other Queens neighborhoods to the AGT marked an important representational moment in a struggle over the political significance of identity and urban space. This struggle engaged activists in Corona–East Elmhurst in a series of efforts to articulate their political interests, identities, and commitments in relation to PANYNJ's regional development strategy and gain access to the instruments of perception and expression that would empower them to construct alliances that transgressed the boundaries of local community.

In their struggle with the Port Authority, activists in Corona and East Elmhurst endeavored to develop and sustain these capacities by reaching out to expert advocacy groups, by collecting and disseminating data about the safety overrun and AGT, and by building political networks or "counter-publics" where they could formulate alternative constructions of their interests and identities within a changing spatial economy.

Whereas activists struggled to project the frontiers of public deliberation and debate, the Port Authority's coalition deployed dividing practices which, by regulating access to the instruments of perception and expression, operated to fragment and limit public opposition. These dividing practices ranged from the manipulation of the mass media and public review process to the utilization of procedures and institutions that tended to convert class differences into varying capacities to "be heard," thereby obscuring common interests across spatial frontiers and class differences.

TALKIN' COMMUNITY: THE DILEMMAS OF "MILITANT PARTICULARISM"

On September 22 the United Community Civic Association (UCCA), led by Rose Marie Poveromo of Astoria, held a town hall meeting at the Lexington School for the Deaf in Jackson Heights. The purpose of the meeting was to give residents an opportunity to voice community concerns before a mass gathering of politicians and city officials. Among the invited panelists were three members of Congress, seven New York State legislators, three City Council members, police precinct commanders, borough commissioners of the Sanitation and Buildings Departments, and the Port Authority's general manager of LaGuardia Airport. Representatives of community boards and civic associations in northern Queens had been invited to confront the public officials with questions and to voice the concerns of their neighborhoods.

The general audience, overwhelmingly white and numbering more than five hundred, filled the auditorium. Politicians and city officials greeted one another on the stage. Audio visual technicians tested microphones, arranged power cables, and set up portable lights for the video crew that would be taping the event. A deaf-language translator waited to the left of the stage for the meeting to begin. The handful of black activists in the audience were all from Corona–East Elmhurst and included Joyce Cumberbatch, Pat Beckles, and Arthur Hayes, president of the East Elmhurst–Corona Civic Association. Cumberbatch and the others from Corona–East Elmhurst hoped that the UCCA town meeting would provide an opportunity to rekindle broad-based opposition to the AGT, which they felt had been undermined by the Port Authority's practice of divide and rule.

Rose Marie Poveromo approached the podium and called the huge gathering to order:

> The purpose of tonight's ambitious town hall meeting on community concerns is twofold: first, to make our distinguished panelists aware of how deeply troubled

we are by the epidemic tide of maniacal violence and the continuous assault and erosion of our fragile quality of life; second, to manifest community bonding in a unified dedication of purpose for the protection and preservation of the communities we serve.

The threat of an "epidemic tide of maniacal violence" and the need for neighborhoods to bond in defense would remain a leading theme in the discourse of activists and public officials during the meeting, registering and reproducing a mode of grass-roots mobilizing that constructs community through the punitive exclusion of outsiders. This "militant particularism," to use Raymond Williams's phrase, locates neighborhood problems and degradation in the inappropriate, if not criminal, behaviors of marked categories of outsiders and stresses the removal and policing of the latter as the primary means by which to restore neighborhood integrity.[2] By imagining that community problems originate through the deviant-coded behaviors of individuals and groups, this discourse of stability would divert discussion and debate away from systems-wide, transneighborhood concerns, such as the AGT, and transpose questions of political and economic power into problems of individual behaviors linked to racial, class, and ethnic differences.

Through an analysis of this case I show how constructions of social deviance linked to race, class, and ethnic identities serve to shield relations of political and economic subordination from contestation. I also direct attention to the state's role in promoting these power-evasive ways of addressing neighborhood problems, in this case through the implementation of a "quality-of-life" policing strategy by city officials.

The format of the town hall meeting allotted community representatives three minutes to voice their area's major concern to one or a number of public officials, who were then asked to respond. Questions from the general audience would be allowed after all the invited representatives had spoken.

George Delis, district manager of Community Board 1 in Astoria, spoke first. Delis observed that although forty-seven thousand cars had been stolen in Queens County in 1993, only fifteen of the fifteen hundred persons arrested for car theft received sentences. "We are the highest auto theft county east of the Mississippi," he argued. "We'd like to know what is being done about this major crime that is affecting everybody here."

State Senator Leonard Stavisky approached the microphone, nodding his head in sympathy as the applause died down. "Barely two hundred people are in the state's prisons for auto theft and related crimes," Stavisky declared. "This is the most expensive crime practiced against the citizenry apart from buying a home [*sic*]," he continued. "Raise your hand if *you* have been the victim of auto theft or car vandalism." A swarm of hands shot into the air, quickly followed by a roar of applause. Stavisky smiled, surveying the audience. "Okay, is it widespread enough for us to be concerned?"

Delis's choice of auto theft as his community's chief concern highlights not only the leading role crime has come to play in the discourse of neighborhood activists but also the rhetorical and policy-making emphasis that governing authorities have placed on "get tough" law enforcement as a strategy for preserving neighborhood quality of life, particularly since the mid-1960s (see Gordon 1990). Stavisky's confirmation of the state's failure to punish car thieves, along with his theatrical invocation of their victims, illustrates the complicity of state officials in cultivating the fear of crime and evoking "defensive communities," constructed in relation to external threats. The emphasis on policing served to elide and depoliticize broader, systemic inequalities by framing multifaceted social issues as *local* violations of neighborhood integrity committed by deviant individuals and social groups. This tendency to condense and represent structural problems through administratively defined categories of social deviance is illustrated in the following discursive exchange.

Ed Babor, president of the Astoria Civic Association, began his statement by pointing to an increased presence of prostitutes and homeless people in Astoria. The latter, Babor explained, were community concerns because of "their public disrobing and bodily relieving of themselves on sidewalks and streets, in front of stores, near subway stops, right in front of people and their families in broad daylight."

Captain Patrick Timlin, commander of the 114th Precinct in Astoria, responded by pointing out that the police department had made "quality-of-life issues," such as prostitution and vagrancy, high priorities. Timlin noted that the 114th Precinct was the first to implement "Operation John," which had resulted in the arrest of five hundred clients of prostitutes in six months.

Timlin continued:

> As for quality-of-life issues in general, we have given out a tremendous amount of summonses. The police department has deployed decibel monitors to target the people who have the loud radios on the streets. We go after the people who are drinking as well. The Queens task force came out and just did a joint operation with us about two weeks ago in Astoria Park, and we made about five or six arrests there and gave out seventy-five summonses that night.

Ed Babor responded:

> What about the homeless? I'm not talkin' about the homeless issue itself, I'm talkin' about them changing their clothes in the middle of the street, right on the corner. When they have to relieve themselves, they go to the nearest tree in broad daylight, women walking by and everything.

Babor's caveat, "I'm not talkin' about the homeless issue itself," at once alluding to and suppressing an alternative way of understanding the homeless problem, highlights the mechanism through which institutional arrangements of power configure the ground of the "sayable," enabling certain dispute trajectories and disabling others. The officials' emphasis on law enforcement as a mode of protecting community integrity made certain problem-solving strategies, mechanisms, and discourses available to activists. However, in pursuing these resources, residents were invited to articulate their interests, identities, and goals through place-bound notions of "community" and "quality of life" that emerge through practices of policing and surveilling space. In short, the state's readiness to respond to community problems through law enforcement practices incited activists to represent and indeed experience their concerns through the tactical logic of controlling community space.

Captain Timlin's response to Babor's qualified concern about the homeless illustrates this "imbrication of the police function into the built environment" (Davis 1990:250):

> We've received complaints about the homeless throughout the entire precinct. We have several liaisons with the Salvation Army and other outreach groups to have these people come down and get these people to go to the shelters. As recently as yesterday, in Atkins Square Park, we had the task force come down there and we swept the park clean. So I'm going to make it a top priority to target specific locations.

Timlin was followed by State Assemblyman Joseph Crowley, who applauded the NYPD's Operation John and pointed out his own contribution to the policing of public space.

> In terms of quality-of-life crimes, which is something I was very active in, I congratulate Pat Timlin. He also mentioned using a bill that I had the pleasure of sponsoring, which was a bill dealing with car and boom box noise. And I'm happy to hear that the police department is securing the instruments that are necessary to read the decibel levels, because, as Pat mentioned, where you find these types of radios, you will find a lot of other problems, whether it's urinating in public, which is a problem not only in parks and not only among people who are drinking. In fact, I saw a little boy being helped by his mother, urinating against a wall, which I found, you know, incredible. These are the types of things I'd like to stress to the police department. Again, they're the little things that, you know, go on on a regular basis.

The rationale for this theory of public order—boom box noise leads to public urinating and other social problems—was concisely elaborated in *Police Strategy No. 5: Reclaiming the Public Spaces of New York*, a report published by the office of Mayor Rudolph Giuliani and the New York City Police Department, directed by William Bratton. The report, released in July 1994, outlined a broad strategy for "reversing the decline in public order" by enforcing "decency" in public spaces (Giuliani and Bratton 1994:5):

> A decent society is one where all people are free to pursue education, enterprise, and entertainment that creates a sufficient standard of living for themselves and their families and contribute to an atmosphere of mutual respect for their fellow citizens. A decent society is a society of civility.
>
> New Yorkers have for years felt that the quality of life in their city has been in decline, that their city is moving away from rather than toward the reality of a decent society. The overall growth of violent crime during the past several decades has enlarged this perception. *But so has an increase in the signs of disorder in the public spaces of the city* (Giuliani and Bratton 1994:4; emphasis added).

Citing the writings of James Q. Wilson and George Kelling, *Strategy No. 5* advances the thesis that signs of unaddressed disorder in public spaces, such as street prostitution, "boom box cars," aggressive panhandling, and grafitti, invite further disorder and more serious crimes by signaling to society that "no one cares" (Giuliani and Bratton 1994:4). This breakdown of decency exacerbates fear among urban residents, causing them both to abandon public spaces and to leave the city. Unaddressed disorder, the report argues, is therefore the first step in the "downward spiral of urban decline" (Giuliani and Bratton 1994:4).

Police Strategy No. 5 provided a revisionist genealogy of urban decline, situating its origins in the crypto-semiotics of fear and "decency," rather than in the structures and processes of urban political economy. At the ideological level, *Strategy No. 5* appropriated the concept and language of "quality-of-life" politics, narrowing its purview to *signs* of disorder that could be read by residents in their local communities.

Whereas neighborhood activists used the "quality of life" concept to refer to a fluid and heterogeneous set of problems and issues, ranging from environmental pollution and school overcrowding to crime, grafitti, and poor municipal services, *Strategy No. 5* reinscribed quality of life as a *moral* category which, eliding the power relations that structure urban life, drew its content from a politically shaped notion of deviance:

> In one sense, this strategy may be viewed as a start toward reversing the trend Senator Daniel Patrick Moynihan has termed "defining deviancy down." Senator Moynihan argues that, as a society, we have become so overwhelmed by crime and disorder that we have "been re-defining deviancy so as to exempt much conduct previously stigmatized." In other words, "we are getting used to a lot of behavior that is not good for us."
>
> In another sense, this strategy may be viewed as an effort at what Police Commissioner William J. Bratton has called "defining decency up." In concert with

other public and private agencies, the courts, and all concerned and committed citizens, the NYPD will work to uphold a uniform standard of civility and mutual respect in all the neighborhoods of the city (Giuliani and Bratton 1994:5).

In order to achieve the goal of "defining decency up," *Strategy No. 5* outlined sweeping changes in policing practices and an enabling legislative agenda. An important objective of the strategy was to provide police precinct commanders with the authority and wherewithal to respond immediately to "disorderly conditions" in local neighborhoods without the mediation of supra-local police or other government agencies, such as the NYPD's Public Morals Division, the Department of Environmental Protection (DEP), or the State Liquor Authority.

Under "Operation Soundtrap," for example, local precinct commanders were provided with the authority and equipment needed to monitor, ticket, and seize boom box cars that were playing music too loudly, thereby lessening reliance on the enforcement actions of the DEP.[3] *Police Strategy No. 5* outlined similar enhancements in the power of local authorities to police other quality-of-life offenders, such as "squeegee cleaners," "panhandlers," "dangerous mentally ill street people," "reckless bicyclists," "illegal peddlers," "graffiti vandals," and "drunk and disorderly party-goers."

Police Strategy No. 5 and its practices of quality-of-life policing provided the institutional foundation for the discourse of militant particularism articulated by activists during UCCA'S meeting, illustrating how institutional power arrangements shape the ways in which activists formulate their interests and construct their collective identities. As Robin Wagner-Pacifici pointed out, "social discourses both reflect and reproduce power relations that 'live' in social structures" (1994:4).

However, not all speakers at the town hall meeting framed their concerns within the place-bound calculus of unaddressed social disorder. Pat Beckles began his statement by charging that the city had failed to replace street signs, install traffic lights, and stop drug selling on Ditmars Boulevard in East Elmhurst. After noting the pollution problem in Flushing Bay, Beckles raised the issue of the AGT. "The light rail system, if it is built as the Port Authority proposes, will be a tragedy. It must not be built on the surface. It must be underground, on the median of the Grand Central Parkway. We *cannot* give more of our community. We need a concerted effort on your part to be sincere to the efforts of our community. Would somebody please look into this?"

Although his statement received considerable applause from the audience, neither the Port Authority's manager at LaGuardia Airport nor any public officials responded. The problem of the AGT proposal was beyond the pale of the "defended neighborhood" (Suttles 1972). Nevertheless, Beckles's suspicions were warranted: one month later the Port Authority would renege on its agreement with East Elmhurst. With the meeting time now running short, Poveromo hastily introduced the next speaker, Adrienne Sumowicz, president of the Jackson Heights Beautification Group.

"We're here to turn the tides," Sumowicz began. "We're not just asking for nice little answers and 'maybe we'll think about it.' We need your help. We're not just playing around." The audience applauded with enthusiasm.

"We fought for landmarking," Sumowicz continued, "not just because of the beautiful homes and buildings that are there, but because it would bring an important stabilizing factor into our community. We had a dual purpose. Our community is falling apart. We have apartment buildings that are turning into tenement slums. And you know what's worse? The politicians don't care!"

Sumowicz called for the formation of a task force of police, elected officials, and community people to investigate the renting of apartments in Jackson Heights to low-income people.

"These apartments should not be *low*-income, *poverty* level," she declared. "I mean, none of us look like we're poverty. And certainly with all of the drugs in our community there's nobody *poverty*." Laughter rose from the audience. Sumowicz continued: "We want people who have the ability, the police units, to go into these apartments and see what's going on. Why do we have to have thirty people in an apartment! There's quality-of-life issues in Jackson Heights because of these apartment buildings. They're coming into our community and now we're saying *enough!*"

Joyce Cumberbatch turned to me looking perplexed. "Who? Who is she talking about?"

City Councilwoman Helen Marshall, representing East Elmhurst and parts of Corona and Jackson Heights, was the first to respond to Sumowicz. Marshall waited at the microphone for the applause and shouts from the audience to die down. The ensuing dialogue reveals the exclusionary and deeply racialized character of this power-evasive discourse of community defense.

> HELEN MARSHALL: I think there's hardly an issue that you've mentioned that a number of us—and we can't operate without the community—that we've all been involved in. The idea of a task force is intriguing and interesting and, if it would help, I think that a task force would be great. You have the community board addressing issues, you have various associations, and even your organization, United—
>
> ADRIENNE SUMOWICZ: No, no, no, Helen. There's state and federal and city money being given to different groups to *place* people here. That has to be stopped.
>
> HM: All right, first of all, I don't know exactly what you mean by people being—
>
> AS: Someone has to sit and look at the statistics that we have. Not just in the—
>
> HM: About people paid to come?
>
> AS: Well, people who are being placed in these rental apartments. They're not the regular *family*. You have doubling up going on. You have the city subsidiz-

ing, helping this. This has to stop. This community can't take it. We can't have quality of life like this. We're *bulging* at the seams. Something's gotta give here.

HM: Well, I think that our—one of our biggest problems is drugs and I know—

Marshall was interrupted by shouting from the audience. A middle-aged man in the rear stood and yelled: "Adrienne, why don't you ask her why she's not changing the immigration laws!" The audience burst into applause, many shouting out in agreement with the man in the rear. Nonplused, Marshall paused. Poveromo returned to the podium and called for order.

HM: Drugs are *clearly* a problem that has plagued our community. It didn't start this year. It's been going on for some twenty or more years. I think that what you're asking now is for some heightened up activity. We can put a task force together. I am sure that *all* of us would agree to do it, if that is the answer. We have educational problems, our schools—

AS: Schools are not the answer.

HM: Well, you said you wanted a task force.

AS: No, I want a task force to look at housing.

HM: Only housing? What about education? Our schools are in crisis and—

AS: My question *here* was focused on housing, and I'm asking for a housing task force. I am asking you to look at these apartments—no one is looking at what is going into our rental apartments—to look at the landlord, to look at the banks, the city, and see what money is being given to *these people*, *bonus* money—I want to know, because this is *our* community.

HM: All right, Adrienne, we cannot *only* look at apartments. If we're going to talk about the problems of housing, we have to look at it all. We've got overoccupancy, and we've got problems all over. And if we're going to talk about a housing committee or a housing task force, that's fine, but let's attack it from all levels.

Congresswoman Carolyn Maloney spoke next, pointing out that Congress had recently passed a ban on assault weapons and that she was supporting a national gun registration law tied to the anticrime bill. This, she said, would help in fighting drugs.

"Now, in response to the gentleman's question in the back," she continued. "Congress does have a task force—and the president has a task force—working on immigration law changes. Likewise in the Congress; the Judiciary Committee is looking at the whole system that is not working" (Figure 8.1).

Sumowicz, who had remained at the microphone, retorted that gun control was not the answer. "I have to go back to our housing issue," she insisted. The audience clapped.

Figure 8.1. Congresswoman Carolyn Maloney responds to audience questions about immigration reform at the United Community Civic Association's town hall meeting. Rose Marie Poveromo stands behind the podium at the far right.

State Assemblyman Ivan Lafayette, representing Jackson Heights, approached the microphone and asked Sumowicz to explain her claim that public funds were being used to place people in apartment buildings.

ADRIENNE SUMOWICZ: People are putting city, state, and federal money into these people.

IVAN LAFAYETTE: I don't know—who are *these people*?

AS: Obviously, the renters—because I'll tell you what. We have documented this. Again, someone who sits with us would be very happy to show—

IL: I'd like to know—you're talking in a public forum. And since you've made this a public issue, and you're saying *those people* and public money, I'd like to know—

AS: Welfare recipients! Group home turnstiles—would you like me to go on? I can give—I can show you children who have been put in for a group home—and I'm not talking disabled. I'm talking rap sheets that are *six feet long*.

IL: Are you talking group homes? Are you talking about group homes?

AS: I'm talking—I'm talking delinquent people that are coming in and getting city-subsidized money and going into these rental complexes without *us* even knowing about it.

[Applause]

IL: Are you saying that the city is giving money to criminals to move into apartments?

AS: To *landlords*. We must look at—

[Applause]

IL: I'm just trying to clarify what you're saying. Are you saying to me that the City of New York is picking up criminals and giving them money to occupy illegal apartments? That's what you're saying?

Jeering is directed at Lafayette, and one man shouts, "Are you an immigration apologist?"

AS: I am telling you—you asked me who is living in those apartments and how, and I am telling you how.

IL: That there are only criminals moving in?

AS: Yes, *sir*. Look at the quality of life we have. You think that that's done by *us*? I mean, be real. We're obviously bulging at the seams.

IL: I don't know who *us* is. And who—

AS: The people that are *here*!

Sumowicz's dialogue with public officials, although representing an extreme position in the discourse of militant particularism, demonstrated the strong nativist tendencies in power-evasive notions of "community." The construction of "us" as the predominantly white and native-born audience was enabled by practices which, like those elaborated in *Police Strategy No. 5*, attributed *structural* determination to the behavior of marked categories of individuals and groups. Thus welfare recipients, immigrants, homeless persons, and "squeegee cleaners" inhabited equivalent positions as subjects in this exclusionary discourse and its related practices of subjugation. If Pat Beckles's appeal for help in holding the Port Authority accountable fell on deaf ears, it was because people were "talkin' community" in a way that excluded difference and rendered power and the politics of class, ethnic, and racial differences invisible. For the "us" that was invented at UCCA's town hall meeting were the white and "decent" citizens of northern Queens.

After the meeting I asked Cumberbatch where she thought things stood in the fight against the AGT as we waited for a taxi outside the Lexington School for the Deaf. "I don't know," she replied. "I don't see much more happening on it. I guess out here they're more worried about immigrants and winos than about the Port Authority."

THE RETURN OF THE AUTHORITY

On the evening of October 20 Community Board 3 convened its monthly meeting at the Louis Armstrong Intermediate School on the border of East Elmhurst and Jackson Heights. Board members took their places at the front of the dimly lit school lunchroom. Community residents settled into their seats at child-sized tables, eying with curiosity the three men in business suits who were taping technical drawings to the green-tiled wall.

"They look like gangsters, don't they?" a middle-aged white man remarked as he took the seat next to me, dropping a manila folder crammed with papers on the table. Shirley Clark, president of the Ninety-sixth/Ninety-seventh Street Block Association, sat across from us and perused the slick *Access* newsletter that a PANYNJ official had just distributed to the audience. John, the president of a Republican club in Jackson Heights, greeted Clark and reached into his folder.

"Shirley, did you see this?" he asked, eyes flashing with excitement as he held up the *New York Newsday* article. Clark frowned with concern and eyed the headline: "Exec's Plunge Off the Edge: Rampage Linked to Port Authority Probe." John turned to me: "Do you believe them? Unbelievable what they'll do."

The *Newsday* article, published that morning, reported the suicide of a former executive of the Frederic R. Harris, Inc., consulting firm, which had been awarded the $10 million contract to manage planning for the AGT (*Newsday*, 20 October 1995). The Manhattan district attorney's office was investigating whether the executive's suicide was linked to the theft of secret Port Authority documents in a bid-rigging scheme.

Before being fired by the engineering and consulting firm, the executive had been working as an in-house consultant to the Port Authority. In his suicide note the executive stated that he had stolen documents from the Port Authority and passed them to his supervisor at Harris to strengthen the company's bid for the AGT contract. Instead of being rewarded for his efforts, he was fired. On September 16 the executive burst into the home of his former supervisor, set it on fire, and shot himself. *Newsday* reported that the Nassau County police were "baffled" when Port Authority officials "mysteriously" arrived at the house while it was still smoking, misrepresenting themselves as the executive's friends and questioning police about the suicide (20 October 1995).

A second article, "PA Rail Link Records Seized," reported that agents from the Manhattan district attorney's office had seized records from the Port Authority's Airport Access Program and observed that the AGT program "was already facing withering opposition from civic groups and residents of Queens and Manhattan who objected to the line being built in their neighborhoods" (20 October 1995).

When Paul Lewis, chairman of Community Board 3, called the meeting to order and introduced the first speaker, John collected the fragments of the *Newsday* exposé and carefully returned them to his folder. First on the community board's agenda was an up-date on the Flushing Bay park and promenade project and the AGT. A representative from the New York City Parks Department, which was charged with developing the promenade, and officials from Port Authority had been invited to speak to the community.

"We are here to be guided by the community," an official with the Airport Access Program began. "In terms of the two alternatives that you will see here tonight, nothing has changed as far as we're concerned."

Shirley Clark looked around the room quizzically. "Two alternatives? What does she mean, two alternatives?"

The PANYNJ official continued. "If you want us to do something different, we're willing to do it." She then introduced a member of the Port Authority's consulting team that had assembled on the left side of the room, next to a huge aerial photograph of the city showing the AGT alignment. Jeff, the consultant, recapped how the Port Authority had worked with the community to develop the plan for the "depressed" or semi-submerged alignment for the AGT in East Elmhurst.

"Now," he continued, "I'm going to begin to describe to you a variation that we were asked to take a look at as a result of the improvements that are planned for this promenade and park area along Flushing Bay." Assisted by a second member of the team, Jeff held up a large technical drawing of the variation. Members of the community board looked on with interest, twisting in their seats to get a better view. "Who the hell can see that!" a woman in the audience blurted. A third consultant stepped forward to support the sagging middle of the drawing.

Jeff described the new option, which proposed siting the AGT at ground level along the median of the Grand Central Parkway, rather than *below* ground on the adjacent parkland fronting on Flushing Bay. The latter "depressed" alignment had been agreed on through the Port Authority's negotiations with East Elmhurst. By the terms of this agreement, the AGT was to be built in a semi-submerged, landscaped tube which Port Authority officials had claimed would serve as a "visual screen" and "noise barrier," shielding promenade users from the sights and sounds of the eight-lane Grand Central Parkway.

While his colleagues fumbled with the profile drawings of the new alignment, Jeff attempted to give them representational authority, presenting the drawings as authentic "snapshots" of a smooth, if not intractable, technological evolution: "These are not in the form of a presentational graphic. These are working drawings that were pulled off the drawing board to bring here and show you how the concepts were developing . . . ah . . . after we had already developed our below-grade alignment along the promenade."

Jeff explained that the Port Authority had discovered that its proposal for the depressed alignment along Flushing Bay was "incompatible" with the New York City Parks Department's plan to develop the promenade. City Councilwoman Helen Marshall had warned Port Authority officials, after the East Elmhurst agreement had been reached, of the importance of coordinating their planning activities with those of the Parks Department.

Stunned, members of the community board listened as the Parks Department's young landscape architect explained that the AGT would take up "valuable green space" on the promenade, interfering with pedestrian use. Holding up a rendition of his department's plan for the promenade, the architect cheerfully declared, "We're going to transform this area into another green space, a better green space, with a continuous bike path and pedestrian path similar to what you see at Battery Park City."

Barbara Coleman, Corona–East Elmhurst resident and a member of the board's Aviation Committee, broke the silence and addressed the Port Authority's consultant:

BARBARA COLEMAN: Let's drop this down into words I can understand. One of the things our committee agreed to was a ditch. And in the ditch went the AGT. Now you're saying you want it to rise to grade level. Is that what you're saying?

PORT AUTHORITY: It's going to be above ground, I believe, but not elevated. It's going to be, from my understanding, above ground level. It will not be elevated as early as it was when it was underground. I don't know why—

BC: Now you're confusing me. Do we have a *ditch* or *don't* we have a ditch?

PA: No, it's on grade.

BC: We were promised a parkland ditch, which the AGT would go in. Now you're telling me it's going to be at grade rather than below grade. Is that what you're telling me?

PA: That's correct.

A flurry of cross-talking erupted among board members and the audience. John, sitting next to me, leaned across the table toward Shirley Clark: "Now it's gonna be underground?" he asked. "No," Clark replied, "its going to be *on* the ground."

A woman raised her hand and asked whether building the AGT on the median of the Grand Central Parkway would require widening the median and, as a consequence, require a scaling down of the promenade. "Numbers and facts can confuse people," she added, pointing to the drawings. "For example, I want everybody in this room to know, I am *not* thirty-five pounds overweight. I am six inches *too short*." The PANYNJ consultants grinned awkwardly and then gave assurances that the parkway's median would not be widened.

Members of the community board launched a barrage of questions, pressing the Port Authority consultants and the Parks Department architect on technical issues pertaining to the two options. The architect restated his agency's concern that the depressed AGT alignment agreed to earlier would take up valuable green space. He added that there was also an important safety issue: the semi-submerged tube and landscaped berm, he claimed, would "isolate" the promenade from public view. "The best way to secure the park space," he explained, "to keep it, you know, safe, is to have eyes looking in on it all the time."

"From where?" asked Hamlett Wallace, chair of the Aviation Committee, frowning incredulously. "From cars?"

"From all over," the architect replied. "I mean, if you've got space, if you have cars, they can keep an eye on the promenade and parkland. That's a major concern of ours."

Wallace responded by revisiting the argument for the "landscaped berm" that had been used by Port Authority officials to win East Elmhurst's support for the AGT project. "The way they were going to do it, the berm would act as a sound barrier for people who walk on the promenade. That's why they—"

The architect interrupted: "It's cutting it off though. It cuts it off from public view."

Catcalls and disgruntled comments rose from the audience. "What we need is some accurate drawings," Wallace continued, "that will actually tell us what is going on."

"That's why *this* drawing is being developed," the Parks Department architect retorted, holding up his poster board. "So we can overlay our program with their program. Then you will be able to see where the tight spaces are and where the conflicts are going to occur." A Port Authority consultant agreed, assuring the assembly that an "overlaid" drawing was now being developed by Port Authority planners.

The audience and board members greeted this announcement of yet another drawing with a new round of outbursts. Ed Lewis, the community board's chair, called for order and addressed the Parks Department architect:

> I'll tell you what my problem with the Parks Department is. First of all, your concern is that this AGT thing will take away some green space that doesn't even exist for us—a promenade that you haven't even built yet! Fifty percent concrete and 50 percent green space is better than what we have now. Second, the Parks Department's concern over parkland in this area is astounding for this community board, because you tripped over yourself to give away parkland in the middle of Flushing Meadows–Corona Park for the United States Tennis Association. It's an amazing contradiction that parkland becomes sacred when it's to our detriment. And when it's to the benefit of some outside entity, then parkland can be just thrown away.

Lewis's comments provoked applause and more questioning. Barbara Coleman asked why the AGT could not be built in a tunnel below the planned promenade. Edward O'Sullivan, Director of the Airport Access Program, replied that the soil was poor and that a tunnel would be too expensive. Lewis asked why groups in Manhattan had received money to study the AGT when "the people of Queens will have to live with it." The PANYNJ official replied that he was not privy to that information.

The woman who had earlier alluded to PANYNJ's manipulation of numbers and facts stood and informed the assembly that the FAA would hold a public hearing the next day to solicit comments on its plan to rescind the High Density Rule (HDR), a regulation limiting the number of flights at airports located in densely populated areas. Turning to the PANYNJ officials, she argued that the repeal of the HDR would render moot their claims of decreased automobile traffic in Queens resulting from the AGT.

"Are you talking to Mr. O'Sullivan?" Barbara Coleman called out. "Because he *did* say that we would not have any more planes at LaGuardia."

The Port Authority officials remained silent and began to gather their drawings. Shirley Clark peered at John, sitting across from her. "Now, how did they expect us to find out about this hearing?" John shook his head. "This is just outrageous." Fuming, he reached into the folder for the *Newsday* article.

Noting the late hour, the board's chairperson closed the question-and-answer period. John protested, wanting to confront Port Authority officials with the bid-rigging scandal that had been exposed in *Newsday*. After a brief dispute, the board moved on to the next item on its agenda. The officials from the Port Authority and the Parks Department took their drawings and filed out of the lunchroom.

"You see," Shirley Clarke said to me, shaking her head. "They don't want us to say anything." John stood and collected his things to leave. "They look like gangsters in those suits, don't they?"

HEGEMONY AND THE POLITICS OF THE PUBLIC SPHERE

Nothing is more difficult than the art of maneuver.
(Sun Tzu)

Corona–East Elmhurst's struggle against the Port Authority did not end in defeat. On June 1, 1995, George Marlin, PANYNJ's executive director, announced that the proposed twenty-two-mile AGT plan was "dead" (*New York Times*, 1 June 1995). Marlin, appointed by the newly elected governor, George Pataki, cited soaring cost estimates for the AGT as a prime reason for scrapping the original plan. Port Authority officials feared that the AGT's cost, now estimated at $5 billion, could not be raised from the Passenger Facility Charge as first claimed and would require massive public subsidization. A *New York Times* article, reporting on the AGT's demise, noted that the AGT proposal had drawn strong criticism from transportation experts and "stirred a backlash on the Upper East Side of Manhattan" (1 June 1995). Not surprisingly, opposition to the AGT in Queens was not mentioned.

One year later the Port Authority's board of directors approved a new, smaller-scale plan for an elevated, light rail airport access system that would bypass LaGuardia Airport. Under the $1 billion plan, an 8.4-mile rail link would be built between Kennedy Airport and the Long Island Railroad's Jamaica Station in Queens (*New York Times*, 11 May 1996). In this proposal LaGuardia Airport would be served by a high-speed ferry system departing from Manhattan's East Side which would be developed through a separate project (FAA/NYSDOT 1996). "It is a first step," George Marlin told *Newsday*. "There is minimal community opposition. The money is available. The technology is available ... We have to focus in getting it off the drawing boards" [*sic*] (14 May 1996).

Many factors figured in the Port Authority's decision to abandon the plan for the AGT. Perhaps most significant was the system's cost which PANYNJ officials eventually admitted would far exceed revenues generated by the PFC ticket surcharge. The *Times* reported that PANYNJ's executive director had been given a mandate by New York State's newly elected Republican governor to privatize some Port Authority operations and that Marlin "feared that the project would ensnare the Port Authority in a financial fiasco" (1 June 1995). Second, the proposal drew sharp and highly publicized criticism from transportation experts, public interest organizations, and probusiness advocacy groups which, like the Regional Plan Association, argued that the AGT would not provide adequate links to the city's existing transportation system and, consequently, would not serve key zones of the city's business district, such as the Wall Street area and the West Side.[4] Since Port Authority officials had based their arguments for the AGT on claims linking the mobility of capital to the economic well-being of the city, this criticism from the business community was particularly damaging, as well as embarrassing.

Finally, neighborhood-based opposition, most notably from Manhattan's affluent and politically powerful Upper East Side, focused public attention on environmental and other quality-of-life problems associated with the AGT system while raising the specter of protracted and costly legal challenges. The Port Authority's scaled-back proposal placated many of these critics by eliminating the Manhattan terminals, providing access to Pennsylvania Station (and the West Side) via the new system's link to the Long Island Railroad and, perhaps most important, by reducing the project's cost to an estimated $1 billion.

Given the complexity of this political field, it would be difficult to determine the impact that resistance in Corona and East Elmhurst had on the defeat of the AGT proposal. The efforts of Joyce Cumberbatch and other activists did force Port Authority officials to respond to and negotiate community concerns and, in the process, expend resources, parry public criticism, and develop planning alternatives which, however disingenuous, provoked wider resistance from other areas of Queens. This opposition added to the political as well as economic costs of the project which, in the end, led to the abandonment of the twenty-two-mile AGT system.

Nevertheless, the Port Authority's practices of managing opposition were effective in shaping the terms and trajectories of neighborhood opposition in Queens, inciting the formation of local, place-bound constructions of identity and interests, and imbuing certain courses of action with macroeconomic authority and technical necessity. To these ends, the Port Authority and its boosters worked to command the multiple sites in the public sphere where social issues and meanings are publicly elaborated, contested, and communicated.

In their meetings with activists PANYNJ officials utilized a discourse of technical feasibility, verbal and visual, to lend authority to specific constructions of the built environment and to anchor activists to equally specific narratives of their spatial identity. Recall the PANYNJ consultant's remarks concerning the fantasy image of the landscaped berm: "I think that one should imagine a promenade there. . . . this, by the way, is a mechanically drawn, very accurate perspective, using all the dimensions and plans and profiles that are there. It's a very accurate representation because we don't want to fool ourselves, and we don't want to fool you."

This and other invitations to imagine place, incorporated into Port Authority narratives of negotiated progress, served to depoliticize issues regarding the AGT's systemic appropriateness and impact by projecting them beyond the borders of the imagined community. The charge, repeatedly made by activists, that the Port Authority was using divide-and-conquer tactics accurately captured the political significance of the Port Authority's practices of cultivating and legitimating local, place-bound constructions of political identity and interest.

These processes of governing dissent extended beyond the borders of Corona–East Elmhurst to implicate other relations of power and discursive sites in the wider public sphere. Through the mass media, PANYNJ officials invoked the ideology of global competitiveness to cast the interests of Queens activists as local and therefore subordinate to broader needs of the regional economy and antithetical to those of other localities such as Manhattan, origin of the "business traveler." With few exceptions, the process of "story making" in the mass media privileged the accounts of issues and disputes provided by elected officials and by influential and typically Manhattan-based organizations. As a result, although activists in Queens shared a systems-level critique of the AGT with their counterparts in Manhattan, their opposition was framed in the mass media as focusing on local environmental effects such as noise, vibration, and blocked "view corridors." Moreover, the concerns of Queens activists were regularly presented in the mass media in the form of direct quotations taken from *individual* activists, rather than in the more authoritative form of organizational "positions" with the consistency to be paraphrased by reporters.

If the Port Authority's campaign for the AGT demonstrates generally the variety of practices, discourses, and institutional locations utilized in the hegemonic process, the organizing experience of activists in Corona and East Elmhurst illuminates the complex relationship of that process to power differentials grounded in class and racial hierarchies. On the one hand, differences in political capital tied to class position weakened the relative ability of Queens activists to contest the forms of technological and macroeconomic authority exercised by the AGT coalition. On the other hand, nativist constructions of racial, ethnic, and citizenship differences at UCCA's town hall meeting, braced and enlivened by *Police Strategy No. 5*, weakened possibilities for forging common interpretations of political problems and interests beyond the boundaries of the "defended neighborhood." Racial and ethnic categories were not explicitly named in the discourse of unaddressed disorder. Nevertheless, framing neighborhood problems as emanating from the behaviors of "outsider" groups, such as immigrants, welfare families, and the homeless, not only affirmed racial and ethnic bigotries but also promoted the view that community integrity required the exclusion, rather than negotiation, of differences. Race- and class-structured power hierarchies and discourses thus served to enhance the Port Authority's ability to divide its opposition and command the terms and directions of public discussion and debate on the AGT and other airport-related issues.

The making of hegemony relies precisely on these diverse and multisited practices of governing public deliberation and dissent. What makes the hegemonic process effective is less its "taken for grantedness" or coherence as a belief system than its capacity as an ensemble of political relations and practices to command the social processes through which meanings are publicly articulated, communicated, and invested with contextual authority and social legitimacy (cf. Eley 1992).[5] Hegemony works less on the hearts and minds of the disempowered than on their ability to articulate and exercise a political identity able to realize the social force necessary to change the order of power relations. Hegemony is the power to make and remake political subjects.[6]

The case of Corona–East Elmhurst's struggle with the Port Authority suggests that political elites are less successful at imposing (or concealing) dominant worldviews than they are at strategically governing the public articulation of meanings and symbols, that is, at regulating the social processes through which meanings are brought to bear in specific contexts to constitute collective and potentially empowering constructions of political interests and identity. Activists were well aware that the Port Authority's claim of the link between airport access and the city's ability to compete in the global economy was a gross simplification of complex economic and political forces. They also knew that PANYNJ's assurances that the AGT would spur job creation were well-worn ploys to win community support for objectionable urban policies. Years of negotiating with public- and private-sector officials, researching urban issues, and, in some cases, reviewing community development budgets had taught activists a great deal about how government works and about the impact of state policies on economic processes. What they lacked was less a grasp of the relationship between neighborhood issues and the global economy than the political resources and space needed to convert those understandings into an empowering and broad-based political identity and social movement. And it was precisely those resources and that political space that were the targets of the Port Authority.

CHAPTER NINE

Conclusion

Today, when we look back over our oppression, we try to
measure the amount of freedom we have obtained thus far.
We perceive, through close observation, that such men
as Nat Turner, Gabriel Prosser, Denmark Vesey,
Frederick Douglass, and preachers from the
Old Testament did not talk about loving the enemy
but rather about the importance of freedom.
(Arthur Hayes, East Elmhurst–Corona Civic Association)

JOHN BELL had invited me to the East Elmhurst–Corona Civic Association's 1995 Scholarship Dinner Dance held at the flamboyant Starlight Ballroom in Jackson Heights. Bell was being awarded the Civic Association's Pioneer Award for his community activism over the past forty years. Dressed in a crisp tuxedo, he whisked back and forth between the glitzy lobby and the ballroom, escorting guests to the four tables he had reserved for the occasion. Two were filled with people from the Corona Congregational Church where Bell worshiped. His extended family, some visiting from North Carolina, sat at a third. Bell seated me at the last table with an assortment of friends from various times and places.

"Well, look who's here!" Selma Heraldo declared, twisting around in her chair to greet me. "I was just asking about you the other day." Heraldo, a vivacious African-American woman, had been a neighbor and close friend of Jake Govan. She had taken me on as a protégé when I first began my research in 1987. Retired from the telephone company, Heraldo had been raised in Corona and knew everyone and everything. She had a keen interest in community history and had helped me to figure out relationships between people, places, and events.

Although the eight people at our table were all friends of John Bell, no one knew anyone else. We sat through the salad course in silence to the music of Ellington's "Take the A Train." When the prime rib arrived, Heraldo struck up a conversation with Phil Sillman, a big, bald, and gregarious Jewish/Italian-American man in his early eighties who had worked with John Bell in reform politics during the 1960s. A retired lithographer, Sillman had been a union organizer and talked about Bell's work in the Furriers' union and about the future of the labor movement. When it was discovered that Sillman and most of the others at the table had attended P.S. 92 in Corona, a spirited discussion ensued as people recalled and matched events and persons from the past.

"Don't I know you?" Heraldo asked a woman sitting across the table. "Yes, you do look familiar," responded Antoinette Wallace. Wallace had lived in East Elmhurst until the 1970s when she moved to New Jersey. The two women exchanged the names of family, friends, and streets until Heraldo placed Wallace as the aunt of a well-known community activist. When dessert arrived and the awards presentation was about to begin, everyone at the table had been securely planted in Corona's past. Heraldo turned to me, fork in hand, and smiled: "You see, I do know everybody."

Like the conversation at our table, the Civic Association's annual dinner dance was an occasion when Corona–East Elmhurst made itself a community by recollecting people, events, and meanings from its past and fashioning them into a shared, yet far from seamless, vision of the future. A pleasurable pause in the arduous work of everyday activism, the dinner dance provided a venue for summarizing and reworking the social meanings of community, black identity, political commitment, and struggle. The dance was very much a story residents "[told] themselves about themselves," as Clifford Geertz put it (1973:448).

In February 1995 this story was not a heartening one. The previous November, Democratic Governor Mario Cuomo had been defeated by George Pataki, an upstate Republican who pledged to make deep cuts in social services and pursue an otherwise conservative policy agenda (Figure 9.1). The year before that the city's first black mayor, David Dinkins, had been defeated by Rudolph Giuliani, a fusion candidate who was pursuing an equally aggressive budget-cutting agenda buttressed by a "law and order" policy of intensive public policing. Corona–East Elmhurst, like the city's other low- and middle-income communities, would bear the brunt of these reductions in education, community development programs, and other public services. The appeal of Arthur Hayes to Nat Turner, Gabriel Prosser, and other race rebels in his presidential address for the event underscored Black Corona's sense of alarm, foreboding, and outrage.

In their acceptance speeches the six awardees echoed this alarm, stressing the themes of community empowerment and service. Two awards were given to women—one a block association organizer, the other a local Baptist minister. Three were given to men—a marine geologist, a police detective, and an actor—all of whom had been raised in Corona–East Elmhurst, moved away, and returned "home" for the event to reaffirm their ties to the neighborhood. When John Bell received his Pioneer Award for community activism, he recounted the contributions that had been made by John Booker, Jake Govan, and others who, up to their deaths, had stressed the importance of being vigilant and informed about struggles for social justice (Figure 9.2).

Figure 9.1. City Councilwoman Helen Marshall (*center*) discusses election returns with campaign workers at the Frederick Douglass Democratic Association on election night, 1994.

After the ceremony Bell came over to our table and showed us the plaque he had just received. Selma Heraldo congratulated him and then frowned. "Why do you always have to give such a long speech and hold up the dancing." She gestured at the band reassembling on the stage.

Bell looked to me in mock frustration. "You see, that's the problem with this country. Nobody ever wants to talk about politics. We need to use events like this to educate people about what--"

Heraldo interrupted: "Don't you go and give us another one of your speeches. We just got finished with the last one!"

Glasses rattled as we all broke into laughter. Bell grinned and watched the dancers line up for the "electric slide."

It was at events like the Civic Association's dinner dance that the concepts of community, identity, and culture seemed most concrete to me, most dynamic, and most insinuated in the practice of politics. For it was by recollecting past struggles and achievements, producing shared meanings about the present, and dancing the electric slide that residents of Corona and East Elmhurst constructed a black community with complex and deeply historical commitments to social activism. And it was in shared laughter, as much as shared suffering, that Selma Heraldo, John Bell, and others found the strength and endurance to press these beliefs and commitments into the future.

Figure 9.2. Arthur Hayes (*center*) presents John Bell (*left*) with the East Elmhurst–Corona Civic Association's Pioneer Award for lifelong community service at the association's 1995 Scholarship Dinner Dance.

It is precisely this relation between history, culture, and politics that has been ignored in most narratives of life in the "black ghetto" and its close cousin the "inner city." And though this elision has often been justified in the name of exposing the "grim realities" of urban poverty and joblessness, it has all too often obscured the ways in which race, class, and other social hierarchies shape contemporary urban life; equally important, it has kept us from learning from the everyday struggles of American-Americans for social justice.

My purpose in writing this book was not simply to convey or illustrate the diversity of African-American life and experience, to argue, as many have before me, against the conflation of black identity, poverty, and pathology. For if, as Audre Lorde warned, there is danger in building one's house with the master's tools, we face similar pitfalls when dismantling this house that racism built (1984). Merely to unmask or deconstruct the arsenal of images, tropes, and narratives that have been used for eons to represent the disempowered risks engaging us in the endless remodeling of a structure that needs to be razed. All social groups are diverse, all poverty is political, and the concepts "black ghetto" and "inner city" are at best empty and useless tropes. Period.

More important, the struggles of activists in Black Corona contributes to our understanding of the social processes through which collective identities and shared political commitments are historically constructed, practiced, and disabled across multiple and crosscutting hierarchies of power. In their struggles for political power, neighborhood services, and environmental justice, black activists strove to construct common definitions of need, empowering social identities, and alternative political spaces in which to negotiate interests and allegiances across racial, ethnic, and gender lines. In contrast, their adversaries—sometimes the state, sometimes capital, and often a complex amalgam of the two—worked to undermine this empowering politics of identity by employing practices of divide and conquer which constituted and braced disabling and power-evasive constructions of racial, class, and spatial identity.

It is these strategies and practices, the nuts and bolts of political resistance and domination, commitment, and indifference, that we stand to learn from the people of Black Corona.

Chapter 1
Introduction

1. For discussions and critiques of conservative analyses of urban poverty and their political use in attacking social welfare programs during the Reagan and Bush presidencies, see Piven and Cloward (1982), Omi and Winant (1986), Block et al. (1987), Katz (1989), Phillips (1991), and Williams (1992). See Collins (1989), Fineman (1991), Reed (1991), and Williams (1994) for critical analyses of the "welfare mother" trope in discourses about urban black poverty. See Gordon (1991) for an analysis of increases in law enforcement spending and prison construction, beginning roughly with the Nixon administration.

2. *New York Times*, 3 May 1992. See Davis (1990) and Gregory (1994) for case studies of the use of discourses of black family pathology and black rage to depoliticize social justice issues. On the concept of "depoliticization" as it relates to discourses about family and domestic stability, see Fraser (1989:161–171).

3. See Gilder (1981) and Murray (1984) for examples of this perspective.

4. In a 1991 article Wilson summarized the impact of economic restructuring on the minority poor:

> The shift from goods-producing to service-producing industries, increasing polarization of the labor market into low-wage and high-wage sectors, innovations in technology, relocation of manufacturing industries out of the central city, periodic recessions, and wage stagnation exacerbated the chronic problems of weak labor-force attachment among the urban minority poor. This resulted in accelerated increases in the rate of joblessness (unemployment and nonparticipation in the labor force) among urban blacks, despite the passage of antidiscrimination legislation and despite the creation of affirmative-action programs. The sharp climb in joblessness helped to trigger other problems such as the rise in concentrated urban poverty. (6)

5. See Massey and Denton (1993) and Oliver and Shapiro (1995).

6. For critiques of this middle-class role model view, see Reed (1991), Trotter (1993), Kelley (1994), and Duneier (1992).

7. See, in particular, Reed (1988) and Williams (1992). The gendered logic of this "failed family" model registers and reaffirms what feminist scholars have described and critiqued as the "double standard" of welfare provision (Pearce 1985; Nelson 1990; Fraser 1989; and Gordon 1990). Linda Gordon argued that a key source of this double standard is the "family wage system" which constructs women as domestic dependents of independent, wage-earning men (1990). As a result, not only are women who receive means-tested relief stigmatized and administratively penalized for presiding over "deviant" households, but their needs are constructed narrowly as the absence of a male wage.

8. See Williams (1992), Trotter (1993), and Jackson (1993) for critiques of this "Golden Age" view of black class relations before civil rights–era reforms.

9. Rainwater accounted for the function of this autonomy in peculiarly psychological terms:

> This functional autonomy of the lower-class Negro subculture is in the interest of both the larger society and of the group itself. The ghetto requires breathing-room free from the oppressive eye of conventional society, and therefore from the oppressive application of conventional norms. Conventional society is freed from the necessity to face up to the pain and suffering that it has wrought; conventional culture is relieved of the necessity to confront the fact that in the ghetto its norms are constantly flaunted and that the social control mechanisms that are supposed to insure observance cannot operate effectively. (1970:6–7)

For critical discussions of this focus on the ghetto poor in ethnographic studies of black urban life, see Green (1970), Valentine (1971), and Williams (1992). Historians have also criticized this ghetto focus in scholarship on black urban history. See Trotter (1985) and Kusmer (1991). Notable exceptions to this research focusing on the ghetto and its poor include DuBois (1996 [1899]; 1969 [1901]), Johnson (1968 [1930]), Drake and Cayton (1945), Frazier (1962), Williams (1988), and, in black urban history, Curry (1981), Trotter (1985), Gatewood (1993), Lewis (1991b), and Kelley (1994).

10. See Hannerz (1973) and Williams (1992) for reviews of 1960s research on the black ghetto.

11. Mitchell Duneier's recent account of black working-class masculinity, *Slim's Table*, challenges the tendency to treat African-American class structure as a "middle class–underclass" dichotomy but affirms the view that the ghetto is a morally and socially disorganized region from which black men must escape in order to realize their respectability and moral virtue. "The wider society," Duneier notes, "rather than simply being a civilizing influence for these men, is a vehicle for them to express their own civility" (1992:159). In Duneier's moral cartography, this "wider society" provides social and moral order that once existed in the ghettos of old: "The greater order that is embodied in cafeteria life [i.e., the research site] was once a characteristic of ghetto life as well and, despite some stereotypes, still exists in some parts of the ghetto. Participation in the wider society ultimately confers on regulars the respectability of their own cultural traditions" (1992:160).

12. See Trotter (1985) and Kusmer (1991) for an analysis of the contribution of race relations research to understanding black social organization.

13. For examples, see Wilson (1987), Wacquant and Wilson (1989), Anderson (1990), and Duneier (1992). See Valentine (1972), Williams (1992), Gregory (1992), and Jackson (1993) for critiques of this neglect of institutional life and power relations in research on ghetto poverty.

14. Notable exceptions to this tendency are King (1981) and Lipsitz (1988).

15. See, for example, Dean (1991) and Ward (1989). For a discussion of this notion as it has pertained to the study of social movements, see Escobar and Alvarez (1992).

16. I use the term *black Americans* to emphasize the ethnic diversity of Corona's population of African descent, which includes U.S.-born African-Americans as well as first- and second-generation black immigrants from the Caribbean, Latin America, and the continent of Africa.

17. See Bender (1978), Young (1990), and Rouse (1991) for critical discussions of the concept of community.

18. Gerald Suttles (1972) develops a concept of community that captures the multiple and dynamic social attachments of urban residential groups:

> In the present account it is argued that our folk and sociological representations of the urban community are especially likely to underestimate the role of external organizations and populations in the definition and solidarity of residential groups. This underestimate applies especially to governmental units and the way in which they must create the local groups to which government itself must respond. Furthermore, it is suggested that the contemporary local urban community need not be seen as a detached and primordial solidarity but is best conceived of as a pyramid of progressively more inclusive groupings, in which each level of sociocultural integration parallels the hierarchy of "adversaries" or "advocates" who face residential groups. (1972:45)

19. See, for example, hooks (1990), Hall (1985), Gilroy (1987), Rutherford (1990), Anzaldua (1987), Kondo (1990), and Butler (1993).

20. See Wallace (1979), hooks (1990), Mercer (1994), Hall (1990), and Harper (1996).

21. See Foucault (1983), Hall (1992), and Butler (1993).

22. Historians have been much more attentive to politics and its relation to the formation of black identities. See, for example, Trotter (1985), Lipsitz (1988), Kelley (1990; 1994), and Higginbotham (1993).

23. See Rosaldo (1980), Thelen (1990), Bodnar (1992), and Kaplan (1992).

24. See Cohen (1985) for a discussion of "identity-based" new social movements approaches in relation to Marxist and "strategy-based" approaches to social movements.

25. See Escobar and Alvarez (1992) for a discussion of this problem in relation to Latin American contributions to social movement theory. This issue has been raised most pointedly in relation to the "newness" of new social movements (Melucci 1994).

26. The lack of attention to history and historical scholarship in contemporary ethnographic accounts of black urban communities is striking. The notable exception in postwar research is, not surprisingly, Drake and Cayton (1945).

27. I use this notion of the "civil rights period," or "era" to refer to the period between the 1954 Supreme Court decision in *Brown v. Board of Education* to about 1970. This usage, although arbitrarily delimited, corresponds roughly to the ways in which activists name and periodize diverse forms of social activism in Corona during the 1950s and 1960s tied to the civil rights and black power movements, and to collective mobilizations associated with the War on Poverty.

28. See, for example, Piven and Cloward (1971), Mollenkopf (1983), Jackson (1993), and Reed (1979).

29. See also Davis (1990) and Abu Lughod et al. (1994) for analyses of race and class-inflected struggles over urban space.

30. As Anthony Cutler et al. (1977) have pointed out: "Class 'interests' are not given to politics and ideology by the economy. They arise within political practice, and they are determined as an effect of political practice. Political practice does not recognize

class interests and then represent them: it constitutes the interests which it represents" (quoted in Laclau and Mouffe 1985:120).

31. See Laclau and Mouffe (1985), Aronowitz (1990), and Hall (1980; 1985) for discussions of the irreducibility of race, gender, and other social differences to "the economic." See Block (1991) for a related critique of "instrumental" treatments of the state and an analysis of the ways in which the state apparatus often conflicts with the particular interests of capitalists.

32. For a discussion of contemporary practices of discrimination in the banking industry, see Williams (1994), Massey and Denton (1993), and Oliver and Shapiro (1995). Discrimination in the delivery of public services is widely documented (see Massey and Denton 1993). For discussions of environmental racism, see Bullard (1990; 1993).

Chapter 2
Making Community

1. More than likely Margaret was a boarder who may or may not have exchanged her labor for some form of remuneration. See Haynes (1968 [1912]) for a discussion of the practice of taking in boarders among African-Americans in New York during the period.

2. Earl Lewis (1991c) noted the high percentage of black women employed in manufacturing in Norfolk, Virginia (claiming 50 percent of the city's manufacturing jobs in 1920), but pointed out that many of these jobs, like dressmaking, were paid by the piece and performed in nonfactory settings. In New York City Haynes reported that, in 1900, dressmaking employed the highest number of black women (813) after "servants and waitresses" (10,297) and "laundresses" (3,224) (1968 [1912]:72).

3. The black press played an important role in recruiting southern black female labor. Joe William Trotter records an advertisement placed in the *Wisconsin Afro-American*, beginning in 1892: "To Our Southern Readers": "Any one desiring to obtain work as a domestic, no matter where your home is, write to us, at this office, we will make for you all arrangements" (1985:12). DuBois noted the disproportionate number of African-American women among New York's black population, six to five, and observed that "the demand for Negro housemaids is unbalanced by a corresponding demand for Negro men" (1903:43).

4. Boarders included a Swedish-born engineer, an attorney from Massachusetts, a railroad clerk, and two middle-aged and self-described "capitalists."

5. In another curious case a fifty-three-year-old New York–born black laborer was recorded as married to a New York–born black woman for whom "Germany" was reported as the birthplace of her parents. An error notwithstanding, one could speculate that either one or both her parents were in fact "colored" Germans or that the woman was "white" and had, in the mind of the enumerator, become racialized through intermarriage.

6. However, as Curry (1981) noted, African-Americans faced serious social and legal occupational barriers throughout the city and were disproportionately employed as servants. Between 1826 and 1930 more than one-sixth of the 15,540 applications for positions as house servants processed by the New York Society for the Encouragement

of Faithful Domestics came from free blacks, although they accounted for less than 7 percent of the city's population (Curry 1981:22).

7. This public protest followed a long tradition of black resistance to compulsory colonization schemes, such as those advanced by the American Colonization Society established in 1817. For example, at a New York meeting in the 1830s African-Americans declared, "[W]e claim this country, the place of our birth, and not Africa, as our mother country, and all attempts to send us to Africa we consider gratuitous and uncalled for" (quoted in Curry 1981:235).

8. African-Americans from Corona, Flushing, and surrounding areas were also employed in service occupations associated with hotels, saloons, and other pleasure resorts along Flushing Bay during the 1870s and 1880s, and, earlier, at the Fashion Race Course located in what today is North Corona. See Seyfried (1986) for a discussion of these recreational areas.

9. Curry disputed the assertion that black occupational exclusion was strongly linked to increasing immigrant populations after the 1830s, noting that "discrimination, even in unskilled occupations, had been obvious well before the swelling waves of Irish immigration began to break on American shores" (1981:20).

10. See Osofsky's discussion of the difficulty of estimating black populations during this period resulting in part from the use of the census category "Colored" to include Asians, Native Americans, and Blacks (1971:220–221).

In 1890 African-Americans in Queens numbered 3,582. By 1900, however, this figure had dropped to 2,611, rising again to 3,198 in 1910 (Osofsky 1971:220). Although difficult to interpret, this drop and increase might suggest an out-migration of locally born blacks, closely followed by an immigration of African-Americans from the South. None of the city's other four county's experienced this drop in population between the years 1890 and 1900.

11. Osofsky wrote of the event:

The word spread that a "nigger chase" was on. Up and down the streets, through hotels and saloons, in cellars and streetcars, Negroes were attacked and beaten. White street gangs mobbed the electric cars on Eighth Avenue . . . pulled Negroes off at random and beat them: "Every car passing up or down Eighth Avenue . . . was stopped by the crowd and every negro on board dragged out . . . The police made little or no attempt to arrest any of [the] assailants," *The New York Times* noted. One man brought a clothesline, tied it to a lamppost, and looked for someone to lynch. (1971:48)

12. See Scheiner (1965) for a discussion of San Juan Hill and the race riot in 1905. W.E.B. DuBois, writing in 1901, described the restricted housing market faced by African-American New Yorkers at the turn of the century. "[In] the Tenderloin district, where the newer Negro immigrants must needs go for a home, the average family occupies three small rooms, for which it pays $10 to $15 a month. If the family desires a home further from the vice and dirt of New York's most dangerous slum, it must go either to Brooklyn or, far from work, up town, or be prepared to pay exorbitant rents in the vicinity of Fifty-third street" (1969 [1901]:148).

13. Responding to the *New York Age* editorial, Eugene Kinckle Jones, executive secretary of the National Urban League and a resident of Flushing, wrote: "[T]he Na-

tional Urban League accepts your challenge and will seek further to extend its work so as to be at least to meet more adequately the industrial need of the colored people." Among the points in the League's program for the establishment of a National Industrial Department were the following: "To help through available channels of information to ascertain points at which there is need of Negro labor and points at which there is an over-supply of Negro labor and to use existing agencies of publicity and placement to direct Negro labor, including migrants to those points where they are most needed and where their families most easily become adjusted" (*Age*, 9 February 1924).

14. Residents interviewed who arrived in Corona during the early decades of the century discounted the significance of racial covenants, at least in northern sections of Corona where most African-Americans settled.

15. Drake and Cayton, citing similar comments concerning the lack of prejudice in prewar Chicago, contend that much of such "testimony must be discounted as retrospective myth," sometimes associated with old settler beliefs that southern migrants "spoiled things" (1945:74–75). Though such reconstructions may have been tinged with nostalgia for the "good old days," as well as by infra-racial animosities, racism operates unevenly, shaping different arenas of social relations differently. Govan and other residents who minimized the impact of racial prejudice in everyday interactions with neighbors nonetheless emphasized racism at the workplace and in institutional contexts.

16. John W. Rapp was president of the Empire Art Metal Company, which manufactured fireproof doors and window frames and, during World War I, was contracted by the War Department to produce hand grenades.

17. Some residents reported that Long Island City–based commercial laundries servicing the railroad were an important source of employment for black women in Corona.

18. As Kenneth Kusmer pointed out: "From the very beginning, racism has run like a dark thread through American history, and it has repeatedly scarred the lives of black city dwellers. Yet racial antagonism has varied in intensity over both place and time; its effects have been channeled in distinctive ways in different types of communities; and it has impacted upon various elements of the black community in different ways" (1991, 5:99).

19. See Higginbotham (1993:76) for a discussion of the role of the Baptist press in building "racial community" and women's communities.

20. Correspondences from other communities during this period similarly noted the flu pandemic of 1918 and often provided sick lists. Seyfried (1986) reported that the influenza death rate in October 1918 was so high in Queens that local newspapers carried three columns of obituaries. By November, following a mass vaccination program, the outbreak had died down.

21. W.E.B. DuBois, in "The Problem of Amusement," captures the spirit of this secession and its underlying politics of pleasure, which frequently placed middle-class respectability, grounded in the church, at loggerheads with more secular black youth culture (cf. Kelley 1994):

I have heard sermon after sermon and essay after essay thunder warnings against the terrible results of pleasure and the awful end of those who are depraved enough to seek pleasure. I have heard such a fusillade of "don'ts" thrown at our young people: don't dance, don't play cards, don't go to the theatre, don't drink, don't smoke, don't sing songs, don't play kissing games, don't play billiards, don't play foot-ball, don't go on excursions—that I have not been surprised, gentlemen and ladies, to find in the feverish life of a great city, hundreds of Negro boys and girls who have listened for a life-time to the warning "Don't do this or you'll go to hell," and they have taken the bit between their teeth and said, "Well, let's go to hell." (1978:226–227)

22. "Many members of the Congregational Church," Drake and Cayton reported for Chicago, "stated that they liked their church because it was progressive and had a community program. But to the upper class, the church is not primarily a religious institution; it is rather a status attribute" (1945:538). Corona residents also emphasize the social consciousness and education of church members when discussing their reasons for belonging to the Congregational Church; both these qualities, of course, remain central attributes tied to black upper-class identity. Interestingly, George Lopez and many other Corona and Flushing youth who participated in the Congregational Church's Young People's Christian Endeavor, were never church members. The Lopez family, for example, attended the Resurrection Episcopal Church, which in Corona and elsewhere was also associated with elite identity and attracted many persons of West Indian descent. For some Corona youth, no doubt, participation in the Christian Endeavor offered status and entry into the exclusive cultural sphere of the "socials."

23. Drake and Cayton's account of Chicago's "upper class" society holds true for Corona's pre-depression elite as well. "Bronzeville's upper class is 'home-centered,' stressing an ordered and disciplined family life. Its style of living demands enough space and enough income to allow for frequent entertaining. The wives maintain the social ritual, and small cliques of women, or of women and their husbands, constitute the basic non-family social units" (1945:531).

24. The "four hundred" is an allusion to the black elite of Washington, D.C. (see Gatewood 1993).

25. Frazier wrote in *Black Bourgeoisie*:

The numerous "social" clubs and other forms of voluntary associations which have existed among them provided a form of participation that compensated for their reflection by the white community. At the same time these various "social" clubs have been a part of the struggle of Negroes for status within their segregated communities. The elite, who have set themselves apart as Negro "society" and have attempted to maintain an exclusive "social" life, have been extremely conscious of their inferior status in American life. For them "social" life has not only provided a form of participation; it has represented an effort to achieve identification with upper-class whites by imitating as far as possible the behavior of white "society." (1962:169)

26. See Kaplan (1992) and Blee (1991) for discussions of political culture and the role of everyday cultural practices in articulating social activist networks.

27. The 1940 figures for professional positions among whites were 7.8 percent male and 10.4 percent female; among blacks, 2.7 percent male and 3.2 percent female. The figures of that year for clerical jobs among whites were 24.6 percent male and 48.8 percent female; among blacks, 11.6 percent male and 8.9 percent female.

28. Queens received a large share of WPA resources. In addition to the building of LaGuardia Airport, the most costly project handled by the WPA in the United States, WPA labor constructed or rebuilt 240 miles of roadways in Queens, laid out public

parks and playgrounds, reconstructed the lower level of the Queensborough Bridge, and completed Queens General Hospital (Millett 1938).

29. Millett (1938) reported that although workers were generally centrally assigned by the Division of Employment and Resources of the city's Emergency Relief Bureau, some consideration was given to a worker's proximity to job location. Moreover, workers could request transfers on such grounds as "excessive car fare to the work site."

30. See Millett (1938) for a description of the WPA's organizational structure and operational procedures.

31. See Drake and Cayton (1945), Spear (1967), Kusmer (1976), and Trotter (1985).

32. This 1957 population figure is for health areas 11 and 15, which roughly coincided with the commonly understood boundaries of Corona proper. Health areas are population units that were used by the New York City Department of Health and other city agencies for the tabulation of vital statistics. However, by 1957 an additional ninety-nine hundred black residents were living to the north of Northern Boulevard in what had become known as East Elmhurst.

Chapter 3
The Movement

1. As Evelyn Higginbotham pointed out: "On the one hand, uplift meant accommodation and surrender to the concepts, principles, and ideals of the dominant society. On the other, uplift was a denial of what white society meant by accommodation, for it spoke of a possibility to move beyond the limits prescribed by the dominant society" (1993:18).

2. The depression brought about a virtual halt in the construction of residential housing, and, although the housing construction industry had begun to recover by 1940, World War II ended it once again (Massey and Denton 1993). See Hirsch (1985) for a discussion of the impact of this postwar housing shortage on African-Americans in Chicago.

3. The Fair Housing Practice, or Sharkey-Brown-Isaacs Law, exempted owner-occupied, two-family buildings and housing developments of fewer than ten private homes.

4. See Nancy Fraser (1989, 1992) for a discussion of the concept of politicization.

5. The white insurgents were Judah Kline, candidate for male assembly district leader (Part B), and Milton Norman, candidate for the New York State Assembly, Fifth A.D.

6. An incumbent Democrat, Seymour Boyers, also stood for election.

7. Ben Davis, Jr., a prominent Harlem Communist, took Adam Clayton Powell's seat on the City Council in 1944 following the latter's resignation to run for Congress (Naison 1984).

8. See also *New York Times*, 13 August, 15 August, and 2 September 1964.

9. In 1950, 21 percent of the residents of Woodside, Jackson Heights, and Elmhurst (distinct from East Elmhurst) were foreign-born whites (Community Service Council of Greater New York 1958).

10. In fact the initial proposal to pair P.S. 149 and P.S. 92 had been made by white liberal members of P.S. 149's executive committee in concert with top officials of the

United Parents Association, the coordinating body of most of the school parents associ-ations in the city (Rogers 1969).

Chapter 4
The State and the War on Politics

1. See also Piven and Cloward (1971), and Reed (1979).

2. Rioting had broken out in Harlem and Brooklyn's Bedford Stuyvesant in mid-July only weeks after the July 3 signing of the 1964 Civil Rights Act. In July 1966 racial clashes between blacks and whites in East New York, Brooklyn, prompted newly elected mayor John V. Lindsay to create a Summer Task Force to keep the peace (Katznelson 1981).

3. See Gilman (1985) for a discussion of how metaphors of degeneration and disease have been used to represent racialized population groups and to naturalize political processes. For an extraordinary case study illustrating the conflation of race, space, and disease in public policy practice, see McClain's analysis of the bubonic plague outbreak in San Francisco's Chinatown in 1900 (1988; see also 1994).

4. Katznelson (1981) pointed out that the impetus for creating the Urban Action Task Force was a series of racial clashes that occurred in East New York, Brooklyn, during the summer of 1966. Barry Gottehrer, who served as an assistant to the mayor wrote: "It was time to concentrate on neighborhoods, the poorest neighborhoods, before troubles blew up in our faces eight or ten months later. We were under pressure to alleviate the long term injustices of inadequate housing, health care facilities, sanitation collection, job opportunities. For these needs we required a massive infusion of state and federal funding, as well as planning; but with or without those funds, we needed to head off the confrontations in the streets that now seemed inevitable" (quoted in Katznelson 1981:137–138).

5. The Corona–East Elmhurst Planning Committee, precursor to the development corporation, was already receiving OEO funding. The committee was awarded $34,115 in July 1968 to operate seven programs serving 2,050 residents (Long Island Press 1968).

6. Phrase taken from Miller and Tomaskovic-Devey (1983) and quoted in Castells (1989:379).

7. The use of quasi-public development agencies, such as the city's Public Devel-opment Corporation (PDC), the state Urban Development Corporation (UDC), and the Port Authority of New York and New Jersey (PANYNJ), as lead sponsors in ma-jor projects enabled the city to override local planning review and insulated develop-ers from community opposition associated with the complex approval process (Mol-lenkopf 1992; Fainstein 1994). For example, the state UDC, created to develop low-and moderate-income housing, retained its original power to override local zon-ing and citizen participation requirements despite its rebirth as an economic develop-ment agency. The PDC, renamed the Economic Development Corporation in 1991, played a lead role in development during the 1980s, participating in two hundred projects in 1987 worth $13 billion. Although the Department of City Planning "tech-nically has responsibility for land-use planning," Susan Fainstein pointed out, it "largely deferred to the PDC/EDC's definition of the city's development strategy" (1994:116).

Robert Fitch provided a synopsis of how public development agencies were mustered to the service of development interests to build the fifty-story Citicorp building in Long Island City, Queens, during the Koch era.

Citibank, reeling from its bad real estate loans, forced to sell off its signature midtown headquarters to the Japanese, shifted to its [Long Island City] property to build a new tower. To speed development, Urban Development Corporation (UDC), PDC and the Port Authority were brought in: UDC to over-ride zoning laws; Port Authority to float bond issues that don't have to be approved by the voter for infrastructure; PDC to "help Citicorp take advantage of an array of city-sponsored financial incentives." (1993:48)

Through the aggressive deployment of zoning bonuses, public subsidies, tax incentives, and other regulatory and institutional incentives, the Koch administration promoted a development of the built environment that privileged the advanced corporate services sector of the city's economy tied to Manhattan's central business district. "The net effect, though not the avowed purpose," Mollenkopf wrote, "of Koch's development policy was to promote the postindustrial transformation of the New York City economy" (1992:149–150).

8. The Council Against Poverty was established in 1965 to allocate federal and city funds to twenty-six community corporations which in turn contracted with delegate agencies to provide services (see chapter 3). In 1977 the U.S. Community Service Society suspended the council's funding on the grounds that many of its corporations had failed to comply with federal guidelines pertaining to the election of board members and some had financial irregularities (Mollenkopf 1992).

9. See Jackson (1993) for a discussion of the limited political base of the War on Poverty; see Piven and Cloward (1971) for a discussion of the cautious rhetoric adopted by War on Poverty planners; see Omi and Winant (1986) for a discussion of the Reagan-Bush era assault on race-based "group rights" principles and interests.

Chapter 5
Race and the Politics of Place

1. In the late 1940s the dump was cleaned up and Quonset huts were constructed to provide temporary housing for World War II veterans and their families (*New York Daily News*, 14 February 1982).

2. See Hall et al. (1978) for an analysis of the development of an ideology of black crime in Britain during the 1970s, and see Rieder (1985) for a discussion of how blacks, welfare, and "mugging" were conflated in the activist ideology of whites in Canarsie, Brooklyn.

3. "Scatter-site" housing was a federal housing initiative designed to integrate the black poor into white middle-income neighborhoods by requiring cities to devote a portion of their federal housing funds to the construction of low-income housing projects in white communities. In 1966 the New York City Housing Department designated a site in Corona for low-income housing. Subsequent protests led to the replacement of the Corona site with one in nearby Forest Hills. For a discussion of both controversies, see Cuomo (1983:3–23).

4. See the minutes of 8 January District Service Cabinet meeting, Office of Neighborhood Government, New York City Mayor's Office, page 3. The Neighborhood Stabilization Committee was formed within the structure of the Corona–East Elmhurst District Cabinet, which operated under the authority of the Office of Neighborhood Government.

5. The only day care center located within Lefrak City in 1987 charged $85 per week and fined parents for picking up children late.

6. For example, a white resident of a middle-income housing complex in Brooklyn, responding to a 1987 court order requiring its owner to end discrimination against blacks, declared: "We're being dumped on. We worked so hard to keep this place the way it is. Why bring in the garbage?" (*New York Newsday*, 7 May 1987).

7. In fact Claire Shulman, the borough president of Queens, had spoken about the garbage barge and the political crisis it instigated at the "kick-off" ceremony for the cleanup competition, which Baskin and her crew attended.

8. Nancy Fraser, in her analysis of the politics of needs interpretation, highlights three axes, or "moments," of political struggle that prove helpful in conceptualizing the activist work and accomplishments of CCA:

> I take the politics of needs to comprise three moments that are analytically distinct but interrelated in practice. The first is the struggle to establish or deny the political status of a given need, the struggle to validate the need as a matter of legitimate political concern or to enclave it as a nonpolitical matter. The second is the struggle over the interpretation of the need, the struggle for the power to define it and, so, to determine what would satisfy it. The third moment is the struggle over the satisfaction of the need, the struggle to secure or withhold provision. (1989:164)

Chapter 6
A Piece of the Rock

1. For example, Nicholas Lemann, addressing the origins of the underclass, writes:

> The way that the two versions of black life since the sixties fit together is through the idea of the bifurcation of black America, in which blacks are splitting into a middle class and an underclass that seems likely never to make it. The clearest line between the two groups is family structure. Black husband-wife families continue to close the gap with whites; their income is now 78 percent as high. But the income of black female-headed families, adjusted for inflation has been dropping. The black female-headed family represents an ever larger share of the population of poor people in America: 7.3 percent in 1959 and 19.3 percent in 1984. (1986:33)

2. By emphasizing the role of neighborhood-based relations and processes in shaping black class dispositions or identities, I argue against the tendency to view community-based struggles and forms of consciousness as "nonclass" in nature, or lacking in "class content" (see Kling and Posner 1992).

3. There were thirty-six persons in the "white" category, ninety-two in "black," and forty-nine in "other."

4. Queens Community District 3 includes East Elmhurst and predominantly white and Latino Jackson Heights to the west. Community District income data is derived from *Community District Statistics: A Portrait of the 1980 Census* (City of New York, Department of City Planning, 1984).

5. In fact 24 percent of Govan's employed neighbors worked in "protective service" occupations, which underscores the growth of uniformed security guard work as a source of low-paying service work for minorities. See Davis (1990) for a discussion of this phenomenon in Los Angeles.

6. Computations of organized block faces were developed from a list of block associations and their catchment areas prepared by the office of State Assemblywoman Helen Marshall in 1987. "Block face" here refers to one of the four sides, or "faces," of a rectangular city block.

7. At the other end of the scale, 18 percent of the blocks listed in North Corona census tracts showed owner occupancy rates of less that 25 percent, compared with only 3 percent of the blocks in East Elmhurst census tracts.

8. In his first "State of the Church" statement in the Corona Congregational Church's *Parish Post*, Bryer outlined his agenda:

Since May 1, 1987, I have been your pastor and wish to take this time to report that the church and its related ministries can and will be lifted to the glory of THE LORD. I find the worship life of the congregation to be very strong, however, the absence of youth and young adults creates a serious void in the Corona Church Family. I hope that each auxiliary, board, and committee within the Corona Church Family understands its role in correcting this condition. We must make room for and invite youth and young adults to participate actively in the ministry of the family. Also, we need to be involved in all levels of the United Church of Christ. Some of the issues we need to be more involved with within the wider church society are the Women's Fellowship, United Black Christians, the Task Force on the Ministry, Apartheid in South African, AIDS and racism--you and I have in our hands the present and future of not only the Corona Congregational Church family but surrounding communities as well.

9. The names Lillian and William Clark are pseudonyms.

Chapter 7
Up Against the Authority

1. Helen Marshall was elected to the New York City Council in 1991 after serving for nine years in the New York State Assembly.

2. As Logan and Molotch point out, "local growth does not make jobs; it only distributes them" (1987:89).

3. A *Newsday* reporter who covered the AGT issue told me that the story was not developed from an "official" political source or press release. He would not, however, reveal its source.

4. The "tunnel to nowhere" is a reference to the Port Authority's attempt to build an airportwide, underground baggage sorting and distribution system at JFK International Airport. The project was canceled before completion at a cost of $21 million.

5. Pierre Bourdieu has called attention to this "censorship effect" of the political field:

> Because the products offered by the political field are instruments for perceiving and expressing the social world (or, if you like, principles of division), the distribution of opinions in a given population depends on the state of the instruments of perception and expression available and on the access that different groups have to these instruments. This means that the political field in fact produces an effect of censorship by limiting the universe of political discourse, and thereby the universe of what is politically thinkable, to the finite space of discourses capable of being produced or reproduced within the limits of the political *problematic*, understood as a space of stances effectively adopted within the field—i.e., stances that are socio-logically possible given the laws that determine entry into the field. (1991:172)

Chapter 8
The Politics of Hearing and Telling

1. An indication of this difference in wealth between the two areas can be gleaned by comparing housing values. Whereas the median housing value for owner occupied units in Community Board 3 (East Elmhurst and Jackson Heights) was $209,700 in 1990, the comparable value for boards 5, 6 and 8, comprising the Manhattan Task Force, was $500,001 (Department of City Planning 1992).

2. See Harvey (1995:71).

3. Section 375(47a) of the Vehicle and Traffic Law prohibits the amplification of vehicular sound in excess of eighty decibels when measured from fifty feet. In 1993 the NYPD conducted eleven Operation Soundtraps, summoning and seizing (for evidence) 147 vehicles.

4. In its *Written Reevaluation/Technical Report on Changes to the Proposed JFK Airport Access Program*, the Federal Aviation Administration and the New York State Department of Transportation cited both financial costs and public opposition as reasons for abandoning the original twenty-two-mile project: "In response to issues raised during the NEPA review process and in light of the anticipated level of funding for construction of the project, the Project Sponsor has concluded that an 8.4-mile long portion of the original system in Queens, using the same general alignment between Jamaica Station and JFK, an airport link to Howard Beach Station, and within the JFK CTA, all of which were evaluated in the DEIS, is the proposed action" (FAA/NYSDOT 1996:1.1).

5. Here I shift attention away from the problematic of how explicit or implicit, visible or hidden, conscious or unconscious "worldviews" are for their holders. This is fundamentally a psychological question that not only begs a philosophy of the subject but also focuses attention on the "forms" in which a hegemonic worldview is cast, rather than on the latter's social mechanics (cf. Comaroff and Comaroff 1991). For example, the Comaroffs (1991) write, "[H]egemony is a product of the dialectic whereby the content of dominant ideologies is distilled into the shared forms that seem to have such historical longevity as to be above history—and, hence, to have the capacity to generate new substantive practices along the surfaces of economy and society"

(1991:30). Where for the social scientist the task is one of "reading" hegemonic forms and their modes of representation, for the agents of social transformation, the counter-hegemonic struggle is one of exposing or recognizing hegemonic worldviews as ideological and therefore subject to contestation (28). Although this emphasis directs attention to the problem of consciousness and the cultural forms and modes of representation that bear it through history, it risks attributing undue agency, or determinacy, to the contents and "enduring forms" of knowledge ("the commodity form," "linguistic forms," and "epistemological forms") at the expense of the power relations and practices that not only articulate them but also insinuate them with authority and efficacy relative to alternative forms of knowledge. This fetishization of the *form* of hegemonic knowledge is evident not only in the tendency to speak of hegemonies as if they were "independent beings endowed with life" but also in the appeal to optical tropes to describe, if not account for, the dialectic of hegemony and resistance (Marx 1967:72).

6. For example, to represent homeless people as problems rather than as symptoms of broader social injustices suggests not the "taken for grantedness" of the notion for its bearer, but rather *recognition* of its efficacy as a discursive act within a wider political field. The activist who raised the problem of the homeless was well aware that he was construing a particular view of the problem among possible others: "I'm not talkin' about the homeless issue itself, I'm talkin' about them changing their clothes in the middle of the street, right on the corner." The activist's statement was less a reflection of a dominant ideology than an appeal to a specific configuration of power (represented by police commanders and elected officials) and political interest (operationalized in *Police Strategy No. 5*) which imbued positions taken within the discourse of unaddressed disorder with authority and above all practical efficacy.

References Cited

Newspapers

Crisis, 1935–1939
Long Island Daily Press, 1935
Long Island Post, 1965
Long Island Press, 1967–1976
Long Island Star Journal, 1957
New York Age, 1917–1952
New York Daily News, 1982

New York Herald Tribune, 1964
New York Newsday, 1987–1996
New York Post, 1969
New York Times, 1922–1995.
Newtown Register, 1911–1915
Queens Chronicle, 1994

Unpublished Documents

Ad Hoc Committee for Voter Registration. 1964. Letter, 7 July. Typescript, files of the author.

———. 1964. Newsletter, July 21. Typescript, files of the author.

———. N.d. Letter. Typescript, files of the author.

Clarion. 1988. Concerned Community Adults, eds. Vol. 1, no. 2. Typescript, files of the author.

East Side Coalition on Airport Access. 1994. "Testimony before a Joint Hearing of the Federal Aviation Authority and the New York State Department of Transportation." Letter, July 28. Typescript, files of the author.

Environmental Defense Fund. 1994. "Comments of the Environmental Defense Fund on the Port Authority's Proposal to Provide Transit Access to LaGuardia and JFK Airports." Letter, July 28. Typescript, files of the author.

Independent Citizens Committee. 1963. Letter, October 24. Typescript, files of the author.

Independent Citizens for Good Government. 1964. Newsletter, January. Typescript, files of the author.

———. 1964. Press release, October 17. Typescript, files of the author.

Julian I. Garfield Democratic Association. 1962. *The Second Anniversary Testimonial and Awards Banquet Honoring Corinne K. Harris* (pamphlet). Corona, N.Y.: Julian I. Garfield Democratic Association.

Lefrak City Tenants Association. 1988. *The Lefrak City Tenants Association Presents Its Sixth Annual Awards Dinner Dance* (pamphlet). Corona, N.Y.: Lefrak City Tenants Association.

Regional Plan Association. 1994. "Comments on the Draft NEPA Environmental Impact Statement and SEOR Environmental Impact Statement for the Port Authority of New York and New Jersey's proposed Airport Access Program." Letter, August 8. Typescript, files of the author.

Books and Articles

Abu-Lughod, Janet L., et al. 1994. *From Urban Village to East Village*. Oxford: Blackwell.

Abu-Lughod, Lila. 1989. "The Romance of Resistance: Tracing Transformations of Power through Bedouin Women." *American Ethnologist* 17 (1): 41–55.

Anderson, Benedict. 1983. *Imagined Communities*. New York: Verso.

Anderson, Elijah. 1990. *Streetwise: Race, Class, and Change in an Urban Community*. Chicago: University of Chicago Press.

Anzaldua, Gloria. 1987. *Borderlands: La Frontera*. San Francisco: Spinsters/Aunt Lute.

Aronowitz, Stanley. 1990. *The Crisis in Historical Materialism: Class, Politics, and Culture in Marxist Theory*. Minneapolis: University of Minnesota Press.

Barth, Gunther Paul. 1980. *City People*. New York: Oxford University Press.

Bender, Thomas. 1978. *Community and Social Change in America*. Baltimore: Johns Hopkins University Press.

Betten, Neil, and Raymond a. Mohl, eds. 1970. *Urban America in Historical Perspective*. New York: Weybright and Talley.

Blee, Katherine M. 1991. *Women of the Klan: Racism and Gender in the 1920s*. Berkeley: University of California Press.

Block, Fred. 1991. "The Ruling Class Does Not Rule." In *Unfinished Business*," ed. Socialist Review Collectives, 29–44. New York: Verso.

Block, Fred, Richard A. Cloward, Barbara Ehrenreich, and Francis Fox Piven. 1987. *The Mean Season*. New York: Pantheon.

Blumberg, Barbara. 1979. *The New Deal and the Unemployed: The View from New York City*. London: Associated University Press.

Bodnar, John. 1992. *Remaking America: Public Memory, Commemoration, and Patriotism in the Twentieth Century*. Princeton, N.J.: Princeton University Press.

Bodnar, John, Roger Simon, and Michael P. Weber. 1983. *Lives of Their Own*. Chicago: University of Illinois Press.

Bourdieu, Pierre. 1991. *Language and Symbolic Power*. Cambridge: Harvard University Press.

Bullard, Robert D. 1990. *Dumping in Dixie: Race, Class, and Environmental Quality*. Boulder, Colo.: Westview.

―――, ed. 1993. *Confronting Environmental Racism: Voices from the Grassroots*. Boston: South End.

Butler, Judith. 1993. *Bodies That Matter*. New York: Routledge.

Caro, Robert. 1975. *The Power Broker*. New York: Vintage.

Castells, Manuel. 1989. *The Informational City*. Cambridge, Mass.: Blackwell.

Chamber of Commerce of the Borough of Queens. 1922. *Queens Borough* 8(2).

City Planning Commission. 1963. *Corona–East Elmhurst Area Extension*. New York: City Planning Commission.

―――. 1968. *Community Planning Districts: Boundaries and Procedures for Modification*. New York: City Planning Commission.

―――. 1994. "Calendar No. 4. Resolution on Application C 930505." New York: City Planning Commission.

Cohen, Jean L. 1985. "Strategy or Identity: New Theoretical Paradigms and Contemporary Social Movements." *Social Research* 52 (4): 663–716.

Collins, Patricia Hill. 1989. "A Comparison of Two Works on Black Family Life." *Signs* 14 (4): 875–884.

Columbia University. 1973. *A Community Profile of Queens Community Planning District 3*. New York: Bureau of Applied Research, Columbia University. Photocopy.

Comaroff, Jean, and John Comaroff. 1991. *Of Revelation and Revolution*. Chicago: University of Chicago Press.

Community Planning Board 14A. 1968. *Corona and East Elmhurst: "Chance for a Change."* Queens, New York. Photocopy.

Community Service Council of Greater New York. 1958. *Queens Communities: Population Characteristics and Neighborhood Social Resources*. New York: Community Council of Greater New York.

Connolly, Harold X. 1977. *A Ghetto Grows in Brooklyn*. New York: New York University Press.

Conquergood, Dwight. 1992. "Life in Big Red: Struggles and Accommodations in a Chicago Polyethnic Tenement." In *Structuring Diversity*, ed. Louise Lamphere, 95–144. Chicago: University of Chicago Press.

Cox, Kevin. 1982. "Housing Tenure and Neighborhood Activism." *Urban Affairs Quarterly* 18 (1): 107–129.

Cuomo, Mario. 1983. *Forest Hills Diary: The Crisis of Low-Income Housing*. New York: Vintage.

Curry, Leonard P. 1981. *The Free Black in Urban America, 1800–1850*. Chicago: University of Chicago Press.

Cutler, Anthony, et al. 1977. *Marx's 'Capital' and Capitalism Today*. Boston: Routledge and Kegan Paul.

Danielson, Michael N., and Jameson W. Doig. 1982. *New York: the Politics of Urban Regional Development*. Berkeley: University of California Press.

Davis, Mike. 1990. *City of Quartz*. New York: Vintage.

Dean, Mitchell. 1991. *The Constitution of Poverty*. London: Routledge.

Dear, Michael, and Jennifer Wolch, eds. 1989. *The Power of Geography*. Boston: Unwin Hyman.

de Certeau, Michel. 1984. *The Practice of Everyday Life*. Berkeley: University of California Press.

Dirks, Nicolas B., Geoff Eley, and Sherry B. Ortner, eds. 1994. "Introduction." In *Culture/Power/History*. Princeton, N.J.: Princeton University Press.

Douglas, Mary. 1966. *Purity and Danger*. New York: Praeger.

Drake, St. Clair, and Horace R. Cayton. 1945. *Black Metropolis*. New York: Harcourt, Brace.

Dreyfus, Hubert L., and Paul Rabinow. 1983. *Michel Foucault: Beyond Structuralism and Hermeneutics*. Chicago: University of Chicago Press.

DuBois, W.E.B. 1903. *Some Notes on the Negroes in New York City*. Atlanta, Ga.: Atlanta University Press.

———. 1969 [1901]. *The Black North in 1901: A Social Study*. New York: Arno.

———.1978 [1897]. "The Problem of Amusement." In *W.E.B. DuBois: On Sociology and the Black Community*, ed. Dan Green and Edwin Driver, 226–237. Chicago: University of Chicago Press.

———.1992 [1935]. *Black Reconstruction in the United States, 1860–1880*. New York: Atheneum.

DuBois, W.E.B. 1996 [1899]. *The Philadelphia Negro: A Social Study*. Philadelphia: University of Pennsylvania Press.

Duneier, Mitchell. 1992. *Slim's Table*. Chicago: University of Chicago Press.

Easton, Harriet G. 1967. "History of Fiftieth Anniversary." In *Fiftieth Anniversary: Corona Congregational Church*. Corona, N.Y.: Corona Congregational Church.

Eley, Geoff. 1992. "Nations, Publics, and Political Cultures: Placing Habermas in the Nineteenth Century." In *Habermas and the Public Sphere*, ed. Craig Calhoun, 289–339. Cambridge: MIT Press.

Escobar, Arturo, and Sonia E. Alvarez. 1992. *The Making of Social Movements in Latin America*. Boulder, Colo.: Westview.

Fainstein, Susan. 1994. *The City Builders*. Cambridge, Mass.: Blackwell.

Fainstein, Norman I., and Susan S. Fainstein. 1974. *Urban Political Movements: The Search for Power by Minority Groups in American Cities*. Englewood Cliffs, N.J.: Prentice-Hall.

———. 1983. "Economic Change, National Policy, and the System of Cities." In *Restructuring the City: The Political Economy of Urban Redevelopment*, ed. Susan S. Fainstein et al., 1–26. New York: Longman.

Farley, Reynolds, and Walter R. Allen. 1987. *The Color Line and the Quality of Life in America*. New York: Russell Sage.

Federal Aviation Administration and New York State Department of Transportation (FAA/NYSDOT). 1994. *Draft Environmental Impact and Section 4(f) Evaluation: The Port Authority of New York and New Jersey's Airport Access Program*. New York: FAA/NYSDOT.

———. 1996. *The Port Authority of New York and New Jersey JFK International Airport Light Rail System: Written Reevaluation/Technical Report on Changes to the Proposed JFK Airport Access Program*. New York: FAA/NYSDOT.

Fineman, Martha. 1991. "Images of Mothers in Poverty Discourses." *Duke Law Journal* 42:274–295.

Fitch, Robert. 1993. *The Assassination of New York*. New York: Verso.

Foucault, Michel. 1983. "The Subject and Power." Afterword. In *Michel Foucault: Beyond Structuralism and Hermeneutics*, ed. Hubert Dreyfus and Paul Rabinow, 208–226. Chicago: University of Chicago Press.

———. 1990. *The History of Sexuality: An Introduction*. Vol. 1. New York: Vintage.

———. 1991. "Politics and the Study of Discourse." In *The Foucault Effect: Studies in Governmentality*, ed. Graham Burchell, Colin Gordon, and Peter Miller. Chicago: University of Chicago Press.

Fraser, Nancy. 1989. *Unruly Practices: Power, Discourse, and Gender in Contemporary Social Theory*. Minneapolis: University of Minnesota Press.

———. 1992. "Rethinking the Public Sphere: A Contribution to the Critique of Actually Existing Democracy." In *Habermas and the Public Sphere*, ed. Craig Calhoun, 109–142. Cambridge: MIT Press.

Frazier, E. Franklin. 1939. *The Negro Family in the United States*. Chicago: University of Chicago Press.

———. 1962. *Black Bourgeoisie*. New York: Collier.

———. 1964. *The Negro Church in America*. New York: Schoeken.

Frost, Olivia P. 1947. *Aspects of Negro Life in Queens, New York City*. New York: Urban League of Greater New York.

Fuentes, Annette. 1984. "What's Poverty Got to Do with It?" *City Limits* (November): 13–18.

Gatewood, Willard B., Jr. 1993. *Aristocrats of Color: The Black Elite, 1880–1920*. Bloomington: Indiana University Press.

Geertz, Clifford. 1973. *The Interpretation of Cultures*. New York: Basic.

Gilder, George. 1981. *Wealth and Poverty*. New York: Basic.

Gilman, Sander. 1985. *Difference and Pathology*. Ithaca, N.Y.: Cornell University Press.

Gilroy, Paul. 1987. *Ain't No Black in the Union Jack*. Chicago: University of Chicago.

Giuliani, Rudolph, and William Bratton. 1994. *Police Strategy No. 5: Reclaiming the Public Spaces of New York*. New York: City of New York.

Gordon, Diana R. 1991. *The Justice Juggernaut*. New Brunswick, N.J.: Rutgers University Press.

Gordon, Linda. 1990. "The New Feminist Scholarship of the Welfare State." In *Women, the State, and Welfare*, ed. Linda Gordon, 9–35. Madison: University of Wisconsin Press.

Green, Vera. 1970. "The Confrontation of Diversity within the Black Community." *Human Organization* 29:267–272.

Gregory, Steven. 1992. "The Changing Significance of Race and Class in an African-American Community." *American Anthropologist* 19 (2): 255–274.

———. 1994. "Time to Make the Doughnuts: On the Politics of Subjugation in the 'Inner-City.'" *PoLAR: Political and Legal Anthropology Review* 17 (1): 41–54.

Gregory, Steven, and Roger Sanjek, eds. 1994. *Race*. New Brunswick, N.J.: Rutgers University Press.

Guest, Avery M., and R. S. Oropesa. 1986. "Informal Social Ties and Political Activity in the Metropolis." *Urban Affairs Quarterly* 21 (4): 550–574.

Hall, Stuart. 1980. "Race, Articulation, and Societies Structured in Dominance." In *Sociological Theories: Race and Colonialism*, 305–345. Paris: UNESCO.

———. 1985. "Signification, Representation, Ideology: Althusser and the Post-Structuralist Debates." In *Critical Studies in Mass Communication* 2 (2): 91–114.

———. 1990. "Cultural Identity and Diaspora." In *Identity: Community, Culture, Difference*, ed. Jonathan Rutherford, 222–237. London: Lawrence and Wishart.

———. 1992. "Discussion." In *Black Popular Culture*, ed. Gina Dent, 85–91. Seattle: Bay Press.

Hall, Stuart, Chas Critcher, Tony Jefferson, John Clarke, and Brian Roberts. 1978. *Policing the Crisis: Mugging, the State, and Law and Order*. New York: Holmes and Meier.

Hannerz, Ulf. 1969. *Soulside: Inquiries into Ghetto Culture and Community Life*. New York: Columbia University Press.

———. 1973. "Research in the Black Ghetto: A Review of the Sixties." *Journal of Asian and African Studies*. 9 (3–4): 5–25.

Harper, Phillip Brian. 1996. *Are We Not Men?* New York: Oxford University Press.

Harrington, Michael. 1971 [1962]. *The Other America*. New York: Pelican.

Hart, Robert Lamb, Adam Krivatsy, and William Stubee. N.d. *Local Area Study: Jackson Heights, Corona, East Elmhurst, Elmhurst*. New York: Department of City Planning.

Hart, Robert Lamb, Adam Krivatsy, and William Stubee. 1970. Corona–East Elmhurst Development Program. New York: Corona–East Elmhurst Development Committee, New York City Department of City Planning, the New York City Housing and Development Administration.

Harvey, David. 1978. "Labor, Capital, and Class Struggle around the Built Environment in Advanced Capitalist Societies." In *Urbanization and Conflicts in Market Societies*, ed. K. R. Cox, 9–37. New York: Methuen.

———. 1989. *The Condition of Postmodernity*. Cambridge, Mass.: Blackwell.

———. 1993. "Class Relations, Social Justice, and the Politics of Difference." In *Place and the Politics of Identity*, ed. Michael Keith and Steve Pile. New York: Routledge.

———. 1995. "Militant Particularism and Global Ambition: The Conceptual Politics of Place, Space, and Environment in the Work of Raymond Williams." *Social Text* 42:69–98.

Hayden, Delores. 1984. *Redesigning the American Dream*. New York: W. W. Norton.

Haynes, George Edmund. 1968 [1912]. *The Negro at Work in New York City*. New York: Arno.

Higginbotham, Evelyn Brooks. 1993. *Righteous Discontent*. Cambridge: Harvard University Press.

Hirsch, Arnold. 1985. *The Making of the Second Ghetto*. New York: Cambridge University Press.

Hobsbawm, Eric, and Terence Ranger. 1983. *The Invention of Tradition*. New York: Cambridge University Press.

hooks, bell. 1990. *Yearning: Race, Gender, and Cultural Politics*. Boston: South End.

Jackson, Andrew. 1985. "The Langston Hughes Community Library and Cultural Center." Corona, N.Y.: Langston Hughes Community Library and Cultural Center. Photocopy.

Jackson, Kenneth T. 1985. *Crabgrass Frontier: The Suburbanization of the United States*. Oxford: Oxford University Press.

Jackson, Thomas F. 1993. "The State, the Movement, and the Urban Poor: The War on Poverty and Political Mobilization in the 1960s." In *The Underclass Debate*, ed. Michael B. Katz, 403–439. Princeton, N.J.: Princeton University Press.

Johnson, James Weldon. 1968 [1930]. *Black Manhattan*. New York: Arno.

Jones, Jaqueline. 1985. *Labor of Love, Labor of Sorrow*. New York: Vintage.

———. 1992. *The Dispossessed*. New York: Basic.

Kaplan, Temma. 1992. *Red City, Blue Period: Social Movements in Picasso's Barcelona*. Berkeley: University of California Press.

Katz, Michael B. 1989. *The Underserving Poor*. New York: Pantheon.

Katznelson, Ira. 1981. *City Trenches: Urban Politics and the Patterning of Class in the United States*. New York: Pantheon.

Kelley, Robin. 1990. *Hammer and Hoe*. Chapel Hill: University of North Carolina Press.

Kelley, Robin D. G. 1994. *Race Rebels: Culture, Politics, and the Black Working Class*. New York: Free Press.

King, Mel. 1981. *Chain of Change: Struggles for Black Community Development*. Boston: South End.

Kling, Joseph M., and Prudence S. Posner, eds. 1992. "Class and Community in an Era of Urban Transformation." In *Dilemmas of Activism: Class, Community, and the Politics of Local Mobilization*, ed. Joseph M. Kling and Prudence S. Posner, 23–45. Philadelphia: Temple University Press.

Kondo, Dorinne K. 1990. *Crafting Selves: Power, Gender, and Discourses of Identity in a Japanese Workplace*. Chicago: University of Chicago Press.

Kroessler, Jeffrey A. 1993. "Baseball and the Blue Laws." *The Long Island Historical Journal* 5 (2): 168–177.

Kusmer, Kenneth. 1976. *A Ghetto Takes Shape: Black Cleveland, 1870–1930*. Urbana: University of Illinois Press.

———. 1991. "The Black Urban Experience in American History." In *Black Communities and Urban Development in America 1720–1990*, ed. Kenneth Kusmer, 9:33–64. New York: Garland.

Laclau, Ernesto. 1990. *New Reflections on the Revolution of Our Time*. New York: Verso.

Laclau, Ernesto, and Chantal Mouffe. 1982. "Recasting Marxism: Hegemony and New Social Movements." *Socialist Review* 12, no. 6: 91–113.

———. 1985. *Hegemony and Socialist Strategy*. New York: Verso.

———. 1991. "Recasting Marxism: Hegemony and New Political Movements." Interview with Ernesto Laclau and Chantal Mouffe. In *Unfinished Business*, ed. Socialist Review Collective, 53–67. New York: Verso.

Lemann, Nicholas. 1986. "The Origins of the Underclass, Part 1." *The Atlantic Monthly* (June): 33.

Lewis, Earl. 1991a. "Afro-American Adaptive Strategies: The Visiting Habits of Kith and Kin among Black Norfolkians during the First Great Migration." In *Black Communities and Urban Development in America 1720–1990*, ed. Kenneth Kusmer, 5:53–66. New York: Garland.

———. 1991b. *In Their Own Interests: Race, Class and Power in Twentieth-Century Norfolk, Virginia*. Berkeley: University of California Press.

———. 1991c. "Expectations, Economic Opportunities, and Life in the Industrial Age: Black Migration to Norfolk, Virginia, 1910–1945." In *The Great Migration in Historical Perspective*, ed. Joe William Trotter, Jr., 22–45. Bloomington: Indiana University Press.

Lipsitz, George. 1988. *A Life in the Struggle: Ivory Perry and the Culture of Opposition*. Philadelphia: Temple University Press.

Logan, John R., and Harvey L. Molotch. 1987. *Urban Fortunes*. Berkeley: University of California Press.

Lorde, Audre. 1984. *Sister Outsider*. Freedom, Calif.: Crossing.

Mannheim, Karl. 1952. *Essays on the Sociology of Knowledge*. London: Routledge and Kegan Paul.

Marx, Karl. 1967. *Capital*. Volume 1. New York: International.

Massey, Douglas S., and Nancy A. Denton. 1993. *American Apartheid: Segregation and the Making of the Underclass*. Cambridge: Harvard University Press.

McAdam, Doug. 1994. "Culture and Social Movements." In *New Social Movements*, ed. Enrique Larana, Hank Johnston, and Joseph R. Gusfield, 36–57. Philadelphia: Temple University Press.

McClain, Charles. 1988. "Of Medicine, Race, and American Law: The Bubonic Plague Outbreak of 1900." In *Law & Social Inquiry* 13 (3): 447–513.

McClain, Charles. 1994. *In Search of Equality*. Berkeley: University of California Press.

Meir, August, and Elliott Rudwick. 1976. *Along the Color Line: Explorations in the Black Experience*. Urbana: University of Illinois Press.

Melucci, Alberto. 1989. *Nomads of the Present*. Philadelphia: Temple University Press.

———. 1994. "A Strange Kind of Newness: What's 'New' in New Social Movements?" In *New Social Movements*, ed. Enrique Larana, Hank Johnston, and Joseph R. Gusfield, 101–130. Philadelphia: Temple University Press.

Mercer, Kobena. 1994. *Welcome to the Jungle: New Positions in Black Cultural Studies*. New York: Routledge.

Miller, Seymour Michael, and Donald Tomaskovic-Devey. 1983. *Recapitalizing America*. Boston: Routledge and Kegan Paul.

Millet, John D. 1938. *The Works Progress Administration in New York City*. Chicago: Public Administration Service.

Mollenkopf, John H. 1983. *The Contested City*. Princeton, N.J.: Princeton University Press.

———. 1992. *A Phoenix in the Ashes*. Princeton, N.J.: Princeton University Press.

Moore, Shirley Ann. 1991. "Getting There, Being: African-American Migration to Richmond, California, 1910–1945." In *The Great Migration in Historical Perspective*, ed. Joe William Trotter, Jr., 106–126. Bloomington: Indiana University Press.

Morris, Aldon D. 1984. *The Origins of the Civil Rights Movement*. New York: Free Press.

Murray, Charles. 1984. *Losing Ground: American Social Policy, 1950–1980*. New York: Basic.

Naison, Mark. 1984. *Communists in Harlem during the Great Depression*. New York: Grove.

Negt, Oskar, and Alexander Kluge. 1993. *Public Sphere and Experience*. Minneapolis: University of Minnesota Press.

Nelson, Barbara J. 1990. "The Origins of the Two-Channel Welfare State: Workman's Compensation and Mothers' Aid." In *Women, the State, and Welfare*, ed. Linda Gordon, 123–151. Madison: University of Wisconsin Press.

Oliver, Melvin L., and Thomas M. Shapiro. 1995. *Black Wealth/White Wealth*. New York: Routledge.

Omi, Michael, and Howard Winant. 1986. *Racial Formation in the United States*. New York: Routledge.

Osofsky, Gilbert. 1971. *Harlem: The Making of a Ghetto, 1890–1930*. New York: Harper Torchbooks.

Pearce, Diana. 1985. "Welfare Is Not *for* Women: Why the War on Poverty Cannot Conquer the Feminization of Poverty." In *Women, the State, and Welfare*, ed. Linda Gordon, 265–279. Madison: University of Wisconsin Press.

Pecorella, Robert F. 1994. *Community Power in a Postreform City*. Armonk, N.Y.: M. E. Sharpe.

Phillips, Kevin. 1991. *The Politics of Rich and Poor*. New York: Harper Perennial.

Piven, Frances Fox, and Richard A. Cloward. 1971. *Regulating the Poor*. New York: Pantheon.

———. 1982. *The New Class War*. New York: Pantheon.

Plotkin, Sidney. 1990. "Enclave Consciousness and Neighborhood Activism." In *Dilemmas of Activism: Class, Community, and the Politics of Local Mobilization*, ed. Joseph M. Kling and Prudence S. Posner, 219–239. Philadelphia: Temple University Press.

Port Authority of New York and New Jersey. 1994a. "Message from the Executive Director." *Access* 1 (1): 1–2.

———. 1994b. "Hearings Held on Draft Environmental Statement." *Access* 1 (4): 1–4.

Powledge, Fred. 1964. "'Mason-Dixon' Line in Queens." *New York Times*, magazine section, 10 May.

Rainwater, Lee. 1970. *Behind Ghetto Walls*. Chicago: Aldine.

Ravitch, Diane. 1974. *The Great School Wars*. New York: Basic.

Reed, Adolph. 1979. "Black Particularism Reconsidered." *Telos* 39 (Spring): 71–93.

———. 1988. "The Liberal Technocrat." *The Nation* 246:167–170.

———. 1991. "The Underclass Myth." *The Progressive* 55 (August): 18–20.

Ricourt, Milagros. 1995. "The Creation of Pan-Latino Ethnicity: Gender, Class, and Politics in Corona, Queens." Ph.D. diss., City University of New York, Graduate Center.

Rieder, Jonathan. 1985. *Canarsie: The Jews and Italians of Brooklyn against Liberalism*. Cambridge: Harvard University Press.

Rogers, David. 1969. *110 Livingston Street*. New York: Vintage.

Rosaldo, Renato. 1980. *Ilongot Headhunting*. Stanford: University of California Press.

Rose, James. N.d. *African-Americans in Queens County, New York*. New York: Store Front Museum/Paul Robeson Theater.

Rouse, Roger. 1991. "Mexican Migration and the Social Space of Postmodernism." *Diaspora* 1:8–23.

Rutherford, Jonathan, ed. 1990. *Identity, Culture, Difference*. London: Lawrence and Wishart.

Rydell, Robert W. 1993. *World of Fairs*. Chicago: University of Chicago Press.

Sacks, Karen. 1988. *Caring by the Hour: Women, Work, and Organizing at Duke Medical Center*. Urbana: University of Illinois Press.

———1994. "How Jews Became White Folks." In *Race*, ed. Steven Gregory and Roger Sanjek, 78–102. New Brunswick, N.J.: Rutgers University Press.

Sahlins, Marshall. 1981. *Historical Metaphors and Mythical Realities*. Ann Arbor: University of Michigan Press.

Sanjek, Roger. 1993. "After Freedom in Newtown, Queens: African Americans and the Color Line, 1828–1899." *The Long Island Historical Journal* 5 (2): 157–167.

Scheiner, Seth M. 1965. *Negro Mecca*. New York: New York University Press.

———. 1991. "The New York City Negro and the Tenement, 1880–1910." In *Black Communities and Urban Development in America 1720–1990*, ed. Kenneth Kusmer, vol. 4, part 2, 194–205. New York: Garland.

Scott, James. 1990. *Domination and the Arts of Resistance*. New Haven: Yale University Press.

Seyfried, Vincent F. 1961–66. *The Long Island Rail Road*. Part 7: The Age of Electrification. Garden City, N.Y.: Vincent F. Seyfried.

———. 1986. *The Story of Corona*. Garden City, N.Y.: Vincent F. Seyfried.

Shefter, Martin. 1992. *Political Crisis, Fiscal Crisis*. New York: Columbia University Press.

Smith, Michael Peter. 1988. *City, State, and Market*. Cambridge, Mass.: Blackwell.

Soja, Edward W., and Barbara Hooper. 1993. "The Spaces That Difference Makes: Some Notes on the Geographical Margins of the New Cultural Politics." In *Place and the Politics of Identity*, ed. Michael Keith and Steve Pile, 183–205. New York: Routledge.

Spear, Allan H. 1967. *Black Chicago: The Making of a Negro Ghetto, 1890–1930*. Chicago: University of Chicago Press.

Sugrue, Thomas J. 1995. *The Origins of the Urban Crisis*. Princeton, N.J.: Princeton University Press.

Suttles, Gerald D. 1972. *The Social Construction of Communities*. Chicago: University of Chicago Press.

Thelen, David. 1990. "Introduction." In *Memory and American History*, ed. David Thelen, vii–xix. Bloomington: Indiana University Press.

Tobias, Andrew. 1973. "Someday We May All Live in Lefrak City." *New York* (May 12): 36–42.

Trotter, Joe William, Jr. 1985. *Black Milwaukee*. Urbana: University of Illinois Press.

———. 1991. "Race, Class, and Industrial Change: Black Migration to Southern West Virginia, 1915–1932." In *The Great Migration in Historical Perspective*, ed. Joe William Trotter, Jr., 46–67. Bloomington: Indiana University Press.

———. 1993. "Blacks in the Urban North: The 'Underclass Question' in Historical Perspective." In *The Underclass Debate: Views from History*, ed. Michael Katz, 55–81. Princeton, N.J.: Princeton University Press.

United States Army Corps of Engineers. 1992. *Request for Public Comment and Announcement of a Public Hearing*. Public Notice Number: 92-11400-Y5 (11 December). New York: Army Corps of Engineers.

United States Bureau of the Census. 1980a. *Census of Population and Housing*, Summary Tape File 3A (New York). Prepared by the City University of New York Data Service.

———. 1980b. *Census of Population and Housing*. Summary Tape File 1B (New York). Prepared by the City University of New York Data Service.

Valentine, Charles. 1971. "The Culture of Poverty: Its Scientific Implications for Action." In *The Culture of Poverty: A Critique*, ed. Eleanor Leacock, 193–225. New York: Simon and Schuster.

———. 1972. *Black Studies and Anthropology: Scholarly and Political Interests in Afro-American Culture*. A McCaleb Module in Anthropology. Reading, Mass.: Addison-Wesley.

Vavruska, Mary. N.d. "Statement of Complaint: Mary Vavruska, Complainant against the Chancellor and the Board of Education of the City of New York." Photocopy.

Wacquant, Loic J. D., and William J. Wilson. 1989. "The Cost of Racial and Class Exclusion in the Inner City." *Annals of the Academy of Political and Social Sciences* 501:8–25.

Wagner-Pacifici, Robin. 1994. *Discourse and Destruction*. Chicago: University of Chicago Press.

Wallace, Michelle. 1979. *Black Macho and the Myth of the Superwoman*. New York: Dial.

Walsh, Annmarie Hauck. 1990. "Public Authorities and the Shape of Decision Making." In *Urban Politics New York Style*, ed. Jewel Bellush and Dick Netzer, 188–219. Armonk, N.Y.: M. E. Sharpe.

Ward, David. 1989. *Poverty, Ethnicity, and the American City, 1840–1925*. New York: Cambridge University Press.

Westwood, Sally. 1985. *All Day, Every Day*. Urbana: University of Illinois Press.

Williams, Brett. 1988. *Upscaling Downtown*. Ithaca, N.Y.: Cornell University Press.

———. 1991."Aliens in our Midst." *The Progressive* 55:40–42.

———. 1992. "Poverty among African Americans in the Urban United States." *Human Organization* 51 (2): 164–174.

———. 1994. "Babies and Banks: The 'Reproductive Underclass' and the Raced, Gendered Mask of Debt." In *Race*, ed. Steven Gregory and Roger Sanjek, 348–365. New Brunswick, N.J.: Rutgers University Press.

Wilson, William J. 1978. *The Declining Significance of Race*. Chicago: University of Chicago Press.

———. 1987. *The Truly Disadvantaged*. Chicago: University of Chicago Press.

———. 1991. "Studying Inner-City Social Dislocations: The Challenge of Public Agenda Research." *American Sociological Review* 56 (February): 1–14.

———. 1996. *When Work Disappears: The World of the New Urban Poor*. New York: Knopf.

Wolters, Raymond. 1974. *The Negro and the Depression*. Westport, Conn.: Greenwood.

Young, Iris. 1990. *Justice and the Politics of Difference*. Princeton, N.J.: Princeton University Press.

Abu-Lughod, Lila, 133

activism: and age, 159–60; and identity, 11–12; political culture of, 160

Amenia Conference (1933), 44

Area Policy Boards: election of, 128–32; origin of, 103

Black Bourgeoisie (Frazier), 259n.25

black ghetto: and formation of white middle-class identity, 83; trope of, 5, 10, 12. *See also* inner city

black identity. *See under* identity

Black North in 1902, The (DuBois), 20

Black Panther Party (Corona), 83, 96–97

block associations, 97, 146–56, 188–91; coalition building of, 192–93; and environmental justice groups, 191–93, 202; and homeownership, 147, 151; political effectiveness of, 147–48, 150–52, 154; and public culture, 160, 168–73

block busting, 62

block clubs. *See* block associations

Blumberg, Barbara, 43

Bourdieu, Pierre, 265n.5

Bratton, William, 232–34

Caro, Robert, 60

Castells, Manuel, 195

Cayton, Horace, 40, 56, 258n.15, 259nn. 22 and 23

church, black: civil rights era activism of, 69–70, 72; political role of, 167

civic associations. *See* block associations

civil rights movement, 55; impact on formation of black middle class, 144; influence of, in Corona, 66–70, 72–73

class
—black class formation, 17–18, 47–48, 53–54, 65, 140–141; and gender, 54; impact of politics on, 145–46, 149–50
—black class identity, 140, 155–56; and access to political resources, 223, 225–29; and residential location, 65–66
—black class stratification, 63–65, 144–46; bifurcated model of, 12, 140, 263n.1; impact on political institutions, 161

—black class structure, 7–8; and civic association culture, 176-77
—white class identity, 80–83

coalitions, and broadening of public sphere, 201–3

Comaroff, Jean, 265n.5

Comaroff, John, 265n.5

community: concept of, 11, 255n.18; contested character of, 216; nativist constructions of, 230, 238; and segregation, 65

Community Action Program, 97–98

Community Development Block Grant Program, 98, 101

Corona: black population of, 48–49, 53, 57, 60, 63, 67; black settlement in, 20–26, 28, 32, 36, 48–49, 60

Cox, Philip, 147

crime, black: ideology of, 113–14, 123; rhetorical use of, 231

culture of poverty thesis, 8, 10

Cuomo, Mario, 114

Curry, Leonard, 256n.6, 257n.9

Cutler, Anthony, 255n.30

Davis, Mike, 215, 232

de Certeau, Michel, 143–44, 182

decentralized city government, 99–100

Declining Significance of Race, The (Wilson), 7

deindustrialization, 7, 105–6

Dirks, Nicholas, 12

discrimination, 17, 24, 29–30; in employment during Depression, 40–44; and federal housing policies, 61; in housing, 59, 112–13; and 1939 World's Fair of, 44–45. *See also* segregation

Drake, Sinclair, 40, 56, 258n.15, 259nn. 22 and 23

Dreyfus, Hubert, 222

DuBois, W.E.B., 20, 44, 80, 256n.3, 257n.12, 258n.21

Duneier, Mitchell, 254n.11

East Elmhurst: black middle class of, 144–46; black settlement in, 63–65

economic restructuring, 106

education: and blacks in Corona, 49; as credentialed security, 75–76

Eley, Geoff, 12

elite, black (Corona), 32–33; lifestyle and occupations of, 36–40; and race consciousness, 37; and reckoning of status, 36–39, 259nn. 22 and 23

enclave consciousness, concept of, 115

environmental justice, 191–92

ethnicity, black, 175–76

family, black: and "failed family" model, 253n.7; notion of weakened values of, 5; pathological model of, 111, 114–15, 137; as political model, 134

Federal Housing Administration (FHA), 59, 61–62

fiscal crisis of 1975 (New York City), 101–2

Fitch, Robert, 261n.7

Forest Hills housing controversy, 113–14, 262n.3

Foucault, Michel, 85–86

Fraser, Nancy, 104, 263n.8

Frazier, E. Franklin, 39, 259n.25

Frost, Olivia, 43–44, 49

garbage, as symbol of social disorder, 125–26

Gatewood, Willard, 36–37

Geertz, Clifford, 249

gender: and black class formation, 54; and political strategy, 132–35

ghetto poverty, persistence of, 5–8

ghetto subculture, concept in academic research, 8–10

ghetto underclass, 7–8, 10, 253n.4

Gilman, Sander, 261n.3

Giuliani, Rudolph, 232–34

global competition: activists's critique of, 215–16; ideology of, 193–95, 245

Gordon, Linda, 105, 253n.7

Great Depression: and black class formation, 47; and black employment, 40–44; Corona during, 41–43

Great Society. *See* War on Poverty

Hall, Stuart, 18–19

Hannerz, Ulf, 9

Harrington, Michael, 86

Harvey, David, 17

hegemony: and construction of identity, 202; and governing of public debate, 246, 265n.5; as power to make and remake subjects, 246

Higginbotham, Evelyn, 36, 54, 260n.1

Home Owners Loan Corporation (HOLC), 59, 61

homeowner activism, 154–56

homeownership, black: as benchmark of progress, 55; impact of Depression on, 43; in Queens, 49

Hooper, Barbara, 202

housing conditions: for blacks, 25, 60; and postwar housing shortage, 58–59

identity: and critique of essentialism, 12; and history, 13; political formation of, 16, 18; and social theory, 11–14. *See also* political identity

—black identity: binary model of, 12, 140; and black press, 38–39; construction of, 144–46, 215–16; diversity of, 53, 176; and middle class, 56, 145, 150, 155–56; politics of, 12–13

—white identity, 31–32; and racial segregation, 80–81, 83

immigrants: and black civic institutions, 177; and social deviance, 235–38

inner city: concept of, 5; crisis in, 5–6; views of black poor in, 10. *See also* black ghetto

integration: benefits of, 57–58; and Corona schools, 76–79 (*see also* Princeton Plan); and "scatter site" housing, 113–14, 262n.3; weakness as strategy, 82

Jackson, Thomas F., 97

Jackson Heights school integration controversy, 78–82

Johnson, James Weldon, 20

Katznelson, Ira, 94, 99, 261n.4

Kelley, Robin, 15, 39

King, Martin Luther, Jr., 55

Koch, Edward, 102; post-fiscal-crisis policies of, 103–5, 261n.7

Ku Klux Klan, 30–31, 139

Kusmer, Kenneth, 258n.18

Laclau, Ernesto, 19, 215

Latinos, and black institutions, 177

Lefrak City: population of, 111–13; as symbol of black pathology, 113–16, 123, 137; as "welfare haven," 113

Lemann, Nicholas, 263n.1

Lewis, Earl, 256n.2

Lindsay, John V., 94
Logan, John R., 194
Lorde, Audre, 251

Malcolm X, 76
Mannheim, Karl, 160
Marx, Karl, 266n.5
McClain, Charles, 261n.3
Melucci, Alberto, 135
memory, public: and activism, 174; and identity, 13–14; social production of, 173–76; and "southernness," 174–75
middle class, black: exodus of, 7–8, 10; growth of, 40, 47–48; and identity, 56, 145, 150, 155–56; political formation of, 215–16. *See also* class
migration, black: pre–World War I, to New York City, 23–25; and public memory, 174–75; to Queens, 24, 26, 49; from the South after World War II, 58
militant particularism, 230, 234
Mollenkopf, John, 88, 93, 103–4
Molotch, Harvey L., 194
Moses, Robert, 59, 182
Mouffe, Chantal, 19, 215

Nation of Islam, 76, 83, 97
National Association for the Advancement of Colored People (NAACP), 41, 50–51, 58, 61, 96; and 1939 World's Fair, 44–45; youth divisions of, 46
National Urban League, 44, 257n.14
nativism, 30–31
neighborhood stability, racialized constructions of, 110, 217, 230
New Deal, 44. *See also* Great Depression; Works Progress Administration
New York Age, 33, 38
New York World's Fair (1939), 44–45
not in my backyard (NIMBY), ideology of, 149, 191–92, 199

occupations, black: in Corona, 20, 23–24, 27–28; in East Elmhurst and Corona, 145; and Great Depression, 40–41
Office of Economic Opportunity, 96–98
Oliver, Melvin, 17
Ortner, Sherry, 12
Osofsky, Gilbert, 23–24, 257n.11

Parents and Taxpayers (PAT), 78–79, 81
place, social construction of, 144

place-based identities: political formation of, 201, 204, 213–16; weaknesses of, 195
Plotkin, Sidney, 115
policing: and black youth, 123; and social deviance, 234; strategies of, 232–34, 238
political capital, and class position, 225–27, 246
political clubs, 51–52, 67–68
political culture, 160, 176; changes in, 48; heterogeneity of, 74, 176
political identity, 155–56; cultural production of, 135, 170, 173, 176; diversity of, 83–84; fluidity of, 202, 215; and history, 106
politicization, concept of, 66–67
politics: and construction of identity, 13; definition of, 13; of pleasure, 39–40; of representation, 16, 126; representational, paradox of, 135
Port Authority of New York and New Jersey (PANYNJ): "divide and conquer" practices of, 201–2, 206–7, 214–15, 229, 245; and formation of place-bound identities, 201, 204, 213–16; and management of public protest, 204–5, 213–15, 220–21, 229, 245; origin of, 183
poverty, black: knowledge about, 86; origins and persistence of, 5–8. *See also* ghetto poverty
press, black: and community solidarity, 33–35; and identity, 38–39
Princeton Plan, 77–79, 81–82, 157–58
property values, rhetoric of, 155–56
public culture, and formation of political constituencies, 170–72, 176. *See also* political culture
public sphere: concept of, 195; governing of, 215–16; policing of, 231–34; widening of, 136–38

quality of life, discourse of, 154, 233

Rabinow, Paul, 222
race riots, 24–25
racial uplift, ideology of, 57, 260n.1
racism, white, 29–31, 79–83
Rainwater, Lee, 8, 9, 254n.8
redlining, 17, 61–62
Regional Plan Association, 223, 225–26, 244
restrictive covenants, 26, 59
Rieder, Jonathan, 115
Rydell, Robert, 44–45

Sacks, Karen, 133
Sahlins, Marshall, 15
school boycott, in East Elmhurst–Corona, 76–77
school pairing. *See* Princeton Plan
Scott, James, 172
segregation, 24, 29, 55, 57–58, 60–63; and black class formation, 53; and gender asymmetry, 54; in schools, 74–75, 77; and white identity, 80–82, 83. *See also* discrimination
Seyfried, Vincent, 258n.20
Shapiro, Thomas, 17
Slim's Table (Duneier), 254n.11
slum clearance, 58–59
Smith, Michael, 101, 105
social clubs, 37–40, 259n.25
social deviance: discourse of, 230–231, 233; policing of, 234
social movements theory, 14
Soja, Edward, 202
Soulside (Hannerz), 9
southernness, discourse of, 174–75
suburbanization, 87
Suttles, Gerald, 255n.18

Thelen, David, 13
Trotter, Joe William, Jr., 32, 256n.3
Truly Disadvantaged, The (Wilson), 6–8

Uniform Land Use Review Procedure (ULURP), 185–88

urban blight, discourse of, 89–92, 105, 146, 164
urban renewal, 59, 85, 88, 89–94

voluntary associations, 35–36; and civil rights activism, 68–73; impact of War on Poverty on, 95–99

Wagner-Pacifici, Robin, 234
Walsh, Annemarie Hauck, 183
War on Poverty, 86, 88, 93–95, 129–30; and black class formation, 146; and black public sphere, 141; dismantling of, 101; impact on community-based institutions, 96–99, 104–5
welfare dependency, ideology of, 7, 111, 113–14, 253n.7
welfare mother, trope of, 6, 111, 114, 253n.1
welfare state, conservative attack on, 5–6, 253n.1
white flight, 60, 62
white identity. *See under* identity
white violence, 25
Williams, Raymond, 230
Wilson, William Julius, 6–8, 253n.4
Wolters, Raymond, 40–41
women, black: impact of Great Depression on, 41; occupations of, 20, 256n.3; and politics of respectability, 38–39; social activism of, 36, 54
Works Progress Administration (WPA), 4, 42–43, 49, 259n.28

youth, black: representations of, 123, 137

PRINCETON STUDIES IN
CULTURE/POWER/HISTORY

High Religion: A Cultural and Political History of Sherpa Buddhism
by Sherry B. Ortner

A Place in History: Social and Monumental Time in a Cretan Town
by Michael Herzfeld

The Textual Condition *by Jerome J. McGann*

Regulating the Social: The Welfare State and Local Politics in Imperial
Germany *by George Steinmetz*

Hanging without a Rope: Narrative Experience in Colonial and
Postcolonial Karoland *by Mary Margaret Steedly*

Modern Greek Lessons: A Primer in Historical Constructivism
by James Faubion

The Nation and Its Fragments: Colonial and Postcolonial Histories
by Partha Chatterjee

Culture/Power/History: A Reader in Contemporary Social Theory *edited by
Nicholas B. Dirks, Geoff Eley, and Sherry B. Ortner*

After Colonialism: Imperial Histories and Postcolonial Displacements
edited by Gyan Prakash

Encountering Development: The Making and Unmaking of the Third World
by Arturo Escobar

Social Bodies: Science, Reproduction, and Italian Modernity
by David G. Horn

Revisioning History: Film and the Construction of a New Past
edited by Robert A. Rosenstone

The History of Everyday Life: Reconstructing Historical Experiences and
Ways of Life *edited by Alf Lüdtke*

The Savage Freud and Other Essays on Possible and Retrievable Selves
by Ashis Nandy

Children and the Politics of Culture *edited by Sharon Stephens*

Intimacy and Exclusion: Religious Politics in Pre-Revolutionary Baden
by Dagmar Herzog

What Was Socialism, and What Comes Next? *by Katherine Verdery*

Citizen and Subject: Contemporary Africa and the Legacy of Late
Colonialism *by Mahmood Mamdani*

Colonialism and Its Forms of Knowledge: The British in India
by Bernard S. Cohn

Charred Lullabies: Chapters in an Anthropography of Violence
by E. Valentine Daniel

Theft of an Idol: Text and Context in the Representation of Collective
Violence *by Paul R. Brass*

Essays on the Anthropology of Reason *by Paul Rabinow*

Vision, Race, and Modernity: A Visual Economy of the Andean Image World
by Deborah Poole

Children in Moral Danger and the Problem of Government in Third
Republic France *by Sylvia Schafer*

Settling Accounts: Violence, Justice, and Accountability in Postsocialist
Europe *by John Borneman*

From Duty to Desire: Remaking Families in a Spanish Village
by Jane Fishburne Collier

Black Corona: Race and the Politics of Place in an Urban Community
by Steven Gregory

Welfare, Modernity, and the Weimar State, 1919–1933 *by Young-Sun Hong*

Remaking Women: Feminism and Modernity in the Middle East
edited by Lila Abu-Lughod

Spiritual Interrogations: Culture, Gender, and Community in Early African American
Women's Writing *by Katherine Clay Bassard*

Refashioning Futures: Criticism after Postcoloniality *by David Scott*

Colonizing Hawai'i: The Cultural Power of Law *by Sally Engle Merry*